The Civilizations
of Ancient America

The Civilizations
of Ancient America

Selected Papers

of the XXIXth International Congress of Americanists

Edited by

SOL TAX

With an Introduction by

WENDELL C. BENNETT

COOPER SQUARE PUBLISHERS, INC.
NEW YORK • 1967

PREFACE

While Europe was in its dark ages there flourished in America, from Mexico to Chile, a series of civilizations no less striking than those of ancient Europe and Asia. The names Aztec, Maya, and Inca are familiar to all; these were late and local examples of cultural phases through which the Indians of "Nuclear America" passed. What anthropologists know about these civilizations, mostly digging into their remains, is the subject of this book.

This is one of three volumes of papers prepared for the *XXIXth International Congress of Americanists* held in New York from September 5-12, 1949. The others are *Indian Tribes of Aboriginal America*, and *Acculturation in the Americas*. An account and explanation of the Congress itself is contained in its official *Proceedings* published in the volume entitled *Acculturation in the Americas*.

Although there is very much in common among the ancient civilizations of Middle and South America, they have never received treatment, in all their phases, between the covers of one book. The important *The Maya and Their Neighbors* and the monumental *Handbook of the South American Indians* each reach toward the other. The present volume provides a meeting place. Wendell C. Bennett's introduction not only gives unity to the papers included, but puts these studies of American civilizations into historical perspective.

The Wenner-Gren Foundation for Anthropological Research, which sponsored the XXIXth Congress, also provided the funds which make possible publication of this volume. The University of Chicago contributed my time and innumerable facilities.

This volume could never have appeared, however, without the intelligent and devoted collaboration of Mrs. Constance Shimbel, who became my assistant immediately after the Congress and has carried through to the stage of proofreading. Others, notably Miss Betty Starr and Mr. Stuart Johnston, have helped her and me. Mr. Manning Nash assisted in the final stage. To all, and for the patience of the contributors to this volume, my thanks.

SOL TAX

UNIVERSITY OF CHICAGO
January 31, 1951

TABLE OF CONTENTS

INTRODUCTION[1]

Wendell C. Bennett

NUCLEAR AMERICA

In pre-Columbian times, the highest cultural development in the Western Hemisphere was found in the regions now designated as Mexico, Central America, and West Coast South America. Unique and fascinating cultural achievements are found elsewhere, as exemplified by the Arctic Eskimo hunters, the Northwest Coast salmon fishers, and the Amazonian horticulturalists, but cultural complexities of a magnitude that could properly be called civilization, were found only in the central region of the Americas. Historical evidence for this development starts with the arrival of the first Spaniards, who left impressive records of the political and religious institutions which they encountered in this central area. It has since been confirmed by extensive archeological work, which shows that the high civilization in this area was not a phenomenon of only slightly pre-Conquest time, but rather extends back through centuries. Finally, it is in this region that the greatest residue of native population is still to be found, carrying on in part their ancient culture, although modified and merged with a contemporary world.

The term "Nuclear America" is used to refer to this extended area of high civilization. Broad studies of the Western Hemisphere, such as those by Wissler (417),[2] Kroeber (164), and Nordenskiöld (253), have shown, through distribution maps and reconstruction of cultural history, that this nuclear area was, in many ways, a center of distribution. These distribution studies reflect the fact that the high civilizations were located approximately in the geographic center of the western hemisphere, but the geographic position as such would not account for the unique development. The west coast of South America and Middle America share certain environmental features, such as rich soils, mountain

[1]. At the sessions of the XXIX International Congress of Americanists, papers dealing with many aspects of the archeology of Mexico, Central America, and western South America were presented in several special symposia as well as in the open sessions. For the purposes of publication, however, these papers have been brought together in a single volume. This is a traditional practice and has the advantage of grouping papers which deal with the same subject interest. However, one of the objectives of the symposia at the Congress was the recognition of the relationship of archeology to history and ethnology and it is hoped that this subject matter rearrangement will not destroy the fundamental merits of that concept.

This introduction is not intended as a review of the papers included, but rather as a general background framework for them. The scope of coverage in the papers is enormous, both in space and subject matter, but the scope of prehistory of the high civilizations is equally broad.

[2]. Numbers refer to items listed alphabetically in the Bibliography at the end of the volume.

domination, and volcanic ash deposits, but the dissimilarities seem more impressive, especially if one contrasts the desert coast of Peru and the tropical jungle of Central America. In sum, the fact of the high development of civilization in Nuclear America is well established: the causes remain obscure. In any event, the contrasts with other regions of the Western Hemisphere are sufficiently great to justify separate consideration of this nuclear region.

SUBDIVISIONS

Although Nuclear America forms a unit within the Western Hemisphere as a whole, subdivisions of this extensive region have always loomed important. In fact, in terms of research work, the subdivisions have received much greater attention than the total area. Of the vast number of scholars who have devoted their attention to this field, only a handful have worked in the two major subdivisions, Meso-America and the Central Andes. These are, to be sure, the most widely separated subdivisions, and also each had its own distinctive manifestations of civilization. Such factors make it difficult to specialize in both subareas.

Meso-America, as here defined, includes Central Mexico, Guatemala, and Honduras, but excludes Northern Mexico and lower Central America. The Central Andes corresponds generally to the mountain and coastal sections of present-day Peru, with an overlap into the high plateau of Bolivia. A third subdivision covers the intermediate region, namely lower Central America, Colombia, and Ecuador. The remaining subdivisions are marginal; the Southern Andes of Chile, Bolivia, and Northwest Argentina; and Northern Mexico, perhaps including the Pueblo area of the United States southwest.

Meso-America and the Central Andes are clearly the basic components of Nuclear America. Both subdivisions represent intensive culture areas with time depth, for which the term "area co-tradition" has been proposed (38). Some scholars would favor the elimination of the two marginal subdivisions on the grounds that they present problems of a different nature, and at least one scholar, Julian Steward (323), has proposed placing the intermediate subdivision with Venezuela and the West Indies as a Circum-Caribbean unit and thus eliminate it from Nuclear America. Thus the emphasis here on the Meso-America and the Central Andes subdivision is not only a reflection of the interest of scholars but is also justified by the distinction and complexity of the archeological remains in each.

Both Meso-America and the Central Andes have recognized major temporal divisions, although the names for these vary considerably. For Meso-America, Armillas (17) uses the terms "Formative, Florescent, Transitional and Militarists." For the Central Andes, Willey (413) has proposed a three-fold division, designated "Formative, Regional Classic, and Expansionistic." For both subdivisions, scholars are in general agreement on the major time periods, although most prefer greater refinements.

MESO-AMERICA AND THE CENTRAL ANDES

The relationships between Meso-America and the Central Andes have been a challenge to scholars for many years and they are still far from satisfactorily resolved. Twenty years ago Nordenskiöld (253) presented the problem succinctly and his statement still stands. There are many obvious parallels in the cultural developments of these two subdivisions of Nuclear America. Both share a subsistence pattern of intensive agriculture, based on corn, beans, and squash. The basic crafts of ceramics, metallurgy, and weaving are equally developed. In architecture, the areas are similar in their use of stone masonry, planned ceremonial centers utilizing step-sided pyramids, sunken courts, enclosures and altars, as well as in such specific construction techniques as fill behind dressed stone facings and the corbeled arch. Stone carving is found, both as free standing statues and as a decorative device for buildings. There is evidence in both subdivisions of elaborate social, military, and religious organization. Some of the shared food plants, such as maize, sweet potatoes, peppers, peanuts, and tobacco, are of the same species which implies diffusion, in this case probably from South America. However, other plants, such as squash, beans, tomato, and cotton, are of different species in the two subdivisions, which suggest independent domestication.

In spite of these numerous parallels, all concomitants of high civilization, there are equally important contrasts between the two regions. The Central Andes alone had such important plants as quinoa, oca, potatoes, manioc, and other root plants, while cacao was limited to Meso-America. The calendrical elaboration, the recorded dates and the developed forms of writing of Meso-America are notably absent in the Central Andes. Other contrasting features may be attributed in part to cultural emphasis, but are nonetheless distinct. For example, the Central Andes emphasized textiles and metallurgy, while Meso-America stressed stone architecture and carving.

There is general agreement among scholars that Meso-America and the Central Andes had a common cultural basis from which both developed, more or less in an isolated and independent manner. In the past, this common base culture was designated the Archaic, although now the name Formative is more popular. This assumption is certainly logical, but there is actually little factual confirmation for it. A Formative epoch can be isolated, both in the Central Andes and in Meso-America, but the relationship between these two epochs is far from clear. Furthermore, the later developments in the two regions also show many similarities, but no one knows whether these are instances of rather unique parallels or the results of direct historic connections. Nordenskiöld (253) concluded that the common cultural basis was due to migrations while the later parallels represented the diffusion of ideas only. Lothrop (202a) has suggested that the Amazonian Arawaks represent the original intermediaries. No new evidence is available to confirm or deny these suggestions.

Two types of studies would aid in the solution of such problems. The first, and most obvious, is more extensive work in the intermediate subdivision. Although much has been accomplished, there is still far too little to solve relationship problems. The second is to pay greater attention to the refinements of comparisons. Such an approach would require new types of comparative studies. These two avenues to the understanding of the relationship between Meso-America and the Central Andes are taken up separately in the following sections.

The intermediate subdivision between Meso-America and the Central Andes has few elaborate surface constructions and in general less dramatic cultural manifestations. Relatively little scientific investigation has been accomplished. As a consequence, in most parts of this extensive area, established sequences are rare and most information is based on isolated sites or miscellaneous undocumented collections. Fortunately, this situation has been changing in recent years and more attention has been given to describing excavations. Nonetheless, there are still vast areas in which no scientific work has been done, and there is still inadequate material for proper reconstruction.

In Ecuador, most of the archeological knowledge is based on the earlier work of Saville, Jijón y Caamaño, and Uhle. This has been supplemented in recent years by the work of Collier, Murra, and Bennett in the Southern Highlands, by the surveys and excavations of Edwin Ferdon, as yet unpublished in their entirety, and by some explorations of local Ecuadorian scholars. On the basis of all evidence, a tentative sequence for Ecuador as a whole can be established with appropriate regional modifications. The historical picture presented is comparable, in some ways, to the developmental sequence of Peru, but most scholars have been more impressed by the basic distinctions between Ecuador and Peru. Some of the periods in Ecuador appear to have a reasonable antiquity, but these furnish few specific leads towards linking Meso-America and the Central Andes. Uhle (388), to be sure, was impressed by the Maya influence in Ecuadorian materials, but his evidence was based on vague stylistic strains and has not been finally accepted. The numerous and varied clay figurines from the Esmeraldas coast are suggestive of Middle America, but unfortunately they are not placed chronologically.

The extensive highlands of Colombia have only been sampled by the excavator's spade. The excavations of Preuss at San Agustín and of Mason at Santa Marta are still basic. In recent years, considerable excavation and exploration have been carried out by Hernández de Alba, Cubillos, Duque, Lehmann, Pérez de Barradas, Ford, and Haury, to mention but a few. In spite of the quantity and quality of this work, the over-all picture of Colombian prehistory is far from satisfactory. In general, ceramic styles and cultural complexes have strictly local distributions; which makes even relative matching for reconstruction of the total picture exceedingly difficult. Stratigraphic sequences of any magnitude are yet to be discovered, nor is there convincing evidence of any great antiquity to the known finds. The spectacular stone carving of San Agustín has long been known, and comparisons have been made of its varied styles, with both Peru and Central America. However, little is yet known about the antiquity of San Agustín and it is not even certain that it is a single cultural manifestation.

The Chibcha development has often been classed, with the Inca and Aztec, as a third high civilization of the New World. Evidence for this is based largely on the accounts of the early Spanish conquerors. The archeological data do not verify this high development, and the recent excavations by Haury have failed to reveal any significant time depth to the known Chibcha materials.

From a logical point of view, Colombia should contain evidence for any land movements of peoples or cultural influences between Meso-America and the Central Andes, but the archeological refinements at the present time are not sufficient to reveal these.

The archeological situation in lower Central America is like that in Colombia. The work executed by such scholars as Spinden, Strong, Kidder, Paul, Stone, Popenoe, Longyear, Yde, and especially Lothrop, is of excellent quality, but still inadequate in quantity when one considers the size and complexity of the area covered. With the exception of some Maya sites which belong properly with Meso-America, there are numerous local styles, some of considerable distinction, scattered surface ruins and stone sculpture, and some floating sequences. However, it is not yet possible to fit this miscellaneous evidence into a consistent historical framework. Few of the sites are considered to be very ancient, and some, like Coclé in Panama, are dated as only slightly pre-Spanish. There are, however, some exceptions which hold promise for future investigation. The Playa de los Muertos complex in Honduras is stylistically and stratigraphically consistent with the Formative epoch, and recent coastal finds at Monagrillo in Panama seem stylistically early.

Future investigation in the intermediate subdivision may well reveal evidence for early connections between Meso-America and the Central Andes, and at least fill out the picture of an Archaic or Formative epoch. It seems less likely, however, that work in the intermediate subdivision alone will solve the problems of subsequent parallels between the two major areas. Thus it is appropriate to review various types of comparative studies which should point up the kinds of evidence one might expect to find.

COMPARATIVE STUDIES

The Nuclear America field is a rich one for anthropological research in all of its aspects, particularly in terms of the two major subdivisions. In each the archeological records show a long period of development, estimated as approximately 5,000 years duration. Furthermore, the archeological picture presents a certain uniformity in its major outlines. This does not mean that Meso-America

and the Central Andes, unlike other regions, were not subjected to many outside influences, but rather that they were distinctive enough centers to mold
these into a local expression. Both areas furthermore present a cultural con-
tinuum from their archeological past through Colonial and Republican history
to the present. In many areas the relationship of contemporary or historical
native peoples to the past cultures revealed by archeologists is uncertain or
speculative, but in Nuclear America the record of continuity is well established.
Finally, the Indian-derived population is still sizeable in Peru, Guatemala, and
Mexico, and presents problems of a sociological, economical, and political
nature to the modern countries.

In brief, Nuclear America presents ample material for the archeologist, historian, physical anthropologist, linguist, and ethnologist, to mention only those
classically associated with anthropology. More important still is the fact that
the work of all these specialists can be linked together as parts of common problems for investigation. It is, therefore, of considerable interest and concern to
examine ways of utilizing this unusually rich record for the advancement of
social science knowledge.

No great uniformity should be anticipated in studies labeled as "comparative." As every scholar realizes, comparison is a technique, and as such depends
on a problem or a concept for its significance. Comparisons can be and are made
for all sorts of purposes and the particular technique used varies in accordance
with the particular purpose. To insist that comparative studies conform to a set
series of rules would be meaningless. However, in this particular review, the
comparative studies refer to Meso-America or the Central Andes, which offers
at least regional and subject unity.

It is hoped, however, that the comparative studies can be examined and
analyzed in a way that will present at least some unity. It is recognized immediately that comparative studies, whatever their nature, express a relationship
whether it be chronological, artistic, technological, functional or some other.
An examination of the nature of these relationships, and a discussion of how
they might be applied to give greater unity to the studies, in terms of knowledge
of human and cultural behavior, is desirable. As a basis for this, some of the
types of comparative studies which have been applied to Nuclear America are
reviewed.

1. *Chronological.*—The commonest types of comparative studies employed by
the archeologists have been directed towards the establishment of relative
chronologies in the areas. These are either sequential, that is, the superimposed
sequences in a single site, or regional, the matching of local site sequences. In
the first, a relative scale is established by the excavations and the comparisons
are directed toward factoring out evidence of cultural change. In the second,
comparisons are based on the distribution of specific styles or artifacts and
similarities are stressed for matching purposes. In recent work, the comparisons
in both cases have been weighted by percentage frequencies of occurrence.

It seems clear on the face of it that these types of comparative studies are essentially substitutes for absolute time records, rather than contributions to social science in themselves. Once acceptable methods of dating are available, like the Maya calendar and a refinement of radiocarbon techniques, such comparative studies would no longer be so valuable. This is evident once the historical period is reached. To be sure, by-products of comparative studies for relative chronologies involve concepts of development and diffusion, but if these were the principal aims, the comparative techniques would have to be reformulated.

2. *Continuity.*—Comparative studies for establishing continuity of culture or occupation are similar in some respects to those for site sequences, but the ultimate purpose is different. Ford (118*a*) has demonstrated this approach in Viru Valley. The frequency occurrences of all ceramic types in each chronological level are charted for comparison. If the types increase or decrease gradually, continuity is assumed. If the breaks are sharp, discontinuity is implied. Both chronological sequences and knowledge of cultural continuity are basic for many other studies of culture change and process. While the Ford approach has been limited thus far to archeological cultures, it could profitably be applied to historical ones as well.

3. *Horizons.*—The comparative studies of chronology have established certain widespread styles which serve as convenient dating marks, and in Peru these have been termed horizon styles. Willey (413) has defined the horizon as "an abstraction based upon the recurrence of specific features of style or manufacture in prehistoric artifacts, mainly pottery, from one region to another. . . ." In general the horizon styles are but a detail of comparative chronological studies, but Willey in the same paper adds a consideration of the functional significance of the distribution of these styles and complexes. This involves a comparison of the cultural forces—the economic, political, and religious conditions—which favored the distribution and acceptance of the horizon components. Here again is an approach in comparative studies which might well be applied to the historical scene not only to enlarge our knowledge of cultural processes, but to clarify the history as well.

4. *Developmental.*—Trends in the development of prehistoric regional sequences have long been recognized. For example, Larco (179) and Strong (332) have dealt with Peruvian North Coast sequences, Bennett and Bird (40) with the Central Andes, and Armillas (17) with Meso-America. This developmental comparison is based on relative achievements on economic, technological, political, religious, and artistic levels. As applied to the Peruvian North Coast sequence it is basically chronological, but the criteria are not, as is revealed when the developmental classifications are compared more widely. For example, Strong (332) writes, "What is meant here by Florescent is the climax-period wherein the highest, but most standardized, artistic individuality is attained." With such criteria, Florescence might occur at any time period for a

given culture, or not at all. Thus the comparative developmental is in reality a different approach from the comparative chronological. Steward (323) has demonstrated this, and used such a comparative approach in an attempt to reveal causal factors in culture process. In its over-all significance the comparative developmental approach is important, but at the present time it needs more rigorous, and less subjective, criteria.

5. *Technological.*—Comparative studies of techniques, such as ceramics, metallurgy, and weaving, differ from others by virtue of greater exactness in measuring accomplishment. The advantage of such study is that the technique is implicit in the analysis of the object. In reference to Nuclear America studies it would seem logical to make greater use of technological standards in evaluating the developmental achievements.

6. *Functional.*—Comparative studies on a functional level have not been extensively followed, although functional concepts have been used in some of the approaches. In contemporary studies some gross classifications have employed functional terms, such as herding communities, small farmers, and mining communities. Archeologically little has been done comparatively beyond mentioning gross types of sites, such as fishing sites, camp sites, house clusters, and villages. Presumably, it would be profitable to make such comparative studies, for example, of fishing sites, throughout time, from preceramic to modern.

7. *Areal.*—The Viru Valley Program in Peru represents an approach to comparative study of the successive occupations of a single isolated area, in this case a coastal valley. Using the valley as a constant, comparisons are made of its use by different occupants from preceramic to modern times. Such an approach should be applied elsewhere, not only in valleys but in highland basins.

8. *Interregional.*—It is quite clear that the comparative criteria used to demonstrate the cultural unity of the subdivisions of Nuclear America at different time periods do not express adequately the relationship of these divisions with adjacent areas or with each other. For example, both for Ecuador and Northwest Argentina a parallel development with Peru is noted, but the nature of these relationships has yet to be determined. Obviously new criteria are needed since those of identifying similar styles will not apply. This is even more true of the relationship of Peru with the upper Amazon. It is common to point out the sharp division between Andean cultural development and that of the tropical forest. However, there must have been constant contact between Andean and Amazonian peoples and mutual influences must have occurred. This interregional type of comparison would seem desirable in order to get away from the overemphasis on tangible influences as expressed by trade objects and decorative styles.

SUMMARY

A review of the existing evidence shows that the relationships of the cultural developments in Meso-America and in the Central Andes are still far from clear. The studies thus far deal either with gross parallels in the over-all development or are reduced to the examination of specific stylistic features. The latter are suggestive, but not convincing. It is interesting to consider the implications of this frustrating problem. While reasonably separated geographically, the two major subdivisions of Nuclear America share many common features and trends. Communication routes between the two areas, although difficult, were certainly possible, both by land and sea. Still with all the work that has been accomplished, a satisfactory statement of the relationship cannot be formulated. One suspects, but cannot prove, diffusion and historical contacts.

If scholars cannot solve this problem where conditions are reasonably favorable, it raises a real question about the validity of wider comparisons. Trans-Pacific parallels were discussed at the Congress, and the American Museum of Natural History arranged a special exhibit of Old and New World similarities. No specific conclusions were drawn, but by placing comparable objects in juxtaposition, it was left to the imagination of the observer to outline the problem. However, it seems reasonable to insist that scholars solve first the relationships between Meso-America and the Central Andes before struggling with Old and New World parallels, which involve distant ocean voyages, distinctly different time periods, and other complicating features.

INVESTIGATIONS
THE XXIX CONGRESS

The high civilizations of Nuclear America have always been one of the major interests in the International Congresses of Americanists. In fact, the Proceedings of the Congress are recognized as one of the valuable bibliographic source works for generalized, as well as specific, reports in this field. A comparison of the present Congress with the previous one in New York, some twenty years before, shows that a respectable number of articles on the Nuclear America field were presented in each, specifically thirty-two in 1928 and fifty-five in 1949. The distribution of these papers by subdivisions of the area was also in roughly the same proportion. Meso-America leads by far in both cases, the Central Andes follow, and there were only scattered papers on the intermediate and marginal areas. Papers dealing with Nuclear America as a whole were limited to one in 1928 and five in 1949. Likewise, the major topics covered by these two Congresses were about the same. All of this would seem to imply that the interests had not diverged greatly in the past two decades. However, a closer examination shows that there are significant differences in the concepts and the approaches.

A comparison of the two Congresses held in New York is of some interest but does not reflect the total situation nor clarify adequately the trends and changes in a field. For example, the attendance at the last Congress was considerably larger than at the earlier one, which resulted in almost twice as many papers being presented. Moreover, at the 1928 Congress, there was a better distribution of representatives, particularly from the South American countries. In any

Congress, organizational restrictions affect the numbers and types of papers. Most delegates feel that an important international meeting requires a generalized paper, a summary of considerable work accomplished, rather than a descriptive report on a detailed study or excavation. Specialized symposia, a common feature of the 1949 Congress, require specific papers from the invited participants. While there are open sessions which allow opportunity for a representative to express his own interest, it is often necessary, as in the past Congress, to restrict the number of papers which an individual can present.

In recent years, specialized international conferences dealing with specific problems have taken over functions formerly served by the Congresses. For example, in 1949 a group interested in contemporary cultures of Meso-America met for a week at the Viking Fund preceding the Congress sessions and only a summary of their results was presented at the Congress. Similar conferences have been held in recent years on Peruvian problems, physical anthropology, and other specialized subjects.

In the light of all available evidence, it is clear that there has been a great increase of interest in the Nuclear America field in the past twenty years. Equally evident is the fact that the number and variety of scholars interested in the Meso-American subdivision greatly outstrips all others, in spite of the increased number of students now working in the Central Andes, the intermediate, and the marginal subdivisions.

This greater emphasis on Meso-American studies has a deep historical basis. For many years before their discovery by the Spaniards, the peoples of Meso-America had placed great emphasis on the calendar and on writing. The stelae inscriptions of calendrical dates have survived the ravages of time and three of the native codices have also been preserved. This interest in records continued into the post-Conquest times when the Indians learned to write in the Spanish manner. Such records have long attracted scholars of many disciplines, who are interested in the problem of deciphering and interpreting. Such documents are lacking in the Central Andes and other subdivisions.

The accounts of both Spanish and Indians in the sixteenth and seventeenth centuries furnish valuable materials for the study of the Central Andes and Meso-America by historians, archeologists, and ethnologists. Likewise, in the eighteenth and nineteenth centuries, European travelers visited and described many parts of Nuclear America, but, on the whole, all of these accounts are of better quality for Meso-America than for the Central Andes. Finally, scientific excavations and publications began earlier in Meso-America than elsewhere, and, due in part to more adequate financing, have continued to lead the field in quantity and quality.

One of the results of this emphasis on Meso-America has been more specialization. Commonly a student will concentrate on Old Empire Maya or the Valley of Mexico rather than on the region as a whole; on architecture or ceramics rather than on the total archeological complex. In the Central Andes, on the other hand, the tradition of non-specialization started with Bandelier, Uhle, and Tello at the turn of the century and has been maintained ever since. This may explain, in part, the relative clarity and unity in the reconstruction of Central Andean prehistory in contrast to the complexities of Meso-America. It should be noted that the Meso-American specialists are now expanding their interests to the total region, although any extensions which would include the intermediate subdivision or total Nuclear America are still rare.

OLD INTERESTS CONTINUED

A broad review of scholarly work in Nuclear America over the past two decades shows many old interests which have continued to attract attention, as well as some new trends. The review is based on the comparison of different Congress Proceedings, on results of special conferences, on publications, and on field work.

The study of the recorded calendars of the Maya and others has continued to hold the attention of specialists. While there is not, as yet, total agreement in the precise correlations of the Maya and Christian calendars, much progress has been made, and the significant factors involved in such a correlation are being sharpened. Some continue to restrict their interest to the calendrical systems alone, but there are an increasing number who relate their findings to other archeological data. In fact, new problems are constantly being raised by the "dirt" archeologists when they attempt to relate the stratigraphic data to the time chronology as deduced from recorded dates.

Interest in relative chronology established by stratigraphy continues to dominate the field. In all subdivisions of Nuclear America local sequences are being established by the field workers. These local sequences may momentarily add complexities for the over-all picture, but, at the same time, they offer material for ultimate solutions of historic reconstructions.

Description of sites and artifacts is the basis of archeological work. New methods of classification are being devised in terms of specific problems. Likewise, attention is being turned to new descriptive techniques. In Peru, the government is systematically mapping the coastal region from the air, and the resulting air photographs and mosaic maps present new vistas for archeological interpretation. For illustration, the air map allows the study of the relationship of sites, not only to each other but to the topography of the valley, to ancient roads, many invisible from the ground, to irrigation systems, and to other features. Air photos are invaluable for architectural studies. Such air surveys have been used for many years in Meso-America with excellent results.

Interest in historical documents also continues. Historians have long utilized these documents in their studies of the Spanish Empire in the New World, but now many are combining archeological and documentary records. Contact history obviously presents the best opportunity for combining these interests, but it is also being demonstrated that many patterns derived from historical sources can be traced back into the archeological past.

The variety and quality of ceramics, stone sculpture, architecture, metallurgy, and textiles in Nuclear America have always attracted students interested in techniques and art. In fact, specialized papers on such techniques are a feature of every Congress. Quite legitimately these craft objects can be treated as artistic productions in themselves. Better documentation of many such specimens has, however, allowed the study of art styles in a chronological and cultural framework. Such studies are of immense value in enriching the cultural records.

Inevitably and logically, new exploration and discovery continue to be dominant interests. The number of sites to be recorded and the amount of material yet to be excavated are almost beyond conception. There are still extensive areas for which there is no scientific evidence of any kind. Archeologists of Nuclear America have sometimes been criticized for placing too much attention on new discovery and too little on interpretation. In a sense, this criticism is justified and the situation is now being remedied in those areas where sufficient discovery makes sound interpretation possible. However, even when archeologists, geographers, historians, and ethnologists combine their efforts in a concentrated study of one region, such as the Viru Valley in Peru, their interpretations are still limited by the lack of discovery in adjacent areas. Consequently, new discovery must always be encouraged, even though the perpetrator gains thereby the title of adventurer, rather than scholar.

SOME NEW INTERESTS

The distinction between old and new interests in a field of this kind is obviously artificial. Variations in technique, interpretation, and emphasis are seldom totally new and inevitably based on past experience. Consequently, nothing spectacular is implied by this division. As will be noted, many of the items are new only in reference to Nuclear America.

Early man in the Americas has always been a subject of interest to scholars but most of the evidence has come from areas outside Nuclear America. This is, in part, due to the intensity of occupation in these centers of high civilization, which tends to obliterate or obscure remains of the earliest occupants. It is also due to the vast amounts of readily discoverable material present in this area. It is difficult for a trained archeologist to ignore masses of material and concentrate on the discovery of early remains. As a result, there has been an enormous gap in time between the dates attributable to such early finds as Folsom and the dates for the earliest cultures known for Nuclear America. While it has been assumed that remains of early man existed in this area, tangible proof was lacking, in spite of certain isolated finds, like the Punín skull in Ecuador, the precise dating of which is questionable, and the footprints of extinct animals and man in ancient lava beds of Nicaragua. However, many of the arguments for assuming earlier occupations, were based on speculation concerning the centers and time of the domestication of plants and guesses at pre-ceramic components.

During recent years, there have been new discoveries and different approaches. One of the outstanding discoveries is Tepexpan Man, found by De-Terra (105) in an old lake bed in Mexico. This is one of the first scientifically documented finds and has every indication of a reasonable antiquity. Concomitant with the discovery of Tepexpan Man, geological examination of the old lake terraces and pollen profile analysis were carried out. There is evidence for rather drastic climatic change in the area which would lead to new interpretations of early settlement and migration.

New efforts have been made to discover cultural levels underlying the ceramic ones. These have been found in several sites in Meso-America, but in most cases the preservation is so poor that it is difficult to get much information for the earlier remains. In the Central Andes, Bird (60) has concentrated his attention on pre-ceramic sequences. His work in the Chicama Valley of northern Peru has been most rewarding. There he encountered levels representing an extensive period of occupation by peoples dependent on agriculture, but without ceramics. It is noteworthy that neither maize nor manioc are included in the list of the early domesticated plants, but appear much later, together with ceramics. This suggests that a thorough review is needed of the history of the high civilizations, since it has long been standard procedure to link their development with maize agriculture. The early levels in these Chicama sites have exceptionally excellent preservation of textiles and other such normally perishable materials, so that there is ample information for cultural reconstruction.

Archeologists have always been concerned with the problem of dating. As mentioned previously, recorded calendrical dates are found in the Meso-American area, but elsewhere, the archeologists have had to rely on relative dating, based on stratigraphic sequences. When the techniques of tree-ring dating were perfected in the southwest United States, hopes were raised at once for the possibility of applying these to Nuclear America. Unfortunately, the attempts thus far have not been successful. In recent years, the chemists have developed a technique of radiocarbon dating and this again arouses the hopes of the archeologist. The radiocarbon technique covers an adequate time range for most of the materials in Nuclear America, and, furthermore, can be applied to any carboniferous substance, such as charcoal, shells, wood, human or animal bones, and fabrics. Up to this time, a number of samples have been dated (18) and the archeologists are now considering these dates in terms of field evidence. More samples are needed and adjustments will have to be made, but the technique seems to have met most of the standards for accuracy and its wider application will revolutionize the interpretation of prehistory. Since the scholars and public alike are accustomed to dealing with absolute dates in history, there is always a temptation to assign years to relative sequences. The tree-ring experience in the

Southwest showed how much in error some of these guess dates could be, and the radiocarbon results are revealing the same.

Many new refinements are being made for the technical studies of ceramics, architecture, metallurgy, and weaving. Detailed studies of weaving, such as those by Bird and the late Lila O'Neale, consider not only the gross classification of the type of weave, but enter into details of the thread fiber, the tightness of twist, the direction of twist, the number of ply, the number of stitches per design unit, the interlinking of threads, the weave count, and many others. Comparisons are made with modern hand weaving, and actual experiments are made on looms similar to the ancient ones in order to get some estimate of the skill and time required for the finished product. Metallurgical analysis has also been refined, so that studies go beyond determination of the base metals employed and their combinations. Through photo-micrographic analysis, the actual process of construction can be determined. Such technical studies can determine the minimum number of steps and the required sequences which were necessary to achieve the final product. Studies of ceramics are now involved with microscopic analysis of clays and tempers and X-ray photographs of construction details.

These detailed technical studies are of great value for formal analysis and comparison and, once they have been done in sufficient number, should contribute new interpretations for the cultural picture. For example, the s-twist in hand spinning seems to have no technological advantage over the z-twist and the preference for one probably reflects the motor habits of the spinner. Thus, it may be possible to demonstrate cultural continuity or discontinuity by the frequency of occurrence of these two types of twists.

The Nuclear America field is now sufficiently advanced so that the archeologists can devote their attention to planned programs and special problems. Reports are placing greater emphasis on interpretation rather than on purely descriptive accounts. This is reflected in an increased interest in the function of artifacts and cultural complexes. A functional approach sometimes eliminates pseudo-chronological interpretations. For example, the various types of stone masonry encountered in the region of Cuzco have frequently been interpreted as representing different building periods. A functional analysis of this Inca masonry, however, shows clearly that the type of stone work coincides with the type of building constructed. Thus, the whole range of masonry techniques can be assigned to a single time period.

New attention is being paid to the nature of regional unity. The interest in horizon styles and ceramic traditions, and the analysis of continuity or discontinuity in stratified sherd series are all reflections of this consideration of cultural and regional unity. The ethnographic concept of the culture area is now being applied to archeological materials with the added feature of time depth. This approach distinguishes those regions in which the component cultures have influenced each other over a considerable period of time, from those in which the development is essentially local or isolated. Such an analysis leads to an interest in sequences which reveal cultural processes. It is now possible to determine developmental sequences in one region and compare them to those in other regions.

One of the most encouraging trends in the Nuclear America field is the breaking away from narrow specialization in favor of collaborative programs and greater awareness of the contributions made by other disciplines. It is now recognized that historians can contribute to archeological interpretations and vice versa. The environmental factors which the geographer deals with today are seen to be equally pertinent for understanding past civilizations. Programs are now in operation which involve the participation of specialists from many fields. This "area study" approach opens new possibilities for more significant studies.

FUTURE INTERESTS

A review of interests, both old and new, furnishes a basis for discussion of future interests. Notable trends have already been discussed, so that only a few points are reconsidered here.

It seems obvious that further exploration and intensive excavation will continue as a dominant interest. Nothing up to the present time indicates that knowledge has reached the point where new discovery will be only repetition or confirmation of the known. Every scholar admits that his current conclusions are handicapped by lack of knowledge. For many large areas there is either no information or at best scattered bits. Even stratigraphic excavations of refuse heaps, admittedly one of the most reliable techniques for establishing relative chronology, furnish only a pit sample of sherds which are not even a decent cultural skeleton. The coast of Peru contains thousands of unexcavated surface ruins. Detailed analysis of sherd stratigraphy combined with sampling pits may reveal the cultural affiliations of some of these sites, but the arduous task of excavating these larger units is vital if we are to have a full understanding of the cultural developments of the given period. Large scale excavations and government sponsored reconstructions have been reasonably numerous in Meso-America, but in the Central Andes, studies of this magnitude have scarcely begun.

Future archeological work should make substantial contributions to the understanding of culture history and cultural processes. It has been popular over the years to point out that archeologists deal with only a fraction of culture, since they deal with extinct civilizations subject to the vagaries of preservation. The archeologists have heretofore accepted this limitation as a handicap to their contributions. However, it is clear that the dominant interest in the study of culture is continuity and change. It is axiomatic that culture is always changing. At the same time, traditions are transmitted from adults to children and these must have enough continuity to justify the title of culture at all. Thus, the student is faced with the problem of studying continuity in a framework of perpetual change. History certainly plays a prominent role in this study and the archeological record is a part of history. Naturally, the archeologist must recognize the limitations of the materials available, but there is no reason why he cannot make valid studies of the processes of cultural change and cultural continuity. Both can be studied through established archeological sequences in terms of specific artifacts, art styles, and pattern arrangements. Spatial studies of sites reveal similarities and changes in the utilization of river valleys and highland basins. In fact, all sorts of sound interpretations can be made within the framework of the existing materials. Up to the present, archeologists have been slow to recognize the potentialities of their subject, but the indications are that the future will change this.

The recent outstanding advances in techniques of analysis and dating indicate much greater development along these lines in the future. The establishment of reliable dates should eliminate much of the drudgery of seeking evidence for relative time placement and should allow more time and energy for enlarging the record in other ways. The new techniques for analysis likewise present a challenge. Techniques are nothing but aids and it is up to the scholar to make the best use of them in his study. The linguists have been slow in taking full advantage of the new recording devices, so some resistance from the archeologists to the new mechanical aids is to be expected. However, such resistance is seldom long lived so advances can be anticipated.

There is certainly a marked trend to establish archeology as a science which deals with peoples and their cultures, and thus forms a legitimate branch of social science as a whole. Once so established, there would no longer be a marked cleavage between the archeologist and the ethnologist and linguist.

ORGANIZATION

The thirty-nine papers included in this volume on high civilizations cover a wide range of topics and regions. They are arranged in a geographical order, namely, Meso-America, the intermediate region, the Central Andes, and finally, the over-all Nuclear America. Within these regional divisions, papers which deal with the same subject, such as the Maya calendar, are grouped together when possible. In general, papers which deal with the subdivision as a whole are placed first, followed by those which deal with excavations, and, finally, by those which deal with topics. It is self-evident that this matter of arrangement is of minor importance compared to the content of the papers themselves.

MESO-AMERICA

TECNOLOGÍA, FORMACIONES SOCIO-ECONÓMICAS Y RELIGIÓN EN MESOAMÉRICA

Pedro Armillas

I

Para llevar a cabo un análisis funcional del desarrollo de la civilización en el área cultural Mesoamérica la historia escrita descifrada hasta la fecha nos proporciona datos que se remontan, según los recientes estudios de Caso, hasta el año 692 de nuestra era (73). El desciframiento de la parte, aparentemente histórica, de los jeroglíficos mayas, aún no descifrada, podría llevarnos un poco más lejos. La arqueología nos ha proporcionado hasta ahora datos que se calcula llegan hasta mediados, por lo menos, del primer milenio antes de Cristo. Con esos elementos podemos reconstruir la historia cultural de Mesoamérica para un período de por lo menos dos milenios, durante los cuáles—y aquí radica el interés teórico de su estudio—los pueblos mesoamericanos pasaron por distintas etapas de desarrollo tecnológico, económico, social, político y religioso, en las cuáles podemos estudiar el proceso de surgimiento de las sociedades urbanas partiendo de una base de barbarismo neolítico.

Ya anteriormente he presentado un ensayo de interpretación de esa secuencia de desarrollo, como base para una comparación de estructuras culturales entre Mesoamérica y el Area Andina (17). Pero en el estado actual de nuestros conocimientos sobre la materia, ensayos de esa naturaleza solamente se justifican como hipótesis de trabajo, destinadas a ser pulidas por la acción de la crítica y de la auto-crítica y ajustadas a nuevos estudios y descubrimientos. Estas consideraciones y los dos años transcurridos justifican la revisión que ahora presento. Aunque basada esencialmente en datos ya conocidos hace dos años, creo que esta revisión muestra un cuadro más dinámico de los orígenes de la civilización en Mesoamérica, una transición de etapa a etapa menos brusca, que se ajusta mejor a la realidad de los fenómenos culturales.

En el ensayo mencionado usé los nombres de Formativa, Floreciente y Militarista para las tres etapas sobre las cuáles tenemos información. La adopción de esos nombres se hizo teniendo en cuenta las denominaciones dadas por mis colegas peruanistas a fases que parecen homotaxiales con aquellas tres, en el Area Andina. He preferido usar ahora los nombres de Formativa, Clásica e Histórica para las mismas etapas, ciñéndome a un uso más general entre mesoamericanistas. La variedad de términos usados para designar diversos *horizontes* arqueológicos en Mesoamérica refleja la dificultad de hallar términos generales adecuados, que se debe a falta de conocimiento suficiente y la misma dificultad se encuentra al tratar de bautizar etapas de desarrollo cultural interpretadas funcionalmente. Cuando sea mejor nuestro conocimiento de los factores causales de esos desarrollos podremos definir más precisamente y denominar más adecuadamente cada etapa.

Puede afirmarse—por lo menos para las zonas focales de las culturas mesoamericanas—que hay en lo general homotaxis sincrónica. En otras palabras, que hay correspondencia en tiempo entre los diferentes aspectos locales de la misma etapa de desarrollo y que en consecuencia las etapas corresponden bastante bien a *horizontes* o grupos de horizontes arqueológicos. Para zonas marginales esto no puede afirmarse por ahora, se necesita mayor estudio.

En parte por razones de espacio disponible y en parte por falta de conocimiento suficiente sobre algunas de las sub-áreas dentro de Mesoamérica la trato aquí como una unidad, haciendo solamente referencias ocasionales a las diferencias regionales en las distintas etapas. Pero las diferencias ambientales dentro de Mesoamérica son muy grandes (16, pp. 85–87); si tomamos en cuenta además la complejidad étnica que la fragmentación lingüística hace patente y combinamos en un solo mapa las áreas naturales con las étnicas, resulta un intrincado mosaico. Correspondiendo, al parecer, en sus lineamientos generales con las diferencias ambientales y secundariamente con la distribución étnica hay marcadas diferencias culturales que hacen quizás inaplicable a alguna de las sub-áreas el esquema-tipo de desarrollo cultural que aquí presento. Dudo mucho, por ejemplo, de que el término "teocracia" defina adecuadamente la situación en el Occidente durante la Etapa Clásica, porque el complejo dioses-templos-sacerdotes no se desarrolló en esa región en la misma forma que en el resto.

Steward ha hecho notar la influencia de las condiciones ambientales y sistema de cultivo en el modo de habitación de los mayas (322, p. 141), en aldeas dispersas alrededor de los centros religiosos, comparados por Kidder con las actuales *vacant towns* de los Altos de Guatemala (158, p. 248). Las probabilidades de que culturas de ese tipo—enormes superestructuras sobre fundamentos tecnológico-económicos insuficientes—sobrevivan a crisis socio-económicas graves parecen ser muy pocas. Seguramente no es accidental que la ruina del poéticamente llamado "Viejo Imperio" del área maya central fuera completa y definitiva, mientras que crisis semejantes fueron superadas una y otra vez en otras regiones de Mesoamérica, surgiendo cada vez de la crisis nuevas sociedades más desarrolladas.

Debemos considerar relacionado con las condiciones ambientales el importante papel que el Valle de México desempeñó en Mesoamérica, al parecer, desde tiempos de la Etapa Formativa. Esa importancia parecería fuera de lugar al considerar la situación geográfica del Valle, próximo a la frontera de la civilización; al borde del territorio de los salvajes, los chichimecas. Indudablemente la razón de su importancia se debe al carácter lacustre de esa gran cuenca. De ello resultaba:

a) la abundancia de caza y pesca. Economía mixta, basada en cultivo y en productos lacustres, explica la permanencia de los poblados arcaicos.

b) condiciones ideales—al menos en los lagos de Zumpango, Xaltocan, Xochimilco y Chalco—para el sistema de cultivo de chinampas, cuya productividad hizo posible la excepcional densidad de población en el Valle.

c) la facilidad de comunicación por agua. Esa facilidad tenía extraordinario valor dado lo primitivo de las técnicas de transporte mesoamericanas. Debido a ella todo el Valle, con 8000 kilometros cuadrados de extensión, formaba una sola unidad económica.

En el aspecto político, las diferencias ambientales señalaron desde los orígenes direcciones de expansión a los pueblos de las tierras altas hacia las tierras calientes donde podían adquirir importantes productos agrícolas que no se dan en tierra fría. Esta razón es muy clara en las relaciones entre el Valle de México y el de Morelos, o en la expansión hacia la Boca-costa y la costa del Pacífico de los pueblos de los Altos de Guatemala. Sal, piedras finas, plumas preciosas y— desde fines de la época Clásica—yacimientos minerales (oro, plata, cobre) fueron otros factores determinantes de las direcciones de expansión.

Veamos ahora las características de la más antigua de las tres etapas, la denominada Formativa.

II

Veamos ahora las características de la más antigua de las tres etapes, la denominada Formativa.

Subsistencia basada en agricultura. Se sabe positivamente que se cultivaba maíz y algodón. Es probable que también fueran cultivados frijol y calabaza y utilizados los productos del maguey y del nopal. Para las tierras bajas, de clirra caliente y húmedo, de la vertiente del Golfo y del Caribe, ha sido sugerida (157a, p. 121) la posibilidad de una agricultura del tipo Amazonas-Orinoco, basada en el cultivo de la yuca como planta principal, antecediendo a la introducción en esa zona del cultivo del maíz. Sobre sistemas de cultivo no hay datos, es posible que solo el sistema de roza fuera generalmente usado y quizás el cultivo en bajiales—es decir, en terrenos periódicamente inundados y fertilizados por las avenidas de los ríos—en las regiones occidentales, de clirra seco.

El uso del algodón en las culturas arcaicas del Valle de México indica seguramente relaciones comerciales con el Valle de Morelos, Guerrero o el sur de Puebla. Es oportuno hacer notar que ello coincide con la distribución de ciertos tipos de figurillas de terracota (los diferentes tipos D de la clasificación de Vaillant).

En los otros aspectos de la tecnología, ya desde esta etapa se encuentra establecido el patrón básico que perduraría—con pocas adiciones o modificaciones—en la sucesión de culturas mesoamericanas hasta la introducción de técnicas europeas (158, pp. 245-46; 157b, p. 72). Tipos de utillaje y técnicas son muy persistentes en Mesoamérica; sin embargo estudios más precisos que los hechos hasta la fecha pueden poner de relieve diferencias significativas que ahora nos escapan, como prueba el trabajo del Dr. Kidder sobre los artefactos de Uaxactún. Estudios en ese campo deben contribuir a precisar el grado de contraste entre tecnología relativamente baja y estructura socio-política y cultura intelectual muy desarrolladas que es aparente en etapas posteriores.

La elaboración de formas, técnicas y motivos de decoración en alfarería indican una tradición muy larga, cuyos antecedentes no se han encontrado hasta ahora. Hay una semejanza genérica entre las cerámicas del Horizonte Arcaico y en algunos tipos semejanzas específicas, pero no son evidencia de comercio. Parecen ser emergencias locales del mismo patrón básico común.

El reciente descubrimiento de Tlatilco añade algo que faltaba en nuestro conocimiento de las culturas arcaicas del centro de México, que hasta ese descubrimiento se basaba principalmente en los trabajos de Vaillant. Según la interpretación de Miguel Covarrubias, que me parece correcta, la cultura de Tlatilco sería un aspecto refinado de la misma cultura que Zacatenco representa en su aspecto rural. En otras palabras, Tlatilco habría sido una villa—o sea un centro regional—y Zacatenco una aldea. En la villa se habría iniciado la diferenciación social—probablemente en grupos, todavía no definidos en el sentido de castas o clases, que podemos caracterizar con el nombre de estamentos—menos manifiesta en la aldea.

A la misma conclusión, mayor complejidad social de las culturas de la Etapa Formativa de la que podía suponerse hace unos años, obligan los nuevos descubrimientos en torno a la cultura de Miraflores, en los Altos y la costa del Pacífico de Guatemala (309; 157). Aunque cronológicamente, y acaso también taxonómicamente, la cultura de Miraflores está en la transición a la etapa siguiente.

Falta, conspicuamente, un simbolismo religioso formalizado, en contraste muy notable con su desarrollo en las fases siguientes. La imagen del dios del fuego—ese señor del tiempo y el hogar o de la permanencia de lo fugitivo a quien con razón los aztecas llamaban Huehueteotl, el dios viejo—que aparece durante esta fase, hacia su final, es más bien que excepción augurio de tiempos nuevos.

Las ideas religiosas de los mesoamericanos durante la fase Formativa se manifiestan característicamente en el culto a la fertilidad probablemente indicado por las figurillas femeninas de terracota. Estas ideas habrían de cristalizar más tarde en el culto a la Diosa Madre, la diosa de la tierra. También las figurillas bicéfalas y sobre todo las máscaras dobles—de la vida y la muerte (314, p. 25)—parecen contener el germen de una idea religiosa muy importante en tiempos posteriores, el principio dual.

Sobre la presencia en esta etapa, por lo menos en la costa meridional del Golfo, de los dioses-jaguar—ligada al problema de la cronología y definición de las diferentes fases de la cultura de La Venta—ya he expresado mi opinión (17, p. 4). Las raíces de ese culto a los dioses de la tierra y de las aguas deben encontrarse en creencias populares de esta etapa, pero el completo desarrollo del simbolismo hierático de los jaguares pertenece taxonómicamente, y al parecer también cronológicamente, a la etapa siguiente.

Otra ausencia significativa es la de pirámides escalonadas como basamento de templos, tan características de tiempos posteriores, que Kirchhoff (160) enumera como uno de los elementos distintivos de Mesoamérica. Es más, cualquier forma de basamento para templos y los templos mismos no corresponden a esta etapa. Asunto diferente son los túmulos funerarios; es mi impresión que el estudio de este rasgo en Mesoamérica puede producir una sorpresa. Los trabajos de Linné en el distrito de Chalchicomula indican su abundancia en esa zona (191, pp. 29, 55); en la faja costera del Pacífico, en Guatemala, el montículo de Finca Arizona, que corresponde al período Miraflores (309), es claramente un túmulo funerario semejante al de Aljojuca excavado por Linné, aunque representativo el de Finca Arizona de una cultura más refinada. Al mismo tipo parece pertenecer—según la escasa información publicada—el de Canchón, en la meseta al sureste de la ciudad de Guatemala, que corresponde a la misma época (157, p. 226).

¿Son los numerosos montículos de Kaminaljuyú pertenecientes al período Miraflores también túmulos funerarios? Esa fué mi impresión respecto al excavado en los dos últimos años por Kidder y Shook. Una característica común a esos montículos—en contraste con los montículos con función de basamento para templo—es la ausencia de revestimiento de piedra y estuco. Parece pues posible que en Mesoamérica los montículos funerarios sean anteriores, en su origen, a los basamentos para templos y se encuentren desde la Etapa Formativa, aunque en rigor los de Miraflores corresponden más bien a la Etapa Clásica, por los motivos que expongo a continuación.

La mayor discrepancia entre mi clasificación en etapas homotaxiales y los *horizontes* arqueológicos generalmente aceptados consiste en la delimitación de los conceptos Etapa Formativa y Horizonte Arcaico (o *Middle Cultures*) en lo que se refiere al comienzo de la Época Clásica, el motivo de la discrepancia está en la diferente base de clasificación. El Horizonte Arcaico se define generalmente con referencia a tipos de cerámica, hacia el katún 14 del baktún 8 de la Cuenta Larga maya (A.D. 317?) ocurrieron en todas partes de Mesoamérica cambios de estilo en alfarería, en el sentido de mayor diferenciación regional. En algunas zonas aquella fecha marca la aparición de cerámicas polícromas, en contraste con las de época anterior generalmente monocromas; en todas partes el cambio se señala por nuevas formas y en las técnicas y motivos de decoración. Las cerámicas anteriores a esas innovaciones son designadas por los arqueólogos con los nombres de *Arcaicas* o *Pre-Clásicas*. Pero antes de que ocurrieran esos cambios, que solamente en el área maya central van acompañados por la erección de estelas con fechas de la Cuenta Larga y la construcción de bóvedas (usados generalmente como norma para fijar el comienzo del horizonte Clásico) habían aparecido rasgos que indican el desarrollo de los factores económico-sociales que darían forma y contenido a la sociedad teocrática, como son:

a) basamentos escalonados para templos, agrupados en centros ceremoniales. Ejemplo: grupo de basamentos de Cuicuilco; Teotihuacán, donde las pirámides llamadas del Sol y de la Luna habrían sido erigidas antes de aquella fecha; el templo E VII inferior, de Uaxactún.

b) grandes necrópolis, unidas a los centros ceremoniales, con señales de grandes diferencias en condición social. Ejemplo: Monte Albán I–II; montículos del período Miraflores de Kaminaljuyú.

c) arte hierático. Ejemplo: mascarones del templo E VII inferior, de Uaxactún.

d) escritura jeroglífica. Ejemplo: estela C de Tres Zapotes(?); Monte Albán (71). Sistema numérico de posición.

Esos rasgos—aunque aparezcan asociados con cerámicas del Horizonte Arcaico—definen una estructura económico-social correspondiente a una fase inicial de la Etapa Teocrática.

III

Una sociedad teocrática cuya base económica permitía un tremendo derroche de energías en el servicio de los dioses y de los muertos sucedió a las sociedades relativamente simples de la Etapa Formativa.

Las razones en que baso mi hipótesis de sistemas de agricultura permanente (chinampas, riego, terrazas de cultivo) como base económica de las sociedades teocráticas mesoamericanas ya han sido publicadas (17, pp. 106–7; 16, p. 91). Las pinturas murales de Tepantitla, en Teotihuacán, descubiertas en mis excavaciones de 1942, representan las plantas más importantes en la economía: maíz, frijol, calabaza; también maguey y nopal y árboles que parecen ser cacao y zapote. Debemos agregar el algodón, puesto que tejidos de esa fibra han sido también encontrados en Teotihuacán.[1]

En tecnología se puede mencionar el uso de taladros huecos, seguramente de hueso, atestiguado en las máscaras de piedra de estile teotihuacano y en objetos de Kaminaljuyú (158, pp. 113–14). La generalización del tallado de jade y de espejos de pirita responde a las demandas suntuarias de la nueva sociedad. En un plano más práctico, el uso de enormes monolitos en la arquitectura monumental parece indicación del uso de rodillos para mover grandes pesos, sin auxilio de los cuáles cuesta trabajo imaginar cómo pudieron ser transportados. Esta suposición cobra verosimilitud cuando recordamos que ya en esa época la rueda era conocida, aunque aplicada solamente a juguetes y no empleada para fines prácticos (114, pp. 472–74; 327, p. 314).

En lo que respecta a alfarería poco o nada sabemos sobre las cerámicas domésticas de esta época. Los estilos de la cerámica de lujo—fabricada para satisfacer las demandas del templo y de la tumba—se diversificaron y polarizaron en tradiciones locales forjadas alrededor de los focos constituídos por los principales lugares sagrados. La difusión de esos diferentes estilos locales nos permite sacar conclusiones acerca de las relaciones entre los diferentes centros de

---

1. Linné (191, pp. 155–60, 180, 191). Algodón y fibra de maguey para tejidos. Ver tambien Kidder *et al.* (15, p. 98) sobre algodón en Kaminaljuyú.

producción. La difusión en unos casos fué por imitación. A esta categoría corresponde en la mayoría de los casos—siendo la posible excepción una parte de los ejemplares de Kaminaljuyú—la difusión del vaso cilíndrico, de fondo plano, trípode, con tapadera cónica, característico de Teotihuacán III y la fase Esperanza de Kaminaljuyú, que con diversas variantes se encuentra en otras zonas llegando hasta los límites meridionales de Mesoamérica. En otra categoría queda la distribución, por comercio, como es el caso de la cerámica Tzakol, característica del área maya central, encontrada en las áreas maya septentrional y maya meridional y hasta en el lejano Teotihuacán (373, p. 4; 158, p. 237; 191, p. 178). Pero la cerámica de comercio más representativa de esta fase (Teotihuacán III—Monte Albán IIIa—Esperanza—Tzakol) de auge de la Etapa Clásica, cuando las relaciones comerciales entre los diferentes focos fueron activas (antes de la interrupción del comercio que señala la fase Teotihuacán IV—Monte Albán IIIb—Amatle Pamplona—Tepeu) fué sin duda la conocida con el nombre de Anaranjada Delgada,[2] cuyo centro de producción es único, no fué ni Teotihuacán, ni Monte Albán, ni Kaminaljuyú, pero llegó por comercio a esos lugares y hasta los límites de Mesoamérica, la remota Colima en el noroeste y Copán en el sureste.

Sabemos del comercio de materias primas, destinadas en gran parte a industrias de lujo (lapidaria, plumaria) pero también para utillaje. A Teotihuacán llegaban conchas de ambos mares, piedras finas (¿de Guerrero?), mica (¿de Oaxaca?) y brillantes plumas del Sur; tambien algodón. A Uaxactún llegaban obsidiana en grandes cantidades, pedernal de fina calidad, metates y manos de granitos y lavas, jade, vasos de mármol, conchas de ambos mares y probablemente plumas de quetzal (157b, p. 73). A Kaminaljuyú llegaban también conchas tanto de la vecina Mar del Sur como de la del Norte, obsidiana verde y alfarería de lujo; además, indudablemente, de productos de la Boca-costa y la costa del Pacífico, como pescado seco, iguanas, aguacates, cacao, algodón (158, p. 249). Parece que en retorno esos centros exportaban principalmente objetos manufacturados de lujo.

Durante el último tercio de la Etapa Clásica el comercio de objetos de metal (tumbaga) como artículos de lujo importados de Panamá o Colombia alcanzó por lo menos al extremo meridional de Mesoamérica. Está probado por hallazgos en El Salvador (Tazumal de Chalchuapa), Honduras (Copán) y en el valle del Motagua, Guatemala (San Agustín Acasaguastlán). Los entierros de El Tazumal con objetos de metal han sido fechados, por relaciones con Copán de la cerámica asociada, en 9.16.0.0.0 (A.D. 751?) (62, p. 42), la figurilla de tumbaga de Copán fué encontrada en la ofrenda bajo la estela H, que lleva la fecha 9.17.12.0.0 (A.D. 782?); ahora no hay duda de que el metal encontrado en una tumba de San Agustín Acasaguastlán corresponde a la misma época (157, pp. 229–30). En todos esos casos parece tratarse de piezas importadas, lo cual no

---

2. En alemán *Dünnwandiger hellgelber Ton;* en inglés *thin orange ware, yellowish-red pottery, eggshell orange ware.*

indica necesariamente, en consecuencia, conocimiento en Mesoamérica en esa época de las técnicas de minería y metalurgia. Sin embargo, como ha hecho notar Kidder, si se acepta la correlación *corta* 11.3.0.0.0 entre las cronologías maya y cristiana, hacia lo cual se marca actualmente una tendencia,[3] habría que aceptar que ya para entonces se conociera en el occidente de Mesoamérica la metalurgia del cobre, puesto que cascabeles de cobre en el estilo del occidente de México alcanzaron a llegar hasta el área Hohokam desde poco después del año 1000 de nuestra era. Pero el tipo de metalurgia del occidente de México (cobre o bronce, plata) indica origen diferente, independiente de ese comercio de tumbaga en el sur de Mesoamérica.

El modo de habitación en esa época parece haber sido generalmente en aldeas dispersas alrededor de centros ceremoniales con función primariamente religiosa, habitados permanentemente por una relativamente reducida nobleza sacerdotal y sus servidores. En ellos se congregaría la población de las aldeas en ocasión de las grandes fiestas (375). El grado en que esa función primaria pueda haber sido superada por otras—como centro político, industrial y comercial— debió variar de unos lugares a otros, de una región a otra y en el transcurso del tiempo. Además de los templos de los dioses, palacios y conventos para los nobles-sacerdotes y los novicios y canchas para el sagrado juego de pelota, había lugar en esos centros ceremoniales para los muertos ilustres, en tumbas suntuosas construídas bajo las plataformas de los templos o agrupadas en extensas necrópolis, el mejor ejemplo de las cuales es Monte Albán. Pero la extensión urbanizada—con calles y plazas pavimentadas y conductos subterráneos de desagüe—en esos centros es, en algunos de ellos, enorme (en Teotihuacán pasaba, probablemente, de 750 hectáreas); no hay duda en tales casos de su carácter plenamente urbano.

El carácter religioso de las construcciones monumentales—en relación con lo cual hubo de existir un bien organizado control de la fuerza de trabajo—y la cantidad e importancia de las efigies de sacerdotes en las representaciones artísticas manifiestan que la religión fué la principal fuerza integradora de esas sociedades. Por ello y por los datos históricos que se refieren a la época inmediatamente posterior (véase más adelante el carácter de la sociedad tolteca) podemos inferir que el poder político fuera ejercido por una nobleza sacerdotal y caracterizar a esas sociedades con el término de teocracias.

Si sobre el monopolio del poder político por la clase sacerdotal durante esta época hay razonable seguridad resulta más difícil establecer, sobre la sola base de los datos que proporciona la arqueología, el tamaño de las unidades políticas.

3. Las dudas sobre la correlación de la Cuenta Larga maya con la cronología cristiana me han decidido a usar para mayor precisión las fechas en el sistema maya. Para beneficio de los no iniciados en el sistema doy entre paréntesis las fechas cristianas que resultarían según la correlación 11.16.0.0.0, generalmente usada durante estos últimos años. Para obtener las fechas correspondientes según la correlación "corta" 11.3.0.0.0 basta sumar 260 años a las que doy entre paréntesis.

Refiriéndose al área maya central (375, p. 148) Thompson se inclina a rechazar tanto la idea de ciudades-estado según el tipo griego como la de un gobierno centralizado y sugiere una especie de federación gobernada por sumos sacerdotes locales, a la cuál compara con el régimen jesuítico en el Paraguay del siglo XVIII. Pero el tamaño de cada una de esas unidades políticas no puede haber sido demasiado pequeño, a juzgar por la cantidad de fuerza de trabajo de que disponían para emplear en actividades no productivas. Sirva de ejemplo la construcción, de una sola vez y en tiempo no muy largo, de la Pirámide del Sol, de Teotihuacán, un caso quizás extremo pero de ningún modo único en cuanto a esfuerzo requerido.

Un arte hierático, muy desarrollado, nos muestra en pinturas murales, en escultura y en la decoración de vasijas ceremoniales, el carácter de la religión. El dragón (jaguar-serpiente-quetzal) de los dioses de las aguas es el símbolo más importante. Con esos dioses se asociaban también buho y la mariposa. Además de los omnipresentes señores de las aguas (*Tlaloc-Chac-Cocijo-Tajín*) se reconocen en las representaciones religiosas deidades de la vegetación (*Xipe Totec*) y del maíz; el viejo Dios del Fuego; un Dios-Murciélago, importante en el sur (Oaxaca y el área maya) y un misterioso Dios-Gordo cuyo culto desapareció con la transformación de la sociedad al final de la Etapa Clásica. Es notorio por su ausencia el culto de los dioses de la guerra; nada se ha encontrado en este horizonte correspondiente al complejo águila solar—sacrificio de corazones que dió carácter y estilo a la religión mexicana en tiempos posteriores. Los sacrificios humanos no parecen haber sido importantes, sin embargo el culto de *Xipe Totec* indica una forma de sacrificio.

Las mayores pirámides escalonadas con función de basamento para templos fueron erigidas en esta época. Sus imponentes masas dieron carácter al paisaje urbano de los centros ceremoniales.

La estratificación social se refleja en las costumbres funerarias. Los nobles-sacerdotes fueron enterrados en suntuosas tumbas, acompañados por mujeres y sirvientes.

Escritura jeroglífica, matemáticas (uso del cero y del sistema de posición en la escritura de numerales), astronomía y calendario marcan el desarrollo de la cultura intelectual; esos conocimientos eran, indudablemente, monopolio de muy reducidas minorías. El intercambio de ideas entre esas minorías fué seguramente activo, sirva de ejemplo el congreso de dieciseis astrónomos representado en el Altar Q de Copán, reunidos en 9.17.5.0.0 (A.D. 776?) para ajustar el calendario; pero los fundamentos de la Cuenta Larga parecen haber sido guardados como valioso secreto en el sur. La caída en desuso de la Cuenta Larga al desintegrarse las sociedades teocráticas del área maya central fué indudablemente un lamentable resultado de ese monopolio.

El auge de la Etapa Clásica, cuando las fuerzas de integración de la sociedad teocrática se habían desarrollado plenamente y antes de que se manifestasen de manera perceptible las fuerzas desintegradoras, duró poco más de tres siglos, o sea desde 8.14.0.0.0 hasta 9.10.0.0.0 de la Cuenta Larga maya (A.D. 317–633?). El horizonte arqueológico correspondiente es Teotihuacán III—Monte Albán IIIa—Esperanza—Tzakol.

Como ya he señalado, hay una fase inicial de la Etapa Clásica antes de 8.14.0.0.0. Después de 9.10.0.0.0 las relaciones de El Petén, en el área maya central, con el mundo exterior parecen haber sido cada vez más difíciles. Sin embargo tanto los centros ceremoniales del Petén como los del extremo sureste (Quiriguá, Copán) persistían en la tradición teocrática. Mientras tanto en el otro extremo del área maya central, en el valle del Usumacinta, se hace patente la importancia cada vez mayor que la guerra iba adquiriendo, demostrada en representaciones de escenas bélicas en pintura y escultura.

Para entonces Teotihuacán, en el Valle de México, había sido incendiado y destruído y las gentes que usaban la alfarería rojo-sobre-bayo del estilo llamado Coyotlatelco vivían entre los arruinados palacios y templos en ese lugar, mientras en la zona de Azcapotzalco persistía un postrer, atenuado foco de la cultura teotihuacana. Probablemente debamos relacionar con esos acontecimientos el comienzo de la 'tiranía' de los Olmeca-Xicalanca en el valle de Puebla (Cholula). Simultáneamente se iniciaba la decadencia de Monte Albán (Monte Albán IIIb), había cesado la actividad constructiva en Kaminaljuyú (período Amatle-Pamplona) y llegaba también a su fin la larga ocupación ininterrumpida de Tres Zapotes. Ya he sugerido (14, pp. 156–57) que corresponden posiblemente a esta época los fosos cavados en la peña viva que rodean el cerro de Xochicalco—el centro ceremonial coronado por el templo adornado todavía con el pacífico simbolismo del dragón de las aguas—y su vecino de la Bodega, que parece ser su ciudadela.

IV

A pesar de la dramática evidencia de la violenta destrucción o súbito abandono de muchos de los centros religioso-políticos de la etapa teocrática y de la rápida decadencia de otros, no debemos pensar en una transformación igualmente brusca de la estructura social. En realidad, como ya he mostrado, las fuerzas desintegradoras de la sociedad teocrática se manifiestan claramente durante el último tercio de aquella era. Por otra parte, tras de esa general subversión, después de 10.4.0.0.0 (A.D. 909?) cuando todos los centros importantes habían sido abandonados hay evidencias de conservatismo, de restauraciones, es decir de altos e incluso retrocesos temporales en el proceso de transformación social, en los nuevos centros políticos que surgen de la confusión. En el centro de México, la presión de los chichimecas en la frontera norte de Mesoamérica hace la situación todavía más complicada. Tras de los trastornos causados por las conquistas de Mixcoatl, el gobierno en Tula de su hijo Ce Acatl Topiltzin, como quetzalcoatl, rey-sacerdote, representa una regresión al patrón anterior, perturbada por las aspiraciones de la casta militar—formada al parecer en gran parte por bárbaros, como el episodio del huasteco indica—y la guerra civil simbolizada en la lucha entre Tezcatlipoca y Quetzalcoatl parece encubrir, bajo un disfraz religioso, esas perturbaciones socio-políticas.

De hecho, la extensión del simbolismo de Quetzalcoatl-Kukulcán durante la fase inicial de la etapa histórica,[4] me parece encerrar en sí una contradicción. El método de expansión y los resultados de las conquistas que difundieron ese simbolismo favorecían los intereses de las nuevas fuerzas sociales pero la estructura gubernamental—según se ve en Tula—se amoldaba todavía a los viejos patrones, incompatibles con los intereses de los grupos cuya fuerza social era fomentada por esas mismas conquistas: los guerreros y los mercaderes. El resultado de esa contradicción se manifiesta en la final destrucción del poderío de Tula. Y es posible que los mismos factores hayan contribuído a la ruina de Chichén y la formación de la Liga de Mayapán, en Yucatán.

Tras de la caída de Tula ocurrieron en la frontera norte nuevas penetraciones chichimecas, facilitadas por la desintegración política consiguiente. Habría que estudiar en qué grado esas invasiones introdujeron factores nuevos en el proceso de transformación social o si fueron sólo un incidente que retardó el proceso hasta que los recién llegados fueron incorporados culturalmente. Finalmente, aunque la religión era todavía una fuerza efectiva de control social en 1519 el poder político había pasado a manos de las nuevas clases—nobleza militar y mercaderes, equiparados a la nobleza—representadas en el estado Culhua Mexica por el *tlacatecuhtli*, el supremo señor, y el *tlalocan*, el consejo supremo.

Terminaré mi análisis con un breve inventario de la civilización meso-americana en 1519:

En agricultura el sistema de roza era generalmente empleado. Además cultivos de regadío (*chinampas*, riego a brazo en huertos a orilla de lagos o con agua de pozos, acequias sacadas de los ríos) en la Mesa Central, la Mixteca, los valles de Oaxaca y en toda la vertiente del Pacífico desde el Río Grande de Santiago (Nayarit) hasta el Río Lempa (El Salvador); cultivos de humedad en terrenos periódicamente inundados y fertilizados por las avenidas de los ríos en el valle del Río de las Balsas, en el extremo noroeste de Mesoamérica (Sinaloa) y posiblemente en otras zonas (6, pp. 85-91). Cacao, algodón, chile, y maíz eran las principales cosechas en las tierras de regadío. En algunos lugares siembra en almácigo (y por consiguiente trasplante) y abonos. En el occidente de México se usaban aperos de labranza de metal ('*coa*' con hoja de cobre).

La mayor parte de las obras de riego de Mesoamérica parecen haber sido empresas locales, construídas y mantenidas con los solos recursos de una comunidad. Esta situación—debida en gran parte a las condiciones ambientales—pudo conducir en algunas regiones (quizá la Mixteca) a una especie de feudalismo de tipo japonés.[5] Pero el estudio de este punto, de gran importancia teórica, requiere más información de la que se ha reunido hasta la fecha.

4. Sobre el significado de ese simbolismo (Armillas, 14a).

5. Sobre ese tipo de feudalismo en México (Wittfogel, 418).

Por otra parte, grandes obras hidráulicas—construcción de presas, canales, diques, acueductos y calzadas—fueron llevadas a cabo en el Valle de México durante el siglo XV, simultáneamente con la integración y desarrollo del 'Imperio,' reuniendo los recursos de varias ciudades-estado.

Utillaje lítico, pero además instrumentos de metal (cobre, quizás bronce) usados por los artesanos: punzones, cinceles, cuchillas, hachas; también agujas y anzuelos y en el occidente se usaba metal para aperos de labranza. Sin embargo, en la mayor parte de Mesoamérica el metal era usado principalmente para propósitos suntuarios. El desarrollo de minería y metalurgia coincide con el surgimiento a un papel activo de dos regiones que hasta entonces parecen haber tenido un papel más bien pasivo en el desarrollo de las culturas mesoamericanas, me refiere a Michoacán, con especialización en la metalurgia del cobre y de la plata,[6] y la Mixteca, especialización en orfebrería.

En algunas regiones una parte considerable de la población vivía en núcleos urbanos. Un estudio reciente (98) asigna a Tenochtitlán-Tlatelolco 300,000 habitantes, 400,000 al área metropolitana Texcoco-Coatlichan-Huexotla-Atenco. Huejotzingo y Cholula parece se acercaban al cuarto de millón y Chalco es posible que alcanzara 100,000. En Colima y áreas vecinas Sauer menciona ocho ciudades, aunque de tamaño mucho menor que las del centro de México. En ellas se concentraba un quinto de la población de aquellas provincias (295).

Estratificación social: (a) nobles, propiedad privada de la tierra, diversas categorías de nobleza; (b) plebeyos, miembros del *calpulli*, propiedad comunal de la tierra; (c) mayeques, condición de siervos, trabajaban las tierras de los nobles; (d) esclavos. Mercaderes asimilados a la nobleza. Los *calpulli* parece eran, en 1519, unidades territoriales, habiendo perdido su carácter tribal, correctamente los españoles los llamaron *barrios;* formación artificial de nuevos *calpulli* al establecer colonias en las marcas fronterizas.

Organización política. En lo interior: poder en manos de la nobleza, oposición de intereses entre nobles y plebeyos manifestada en la oposición de los plebeyos de Tenochtitlán a la guerra contra Azcapotzalco (1428). En lo exterior: política de expansión dirigida por la nobleza militar—cuya hacienda aumentaba por donaciones reales de tierras conquistadas—y por los poderosos gremios de mercaderes. Confederaciones de ciudades-estado para fines de expansión, con tendencia a convertirse en *imperios* bajo la hegemonía de uno de los estados miembros. Organización de los territorios sometidos: guarniciones, colonización. Fortificaciones fronterizas.

Dioses de la guerra, ávidos de sangre humana, forman la ideología adecuada para esas sociedades. El águila solar, emblema de esos dioses, substituyó al viejo dragón de los dioses de las aguas. Se le ofrendan los corazones arrancados de los pechos de los prisioneros. Diferencias de clase en ideología se manifiestan por la continuidad de la devoción popular a los dioses de las aguas.

6. Sobre metalurgia en Michoacán (Borbolla, 284).

AQUATIC SYMBOLS COMMON TO VARIOUS CENTERS OF THE CLASSIC PERIOD IN MESO-AMERICA

J. Eric S. Thompson

The purpose of this paper is to emphasize the underlying unity of the Classic Cultures of Meso-America by calling attention to three symbols or glyphic elements associated with water or rain gods which occur in various centers of the Classic Period, and which I believe to have been derived from a common ancestral culture of the Middle Period. These are the symbols for blue or turquoise, the owl, or rather, some particular species of owl, and the jaguar. I will omit discussion of the ophidian character of rain deities throughout the region, because this is too well known to need emphasis; and I shall not refer to the distribution of representations of Tlaloc, for that presumably represents not a common ancestry, but a later diffusion from a single center.

BLUE OR TURQUOISE SYMBOL

Among the Maya, the names and glyphs for the year refer directly or indirectly to rain. The two names for the year in Yucatec are *tun* and *haab*. The first signifies "jade"; the second "rain," or that which produces it. These terms are really synonymous as jade and water are precious substances and they are both green. Indeed, the jade glyph is used for the day Muluc corresponding to the Nahua *atl*, "water." The glyphs for *tun* and *haab* incorporate glyphic elements corresponding respectively to jade and rain-storm. There are also other glyphic elements used to denote the year, such as a serpent deity, the owl, the earth crocodile, and the old earth god, all of which have marked aquatic associations.

Whereas in Maya, jade symbolizes year, in Nahua, *xiuitl* (*xiuh* in compounds), the primary meaning of which is turquoise, denotes the year. That turquoise or blue, like jade, has the ritualistic value "rain" or "water" is, I think, fairly well accepted. A name for Tlalocan, the abode of the rain gods, was *xiuhcalco*, "the place of the turquoise house," as is given in the hymn to the Tlalocs reproduced in Sahagun; water is described as "celestial blue, clear blue" (288, bk. 6, ch. 37). Chalchihuitlicue, "she of the jade skirt," and whose jade skirt represented water according to Torquemada, was the goddess of water; in Tlaxcala she was called not "jade-skirted" but blue-skirted (Matlalcueye) because blue was the color of water (238, tratado 3, ch. 16), and in Sahagun's illustration she wears a blue dress which is described as painted with lines of water. Accordingly, I think it is a fair assumption that when Nahua-speaking people called the year "turquoise" they were using the word ritualistically to denote rain, just as the Maya did when they called the year "jade."

31

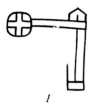

1

2

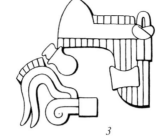

3

4

5

6

7

8

9

10

11

12

13

14   15

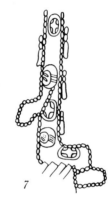

16   17   18

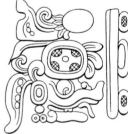

19

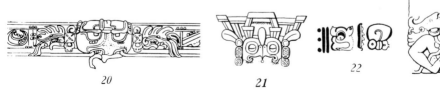

20   21   22   23

Fig. 1

In the Zapotec inscriptions, as Caso (71, 76) has shown, the symbol for year has as its dominant feature a turquoise ornament (Fig. 1, *1, 2*). Caso identifies this element as the *yacaxihuitl*, "the turquoise nose ornament," which is one of the attributes of the Zapotec rain gods, the Cocijos. I would however be inclined to think it was the *xiuhuitzolli*, "the turquoise forehead band and headdress, which is the attribute of Xiuhtecutli in particular, and persons of rank in general. (Fig. 1, *3*). The difference in identification is minor, whether it be the turquoise nose ornament or the front of the turquoise head-band is of small consequence; the point is that the symbol, a cross in a circle, stands for turquoise in both identifications.

If this is the emblem of the Zapotec equivalent of Xiuhtecutli, the old fire god, it is interesting to note that his name means "lord of the turquoise" or "lord of the year," and that despite his igneous dominion, he had his abode in a land of flowers amidst the water, enwrapped in water clouds, and was the lord of the day Atl, "water," corresponding to the Maya day Muluc, represented by jade.

Among the later cultures of central and southern Mexico the year symbol is the trapezoid sign, which, as Seler pointed out many years ago (308, I, 841), appears also as the tail and the identifying feature of the xiuhcoatl, "the turquoise snake," worn by Xiuhtecutli on his back and one of his most characteris-

---

FIG. 1.—Various aquatic elements

1, 2. Element with turquoise symbol identified by Caso as year-bearer symbol in Zapotec writing. After Caso.

3. Emblems of Xiuhtecutli on a stone box in Museo Nacional de Antropología, Mexico. After Beyer.

4. Trapezoid element on tail of stone xiuhcoatl in British Museum. After Joyce.

5. Trapezoid element on tail of xiuhcoatl worn by Xiuhtecutli. Codex Telleriano-Remensis.

6. Falling water with cross-in-circle emblem. Quirigua P.

7. Falling water with cross-in-circle and yax (green) emblems. Yaxchilan 7.

8. Falling water with cross-in-circle and completion emblems. The completion sign has aquatic associations. Quirigua H.

9. Trapezoid and cross-in-circle elements combined to form year-bearer symbol. Xochicalco.

10. Symbol for turquoise. Codex Mendoza.

11. Cross in frame as rain symbol at Teotihuacan. After Armillas.

12. Cross in circle as world direction color. Codex Dresden 31c.

13. Combination of yax (green) and cross in circle. Codex Dresden 18c.

14. Glyph with cross-in-circle affix, probably denoting rainy sky. Yaxchilan L 25.

15. Glyph with yax affix, probably denoting rainy sky. Yaxchilan L 16.

16. Cross in frame below probable water element. Cerro de las Mesas 8. After Stirling.

17. Sky symbol with what is probably elaboration of cross in frame pendant. Slab in American Museum of Natural History.

18. Tlaloc mouth combined with cross in frame. Teotihuacan. After Seler.

19. Earth monster with coefficient of seven, vegetal motifs and cross in circle. Copan D. After Maudslay.

20. Owl perched on celestial planetary band representing the sky. Palenque House E.

21. Owl with trapezoid headdress and earplugs with cross in circle. Piedras Negras 9.

22. Hieroglyph of Moan bird. Dresden 16c.

23. Full-figure representation of Chicchan rain god of number nine showing jaguar paw on temple. Dots on chin are restored. Quirigua D.

tic attributes (Fig. 1, 4, 5). This is also an emblem of the Tlalocs, probably to emphasize their connection with turquoise, a rain symbol.

At Xochicalco we find these two year symbols, the cross-in-circle and the trapezoid element, combined to indicate year (Fig. 1, 9). This would be a form transitional from the early Zapotec to the later Aztec period, reflecting the presumed position of Xochicalco sculpture in the historical sequence.

The cross-in-circle, identified as the Zapotec symbol for turquoise, is a common glyph and art motif in the Maya area. Among other things it represents the color associated with the direction south (Fig. 1, 12). In Yucatan at the time of the Spanish conquest, yellow was the color assigned to that direction, and, accordingly, it has been generally assumed that this cross represents the color yellow. However, there is full and, I think, incontrovertible evidence that its primary meaning in Maya art and hieroglyphic writing is that of water. It appears in what are pretty clearly streams of water, either alone or in conjunction with the symbol yax, "green," an emblem of the rain snakes, the Chicchan gods (Fig. 1, 6, 7), or in conjunction with the completion sign, which also has an aquatic connotation (Fig. 1, 8). As a glyphic affix it is interchangeable with various aquatic elements, among which the yax element and the shell are common. The cleft sky-sign, which with its affixes probably represents falling rain or rainy skies, supplies good examples of this interchangeability with aquatic affixes (Fig. 1, 14, 15). It is also prominently displayed on the head of the earth dragon, a deity with strongly aquatic and vegetal associations (Fig. 1, 19). More detailed reasons for seeing this cross-in-circle as a water symbol are given in *Maya Hieroglyphic Writing; Introduction* (372).

It is possible—and there is other evidence in favor of the thesis—that the Maya color assigned to the south was originally blue-green (they are both called *yax* or its cognates in most Maya languages), and that, as a corollary, the association of yellow with the south was a late and perhaps regional shift which is not reflected in any of the three surviving Maya codices. In that case, of course, we do not know the Maya glyph for yellow. Whether that surmise is correct or not, there is no question that the principal value of the cross-in-circle among the Maya was that of water. It might well have had the original significance blue-green; it can hardly have originally meant "turquoise," for that commodity was probably unknown to the inventors of the Maya glyphs. It often appears in celestial bands in Maya codices, not uncommonly adjacent to the symbol for darkness, thus it might well signify, in contrast, the blue sky of day time. What is probably an elaboration of the turquoise glyph is also associated with the sky in Zapotec art, as Caso has pointed out (76, p. 32; Fig. 80) (Fig. 1, 17), and there, too, it might indicate the blue sky, particularly as the opposite motif, night or death eyes are frequently set in the sky in Zapotec art. Alternatively, it might represent the weeping skies in both cultures.

In classical Teotihuacan this cross-in-circle is again prominent and, as Armillas has noted (15), is most intimately associated with representations of Tlaloc (Fig. 1, 11, 18). Seler somewhat confused the issue by identifying this design with the Maya glyph for Venus (308, V, 440), but the two are quite distinct. There can be little doubt that in Teotihuacan, as at Monte Alban, the symbol represents turquoise and was used ritualistically to denote rain. Turquoise, of course, is a constant feature of Tlaloc in the later horizons of central and southern Mexico.

This turquoise symbol reappears at Cerro de las Mesas. It forms the earplug of Tlaloc on Stela 15, where it must surely indicate that the earplug was of turquoise, and it is prominent on other stelae in association with what may be the glyph for water (Fig. 1, *16*).

According to Codex Mendoza the Aztec glyph for turquoise was something different from the cross-in-circle (Fig. 1, *10*), and there is a glyph depicting turquoise mosaic. However, there is evidence that the old form survived until the Spanish Conquest; in Sahagun's picture of Xiuhtecutli, the god carries a shield which has as its design this cross in yellow on a blue background. This is described in the text as *xiuhtezcatlapanqui ynichimal*, "his shield of turquoise and mirror stone (pyrite?)."

Thus we have this cross-in-circle as a symbol for water and perhaps the color blue in Classic Maya; of turquoise (originally blue-green?) and, by extension, of the year and probably water, at Monte Alban; as an ornament of the Tlalocs, almost certainly with the values turquoise and water, in classical Teotihuacan, and as an earplug design, surely with the value turquoise, at Cerro de las Mesas. This is a wide diffusion of a single element on the classic horizon. In later times the original element varies somewhat in central Mexico, but the example from Sahagun already cited, and the appearance of the element, together with numerous water symbols, on a chacmol from Tacubaya (308, II, 818), show that the old form did survive; a somewhat broken down variant in Codex Xolotl has the value "turquoise" (107).

SCREECH OWL

Among the Maya the moan bird, apparently a variety of screech owl, is intimately associated with rain, not with death, as is generally supposed, although another variety of owl (the *cui*) is an omen of death. Indeed, *moan* in Yucatec means shower. In the art of the Initial Series period, the moan birds perch on the celestial dragons associated with the four world directions who are the senders of rain; the motif is common in Maya art (fig. 1, *20*). On Stela 5, Piedras Negras, the moan bird is set amid cauac (storm) symbols, and has the face of God D, the sky god; on Stela 9, Piedras Negras, he has the trapezoid ornament on his head and the cross-in-circle as ear ornaments (fig. 1, *21*). Indeed, the pluvial associations of this bird in the Maya area are beyond dispute. The double glyph of the moan bird comprises the head of that bird with a coefficient of thirteen and a hook element, likewise a water symbol. The whole apparently refers to *oxlahun-taz-muyal*, "13 layers of clouds," mentioned in prayers. Another form has the St. Andrew's cross also with coefficient of thirteen.

In the art of Teotihuacan, the owl likewise symbolizes rain, for it is intimately associated with the Tlalocs. Representations of Tlaloc may have the owl as a headdress, as a pectoral, or as a general attachment (15, pp. 10–11). Nevertheless, the owl does not seem to be associated with the rain god of Monte Alban nor with the Tlalocs of Kaminaljuyu, but the Tlaloc on Cerro de las Mesas, Stela 15, conceivably has an owl as his helmet. The evidence is uncertain; Stirling regards the head as that of a jaguar, which it may well be, but the angular element center bottom might be the owl's beak. At Monte Alban the glyph of the owl is a day sign, but in several cases it has a coefficient of 13, reminding one that 13 Owl is the Maya glyph of the moan bird and probably stands for the thirteen layers of clouds or skies.

In the case of the owl as a rain symbol there may be linguistic evidence that the concept spread from the Maya area to central Mexico. The Nahua term *Tamoanchan*, the celestial paradise and land of plenty, the abode of the gods, is pure Chiapan Maya; *ta*, "at," *moan*, "the moan bird," *chan*, "sky" or "snake." The complete word means "at the moan-bird sky" or "at the moan bird and snake," a clear reference to this celestial realm of Maya mythology. As the celestial monsters vary from crocodiles to snakes, *chan* could refer either to the sky itself or to the celestial monsters who form it. Seler came near getting this interpretation many years ago, but failed to realize that *chan* is the Chiapan word for sky or snake.

THE JAGUAR

The connections of the rain gods of La Venta, Teotihuacan, and Monte Alban with the jaguar are too well-known to need discussion; less obvious is the incorporation of feline features in the portraits of Maya rain gods. The Maya Chicchan god, deity of the number nine and a serpent god of rain, also has jaguar traits. Spots or a beard on his chin are his distinguishing features, and it is a fair assumption that these indicate jaguar markings, but full figure representations of this head put the matter beyond dispute, for the deity often wears a paw on his temple (fig. 1, 23). This paw, I think, can be accepted without much question as that of a jaguar, especially when we recollect that a common name for the jaguar in Yucatan is *chacmol*, "great paw."

On the other hand, the butterfly, so intimately associated with Tlaloc in the art of Teotihuacan, is, so far as I know, absent from representations of rain gods or snakes in Maya art. Seemingly, it is also unknown in representations of rain deities in Zapotec and La Venta art, although present in Teotihuacan decoration at Kaminaljuyu.

We have, therefore, three rather unusual elements which are closely associated with rain gods in sundry centers of the Classic Period. The turquoise and jaguar elements probably derive from a common ancestor of the Formative horizon; the owl concept may have the same origin, but may have diffused from the Maya area.

EXPLORACIONES EN XOCHICALCO

Eduardo Noguera

Después de haberse practicado prolongadas exploraciones en Xochicalco en el transcurso de los últimos años, se han obtenido resultados de cierta importancia y conclusiones provisionales, además de datos adicionales acerca del significado de esta antigua ciudad los que ya fueron publicados en diversas revistas (246; 247).

Como resultado de estas investigaciones se ha podido comprobar que Xochicalco no guarda siempre constante relación con las culturas del centro de México más que en pequeña proporción y en ese caso esas relaciones corresponden a épocas más recientes. Por el contrario, hay indicaciones de que los orígenes de esta cultura y sus más íntimas influencias deben buscarse en el Sur de México y en lugares muy apartados de Xochicalco.

Gracias a los trabajos emprendidos se observan ciertos contactos con la cultura maya. Existen numerosas características que ofrecen semejanzas con las obras de esos pueblos, tanto en arquitectura y en cerámica lo mismo que en otros rasgos. Todos esos puntos han sido expuestos y dados a la publicidad en las obras citadas, por lo que ahora sólo haremos breve revisión y en vista de que muchos datos son ya conocidos, ahora, como contribución al XXIX Congreso Internacional de Americanistas expondremos los rasgos y características significativas y las relaciones que ofrecen aunque forzosamente incurramos en inevitables repeticiones ya que este escrito constituye, en realidad, el texto de la película que se ha exhibido ante la asamblea, ilustrando en la pantalla todas esas manifestaciones que se descubren en Xochicalco.

Efectivamente volviendo a la zona maya en busca de analogías, tenemos Cobá, primeramente, en donde existe un juego de pelota conservando aún el anillo colocado, en la intersección del talud y el paramento. En Copán se halla una cabeza de guacamaya en ese mismo lugar con la circunstancia de que el perfil es sensiblemente semejante al de Xochicalco.[1] Otro tanto puede decirse del Juego de Pelota de Guaytan en el Valle Motagua, Guatemala (313). En cambio en Piedras Negras, la Estructura K-6 está desprovista del anillo, pero sus perfiles son muy parecidos variando el talud que es de menor inclinación (293). Estrechas o lejanas analogías pueden también establecerse con juegos de pelota de Yaxchilan, la Estructura R-11 de Piedras Negras o con Calakmul, Río Bec, Becan y Uxul de Campeche (285) y fuera de la zona maya con Yucuñudahui, Oaxaca; pero su examen y comparación nos tomaría excesivo espacio.

1. Datos proporcionados por Linton Satterthwaite (293) y Morley (229).

37

A la vez que el monumento explorado ha sido el principal contribuyente al renombre de Xochicalco, sus relieves han motivado varios estudios ampliamente publicados (263, 306, 223, 260, 248) pero todavía su significado no ha sido demostrado de manera absolutamente convincente. (Existen al respecto varias interpretaciones como las de Mena, Palacios Meyer y otras de menor extensión). Por otra parte, como no es el objeto de este estudio intentar ninguna investigación interpretativa, que se hará más adelante cuando se tengan más conocimientos y la región sea mejor explorada, sólo expresaremos en forma concreta nuestra opinión acerca del significado que en resumen expresan estos hermosos relieves. Creemos que se trata únicamente de un registro y corrección caléndarica como así lo asienta Palacios apoyándose de manera preferente en el relieve situado en la esquina N.W. en que se ve parte de una figura humana que colocada dentro del signo *Calli* reune con la mano derecha, abierta sobre el numeral 1. una fecha con otra, por medio de una cuerda, y con la izquierda tira el signo XI *Ozómatli*.

A nuestro entender no sólo expresa el registro de un calendario sino que en forma alegórica anuncia el cambio de todo un sistema, es decir, la adopción de uno nuevo que sería el nahua-mixteco y el abandono del antiguo maya-zapoteca significando, igualmente, la llegada de nuevas gentes o de otras influencias culturales.

En cuanto al estilo de los relieves, en especial el tipo étnico de las figuras humanas, es de un decidido sabor maya mejor que zapoteca. La expresión del rostro, la frente huidiza, al parecer deformada, tratamiento del cuerpo, el elegante y vistoso tocado, la delicadeza de la postura del personaje; no se puede menos que pensar en las obras de los mayas si se buscan analogías, indicios y aun grandes sugerencias ofrecen algunos relieves de la zona maya; indicándonos que de allí es de donde pueden proceder el origen, la inspiración o, en último caso, influencias del arte expresado en Xochicalco.

Al proseguirse las exploraciones se obtuvieron nuevos datos que vienen a corroborar esas relaciones. Al explorar el llamado Edificio "B," contiguo al Juego de Pelota, se han encontrado otros elementos igualmente communes a Xochicalco y a los mayas. Efectivamente, dentro de las cámaras que componen este grupo de estructuras aparece una especie de plataforma o banqueta, adosada al fondo de algunas cámaras y este mismo elemento se encuentra con cierta frecuencia en los edificios mayas. Algunas veces estas plataformas están ornamentadas con pequeños nichos o llevan una serie de losetas a modo de taludes en su parte superior, e igual cosa ocurre en las construcciones mayas. Entre éstas últimas, dichas plataformas fueron quizás evolucionando hasta convertirse en los elaborados y artísticos altares que son frecuentes en Piedras Negras y Copán.

Las semejanzas más estrechas se pueden observar en el altar del Templo E-I de Uaxactun, Guatemala; las banquetas de los cuartos F, B 4; A y B de San José, Honduras Británicas especialmente la cámara B, C 4 que tiene nichos muy semejantes a los de Xochicalco; en Copán, por su altar dentro de la cámara W del templo XXII; por no mencionar más que los de mayor fama, pero igualmente debe existir en otras ciudades mayas este rasgo arquitectónico tan típicamente maya y frecuente en Xochicalco.

Sin embargo; este mismo elemento arquitectónico ocurre también en Tula, pero ya hicimos observar que el Juego de Pelota de esa ciudad es de proporciones, corte y aspecto, semejante al de Xochicalco el que, a su vez, es análogo a los de la zona maya.

Al proseguir las exploraciones y como más reciente información, han aparecido otros materiales que pretenden señalar analogías con la cultura que comparamos a través de algunos nuevos elementos arquitectónicos.

En la porción sur del mismo Edificio "B" que ha sido más intensamente explorado, aparecieron unas cámaras cuyo significado no se pudo averiguar por de pronto. El examen más detenido de esta estructura permite suponer, con bastantes visos de exactitud, que se trata de un temascali. Esta identificación se ha establecido por medio de la comparación de cámaras semejantes en la zona maya.

En efecto, en ciudades antiguas de la cultura maya se han descubierto cierto tipo de construcciones que exhiben determinados rasgos presentando con ello un aspecto muy diferente a los templos y palacios. Esta clase de estructuras según primera identificación de Morley, eran temascalis, los cuales guardan analogía en cuanto a su plano y construcción con los que están en uso en pueblos modernos del centro de México y su forma y proporciones apenas ha cambiado desde épocas antiguas. Por otra parte existe la posibilidad de que estructuras análogas existan en ciudades prehispánicas de estas regiones centrales que, o no han sido identificadas o la exploración no las ha descubierto, si consideramos lo abundante que son en ciertos poblados actuales.

En Xochicalco al sur del patio del grupo sur Edificio "B"—(no. XXXVI) se forman tres pequeñas cámaras (XXXVII, XXXVIII y XXXIX) con niveles de quince centímetros más bajos. La cámara XXXVII tiene una puerta de salida al sur que comunica a un corto vestíbulo (XXXVIII) de alto escalón al S. y en su extremo S. E. colinda con una pequeña cámara (XXXIX) la que a su vez limita con el pasillo que da entrada a la pequeña cámara (XL).

La disposición de una cámara central, cámaras laterales y pasillo (XLI) junto con otros elementos arquitectónicos, parece señalar que se trató de un baño de temascal. Esta suposición se basa en la comparación con los de Piedras Negras y los otros que hemos citado extendiéndose estas comparaciones hasta los modernos temascalis que indudablemente siguieron las tradiciones de los antiguos. Aunque de otras proporciones y otros detalles diferentes, concuerdan en conjunto y obedecen al mismo plano, por lo que salvo que en futuras exploraciones ocurran nuevos datos que nos desmientan, creemos fundada esta suposición.

Por otra parte, si consideramos la situación de esta pequeña cámara al extremo de un gran edificio, que, seguramente, sirvió de habitaciones, es de creerse, como hemos dicho con razones fundadas, que tuvo esa utilidad.

En cuanto a los temascalis de la zona maya, según se encuentran en Piedras

Negras, tenemos la Estructura N-1 excavada por Satterthwaite. Consiste en un cuarto rectangular o sea la *cámara central* situada dentro de un cuarto de mayores proporciones. Hay otra estructura la llamada P-7 que está mejor conservada teniendo aún su techo en buen estado. La cámara central es más pequeña y baja con respecto a los otros edificios.

Las dimensiones de estas estructuras en su interior son de 3.30 a 4.80 metros de largo por 2.15 a 3.20 de ancho. La puerta de entrada a la cámara interior es siempre muy baja y angosta, de 0.90 cms. a 1.13 de alto, por 0.70 a 0.89 de ancho. Todas estas estructuras tienen un dintel cuyas dimensiones por término medio son de 0.76 cms. por 0.34 cms.

Por lo común al fondo de la cámara interior hay una construcción rectangular o sea la cámara de fuego de 1.15 por 0.90 cms. en el caso de la Estructura N-1. La puerta tiene dintel monolítico de 0.70 cms. por 0.83.

Por lo que se refiere a Chichén-Itzá hay dos ejemplos de estas estructuras que se asemejan a los de Piedras Negras y a los del centro de México, por el hecho de estar situada la cámara de fuego al fondo y con un pasaje que conduce a ella. Además en Chichén-Itzá tienen un cuarto exterior en forma de largo pórtico.

Las dimensiones son parecidas en esas distintas localidades y en Xochicalco. En efecto en esta última ciudad arqueológica, la cámara central o de fuego mide 2.60 mtrs. de largo por 1.60 mtrs. de ancho y la pequeña cámara lateral, a la izquierda, 1.40 mtrs. por 1.15 mtrs. Esta última se encuentra dentro de otra cuyas dimensiones son de 3.80 mtrs. por 4.20 mtrs. El pasillo tiene 3.45 mtrs. de largo por 1.10 mtrs. de ancho coincidiendo su semejanza aún en pequeños detalles como es el dintel de piedra de proporciones y aspecto muy parecido al de Piedras Negras y la puerta de entrada a la cámara es de 0.55 mtrs. de ancho por 1.30 mtrs.

Esta clase de construcciones o sean temascalis, no se han encontrado en ciudades antiguas de la Meseta Central o quizás no han sido identificadas, por lo tanto parece ser, un rasgo maya que sólo tuvo desarrollo en Xochicalco y es un dato adicional de las relaciones con la cultura maya aunque surge la posibilidad que exista esta misma clase de construcciones en ciudades del centro de México y que aún no han sido reconocidas por los distintos investigadores.[2]

Por lo que se refiere a las analogías que ofrece la cerámica, antes de las exploraciones y con anterioridad al estudio de la cerámica de Xochicalco, se presumía que ese material ofrecería marcadas relaciones con culturas del centro de México y se tomaba como hecho establecido que no sería más que una repetición de los tipos comunes a Teotihuacán, o culturas post-teotihuacanas (Mazapa, Coyotlatelco, Tlahuica y en general Mixteca-Puebla) o, en último caso, relacionado con culturas conocidas. Pero su estudio y análisis, contrariamente a lo supuesto, conduce a distintos resultados.

El examen de la cerámica de Xochicalco revela varios tipos característicos

2. Todos estos últimos datos fueron dados a conocer en la *Revista mexicana de estudios antropológicos*, Tomo X (México, 1948–49).

muy poco diferentes en cuanto a la clase de barro y sus componentes y de mayor homogeneidad por lo que se refiere a las formas. En cuanto a la decoración ésta es sencilla.

Los tipos más importantes de cerámica son: Anaranjado A, B, C, D, E, F, crema oscura, café claro, crema rojizo, gris, negra y rojo pulido, los cuales ya fueron suficientemente descritas en las publicaciones referidas por lo que sólo expondremos las conclusiones que se obtuvieron de ese material.

En primer lugar la forma especial de cajetes que corresponden a varios tipos de cerámica, que ya hemos descrito y se distinguen por un reborde basal. Esta forma es frecuente en un tipo de cerámica del mismo Estado de Morelos. En las colecciones del Museo Nacional hay un lote catalogado como procedente de Totolapán, Morelos, recogido por el Obispo Plancarte y clasificado como de cultura arcaica que ofrece formas no idénticas, pero sí análogas a las de Xochicalco teniendo en cuenta el reborde aludido y el fondo cóncavo.

Vasijas con este reborde característico y forma semejante se encuentran, igualmente, en Monte Albán I, naturalmente hechas del barro gris propio de esa región. Por su parte, en Xochicalco también ocurren vasijas de barro de ese color aunque en menor cantidad.

Más significativo es el hecho de que vasijas de forma casi idéntica a las de Xochicalco se encuentran en Guaytán, San Agustín Acasaguastlán, Guatemala, que han sido recientemente descubiertas y descritas por Smith y Kidder.

A primera vista parece un poco atrevida esta afirmación tomando en cuenta la enorme distancia geográfica que existe entre estas dos zonas; pero como las regiones intermedias no han sido exploradas y no pudiendo, por ello, establecer los nexos en esas zonas intermedias, tenemos que buscarlas en las más apartadas. No solamente existe semejanza en la forma de las vasijas mencionadas sino que hay otras en esa misma zona de Guaytán que tienen decoraciones de discos rojos que recuerdan mucho lo que es tan frecuente en Xochicalco.

La etapa cronológica a que pertenece esta clase de vasijas sería del Período Lato como así lo llaman Smith y Kidder, y el siguiente el Magdalena de esa región. El período Lato es sensiblemente contemporáneo del clásico Tzakol de Uaxactun y el Magdalena algo más reciente que el Tepeu.

Sin embargo, vasijas con reborde o ángulo basal ocurren asimismo en Uaxactun, desde el período Chicanel, por lo que hay la posibilidad de que este rasgo cerámico llegara posteriormente tanto a Guaytán como a Xochicalco, aunque esto no parece aplicársele a la última zona.

De comparable antigüedad y forma son algunas vasijas que describe Ekholm en el área Tampico-Pánuco y algo semejante se nos ofrece en Tres Zapotes y Cerro de las Mesas correspondiendo a los períodos antiguos respectivamente.

A efecto de esclarecer nuestras suposiciones, el Sr. Alberto Ruz tuvo la gentileza de examinar nuestra colección ya que él ha trabajado con detenimiento en algunas de las zonas de la región maya y tiene gran familiaridad con esa clase de cerámica habiéndo encontrado que tiene un aire mayoide.

En el Tajín, en las colecciones del Sr. Du Solier se encuentra una gran seme-janza en cuanto a la forma de las vasijas, clase de barro y aun motivos decora-tivos en relieve que hallan paralelo con lo encontrado en Xochicalco por lo que se refiere a la cerámica negra y correspondiente a la etapa más antigua.

Es cierto que la forma de las vasijas de Xochicalco no es absolutamente idéntica a todas las que comparamos puesto que hay variaciones en cuanto a la altura, inclinación de las paredes y los soportes, pero junto con la presencia del reborde característico lo predominante son cajetes de aspecto muy semejante.

En cambio el Sr. Pedro Armillas, quien examinó nuestra colección, no encon-tró nada en concreto que pudiera relacionarse con la zona explorada por él en la cuenca del Balsas Medio; pero a su vez, tiene la impresión que Xochicalco está relacionado con culturas más al Sur.

Todo este acervo señala que se trata de una etapa muy antigua comparable al arcaico del Valle de México y de Monte Albán I, y que posiblemente corresponde al período Mamom-Chicanel de la zona maya, a los períodos antiguos de Tres Zapotes y cerro de las Mesas, Vera Cruz, al I y II del área Tampico-Pánuco, y al Período Lato de Guaytan que parece ser un poco posterior a Mamom-Chicanel, puesto que Smith y Kidder lo encuentran contemporáneo con Tzakol.

En resumen y como conclusión repetimos lo que en su oportunidad publica-mos en la revista *Cuadernos Americanos* y que con los nuevos datos obtenidos se refuerzan esas conclusiones en el sentido de que existen presunciones ahora con mejores bases de apoyo de que llegaron influencias culturales mayoides y se establecieron en Xochicalco, dejando allí su sello característico; pero quedaron cortadas por circunstancias desconocidas y posteriormente se establecieron con las del centro.

Esta cultura tiene visos de ser más antigua de lo que se creía, de ofrecer un marcado sabor maya y de haberse desarrollado como un fenómeno aislado, no recibiendo, por causas que no podemos explicar en estos momentos, influencias de las culturas del centro de México, de las que se hallaba rodeada, sino en épocas más tardías.

Finalmente, como asentamos anteriormente, estos resultados tendrán que ser modificados cuando se exploren más detenidamente las regiones intermedias entre Xochicalco y las zonas zapoteca y maya, donde quizás se encuentre la verdadera solución y aparezca el camino por donde llegaron estos elementos.

LAS CERÁMICAS DEL HORIZONTE-CULTURAS LOCALES

E. F. Jacobs Müller

Tres hipótesis de trascendencia para la historia antigua brotan del estudio de la cerámica correspondiente a las dos primeras etapas del Horizonte de las Culturas Locales; etapas llamadas en general Azteca I y Azteca II en los estados de México y Morelos, además del Distrito Federal.

Las tres hipótesis son: (*a*) La cerámica de rojo sobre crema o anaranjado tuvo su origen en Xochicalco. (*b*) El territorio que hoy corresponde a los Estados de México y Morelos estaba dividido en dos zonas: la del poniente y la del oriente. La primera fué territorio de las cerámicas Coyotlatelco y Matlatzinca, cuyo desarrollo fué la Mazapa; la segunda o del oriente, fué de la cerámica Azteca I, que dió origen a la Azteca II. (*c*) Pudo haber habido un foco único de la cerámica Choluteca y polícromo en ese territorio, luego dividido en dos por la intrusión de las cerámicas Coyotlatelco y Matlatzinca por un lado y de la Azteca I por el otro; o a la inversa; establecidas estas cerámicas Coyotlatelco y Matlatzinca y Azteca I se incrustaron las cerámicas Choluteca y Polícroma, así en la zona occidental como en la oriental del territorio del que aquí se trata. Esta última hipótesis doble no puede afirmarse ni desecharse mientras no se hagan exploraciones en el noreste del Estado de México.

Provisionalmente se puede agrupar toda la cerámica de este horizonte en varias familias. La primera y más importante es la de rojo sobre crema o anaranjado, con dos subdivisiones principales:

A. Cerámica Coyotlatelco
B. Cerámica Mazapa

Sigue la familia de Anaranjado, que puede dividirse en dos clases:

A. Azteca I
B. Azteca II

Además hay que enumerar otras de menos importancia, pero también características de este nivel: la de rojo bruñido, la polícroma, con su variación de tipo Laca y Laca firme similares a los de la cerámica Choluteca, la anaranjada fina y la plomiza.

VALLE DE MEXICO

Familia de rojo sobre crema y rojo sobre anaranjado.

A. CERÁMICA COYOTLATELCO

Se caracteriza siempre por una banda roja sobre el labio de la vasija; el resto lleva un baño de color crema o anaranjado. Además, existe un subtipo, que es el negro sobre rojo.

Formas: Se puede dividir en tres clases de "cajetes." La primera se distingue por tener las paredes y el fondo cóncavo, y los soportes, en forma cónica alargada. La decoración principal está en el interior de la vasija. La segunda clase difiere de la primera en que las paredes tienen una inclinación suave. El fondo es plano y los soportes, aunque de forma cónica, pueden ser pequeños, medianos o grandes. En cierto sentido hace recordar la cerámica de rojo sobre café de Teotihuacán. Esta segunda se caracteriza por llevar la decoración en el exterior. Hay un tercer grupo de vasijas sin soportes, poco profundas y de fondo ligeramente cóncavo. En otras palabras: la cerámica llamada del tipo Casquete. La decoración, como ocurre en el grupo segundo, aparece en la parte exterior.

Decoración.—Los motivos son geométricos. Hay diferencia entre los del exterior y los del interior de las vasijas. Los más comunes son: zetas, eses, equis, ganchos, crecientes, ángulos escalonados, casillas como de ajedrez, espirales, puntos limitados por líneas verticales, volutas, círculos de rojo, etc. (378, pp. 51-53, Lams. 11, 18, 19).

Cerámicas asociadas: En las exploraciones hechas hasta la fecha la cerámica Coyotlatelco se ha encontrado, por lo general asociada con:

a) rojo bruñido
b) polícromo-negro, rojo y blanco sobre anaranjado
c) anaranjado de tono rojizo

Una clase de esta última se caracteriza por la decoración de líneas negras gruesas, dibujadas libremente sobre el color natural del barro.

Exploraciones.—Teotihuacán-Tetitla, Santiago Ahuizotla, Atzcapotzalco y Tenayuca. Recolección superficial: El Arbolillo, Cerro de la Estrella, Bosque del Contadero, Texcoco, Papalotla, Chiconautla y Culhuacán (397, pp. 544-45).

Antecedentes probables.—Armillas encontró en la exploración de Tetitla la cerámica Coyotlatelco debajo de la cerámica Mazapa,[1] lo cual parece indicar que es más antigua que la Mazapa en ese lugar. Además, su parecido con la cerámica de rojo sobre café que se encuentra en Teotihuacán desde la época II sugiere que es bastante antigua allí.[2] Sin embargo, Vaillant encontró una cerámica con el borde rojo sobre anaranjado de varios tonos con dibujos burdos en la cultura arcaica desde el horizonte Zacatenco Medio (399, pp. 214, 269, 275-79). Esto indica la antigüedad en esta familia de cerámica en el Valle de México.

VALLE DE TOLUCA

José García Payón halló en el valle de Toluca una cerámica análoga a la de Coyotlatelco. Esta cerámica tiene, por lo general, una banda roja sobre el baño café de la vasija, la cual es de soportes cónicos. García Payón la ha llamado tipo

1. Armillas, Pedro, Semenario de Arqueología. México, D.F., 1944.

2. Exhibición de Cerámica, Salon de Teotihuacán, Museo Nacional de Antropología. México, D.F., 1949.

I-B. En el tiempo se relaciona con el horizonte Teotihuacán II o el Clásico. En el horizonte siguiente se trueca en los tipos 2AY y 3-A (123, pp. 230–31).

Decoración.—Los motivos de esta cerámica, como los de la cerámica Coyotlatelco son geométricos. Aquí se encuentra, asimismo, el sub-tipo negro sobre rojo. Además, se halla la familia de rojo bruñido, que en el Valle de Toluca, se caracteriza por sus soportes del tipo araña. En el tiempo todas estas familias de cerámica se relacionan con el horizonte Teotihuacán IV.

Sigue el tipo 3-B en el cual aparece el rojo sobre crema. Este último se relaciona con el negro y rojo sobre café, o el negro o el rojo sobre baño blanco. También se halló una cerámica roja con decoración esgrafiada, además del tipo Laca y el polícromo, las tres, similares a las de Choluteca I-III.

Exploraciones.—Calixtlahuaca y Malinalco, recolección superficial en todo el Valle de Ixtlahuaca, y el de Jilotepec. Además de la cerámica análoga a la de Coyotlatelco, se hallaron los tipos siguientes: rojo sobre negro o sobre crema, rojo bruñido, rojo con decoración esgrafiada, polícromo y laca similar al Choluteca I (241, pp. 50–54, Lams. 4–8).

Antecedentes probables.—Al examinarse los muchos tepalcates recojidos en los valles de Toluca e Ixtlahuaca no se pudo distinguir si eran Coyotlatelco, Matlatzinca o de Xochicalco. García Payón encontró un tipo de cerámica, el rojo sobre café, contemporáneo de Teotihuacán. Esto parece indicar que el Valle de Toluca no fué la cuna de la cerámica Coyotlatelco.

VALLE DE MORELOS

Desde los niveles más antiguos, en las exploraciones de Xochicalco Noguera encontró una familia de cerámica que se caracteriza por la banda roja sobre el labio de la vasija. Lo que cambia es el baño, que puede ser rojo sobre crema, café claro u oscuro, o anaranjado. Esta familia es la que dió el porcentaje más alto en el total de la cerámica de ese lugar (247, p. 139). Lo grande de su desarrollo, el gran número de sus variantes, y el hecho de que se encuentra desde horizontes más antiguos que corresponden en el tiempo a Zacatenco I del Valle de México— todo esto parece indicar que Xochicalco fué el lugar de origen de esta cerámica.

Formas.—Hay tres clases de cajetes: la primera carece de soportes y tiene la forma de casquete; la segunda tiene soportes huecos de cascabel y la tercera es de soportes cónicos, de tamaños variables.

Decoración.—Además de la banda roja que se encuentra en el labio de la vasija, el baño aplicado es de un pulimento extraordinario. Este baño es de color naranja, crema, café claro u oscuro. La decoración principal se compone de dibujos geométricos: círculos rojos en el interior de la vasija, manchas o triángulos llenos en la pared exterior del cajete. Estos mismos motivos persisten desde el comienzo del horizonte más antiguo hasta el final. Solamente las formas de las vasijas cambian según el horizonte a que pertenezcan.

En el Cerro del Venado, Chimalacatlán, desde el horizonte Mazatepec II se hallaron cajetes en forma de casquete, con la característica banda roja sobre el labio y el baño anaranjado de pulido fino, y otros cajetes con soportes. La decoración principal consta de dibujos geométricos.

En el horizonte Quilamula persisten los cajetes del tipo Casquete, pero sin el pulimento fino. Sobre el fondo natural del barro de color anaranjado, los alfareros antiguos dibujaron líneas y puntos gruesos de color blanco en bandas horizontales (242, p. 45).

En Gualupita, Vaillant encontró en la última época, la cerámica de rojo sobre café, rojo sobre crema, negro, blanco y rojo, la polícroma y otras clases relacionadas con la cerámica Matlatzinca, además de la roja bruñida (401, pp. 88–89, 92, Figs. 26–27).

VALLE DE MEXICO

B. CERÁMICA MAZAPA

Esta cerámica, como la Coyotlatelco, se caracteriza por la banda roja en el labio de la vasija, dibujada sobre un baño crema o café claro.

Formas.—Las principales son cajetes y escasean los soportes.

Decoración.—Es de motivos geométricos. Puede uno dividirla en dos clases: *a* y *b*. La *a* se caracteriza por que son cajetes de muy poco fondo; la decoración se encuentra en el interior de la vasija. Los motivos son: líneas paralelas, rectas, espirales, etc. En la clase *b* los cajetes son más profundos y tienen soportes cónicos grandes con una inclinación. La decoración es de líneas gruesas. Los motivos principales son rayos, ganchos, círculos, etc.

Cerámica asociada con la Mazapa es: el anaranjado, el anaranjado sobre blanco, el laca mate, el anaranjado fino, el rojo bruñido (sobre todo en malacates), el rojizo y el plomizo (189, pp. 78, 126–35).

Exploraciones.—San Francisco Mazapa y Chiconautla. Recolección superficial en la parte septentrional del Valle de México, Chapultepec, Tlatelolco y Chalco. En este último lugar se hallaron figuras del tipo Mazapa aunque estas figuras son bastante raras (397, p. 544).

CERÁMICA AZTECA I

Descripción.—Lo característico es que sobre el fondo natural del barro, que es de un tono rojizo anaranjado, se han pintado líneas gruesas negras en forma libre.

Formas.—Se distingue por la gran variedad de formas: ollas y cántaros con asas de varias clases; platos, cajetes de poco fondo y soportes cilíndricos y molcajetes.

Decoración.—Como en las formas, existe aquí gran variedad de motivos. Entre los más interesantes están las líneales y las figuras geométricas estilizadas, además de dibujos estilizados de la flora, animales, etc. Generalmente forman grandes bandas horizontales en los lados de la vasija y cubren el interior del fondo. Otra característica es la decoración sellada, generalmente en el fondo de la vasija.

Exploraciones.—Tenayuca (249, pp. 143-44) y Culhuacán (243, p. 545). Se ha recojido cerámica superficial en toda la zona de Chalco y Xico (243).

Cerámica asociada: Rojo sobre anaranjado, rojo sobre crema, negro sobre rojo, la rojiza, y la polícroma análoga a Choluteca I-III.

VALLE DE MORELOS

Fué en Tepoztlán donde se encontró un foco de la cerámica Azteca I con sus cajetes de soportes cilíndricos; gran variedad de ollas, cántaros y malacates de forma cónica; así como cajetes de soportes zoomorfos, especialmente en figuras de serpientes análogas a los de Cholula y otras zonas de más al sur (244).

Cerámica asociada de más importancia encontrada en esta región, para este horizonte fué la roja bruñida, rojiza y otras con influencia de la Choluteca.

Posibles antecedentes.—Por la gran cantidad y el desarrollo de tantas variaciones encontradas en Culhuacán, es posible que este sea el lugar de origen. Sin embargo, por la distribución de esta clase de cerámica en el valle de Morelos y otras clases de cerámica de la Mixteca Alta, es posible también que sea una cerámica traída de esta última zona. Solamente más exploraciones pueden aclarar este punto.

VALLE DE MEXICO
CERÁMICA AZTECA II

Descripción.—Cerámica de color anaranjado rojizo; lo más característico es el motivo llamado de Zacatón, que se encuentra en la orilla de la vasija.

Formas.—Como en la cerámica Azteca I, se encuentra aquí gran variedad de formas: ollas, cántaros con asas, platos, cajetes, cazuelas, etc.

Decoración.—Los motivos, por lo general, son lineales; negro, aparte del Zacatón, denota cierto individualismo. Están dispuestos en sentido radial. Hay diferencia entre los motivos del centro y el anular.

Exploraciones.—Las más importantes son las hechas por Noguera en Tenayuca (249, p. 146) y las realizadas en Texcoco, Huexotla y Colhuacán por otros arqueólogos (3, Lam. 11, Fig. 1; Lam. 13, Fig. 14; Lam. 20, Figs. 1, 3, 4, 5, 7, 8, 9, 10, 11).

EL MAPA

Para apreciar la distribución de estas familias de cerámica, se han concentrado todos los datos en un mapa y se han señalado los límites de la expansión de cada familia.

Para que puedan distinguirse con más claridad en el mapa los sitios arqueológicos donde se han hecho exploraciones estratigráficas, se les designa con los números que indica la clave siguiente:

1. Tula
2. Teptihuacán
3. Coyotlatelco
3A. Tenayuca

4. Culhuacán
5. Chiconaulta
6. Calixtlahuaca
7. Malinalco
8. Xochicalco
9. Gualupita
10. Cuernavaca
11. Tepoztlán
12. Chimalacatlán

En el mapa la distribución de cada familia de cerámica se indica con el signo de:

1 Coyotlatelco: − − − −
2. Matlatzinca: . . . .
3. Mazapa: + + + +
4. Azteca I: × × × ×
5. Azteca II: . − . −
6. Choluteca I–III y Policromo: − + − + −

Se ve que la distribución de la cerámica Coyotlatelco señala que los límites de ésta, por el oriente, son: Teotihuacán pasando por Chiconautla, Chalco y Xico; en el sur pasan por Gualupita; hacia el poniente entran por Palo Alto, en Chalma y Malinalco.

Por falta de exploraciones no puede limitarse su extensión en el suroeste del estado de México. Pero parece, dados ciertos indicios, que tal vez por ese lado se extienda hasta Guerrero. Por el poniente, sus límites parecen ser los del estado de México y en el norte se extiende por todos los valles de Ixtlahuaca y Jilotepec para internarse en Tula. Los límites en la región del norte no son muy claros, por falta de exploraciones.

Sin embargo, por los datos reseñados parece que el lugar más antiguo donde se presenta la cerámica de la familia rojo sobre crema o anaranjado es Xochicalco; de modo que ese lugar pudo ser el origen de esta familia. También parece que esta cerámica se desvió por dos caminos: uno pasó por Toluca e Ixtlahuaca y Jilotepec a Tula, y el otro, por Culhuacán, hacia Teotihuacán.

La distribución de la cerámica Matlatzinca por el oriente, comienza con Teotihuacán, sigue el límite del Distrito Federal, para internarse en el Valle de Morelos, a Tepoztlán; pasando por Gualupita sigue el camino de las montañas de Zempoala, pasa por Chalma y llega a Malinalco. No se conocen sus límites en la región del suroeste. Sin embargo, los límites del estado de México parecen ser su lindero del poniente. Por el norte se encuèntra la cerámica en los valles de Ixtlahuaca y Jilotepec; luego se interna para llegar a Tula. Los límites del noreste no se conocen, por falta de exploraciones.

La distribución de la cerámica Mazapa es de mucho interés, porque se concentra en el lado septentrional y oriental del Estado de México y aunque parece tener su foco en Teotihuacán, también se encuentra en Tula y lugares circunvecinos. Sus límites más meridionales parecen ser Xico y Chalco, aunque se encuentra una que otra figurita en Tepoztlán y Morelos.

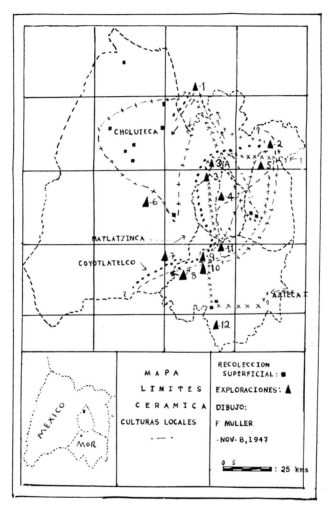

FIG. 1

Como la cerámica Mazapa hallada en Tula y Teotihuacán es posterior a la cerámica Coyotlatelco, tal vez sea el desarrollo más tardío de la familia de rojo sobre crema o anaranjado.

Ahora pasamos a la distribución de la cerámica Azteca I. Aquí tenemos otra cerámica que se encuentra en el oriente del estado de México y Morelos. La zona más oriental que alcanza es La Era, cerca de Chimalacatlán, pasando por Tepoztlán, Culhuacán y Tenayuca para dar la vuelta por Chiconautla. La cerámica Azteca I parece ser producto del oriente, con su foco de origen en Colhuacán o de La Mixteca Alta y la región vecina.

Entonces tenemos la extensión de la cerámica Azteca II. Parece que ésta como la Mazapa es un desarrollo local, cuyo foco es Tenayuca, extendiéndose muy poco. Sus límites parecen ser: Tepoztlán y Gualupita por el sur y Tula por el norte. Su frontera oriental parece ser Xico-Culhuacán.

Por último tenemos la cerámica con influencia Choluteca. Como puede apreciarse, parece que existen dos focos de esta clase de cerámica. El primero se encuentra en el oriente del estado de México y parte de Morelos. Su punto más meridional es Tepoztlán y el más septentrional—Chiconautla. El otro foco se encuentra en el norte del estado de México; su punto más meridional es Ocoyoacac pasando por los valles de Ixtlahuaca y Jilotepec para internarse en el estado de Hidalgo. Son de gran interés estos dos focos de difusión, porque tal vez indiquen el límite de la esfera de influencia que tenía su centro en Cholula.

En resumen se puede decir que parecen surgir los hechos siguientes: que el estado de México se hallaba dividido en dos zonas: la del poniente y la del oriente. Es interesante ver que la cerámica Coyotlatelco y la Matlatzinca coinciden casi en sus limites; que llegan a Teotihuacán y otros lugares vecinos; y que de allí vino el desarrollo posterior de la cerámica Mazapa.

Por el oriente parece ocurrir un fenómeno análogo. Tenemos una cerámica de origen local o del oriente, que se extiende por todo el lado oriental del estado de México, y luego va al norte, hacia el estado de Hidalgo. Como la cerámica del occidente, tiene su desarrollo local posterior, representado por la cerámica Azteca II.

Incrustado entre estas dos grandes familias de cerámica tenemos el grupo de cerámica de influencia Choluteca. No se puede averiguar con los datos presentes, si los dos focos estaban unidos y se separaron por la invasión de los nuevos tipos de cerámica del occidente y el oriente, o si fueron dos ramas de la extensión de la cerámica de Cholula.

En resumen cabe presentar la siguiente hipótesis de trabajo: que toda la cerámica de este horizonte puede agruparse en las familias siguientes:

Familia Monocroma:
    A. Anaranjado de tono rojizo
    B. Rojo bruñido
    C. "Anaranjado fino"

Familia Bicroma:

Rojo sobre Anaranjado o Crema
    A. Coyotlatelco
        sub-tipo negro sobre rojo
        1. Mazapa desarrollo posterior
    B. Matlatzinca
Negro sobre Anaranjado rojizo
    A. Azteca I.
        1. Azteca II—desarrollo posterior

Familia Polícroma:

    A. Polícromo de tres o más colores
        1. Motivos delineados con filete negro
    B. Influencia Choluteca I–III, laca, laca mate y laca firme.

NUEVOS DESCUBRIMIENTOS EN ACAPULCO, MÉXICO

Ignacio Bernal

Exploraciones anteriores llevadas a cabo en Acapulco, especialmente la del Dr. Ekholm, indicaban la existencia de una cultura local bastante pobre en todos aspectos, aunque muy antigua; Acapulco no parecía haber interesado a ningún turista precolombino. Un descubrimiento hecho hace unos meses nos obliga a rectificar esta suposición y a considerar que si los acapulqueños eran unos primitivos cuando menos tenían unos amigos, tal vez venidos de lejos, que no lo eran. Esta nota tiene por objeto estudiar este encuentro.

Los objetos que describiré a continuación fueron en su mayor parte sacados por buscadores de tesoros y solo una mínima parte fué hallada en condiciones científicas. Con todo y este grave defecto me permito presentarlo a la atención de ustedes por tratarse de piezas de particular interés nada usuales en la región de donde vienen; además creo no deben menospreciarse estos hallazgos accidentales pues eso lleva a la pérdida de infinitos datos valiosos.

La bahía de Acapulco está cerrada por una cadena relativamente alta de montañas. Al lado este, sobre la sección llamada Icacos y a unos 300 mts. sobre el mar, se levantan unas piedras rematadas por una de mayor tamaño conocida localmente por el nombre de la Picuda. Estas enormes piedras, resultado de algún lejano cataclismo, dejaron entre sí una serie de oquedades que comunican interiormente entre ellas lo que da la impresión de que se trata de una cueva. El piso está formado en parte por bloques de piedra pero entre unos y otros quedan espacios lienos de tierra poco profunda, pues nunca tiene más de unos 40 cms.

Estos islotes de tierra fueron aprovechados para depositar, casi superficialmente o tal vez enteramente en la superficie, la ofrenda que nos ocupa. Como ya dije la mayor parte de los objetos fué excavado por habitantes locales, pero lo poco que me dejaron demuestra que todos son de la misma procedencia. Ocupémonos primero de los objetos encontrados en condiciones científicas para luego estudiar los demás.

Consta la pequeña colección de fragmentos de cerámica, conchas perforadas, un caracol recortado, puntas de lanza en forma de hoja de laurel, fragmentos de máscaras de madera con mosaico de jade y turquesa, un fragmento de piedra redondo y plano que parece un *tezcacuitlapilli*, probablemente cubierto de mosaico, y cuentas de concha y piedra.

Los fragmentos de cerámica no pasan de cien por lo que no sirven para establecer ninguna tipología. Salvo tres, todos son de ollas gruesas o delgadas. Las gruesas son de barro café muy mal colado con una pintura fugitiva roja o en un caso unas líneas inclinadas y paralelas en el cuello, tal vez formadas por una tela amarrada alrededor de él. Las ollas delgadas son de un barro rojizo arenoso sin *slip* ni decoración. Uno de los fragmentos gruesos tal vez sea de comal y no de olla.

Los tres fragmentos diferentes son: uno también de olla delgada, pulida al exterior y con una decoración de anchas líneas pintadas de rojo; de un color ocre oscuro como el anterior es un fragmento de cajete del que queda el arranque del soporte hueco y globular. El tercer tepalcate es de un barro igual al de las ollas delgadas pero es de cajete con una línea roja en el borde interior. Aunque es difícil estar seguros, parece sin embargo que estos fragmentos corresponden al segundo horizonte hallado por Ekholm en Tambuco o sea al más reciente.

Recogí tres conchas con dos perforaciones cada una y varias rotas todas del tipo *spondylus* y junto con ellas un gran caracol recortado con cuatro perforaciones para colgarlo. Había fragmentos pequeños de muchas más conchas y plaquitas cuadrangulares de conchas rosas asociadas a una placa de pirita, otra de jade y otra de obsidiana. Todo esto seguramente formaba un mosaico, tal vez sobre la "tortilla" de piedra. Hay más de veinte cuentas de concha rosa gruesas que curiosamente son cuadradas y no redondas según lo usual. Con ellas tenemos otras aplanadas con dos perforaciones cada una, como si se debieran pasar dos hilos por ellas. Había también cuentas de piedra que no presentan ninguna particularidad.

Otros objetos de piedra son tres puntas de lanza. La mayor tiene 29.5 cms. de largo y 6 de ancho en su mayor amplitud, es de pedernal café oscuro y tiene como las demás los filos finamente retocados pero es la única que es exactamente simétrica en vez de tener como es habitual una punta más puntiaguda y la otra más redondeada para adaptarse al palo que la sostiene (Fig. 1, *b*).

La segunda es de 25 cms. de largo y de una piedra café más clara mientras la última es casi blanca y solo tiene 17 cms. de largo. Ambas son en forma de hoja de laurel (Fig. 1, *a*, *c*).

Los cascabeles de cobre son todos del tipo indicado en la Fig. 2 y en ningún caso han conservado el "badajo" o posiblemente nunca lo tuvieron por estar muy abiertos. Todos están hechos a base de un alambre de cobre enredado y están decorados sólo en dos formas: los más tienen un alambre en zig-zag puesto a ambos lados representando tal vez una serpiente; los otros tienen dos o tres filas de alambres en zig-zag pero que rodean al cascabel en vez de ir de arriba abajo. Muchos parecen haber sido enterrados ya rotos.

Finalmente entre los objetos encontrados *in situ* están varios fragmentos de máscaras de madera con restos muy claros de mosaico y plaquitas de turquesa y jade.

Entre los objetos que ya se habían sacado de ahí pero cuya proveniencia es casi segura hay muchos que duplican los ya descritos como dos máscaras magníficas de mosaico de las que desgraciadamente no tengo ilustraciones; más de ciento veinte cacabeles de cobre idénticos a los mencionados, conchas y cuentas iguales.

a   *b*   *c*

FIG. 1

FIG. 2

Sólo una pieza es diferente y desde luego única. Parece ser un escudo de madera de 38 cms. de diámetro (Foto 1). En muy bajo relieve está señalada una figura humana con el cuerpo de frente y la cara de perfil. Tanto en las manos como en los pies lleva un cuchillo de pedernal, un tocado o pelo con un mechón al centro, tal vez como el de los guerreros, y una orejera muy adornada. El cuerpo desaparece bajo una rodela con unas como alas con cuatro símbolos, tal vez el

FOTO 1

tonalo, simétricamente colocados. De este, o tal vez del cuerpo atrás de él, cuelga lo que parece el *maxtle* del individuo en un estilo muy mixteco. Una figura parecida hay por ejemplo en el Códice Nuttall (95, p. 12), con pedernales en las manos y un *maxtle* de forma similar aunque se trata de un animal y no de una representación humana.

Aunque es claro que mis excavaciones ya fueron muy tardías sin embargo ni en ellas ni en los alrededores o donde antes se había escarbado encontré un solo fragmento de hueso humano. Todas las preguntas que hice a los demás visitantes del sitio me confirmaron que no habían encontrado huesos y es evidente que de haberlos hallado los hubieran dejado allí mismo o tirado a un lado como hicieron con los tepalcates y fragmentos sin valor comercial. Entonces la conclusión es que no se trata de entierros (que de paso serían muy difíciles en tan poca tierra y espacios bastante limitados) sino de un sitio de ofrendas ¿Cuándo se hicieron, y quienes fueron sus autores?

La época es relativamente determinable. Desde luego los objetos de cobre nos señalan una fecha más bién tardía. Las máscaras de turquesa sobre matriz de madera lo mismo. La única máscara de este tipo hallada hasta ahora en condiciones científicas es la de Coixtlahuaca que encontré en la Tumba 6 de ese sitio y que indudablemente corresponde al último horizonte mesoaméricano, tal vez al siglo XV.

El desconocimiento casi total de la arqueología de Guerrero no facilita una conclusión pero no parece que estos objetos fueran producto local de Acapulco sino de alguna otra parte. Puede ser la región Yopi o la Tlapaneca o ya más lejos, la Mixteca que parece el principal centro distribuidor de las máscaras de madera con mosaico de jade.

POLLEN PROFILES AND CULTURE HORIZONS IN THE BASIN OF MEXICO

PAUL B. SEARS

This paper presents evidence in support of the following thesis:

1. The Basin of Mexico has experienced an indefinitely long series of fluctuations between climates that have been relatively humid and climates that have been relatively dry.

2. The early Archaic or Middle culture and the Aztec culture enjoyed the benefit of relatively humid climates, favorable to the accumulation of organic soils.

3. Between these two cultural periods there occurred a prolonged dry period. The late Archaic or Teotihuacan I culture persisted into this dry period. In the Lake Texcoco area it was covered by a layer of coarse volcanic sand which can be traced stratigraphically under later sediments.

4. Since the dry period referred to continued after the volcanic activity, the later Teotihuacan phases must have carried on for a time under unfavorable moisture conditions. This circumstance must be considered, along with the idea advanced by Vaillant (395) and others, that collapse was due to a failing economic base (see Appended Note).

I shall also try to account for the scarcity of very early human material on the Mexican plateau by showing that such material must have been deposited on the shores of formerly very deep lakes. Most traces of these shores have long since washed downward, and with them, any evidence of man which may have been there.

Finally, I shall show the critical cultural importance of available moisture at the present time within the Basin of Mexico.

The evidence which follows is based upon pollen analysis of lacustrine sediments. The possibilities of this technique for Mexican archeology have already been discussed by Deevey in connection with his preliminary studies of Lake Patzcuaro (103). These studies, which explored about six meters of sediment, indicated recent moist conditions, separated from a still earlier moist period by a dry interval. Our studies in the basin of Lake Texcoco support these findings. Deevey was unable, however, to secure satisfactory pollen counts from his samples in the Mexico City area.

My own studies on the pollen profiles of the Basin were begun in the spring of 1948, through the encouragement of Dr. Pablo Martínez del Rio of the Instituto Nacional de Antropología e Historia. Collections and analyses continued through June, 1948, with the generous assistance of the Museo Nacional, the

Instituto de Geología, Instituto de Biología, and the Instituto Politecnico. Deep samples were made available through the engineering firm of L. Zeevaert.

Collections made in archeological horizons during 1948 were found to have been disturbed by cultivation and fluctuating lake levels. Therefore, a brief collecting trip was made in June, 1949, to the Lake Texcoco area where undisturbed profiles were obtained. Dr. Rubín de la Borbolla kindly placed at my disposal the invaluable services of Sr. Arturo Romano, and we were housed as guests of the Escuela Nacional de Agricultura at Chapingo. The trip was otherwise financed by a grant from the Geological Society of America.

The principal pollen encountered in sediments in the Basin of Mexico, down to a depth of 60 meters, consists of pine and oak, with a lesser showing of fir and alder. These genera are all from the foothill and mountain forests surrounding the Basin. Pollen of the willows, grasses, cat-tails, chenopods, and sedges of the valley floor are present, but in surprisingly small proportion, as a rule.

The altitudinal relations of pine, fir, and oak are such that oak comes further down into relatively moister valleys than does pine. Both oak and fir, when present with pine, occupy the more humid situations, and pine the drier. Alder is found as undergrowth in well-stabilized forests of either pine or oak.

When the relative proportions of various kinds of pollen in the sediments are studied, oak and pine show a very strong inverse relationship. Conditions favorable to a high percentage of oak are unfavorable to a high percentage of pine, and vice versa.

That the oaks of the valley of Mexico are more mesic; i.e., require greater humidity, than the pines, is not merely my own observation. It is also the judgment of Dr. Faustino Miranda, a competent ecologist, familiar with the area. It is further supported by the fact that the high water levels of Aztec time were accompanied by high percentages of oak, while the low water level of late Archaic was accompanied by low percentages of oak and high percentages of pine.

One further point of great importance is that the site at El Tepalcate, near the present low level of Lake Texcoco, is overlaid with coarse volcanic sand. This site, excavated by Apenes (13), was pronounced late Archaic–Teotihuacan I by Noguera (248), who studied the artifacts. We visited this site in 1948, and with the aid of competent workers from the Museo Nacional and the University—Sres. Romano and Aveleyra—confirmed the stratigraphy and character of the cultural material.

Since this volcanic sand constitutes a critical archeological horizon, it was traced, with the assistance of Sr. Romano, during June of 1949. It can be readily identified, not only by its high content of coarse black obsidian grains, but by its tendency to solidify. Being thus resistant to wind-erosion, it forms much of the basin exposed by low water along the eastern edge of the lake. Towards Chimalhuacan at the south it dips below the present surface, being covered with 2 meters of later sediment at our station 1 kilometer north of that town. The same is true at our northernmost station, 3.75 kilometers west of Chapingo.

The late Archaic site at El Tepalcate was almost covered by the high water of 1941, and is believed by Apenes to have been under at least a meter of water in Aztec times (13). However, when the site was occupied during the late Archaic, the water level—as evidenced by stone-work—was at least as low as the present dry-season level, which is due to systematic and prolonged drainage. Unless evidence of major changes in the natural drainage pattern can be produced, we may assume that the low level in late Archaic times was due simply to a lessened rainfall and high evaporation, as the pollen suggests.

Pollen analyses and stratigraphy show that the transition from Archaic to Teotihuacan occurred during a prolonged period of low oak and high pine—a dry period. Since this dry period continued in force for a considerable time thereafter, its relation to the subsequent Teotihuacan phases seems clear.

Preceding this long dry period was a markedly moister one, which should have favored the accumulation of organic matter and the formation of the substantial layer of black soil which, as we know from the Pedregal and other sites, was definitely associated with the Archaic culture. The upper sediments likewise show a moist period, to be associated with Aztec occupation. This is further supported by numerous analyses of last season, including one sample, just below the Aztec floor at Culhuican which showed 17 per cent of oak.

Below these three zones of archeological importance, the alternate banding of moist and dry climate sediments continues, and is quite consonant with the results of our analyses to a depth of 60 meters under the present City of Mexico, although the detailed correlations have not been made. Because of the high content of inorganic colloids, technical difficulties have occurred, but these are being gradually solved.

As supporting evidence of the fundamental climatic pattern of the Basin of Mexico, we have the deep cut of the *Tajo de Nochistongo*. I am indebted to Dr. Maldonado-Koerdell for the opportunity to see this area. The cut shows the bed of a former lake of high elevation, and therefore sensitive to fluctuations in available moisture. We are able to identify at least fourteen successive periods of silt deposit (moist climate, high water level) each with a subsequent period of weathering and soil formation (dry climate, water low or absent). These deposits are, of course, older than those exposed in the basin of Mexico, but the recurring pattern is similar.

In northeastern United States and in New Mexico there is definite evidence of similar fluctuations in available moisture and some reason to believe that these changes can be correlated with retreats and readvances of the late and post-Wisconsin ice. We do not as yet know whether the same fundamental climatic controls were operative in Mexico.

We do know, however, that the present types of vegetation existed in the

Basin during the accumulation of some 60 meters of sediment, extending well back into the Pleistocene. It is chiefly the *proportions* of the oaks and pines that have shifted in response to increasing or decreasing moisture during that time.

These facts suggest that former very high lake levels in various basins of the plateau were not due to revolutionary climatic differences, but rather to physiographic factors. The discovery of a high ancient beach of pebbles in the hills surrounding Tamazulapan in Oaxaca led me to search for similar features elsewhere. There is such a beach at the northern rim of the valley of Oaxaca, indicating that Monte Alban was once an island. Subsequently I found at least four other high beaches to the north. Others are described in the literature, and several geologists have concurred in my supposition that the plateau was once occupied by numerous, very deep lakes, since drained by normal processes. The one at Tamazulapan has been drained by the cutting back of the Río del Oro.

It is my judgment that these circumstances may account for the scarcity of pre-Archaic remnants on the plateau. If the earliest human inhabitants of Mexico lived on the steep margins of deep lakes, most of their traces have long since been washed down into the basins and covered deeply. I would, however, suggest that valuable evidence might be obtained by examining the high ancient beaches for primitive artifacts.

Finally we have tangible evidence that the present culture of Mexico is extremely sensitive to moisture; e.g., the production of food crops and the harvesting of fish near the lake margins which remain today. Dust storms are frequent in the dry bed of Lake Chalco, near the once prosperous village of Xico. Xico was an island until after the completion of the great drainage works in 1900. So far as I could observe, the only crop produced in quantity now is the chenopod *quelite*, whose leaves are used for greens, tiny hard seeds for food, and stems for fencing and thatch. So great is the pressure upon this semi-desert plant that the roots are finally dug up and used for fuel. Xico today is indeed a desolate spot.

There seems no reason to believe that cultures of the past have been any less vulnerable than those of the present. I suggest therefore that the rise and fall of populations and of empire within the valley of Mexico have been profoundly influenced by the changing availability of moisture.

APPENDED NOTE

The detailed technical evidence upon which the foregoing paper is based will be given in subsequent publications. In the meantime considerable new data have been gathered. Much of this is due to the skill and persistence of my associate, Mrs. Kathryn Clisby. She has developed refined methods of separating pollen and spores from the often highly colloidal organic and inorganic sediments, and has also succeeded in finding abundant maize pollen to a depth of 6 meters at the Aztec site under Madero, Mexico, D.F., where the Convent of San Francisco was formerly located. With the refined methods she has developed, it should now be possible to explore lake sediments in various directions and so arrive at some notion of the sequences of maize culture.

In addition, the physical studies of Ing. Leonardo Zeevaert on sediment cores from the basin of Mexico have afforded a striking confirmation of our findings on climatic alternations.

It is now clear that the late Archaic–early Teotihuacan culture, obliged by volcanic activity to shift from the low, moist basin to higher ground northward, must have done so during a relatively dry period. There is reason to believe that this was possible because of abundant ground water sources, traces of which still persist, but at lower levels.

I am indebted to Dr. de Terra for a reminder that the Teotihuacan culture persisted into the moist period which made the subsequent Aztec economy possible. Even so, the deforestation to which Vaillant attributes the downfall of the Teotihuacan culture would certainly have had a disastrous effect on ground water supplies. There is now a deep arroyo some distance south of the pyramids, draining into the Texcoco basin. I have no means of knowing its age, but it clearly contributes to present-day desiccation of the area. If it represents a drainage going back to the time of occupation, it would certainly have intensified the effects of deforestation.

The generous and continuing help of Ing. A. R. V. Arellano remains to be gratefully acknowledged.

THE PYRAMID OF THE SUN IN TEOTIHUACAN
A NEW INTERPRETATION

Rémy Bastien

As early as 1904, the Mexican government of General Porfirio Diaz began feverish preparations for the celebration of the first centennial of the Republic in 1910. Among the items of the program was included the largest archeological excavation as yet undertaken in the Americas: Leopoldo Batres, Chief of the Department of Archeology, was commissioned by the Secretary of Public Education to uncover and rebuild the huge "Hill of the Sun" in the ruined city of Teotihuacan, some fifty kilometers north of Mexico City.

Batres worked hard and resolved the engineering problem of carrying away thousands of tons of soil and stones, surveyed the monument more accurately than it had ever been done before and was able to finish the gross reconstruction on time. If today we cannot praise his skill as an archeologist, at least we must give him due credit for his energy in carrying out his plan of work.

Leopoldo Batres (27) left us only an incomplete account of this huge undertaking. If he ever thought of writing a more detailed report, time failed him. In 1910 the Diaz government was ousted by the revolution and Batres sank into oblivion.

In 1917, the excavations in the city were renewed as part of a vast and exhaustive study of the Valley of Teotihuacan and the results were edited by Dr. Manuel Gamio (120). In the first volume, dealing with the archeological or prehispanic culture, a tentative reconstruction of the city and its principal buildings was proposed with drawings by architect Ignacio Marquina. Marquina (219) reconstructed the Pyramid of the Sun, and his version was readily accepted by scholars writing about Teotihuacan, e.g., Vaillant (395).

From 1945 to 1947, I worked as assistant to the archeologist in charge at Teotihuacan. During that time, I made a detailed study of the Pyramid of the Sun (23). My doubts about the value of Batres' excavation and rebuilding of the monument led me to discover an error which had victimized two generations of archeologists. Besides a number of minor misinterpretations, the whole picture of the monument had been completely misconceived by Batres. It is the purpose of this paper to discuss the most important of these changes, i.e., correction of Batres' reconstruction of the pyramid as a five-bodied structure.

We must look for the cause of those mistakes in the techniques Batres used. He considered it impossible to clear the shapeless mound of its brush, soil, and shambles, and give it back "the form and use it had had in the time of its splen-

FIG. 1.—The author's reconstruction of the pyramid (wood and plastic model)

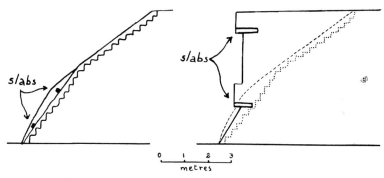

slabs

slabs

0   1   2   3
metres

FIG. 2

FIG. 3

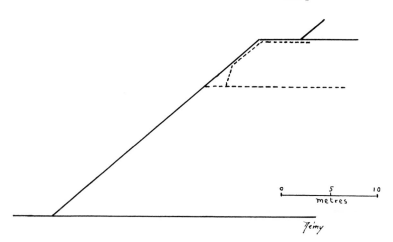

0   5   10
metres

Jemy

FIG. 4

dor" (26). Batres decided to apply a trick which experience had taught him. While digging at Huexotla, Batres (24) had found under the ruined layers of a pyramid the better preserved walls of a smaller construction, quite similar in its layout to the covering one. The discovery made him think that "the Mexican pyramid builders repeated layer after layer the forms which were to be the final shape of the monument with its steps, its stuccoed walls, and landings" (27). The superimposition of buildings was due really to successive improvements, or enlargements of the monuments. This fact was of the greatest value in working out the chronology of the various buildings as, for example, in the Pyramid of Tenayuca. Batres failed to see any chronological importance in that peculiarity; he only grasped a way of making his job easier and quicker—to peel the Pyramid of the Sun and uncover a "smaller one, but in perfect shape like the underskin of an onion" (26).

His hope was in vain. Batres found no inner construction but only managed to further destroy the monument, tearing from it successive layers totaling 5 m. of its original depth. We know by the way in which he explored the western side of the Pyramid (its façade) that he understood his mistake, but he carried on his destructive work on the three remaining sides, up to the third landing. From there to the top, he tried to consolidate the ruined layer as he did on the western slope. In his reconstruction of the façade, he did little to differentiate what was original from what was reconstructed. He aimed at giving the whole façade an air of authenticity. Batres' reconstruction was of stucco, easily discriminated because of its coarse texture from the original remains made of lime and *tezontle* crumbles. He stuccoed newly built staircases and patched parts of the original stucco. However, studying the genuine-looking second body of the façade, I found it had only a $32°$ inclination, instead of the standard $40°$.

On his way up to the fourth landing, on the southern side of the monument, Batres came upon something unexpected and he wrote: "En el tercer cuerpo del costado Sur, han aparecido paramentos verticales hechos de piedras unida con lodo. Es casi seguro que este descubrimiento aumente en un cuerpo mas la Pirámide" (27, p. 10).

It was undoubtedly the most stirring discovery of the excavation. From the sixteenth to the nineteenth century, scores of authors had described the Pyramid of the Sun in Teotihuacan as consisting of four superimposed pyramidal sections, e.g., Castañeda in the sixteenth century in his "Relación de Teotihuacán"; Humboldt (141), who visited the ruins in 1803; and Almaraz (4). Batres was correcting a four-century-old mistake. The pyramid consisted of five rather than four superimposed bodies, as originally supposed. This revision was generally accepted.

The *new* body (actually the fourth) was, however, something strange and unique in the architecture of Teotihuacan. Averaging 5.50 m. in height, it rose first at an almost right angle and then presented a second plane with an average inclination of 40°. Since the narrow steps on its west side follow the general profile of the body, they are very hard to climb (Fig. 2). And yet they were apparently original. Their balustrades showed remains of original red-painted stucco and also remains of slabs or *iztapaltetes*, two on each balustrade, which were used in the classical Teotihuacan cornice. It is these slabs which seem to be responsible for the widespread acceptance of Batres' error. They also figure in Mr. Marquina's tentative reconstruction of the pyramid. A close examination shows clearly that the slab remains are not authentic:

1. By its position in the Teotihuacan cornice, the upper slab "floats" while the lower, built into the slope, is stronger and is more likely to remain *in situ* when the whole cornice breaks. Yet both slabs are actually evident in the fourth body.

2. By their position, the slabs could not be included in the big cornice Mr. Marquina imagined (Fig. 3). Nor could the upper slab extend for over 1.20 m. from the spot where it stuck in the balustrade to the outer ridge of the cornice. Less than 5 cm. thick, the slab could not act as a support and would break at once.

Rejecting the originality of the *iztapaltetes* compelled me to reject the reconstruction of the staircase and of the whole body. What was behind the falsification of the slabs? It seems part of an effort to give to the new body an authentic quality. At the base of all the bodies of the pyramid, on all four sides, it is easy to find original stucco remains. Most often, the lower slab is what indicates the existence of a cornice. Batres knew of both clues, but used them crudely in the new body. Stucco remains are to be seen only upon the balustrades of the staircase and between the slabs, but never at the base of the body where they are usually found.

Outside the staircase, there is one small patch of original stucco, about 30×40 cm. This seems to be part of what Batres took to be the fourth body of the pyramid. It is located on the southern side, approximately at the point where the side changes inclination. This told the whole story.

The original stucco piece is situated in a canal-like depression. When carefully examined, one notices that its surface is not flat. Near the edge of the depression, it makes an angle as if it was part of a canal of a rectangular or square section. It is my opinion that it is the only remains of a drainage canal discovered during the excavations of 1905–10. As a result of his peeling, Batres came upon a section of a drainage canal near the top of the third body. Interpreting it as "paramentos verticales hechos de piedra unida con lodo," he cut the slope at almost a right angle following the plane of the canal. By extending the cut at the same level, Batres created the dwarf body (Fig. 4). One notices that the upper part of the newly created body continues and coincides with the standard 40° slope of the third body.

The use of drainage canals in pyramids is confirmed by the excavations of

Jorge R. Acosta (1, 2) in Tula, state of Hidalgo, where he found in the Pyramid of Quetzalcoatl stone tubes placed under the outer layer of the monument for the purpose of drainage.

Probably more canals existed in the Pyramid of the Sun, but disappeared with the material carted away by Batres.

The presence of a drainage canal on the southern side of the pyramid has one good reason in its favor. The valley floor on which Teotihuacan stands slopes from north to south and the builders of the city laid the axis of their metropolis in that direction, basing their drainage system upon that difference of level. Thus we would expect to find a drainage canal on the southern side of the pyramid.

Besides these material clues which prove the non-authenticity of the fourth body, there exists an important psychological clue. The only time Batres mentions the discovery of a new element which would bring the number of the pyramid's bodies to five is in the sentence already quoted. But in the same report he mentions "the four landings of the pyramid" and draws a general view of the monument with four bodies to show the position of children's skeletons found at its corners: "En cada uno de los ángulos de los cuatro cuerpos de la Pirámide descubrí el esqueleto de un niño al parecer de seis años de edad. ..." (27, p. 22).

Batres' report of 1906 is lavishly illustrated, but a picture of the new discovery is nowhere to be found. It is therefore probable that Batres perceived his error of cutting the third body in two. But instead of admitting his error and repairing it, which he could easily have done with the money and labor at his disposal, he chose to gamble on concealing his blunder and hailing the fabricated fourth landing as an exciting discovery.

The addition of a new body meant also the addition of a new staircase and the modification of the one below it (i.e., the third body). Batres very carefully reconstructed the twin staircases leading from the second to the third landing by covering their balustrades with false stucco. If we accept the convergence of the staircases as Batres reconstructed them, and add the fact that the staircases must have originally been at least 5 m. longer, then we are forced to conclude that the staircases met at the end. Such a design is extremely unusual in Teotihuacan architecture. I strongly suspect that this convergence is another of Batres' fantasies. Plate 24 of the *Memoria* of 1906 (27) reveals that he did not discover more than sections of the first two steps of the northern staircase, and nothing of the southern one!

I have not discussed in this article other problems involved in the study of the monument because no definite solution with regard to them can as yet be reached. I would like, however, to mention briefly some of these problems:

1. The exact shape and construction periods of the smaller pyramid erected at the front base of the great pyramid which Seler (308, V, 430) compares with the *apetlatl* of the Great Temple of Tenochtitlan as described in Sahagun.

2. As a result of the error in slope in reconstructing the second body, the second landing is 5 m. narrower than what must have been its original width.

3. The question of whether the Pyramid had cornices at the top of each of its big four bodies as was the case with the four smaller ones of the *apetlatl*.

4. The size and plan of the shrine at the top of the Pyramid which might possibly be found if excavations were to search for post-holes.

I propose, in Figure 1, a tentative reconstruction of the Pyramid of the Sun based on the new findings. The roof of the temple on top of the pyramid is elevated instead of flat, as Mr. Marquina suggests. This was done because three temples pictured in newly discovered frescoes in Teotihuacan are shown with high straw roofs.

A thorough and detailed reconstruction of the Pyramid of the Sun, one of the most important in prehispanic architecture, must await additional information which can only be obtained by further excavations on the site. It is my hope that this paper may contribute to the acceleration of interest in that direction.

THE TREE OF THE MIXTECA: A SHORT STUDY OF THE HISTORICAL CODICES OF MEXICO

C. A. BURLAND

The savage hunters of late paleolithic times depicted animals and men against an imaginary background of tundra or woodland. To an artist their drawings still convey that world of the imagination. This was truly a great feat by the artists of those distant times.

Rarely indeed was any vegetable form depicted before man had discovered agriculture. The appearance of a tree in a work of art usually means that the artist was one of a community which was able to deal with trees as a matter of everyday experience. When trees come to be reduced in art to conventional forms, we can be sure that they are the product of an old culture with deep roots in an agricultural economy. This is one of the reasons for the title of this paper; to remind us that the people of pre-Columbian Mexico had behind them a long history of social development and high culture.

It was not a constantly evolving culture, for some peoples in Mexico, as else-where, had to recede under the pressure of circumstance from a previously higher level. Such a people, once mighty in their own land, who later fell into captivity, were the Mixteca. From the days of their greatness they retained much of cultural value, including a mythology of truly poetic beauty. "When the world was made, the Ancestors came out of a tree." This is one of the stories they recounted to Father Burgoa when he worked among them after the fall of Mexico to the Spaniards.

In the painted histories that survived the Conquest we find this event depicted, in Vindobonensis (93) and in the Codex Selden (92). In both pictures, the tree is fitted into an old convention of Mexican art, simple and easy to read, which is found in the sculpture of Monte Alban I and also, nearly fifteen centuries later, in the Shield of the Sunrise, one of the beautiful series of turquoise mosaics preserved in the British Museum. This long survival of a convention is a notable matter in art history. Also of interest is the appearance of a geometrical symbol in Monte Alban I which signifies either "a place" or "a building," and which later appears in Teotihuacan glyphs and, in a modified form, in the glyphs of the painted codices where it still retains its original significance.

A quite cursory survey of the surviving codices is sufficient to divide them into groups. The Maya codices have long been a mathematican's delight. The Mexican codices, however, have yielded more solid results. They can be sorted into works dealing with the magical tonalpoualli, some like Codex Laud (91) enshrining complex time counts; the mythologies, best represented by the magnificence of Codex Borgia; and the histories, which, due to Bishop Zumarraga's protection, are the most numerous. These histories, large and small, can be divided into two groups, according to the year-sign used. A square or plain cartouche around the year-bearer day is best shown in Codex Boturini. These codices are all of Aztec cultural origin. The other, and most numerous, series have the year-bearer day sign attached to a cartouche which is pierced by a ray of light like an inverted "V." The writer had assumed that this was restricted to the Mixtecs and kindred peoples of Western Mexico.

Two documents of this series are indisputably of Mixtec origin. Codex Becker I (86), in Vienna, was originally purchased from a Mixtec cacique; and Codex Waecker Götter (Egerton 2895) (94) has a great number of inscriptions in Spanish handwriting but in the Mixtec language. On these inscriptions will depend the tests of accuracy for any attempt to read Mixtec place names. It is also definitive for the Mixtec style of denoting place-glyphs and buildings. Unfortunately, no true facsimile has been published, although an excellent series of photographs is available.

Waecker-Götter is also linked with other codices in that it opens with a procession of symbol bearers of a common type. These appear to be symbolic of the establishment of the Mixtec chieftainships after the fall of Tula. It is surely significant that these processions usually represent the carrying of a sacred bundle associated with the Staff of the Morning Star.

The two codices which include the story of the Tree of the Mixtecs are part of this series. They have not only a year-sign, but both building types and place names in accord with the identified Mixtec styles. For students who wish to consult them, Vindobonensis is available in a splendid facsimile edition, but Codex Selden is available only in photographs or in the inaccurate edition of Kingsborough published in 1831.

There is an immediate temptation to identify the Tree as one of the four directions, as shown by the artist who painted Codex Fejervary-Mayer (90). But in this case the tree has no direction. In Selden it is shown intertwined with serpents; the one a thundercloud serpent of the daytime sky, and the other the star-eyed serpent of the night sky. It is a tree of the heavens arising in the *centre* and extending above and below. This is paralleled in Vindobonensis where the tree is marked on one side with the darts of the Tzitzimime demons of the night and on the other with concentric circles denoting days. This is an interesting confirmation of this writer's view (67) that the dots or colored circles used in the day symbols are not simple numbers but numbers of days—which significantly enough are a group of numerals given a special grammatical form in both the Maya and Mixtec languages.

In Selden the accent is on the heavenliness of the tree. It is the sky. It is in Omeyoacan, guarded by THE TWO—the Creator marked in both his aspects by Cipactli-like jaws as the First.

In the Vienna version the tree is a survivor from the catastrophe of the previous human race. It arises from the burnt soil where flames flicker from little heaps of gray ash. It is rooted on the head of a goddess (female because of the blue comb in her hair) who belonged to the previous order of things, as is shown by her having a tusked mouth, much like the little stone-men who were believed in ancient Mexico to have preceded the present human race. Even the godlings who carve the tree are stupid creatures who wear their collars round their arms and their head plumes hanging down their backs. An old order has passed and a new one is beginning. The heavenly tree has given birth to humanity.

These paintings are full of symbolism, expressive of the thought of great poetry, and yet incapable of being restored fully to words. The imagery is there, and one day a poet familiar with the sonorous and intricate tongue of the Mixtecs may reconstruct a poem on the theme; but undoubtedly he will be influenced by the different world he lives in and so fail to recapture the full meaning of the ancient chant which was recited when the pictures were shown by the priests five centuries ago.

However, we must leave poetry for a very hard fact. Of all the codices we know, Vindobonensis is the most authentically dated. It is pretty certain that it came into Europe before Mexico had fallen in 1521, and that it was collected by Hernando Cortes in 1519; the remarkable year *Ome Acatl*. This means that it could not have been collected from the Mixtecs of Oaxaca. Sahagun, however, tells us that the people of southern Vera Cruz called themselves Mixtecs of the Coasts. The presence among them of a codex in Western Mixtec style would seem to indicate that there was some very real connection. It is significant that the verso side of Vindobonensis contains a history of Eight Deer and the Mixtec dynasties in a different style from the other side of the Codex. It suggests that a later hand continued the story, possibly for the benefit of the strangers. There is evidence of hurry in the last part of the codex in the substitution of dates for pictured events—the stories of dates in living memory could be recited just as easily as pictures of the past could be read. Unfortunately they can give us no clue because the pictures are needed as a guide to the subject commemorated.

On the recto side, the Codex had a special meaning in reference to Cortes, because it dealt with the three Quetzalcoatls in great detail.

There has been some suggestion that Codex Zouche-Nuttall (95) was also presented to Cortes in 1519; but little is known of the adventures of this document beyond the fact that it was in Italy in the mid nineteenth century. Its story is exclusively Mixtec, and in comparison with Selden and Vindobonensis it covers a short period of time.

The scope of the historical codices, from the Beginning of all things, and the Tree of the Mixtecs to the time of the Spanish Conquest, implies a far wider time range than has usually been accepted for these documents. The author, in *Archiv für Völkerkunde* (Vienna), has suggested that Vindobonensis contains a list of the Toltec high-chiefs in Tula, and ceremonies connected with them, and has brought forward a new view of Ixtlilxochitl's account of the Toltec chiefs reigning for fifty-two years.

In conclusion, these historical codices require considerable further study. They are designed in an art style closely akin to the sculptures and paintings of Tula. They are an expression of the art of Vaillant's Mixteca-Puebla complex, which we now know to be rooted in the Toltec "Empire." Do they also take us back to a skeleton history of the Teotihuacanos? Is the family of Tlalocs, which occurs in the early part of Codex Bodley (87) of significance in this connection? If in fact these documents give the history of Mexico as handed down from painter to painter through the centuries, they should be carefully recorded. They will form a handbook which will guide the archeologist on his exploration of the strange distribution of the early cultures of Mexico. Perhaps they will provide a clue as to why the "Toltec" tradition in art seems to be earliest in Tajin, Xochicalco, and far off Santa Lucia Cozumahualpa. The codices are the repositories of the pre-Spanish tradition of Mexico and may well bring our archeological knowledge from prehistory to the stage of recorded fact about known peoples.

EARLY CERAMIC HORIZONS IN YUCATAN

George W. Brainerd

The information on the ceramic chronology of Yucatan which I am about to present has been gathered since 1940 in studies undertaken for the Carnegie Institution of Washington, Division of Historical Research. An outline of the work has been given in summary fashion in *Yearbooks of the Carnegie Institution*, Nos. 39, 40, and 41. Field work was done in 1940, in 1942, and a third season has just been completed.

In addition to the usual function of a ceramic survey in furnishing a reliable chronologic sequence for the placement of other cultural material, it has been hoped that the Yucatan pottery studies would furnish a firmer basis for anchoring the Maya calendric sequence in Christian dating, and that the interrelationships between the Peten Classic, or "Old Empire" culture and the Yucatan Maya could be clarified. These aims have been in a considerable measure accomplished; in their pursuit, the information which forms the subject of this paper has been gathered.

The pottery amassed by workers of the Institution prior to 1940 consisted mainly of large collections excavated during architectural reconstruction at Chichen Itza. There were also smaller collections excavated from test trenches by Henry Roberts at Chichen Itza and elsewhere. While this material was largely confined to the so-called Toltec period of Chichen Itza and to the period of occupation of the ruins of the Puuc area, it also showed a small proportion of quite different and varied potteries. A few of these aberrant sherds were recognizable as similar to pottery of the earlier periods of the Uaxactun sequence.

The discovery of an initial series date of 9.2.0.0.0 at Oxkintok in western Yucatan prompted a ceramic test in 1940 which produced a rich deposit containing not a sherd of any previously recognized type. In 1942, Yaxuna near Chichen Itza, Dzibilchaltun north of Merida, Acanceh and Mayapan southeast of Merida, and the towns, particularly Mani, which border the northern limit of the Puuc hill ranges, all were sampled. These sites were chosen as having a wide geographic distribution and as probably not limited to the two major architectural periods on which we already had material. Particular attention was paid to the cenote and cave springs which must have been, during all human history, the main water sources of the region. During the past season, the survey was extended to the Chenes and Rio Bec areas in eastern Campeche, thus giving much closer connections between Yucatan and the Peten.

Results have been gratifying: we now have defined some twelve to fourteen chronologically sequent phases distinguishable by marked qualitative changes in the ceramics. Most of the interphase changes are in the predominant wares, a few are in forms and minor wares. Most of the phase sequences have been reinforced by stratigraphic evidence, a few are thus far anchored by stylistic placement alone. Although our regional sampling is still sporadic, and there still may be minor shifts in our sequences, the major outline is clear. This chronological outline extends from three sequent Formative phases, here provisionally called Early, Middle, and Late, through the Yucatan Regional and Florescent stages which correspond together to the Peten Initial Series period. Following the Florescent stage come three subdivisions of the Mexican stage, the first of which is the Toltec Chichen Itza phase, the last that of the major Mayapan occupation. We at present know little of the ceramics of the century preceding the Conquest which was followed by Colonial pottery very similar to that of the preceding Mayapan phase, and also very similar to the pottery still in use. The details of this sequence must await publication. I shall summarize some results and implications of the study of the Formative stage.

Three periods have been provisionally defined: Early, Middle, and Late Formative. Early Formative has been found only at the Mani Cenote where it underlay a Late Formative deposit. Middle Formative has appeared at Santa Rosa Xtampak and at Dzibilnocac, both Chenes sites dug the past season in northwest Campeche. Late Formative appears in nearly all sites sampled. Collections of from five hundred to one thousand sherds apiece come from Santa Rosa Xtampak, Dzibilnocac, Chichen Itza, Yaxuna, Holactun, Acanceh, and Mani. Smaller collections come from Dzibilchaltun, Chuburna (near Merida), Mayapan, Kabah and Sayil (in the Puuc area), Xpuhil (in the Rio Bec area of southeast Campeche).

Thus Late Formative deposits have been taken from some fourteen sites. The deposits total about four thousand sherds. Middle Formative in clear cut deposits comes from only two sites and totals about thirteen hundred sherds. Early Formative comes only from Mani, but the deposit totals forty-two hundred sherds. The placement of Early Formative under Late Formative is reinforced by stratigraphy; the placement of Middle Formative between the other two periods rests at present on stylistic grounds which I shall detail. All of this study has been based on refuse deposits of sherd material. I know of no whole vessels of Yucatan Formative pottery.

Although the detailed technical description of the pottery on which these periods are based must await publication, I shall attempt a brief summary for other ceramic workers in neighboring fields.

The Early Formative pottery from Mani consists of over four thousand sherds, the majority in unmixed deposits clearly underlying Late Formative strata. All but two of the sherds come from bottles of a very uniform shape, ranging from 25 to 35 centimeters in diameter. The bottles are handleless, globular, but elongated below into a blunt point, and above into a narrow conical neck capped by a narrow, thickened lip. Capacity is estimated at about 3 gallons, full weight about 30 pounds. This is an unusual size in Yucatan; jars normally range in two groups, one much larger, the other much smaller. One small concurvate sherd bears exteriorly what seems to be a waxy slip of the body color. One watch-glass shaped object was found 7 centimeters in diameter. It may have been a lid. The ware is uniformly of a dull medium brown color, paste medium fine texture with smooth matte surface. The jars are decorated by burnished areas showing but a slight lustre, visible only with good lighting. Decoration is in a combination of stripes and bars 2.5 to 3 centimeters wide, with lined and hachured areas formed by burnished lines only 2 to 3 millimeters in width.

The Middle Formative phases at Santa Rosa Xtampak and Dzibilnocac have not been completely analyzed as yet, and will likely show stratigraphic intergrading with the Late Formative deposits at those sites. There is one sealed deposit from which most of the following criteria have been taken. The two predominant wares are a monochrome with closely adherent slip and medium paste texture, and a brownish-orange ware with allover burnished surface. Some sherds of the brownish-orange ware are in the form of the thus far unique and hence diagnostic Early Formative bottle necks, although the ware is thinner and lighter in color. One of these bottle necks comes from Holactun and another from near Xpuhil. The remainder of this ware is of forms also found in slipped monochrome. The monochromes are predominantly red, with some white, orange, and gray-black. Shapes include a variety of round sided vessels, some with incurving lip; also flare sided, legless flat bottom bowls which never have a sharply outbent lip. Ring form potstands also occur in these phases. The only clearly documented surface decoration is by light incision encircling the vessels in both rectilinear and curvilinear designs. Some unslipped striated jars are in the deposits.

The collections of the Late Formative substage from the various sites show variation, some of it probably regional, some certainly chronological. I shall give a general description. The predominant ware is a slipped monochrome red, orange, white, gray, or black. Often the exterior and interior colors are markedly and certainly intentionally different. Colors show some correlation with vessel forms. The slip at most sites is closely adherent. The pottery of the Late Formative period shows on the average considerably thicker walls than that of the preceding periods. The predominant form is a heavy, large, flat bottomed bowl with flaring sides, often with everted flat lip. Other forms include small-shouldered jars, round sided vessels of various sorts, cuspidor shaped vessels, and globular jars with notch neck. A few large hollow legs occur sporadically. Most sites show a few spouts. There is one flat fabric stamp and one appliqued hand-modeled face from a vessel side. Occasional flanges are found placed sublabially and on vessel sides. Decoration includes very rare blobs of red paint, and much pale trickle paint occurs at some sites. This paint sometimes gives a resist effect, and sometimes is darker than the ground color. A fragment of Usulutan ware occurs. Vessels are decorated by incising and grooving in a considerable variety of patterns: fluting both horizontal and vertical, fingernail impression, impression by a reed or similar hollow circular tool. Decoration in several cases varies significantly between sites. Minor wares include at some sites red slipped over striated jars, at some a thin and highly polished orange ware, but no burnished orange-brown ware like that of the Middle Formative period. Unslipped striated jars form a minor constituent of the samples. Altogether the variety of forms and decoration of this period is somewhat greater than in those that follow.

Following the Late Formative phase at Yaxuna came a phase characterized by a predominance of Flaky Redware. This ware bears a loosely attached slip with a tendency to part readily from the smooth surface of the underlying body. The common bowl form is shouldered or carinated, the bottom strongly curved, in contrast to the predominant flat bottom of Late Formative times. The jar form is also distinctive with a strongly inbent bottom. A red mono-chrome predominates; minor wares include a red on orange dichrome with large scale designs bordered by incision, a redware bearing strongly colored black trickle paint, and an unslipped ware with vegetal tempering. Stylistic evidence, too lengthy to discuss here, suggests that this dichrome was a predecessor of Tzakol style polychrome, where black lines were substituted for the incision and a flange added to the shoulder or basal angle. This phase has therefore been placed in the early Regional stage.

At Acanceh the lowest deposits showed a Late Formative horizon containing small amounts of cream colored Late Formative ware, and of the red slip over striation jar sherds also found in Late Formative at other sites. The adherent slipped redware, which predominates at other Late Formative sites, is nearly completely lacking in favor of Flaky Redware, which occurs in both the typical early Regional forms found at Yaxuna and in the Late Formative vessel shape repertory of the adherent slip ware characteristic of most Late Formative deposits. The Flaky Redware forms and the accompanying Formative and Regional wares show a stratigraphic sequence. Thus a transitional phase is documented between Late Formative and the Regional stage. At Dzibilchaltun was found a small sample of Late Formative Flaky Redware which supports the Acanceh collections.

The occurrence of Formative pottery in Yucatan sites, as explored by this survey, may be characterized as light but remarkably consistent. With a partial exception in the case of the Puuc sites, every major ruin sampled showed pure or nearly pure Late Formative deposits in the bottoms of trenches. The Formative sherds from the ruins, however, seldom exceed a tenth of the total collection. The small size of the Formative collections is obviously influenced by the sampling technique. Our trenches were placed off plaza edges of the latest occupational stage of the ruin. Formative deposits were encountered only by chance, and since the sites, like all Maya sites, grew by both vertical and horizontal accretion during a long time span, only the periphery of the Formative deposits was usually sampled.

There thus seems to have been a well distributed and probably heavy Formative population in Yucatan, and the locations of Formative sites were clung to with surprising tenacity by the later Maya peoples. The ruin locations in Yucatan do not in most cases show such physiographic desirability as to insure their continued choice for this reason alone; the reason, therefore, must probably have been adherence to such a continuing tradition as we know for the later periods.

Our picture of the Yucatan Formative period is lamentably incomplete. Flaked stone artifacts are very rare in Yucatan deposits. A small collection of badly broken, mineralized human bone material came from the Middle Formative deposits at Dzibilnocac. Almost no artifacts save ceramics came from the excavations. In architecture we have been a little more fortunate.

At Yaxuna a high ruin mound of complex shape, measuring about 60 by 130 meters, produced nearly pure Late Formative pottery in four trenches dug around its slopes. The mound seems to have been a raised terrace with several buildings or substructures on it. At Santa Rosa Xtampak a trench dug at the location of the eight Maya stelae of the site pierced several floors, then penetrated 1.5 meters of loose stone fill. By sounding we could estimate that at least 1.5 meters more fill lay below our trench which was stopped because of collapsing rock. All the pottery from under the lower two floors and in the fill is Middle Formative. The extent of this fill is unknown. The plaza in which the trench was dug is about 90 by 100 meters, bounded on one side by the largest pyramid of the site. From this evidence, scarce though it is, it seems reasonable to conclude that at least the Middle and Late Formative periods in Yucatan saw the erection of massive religious centers by the large, well organized groups necessary for such tasks. Certainly this part of the Maya culture pattern began long before the stela cult.

There is no evidence as to the type of habitation of these people, or as to the relationship between their living quarters and their temples, save the evidence available for the other later periods in Yucatan. Since there is also no evidence of change in pattern, generalizations may be valid. The pottery in our collections comes only from ruin groups and water sources, and, with possible exceptions in the Mexican periods, is unquestionably utilitarian, coming from household refuse. In mapping sites and prospecting for pottery deposits, the only evidence of isolated house sites are vague rock alignments resting on the usual 2 to 10 inches of burned over, vegetation churned soil. Pottery does not survive well in such locations. Although occupation at the religious centers may have been seasonal, the refuse suggests that such occupation was extensive and not restricted in social class. The burials with elaborate pottery gifts found in the Miraflores phase of the Guatemala highlands are probably not characteristic of

Yucatan Formative, since not a single whole Formative vessel occurs among the several hundred vessels I have recorded from Yucatan collections.

Although it would be presumptive to reconstruct a culture from the likely biased but tantalizing collection from the Mani cenote, it is difficult to refrain from speculation. The shape and surface treatment contrast strongly with later Yucatan ceramics and are thus far unique in the Maya area. The fact that the deposit is confined to easily portable water containers contrasts with the overlying deposits of the same and other cenotes where a wide form range, including many shallow bowl forms, is universal. There is a suggestion of marked changes in ceramic craft technology as well as in customs of cenote use, changes more radical than those observable over the ceramics of the next thousand years or more.

The Middle and Late Formative periods show characteristics which have become increasingly evident in Middle American Formative phases. In Yucatan there is, thus far, no evidence of strong culture change occurring between the Formative and the following stage, although in the Peten the beginning of the erection of stelae and vaults forms good markers. The available evidence, though meagre, suggests that large religious centers, presumably built under a theocratic government, began by Middle Formative times in Yucatan, and that this pattern continued on the same sites with no major upheavals until the Mexican penetration at about 1000 A.D.

The end date of the Yucatan Formative period is established by ceramic crossties with Uaxactun where the Chicanel ceramic period ended before the carving of the first stela, at about 320 A.D. according to the most commonly accepted correlation. The length of the period in Yucatan is completely unknown. Relative datings with other areas are known only for Late Formative. Mr. Robert Smith has seen all of this material and sees considerable identity and a prevailing similarity between the Yucatan Late Formative and his Chicanel period, although ware proportions are different and various wares are exclusive to one or the other area. There is also a varying amount of similarity between the Yucatan Late Formative collections and Uaxactun Mamom, although these similarities are less marked in every collection than those with Chicanel. Smith sees little resemblance between Middle Formative and the Uaxactun phases. The Early Formative collection thus far relates to nothing else that I know of and has not been found in the strata of Maya sites. Aside from the collections from cenotes which lie near Maya ruins, all excavating has been limited to Maya sites. The beginnings of ceramics in Yucatan as well as the possibility of preceramic cultures have still to be investigated.

AUTHOR'S NOTE, JULY, 1951.—Edwin Shook has written me since the presentation of the above paper that an examination of Guatemala Highland pottery of the Las Charcas and Sacatepequez phases shows the fairly frequent presence of a pattern burnished monochrome generally similar to the Yucatan Mani ware. The evidence of wide distribution suggests that this decorative technique may prove a useful Formative stage early horizon marker.

Robert Wauchope's excellent summary paper of the pre-classic ceramics of Middle America (Middle American Research Records, vol. 1, no. 14, New Orleans, 1950) offers an opportunity for the placement of the above described data from Yucatan in a general scheme. Wauchope's congeries of ceramic traits by stage (see his figure 3) fit perfectly with the Yucatan material. The Yaxuna Early Regional ceramics fit Wauchope's "Urban Formative," and my Yucatan Early, Middle and Late Formative substages all fit into his "Village Formative." My identification of "Large Mounds" beginning in the Middle Formative substage in Yucatan (as well as recent finds in the Guatemala highlands) would seem to add evidence for doubting the suitability of Wauchope's stage names but leaves the value of his general typology unimpaired.

POSSIBLE CHRONOLOGICAL IMPLICATIONS OF THE LONG CERAMIC SEQUENCE RECOVERED AT YARUMELA, SPANISH HONDURAS

JOEL S. CANBY

Important discoveries have been made at the site of Yarumela in Spanish Honduras. Their importance stems from two facts. These are: (1) that the most primitive-appearing ceramics reported to date from Middle America were found, and (2) that this material forms a base for a four-phase ceramic sequence which may extend up to historic times. Both of these facts have considerable bearing upon the problems of general chronology and the correlation of the Maya Long Count with Christian dates. Unfortunately, space does not permit adequate presentation of either matter. In order to include the factual and the speculative material in a single paper, some compromise must be made. Because much of the factual background is available from other sources, only the most salient features will be included here. The theorizing, if it is to stand at all, must rely on rather detailed reasoning. Therefore the stress will be on the latter.

Yarumela is a site which has long been known, but little studied. Its location is in the heart of the Comayagua Valley along the Humuya, a tributary of the Ulua River. From any vantage point in the 10 by 20 mile valley the principal structure of Yarumela can be seen. This is a rubble mound some 20 meters high, 165 meters long, and 100 meters wide, oriented with the long axis roughly east and west. Its shape is quite unusual. At the western end a steep-sided truncated pyramid seems to have been built, while to the east a ramp the full width of the pyramid slopes downward. The west end of the ramp meets the pyramid about midway up its face (some 10 meters); the plane of the ramp slopes very little until reaching the eastern terminus. Here the plane is broken by a rather narrow incline which passes down to ground-level between "balustrade mounds" (extensions of the ramp). No positive trace of terracing or stone facing could be detected on the "Cerrito," but it hardly seems reasonable for such an edifice to have endured so long without protection against the elements. Some of the smaller mounds in the site do have thick river-boulder covering in spots, so apparently the rock-facing technique was part of the culture of the builders.

The site itself covers an area of nearly one and one-half kilometers north and south; one kilometer east and west. Numerous small mounds are scattered over the area, and there are some six ranging in height from five to twelve meters. It is bound on the north and east by the Humuya River which meanders through the valley. In the southeast corner a huge bend of the river once cut its way down nearly 15 meters, aggraded some 5 meters, and graded to the present base-level.

It appears that all this geological activity occurred well within the time of man's first occupation of the valley.

In an effort to recover evidences of such occupation, 25 stratitests were made at Yarumela. In the course of these operations, remains were discovered of one of the most primitive-appearing, ceramic-making cultures so far reported from Middle America. In spite of this, the pottery is far from crude. It is the simplicity of form, lack of formal decoration and slip, and general absence of such modifications as handles, feet, and spouts which make it attributable to a fairly early period in the development of the ceramic art. The lowest levels of several of the trenches yielded material of this early type. The inventory of shapes is nearly exhausted after naming plates and simple jars, for rims from these two categories comprise over 80 per cent of all rims from the horizon. The remainder is composed of simple bowls, a few very coarse pieces, and some jars with slight lip elaboration. The surfaces of these vessels are normally very well burnished. Occasionally some red paint is found crudely applied to the lips of jars and bowls, but no vessel was decorated with anything approaching a formal design. The nearly flat, sideless plates are interesting because of the great variety of lip treatment found thereon. Scarcely any two have similar outlines. Basically, however, all have swollen lips, usually with a marked, but very small, break between the upper face and the thickened lips; the lower portion of the lips is frequently set off from the unburnished base by a pronounced groove. The jars are small with globular bodies and cylindrical necks. Material to supplement the ceramic elements of the culture is extremely scarce. Only a few obsidian blades and flakes and one hollow figurine head were recovered. This latter consists of the lower portion of a face; originally the artifact was undoubtedly rather large (possibly 15 centimeters high). These ceramic remains are, then, much less sophisticated in concept than any previously reported from Middle America (Cf. Vaillant, 440, 398; Ekholm, 114; Caso, 74; Drucker, 110, 111; Thompson, 360; Smith, 312, 311; Ricketson, 276; Butler, 66; Shook, 310; Kidder, 158, 157; Lothrop, 202, 198; Longyear, 193, 195; Popenoe, 269; and Strong, Kidder, and Paul, 335). The only exception, on the basis of a very brief reference, is the "Yojoa Monochrome" mentioned in Strong, Kidder and Paul (335, pp. 111–15). Inspection of their material, however, reveals that it is so badly eroded that little or nothing can be determined about its original nature. One fragment of an annular base, which was included in the collection, seems to point to a later stage of development than the earliest phase at Yarumela. The "Guañape" ceramic complex from the Chicama and Viru valleys of Peru (60) probably approaches most nearly the same developmental stage.

At Yarumela, immediately above levels yielding artifacts assigned to the first horizon, there was encountered material of a more advanced, but obviously contiguous nature. Percentages of plates and jars diminished so that these forms comprised less than 50 per cent of the rim types, plates declining in numbers most radically. New forms had evolved by this second horizon, the most conspicuous being a rather heavy, moderately well-burnished bowl with a flat base and sharply flaring lip. The upper surface of the lip was frequently painted red. The second diagnostic was the occurrence of pattern-burnishing. This surface treatment occurred most frequently on bowls with gently flaring sides and on jar necks. Some of the rims may have been from vases, but the sherd material did not permit definite determination of this point. The pattern, usually appearing black on a smooth gray background, was commonly a band at the rim and base of side or neck with vertical lines of no particular spacing running between the bands. In the second horizon there are more crude, heavy vessels than in the first. Handles appear in small quantities, and a very few grooved bichrome sherds and spouts, presumably imported, are found. The miscellaneous artifacts are as infrequent and undiversified as in the earliest horizon. Besides the obsidian blades and flakes, one solid figurine head of the "Playa de los Muertos" or "Lenca" type is assigned to this phase (328, Fig. 1, c–e; 45). The head came from the only burial discovered during the season; its chronological position is not definitely established. The ceramics from the second horizon are also less advanced stylistically than the earliest materials from other areas (see references above).

The uppermost strata in the majority of trenches excavated at Yarumela revealed a culture well known to Middle Americanists. This is the so-called "Middle Culture" material typified by the presence of Usulutan ware with solid nipple tetrapod supports (202). Most, or all, of the mound-building is attributed to this phase. The culture shows such great strides forward, ceramically and architecturally, that it is necessary to consider the possibility of ethnic movements into the Comayagua Valley for an explanation. This culture, from whatever antecedents, is identical with the "Ulua Bichrome" phase encountered further down the Humuya River at Santa Rita in the Ulua Valley (335). Besides the high percentage (24 per cent) of Usulutan ware (generally flaring-walled bowls of diverse design), several other distinctive pottery types appear, but in lesser quantity. Outstanding among these are: (1) jars with vertical necks coarsely incised in hatch-pattern on the exterior; lips markedly out-clubbed, rather square, painted red-orange; (2) neckless jars with incising or rocker stamping in horizontal bands; (3) cruder neckless jars with rims thickest at the lips and tapering downward, and (4) club-lip bowls with nearly vertical sides, paste a very light color and well burnished; neatly applied red paint covering the lip. There are other vessels which carry on the earlier traditions, such as the plates (in extremely small numbers), simple jars, flare-lip bowls, and heavy jars and bowls. Pattern burnishing disappears. Handles become an integral part of the "Archaic" ceramic complex. Considerably more imports are found, such as Playa de los Muertos figurines (these do not occur in sufficient numbers to be considered as part of the local Archaic), spouts, and painted ware with color-areas set off by grooves. No startling additions are made to the non-ceramic inventory. In regard to comparative material, it is most important to note that this horizon, on the basis of identical shapes and the treatment of Usulutan ware, must be equated with the Copan Archaic (195). It is apparently also the coeval of the Cerro Zapote, Eastern El Salvador, material discovered under great quantities of volcanic ash by Lardé and Lothrop (202). The determining of its relationship with the Highlands of Guatemala must await more detailed publications of those finds. It is assumed, however, that the Yarumela Archaic is at least in part contemporaneous with the Early Chukumuk (198) and Miraflores (158) phases, again on the basis of presence of Usulutan ware with nipple feet.

The final horizon from Yarumela was encountered only on the periphery of the site. This phase is called the "Classic" and is part of the well-known Ulua-Yojoa polychrome complex. Time does not permit the full description of the wares of this late horizon (see 133, 421, 335, 328). It can be stated only that the idea of a Highland sphere typified by "Bold Animalistic" and a Lowland sphere typified by "Mayoid" and "Bold Geometric" is adequately supported by the evidence encountered at Yarumela. Pottery belonging to the Ulua-Yojoa complex has been encountered at Copan with local wares assignable to the Late Full Classic.

At this point a word must be said in reference to the nomenclature suggested for the sequence just outlined. Because of the fact that Copan holds the best, if not the only key to the problem of dating in Honduras, a terminology for the horizons at Yarumela has been devised to follow as closely as possible that employed by J. M. Longyear, the authority on Copan stratigraphy. As will be seen, the resemblance is not great. (These phase-names correspond to Longyear's latest ones [195], not those which appeared in his first, unpublished, account [193].) The period of florescence of the Maya culture has been designated the "Classic"; this is further divided into "Early Classic" and "Full Classic." Because no phase comparable to the "Early" has been revealed in Honduras (except at Copan), the Yarumela florescent horizon is termed simply "Classic." Preceding the Classic at Copan is the "Archaic." Because of the great similarity in the outstanding ceramic type there and at Yarumela, and because the term "Archaic" is generally understood to mean "before the Classic," instead of "primitive," the same term has been adopted for the pre-Classic horizon at Yarumela. The "Pre-Archaic" horizons offered more of a problem. These cultural complexes actually seem to fit into the pattern of the Archaic—certainly they are not to be thought of as "Developmental." Therefore, it was desirable to find names indicating this fact. The differences are so great between the full Archaic and the lower phases, however, that a simple numbering of Archaic I, Archaic II, etc., did not seem in order. To denote the more exact relationships, the terms "Proto-Archaic"—leading up to the Archaic—and "Eo-Archaic"—dawn of the Archaic—were decided upon. The latter is the earliest found at Yarumela. Thus the Longyear terminology has been distorted, possibly beyond recognition, but it is felt that this system will be of value in bringing some order out of the chaos of local names generally applied to ceramic horizons in Middle America. This system is flexible, for developmental stages, rather than chronological periods, are indicated by the names. They may be used to include as great or as limited a sphere as desired simply by prefixing the phase with the site, cultural, topographical, or regional name (e.g., Yarumela-, Lenca-, Highland-, or Honduras-Archaic).

With these few remarks as background, we can now proceed to the matter of chronology. The Yarumela-Classic is datable by the Maya Long Count to 9.16.0.0.0, or as the latest possible beginning, to 9.18.0.0.0; this, of course, being based upon the finds of Ulua-Yojoa polychrome in Late Full Classic deposits at Copan (193, pp. 185–94). Actually, the beginnings could be placed even earlier. A lengthening of the time-span for the Ulua-Yojoa Classic would lead to nearly insoluble problems.

It is becoming a well established fact that Classic material occurs in abundance in the uppermost levels of nearly all stratigraphic excavations made in the Ulua-Yojoa-Comayagua region of Honduras (335, 69). The one exception seems to be the Contact material of Mexican origin found at Naco (335, pp. 20–34). Even in this one-phase site, however, a few sherds assignable to the Ulua-Yojoa polychrome complex were recovered (ibid.). The early historians all agree that the Ulua and the Comayagua Valleys were densely populated at the time of the Conquest (21, p. 77; 421, p. 11). This dense population must have left abundant remains, and these should appear on or near the surface, or at least overlying all earlier material. With the possible exception of Naco, the Ulua-Yojoa polychrome fits this description exactly. At Yarumela, the Classic material was found in loosely consolidated ashy soil overlying all other deposits. At both the Lake Yojoa and Ulua Valley sites excavated by Strong, Kidder and Paul (335) the Classic sherds invariably capped the plainer wares. On the basis of present evidence, then, it seems fair to assign the Ulua-Yojoa ceramic complex to the people occupying the area at the time of the Conquest.

Such late dating for the Classic certainly is contrary to present postulates about the correlation of the Long Count with the Christian calendar. Using the generally accepted Thompson-Goodman-Martinez 11.16.0.0.0 correlation (396, Table III) for the terminal date, and 9.18.0.0.0 as the latest possible initial date, the Ulua-Yojoa complex would be required to fill a time-span of some 760 years. That would be a period about equal to the time attributed to the entire development of the Maya Archaic and Classic combined.

Something is obviously amiss when a culture as uniform as the Ulua-Yojoa must be assigned such a long duration. There are only two solutions. They are: (1) to deny that the Honduras Classic lasted to the Conquest, or (2) to admit that the 11.16 correlation is untenable. The first alternative has been tried, and the basic assumption of the present theory is that the Ulua-Yojoa complex did endure until the coming of the Spaniards. Therefore, if one accepts the basis for the theory, one must reject the 11.16 correlation.

Even the rather daring 11.3 correlation (396, Table IV) does not help the situation very much. Some 260 years are subtracted from the total 760 year span, thus reducing it to "only" 500 years. Even this figure seems unreasonable. There are, admittedly, differences in the Ulua-Yojoa complex. These differences are due, apparently, to spatial rather than temporal distribution (69; 335, pp. 121–25). It is, therefore, suggested that the 10.10 correlation (396, Table V) best explains the chronological position of the Ulua-Yojoa Classic culture or, assuming a break in the Maya dating system, some point between 11.3 and 10.10 would be more defensible (communications with D. H. Kelley).

The remarks are made from the viewpoint of a dirt archeologist, completely disregarding the strong historic and epigraphic evidence against such a radical change in the correlation (157c, 356). Arguments against the idea can certainly be piled high enough to counterbalance the ones set forth here. However, on ceramic evidence alone, the 10.10 or, say, 10.15 dating is reasonable. Without this interpretation there is chaos requiring the presence of almost mythical groups, such as the Jicaque (329, 203, 194) to occupy the Ulua Valley in "Post-Classic" times. Unfortunately, the problem of linguistic associations cannot be taken up in the present paper. It is a vital matter, however, deserving attention.

Any further remarks, after the rather unorthodox conclusions reached above, may seem anticlimactic. However, there remains one more point in regard to dating in Middle America. That is the placement of the Highland Archaic culture(s)—as characterized by Usulutan ware—in the temporal framework. Copan again furnishes the necessary clues. Two facts are of primary importance: (1) the Copan Archaic is characterized by Usulutan ware with nipple feet; and, (2) the evidence from Copan indicates that the true Archaic was of very short duration, being affected by the Maya Early Classic almost upon its establishment along the Copan River. Evidence of the latter statement is found in the rapid development from nipple to mammifeet (mammiform) supports on the Usulutan ware, and the importation of basal flange polychrome bowls. Mammifeet characterize Holmul I pottery (225, pls. 18, 19), and basal flange bowls are the hallmark of the Maya Early Classic (312, Tazkol, pp. 13–21).

The assumption is that the Copan Archaic, an extension of the Highland Archaic, existed during a time when the Lowland Mayas were in a stage of development corresponding to the Early Classic. At the time the Copan area first became occupied by the Archaic peoples, Mayans who were far more advanced culturally, immediately began trade with the Highland enclave, and probably soon moved in a group to join this more primitive population. The proof of this is the fact that rapid "Maya-ization" occurred during the rather brief Copan Early Classic. The relatively retarded nature of the cultural progress at Copan seems indicated also by the fact that the earliest dated stela there seems to be 9.1.10.0.0 whereas the first dated stela at Uaxactun bears an 8.14.10.13.15 inscription (228, Table V). On these grounds, it seems safe to conclude that the Highland Archaic is in part, if not entirely, contemporaneous with the Lowland (Maya) Early Classic. In order to dissolve the hiatus which would occur between the beginning of the Honduras Highland Classic and the end of the Highland Archaic (if earlier dating were admitted), it is necessary to move the terminal date for the Archaic up to about 9.16.0.0.0, or Late Full Classic in the Lowland Maya area. This proposal, assuming as it does a long period of relatively retarded progress in contrast to the Maya Lowlands, would help explain the appearance of Usulutan ware at Chukumuk into late times (198) and would make the high ceramic accomplishments of the Miraflores and earlier cultures more understandable. It would not, however, justify the break between the Miraflores and the later Esperanza phase at Kaminaljuyu, the latter being of demonstrated Maya Early Classic date (158, pp. 250–51).

The ideas of a sloping horizon of cultural development, and of highland peoples being culturally retarded are not radical concepts. Attributing retardation of some 400 to 500 years to Highlanders, in a region known to have had considerable intercourse with the more advanced cultures of the time, seems difficult to accept. Seen from Yarumela, these schemes for an upward revision of the Highland dating seem perfectly in focus. Even the "primitive" Eo- and Proto-Archaic cultures need not be assigned any great age, for the two meters of deposits do not necessarily imply antiquity and the geological data point to a very rapid development of the present course of the Humuya river. The thick ash overburden of the Archaic in Eastern Salvador is easily explained: volcanic activity is famous for the speed with which it can modify land features. Finally, it must be repeated that this paper is presented from the view of an excavator, not from the vantage point of the historian, epigrapher, or mathematician. It is hoped, however, that some of the ideas included here will prove useful in formulating programs of future research and as frames of reference in which more logical historical interpretations of Middle America archeological material can be made.

A HISTORICAL INTERPRETATION OF COPAN ARCHEOLOGY

John M. Longyear III

The recovery and classification of ancient materials is no longer the major concern of archeologists. Instead, modern field workers have occupied themselves more and more with the reconstruction of history and society as these aspects of human activity are reflected by the material culture of vanished peoples. Obviously, we cannot reconstruct a culture in its entirety from material remains alone: architecture, monuments, and artifacts of pottery, stone, bone, and shell can reflect only a small part of the total culture which produced them, even when they are supplemented by certain historical sources. Still, we must do what we can with what we have, for the intrinsic value of our excavated specimens alone rarely justifies the time and money spent in digging them up.

In the American field generally, and in the Middle American field particularly, this recent trend in archeology is reflected in essays such as Taylor's *Study of Archaeology* (337), and in the latest field reports of Kidder (158), Wauchope (408), and others. In the present paper, I wish to supplement these studies with a summary of the history of aboriginal Copan, as I believe it to be revealed by the archeological evidence recovered there by the Carnegie Institution of Washington over the past fifteen years. In a paper of this length, I cannot do more than skim over the listing of the actual specimens; emphasis here will be on interpretation rather than on description.

The general location of Copan is familiar to all students of Middle American archeology. I would like to particularize, however, on a few geographical facts which appear to have had an especial influence on Copan's history. In the first place, although the immediate vicinity of Copan comprises a level, fertile valley, the surrounding country belies this pleasant intervale. The Copan river enters and leaves the valley through narrow, rugged gorges which extend for several miles in both directions, and on all sides rise steep hills and mountains, covered with heavy bush and jungle. Not only, then, would the very existence of Copan valley be almost undiscoverable from an inspection of its surrounding country, but the valley also, once found, would be quite difficult to reach. In the second place, Copan does not appear to lie on the path of any of the major Middle American migration or trade routes, insofar as these latter are controlled by purely geographical factors. From its location, therefore, one would expect the Copan valley to be isolated, perhaps even a refuge area, and not easily brought into contact with the outside world. That it became, on the contrary, one of the

86

greatest centers of the Maya civilization should surely have importance to those who seek the relation between culture and environment.

The human occupation of the Copan valley may be grouped into four periods which I have named, from early to late, Archaic, Early Classic, Full Classic, and Post-Classic. These divisions, of course, have been established by archeological criteria, but I also believe, and will endeavor to show, that they have historical implications. For brevity's sake, the outstanding features of each period will be presented below in outline form, before the interpretative discussion. A full description of the artifacts must await the final report.

ARCHAIC PERIOD

Architecture.—None known.

Dated monuments.—None known.

Pottery.—Coarse ware storage jars, bowls, comales, and an incensario. Burnished ware jars and tetrapod bowls with decoration in Usulutan technique. A few hand-made figurines.

Stone.—Many irregular obsidian flakes, very few true blades. Presence of metates and manos postulated.

Domestic refuse.—Quantities of animal bones and fresh water snail shells.

Burials.—None known.

As with other sites in the Maya area, no sure evidence of pre-pottery peoples has ever come to light at Copan.[1] We must, therefore, assume on the evidence that our Archaic Period represents the earliest occupation of this valley. The culture is represented most abundantly by its pottery, which is of advanced technique, well-formed and fired, and tastefully decorated. The principal method of decoration is by Usulutan technique, which results in series of parallel, wavy lines, showing either light or dark against the background. This technique is found on almost all burnished ware vessels. On coarse ware, filleting and simple painting in one color are used.

The Archaic inhabitants used obsidian in considerable quantities, but recognizable tools, such as blades, are few. These last may have resulted from importation, or perhaps came from the workshops of one or two local artisans, more gifted than the rest.

No mounds, buildings or dated monuments can be correlated with the Copan Archaic, so we must suppose that these peoples had no knowledge of formal architecture or calendrical systems. Since no burials have been found, we lack information on the Archaic physical type and their method of disposal of the dead. Other evidences of ceremonial activity are rare, also, consisting of one crude vessel, which may be an incensario, and a few hand-made figurines, almost certainly imported from the Ulua Valley and El Salvador.

From the above, what can be deduced about the life of these Archaic Copanecos? Surely, it was not a complicated one. The people probably lived in

1. But see Longyear (197) for indications of a possible pre-ceramic complex.

small, thatched huts, clustered in family bands, and so scattered throughout the valley that each group had ready access to both water and the family's corn-fields. That these people grew corn may be inferred from the presence of comales in their pottery debris, and I have further postulated that they ground their corn with metates and manos, although the latter have yet to be definitely associated with Archaic deposits. Aside from corn, wild game and fresh water snails were eaten in abundance, to judge from the quantities of bones and shells found in the refuse.

It is dangerous to speculate on the division of labor in these little communities, but it appears probable that the men took care of the fields, hunted and fished, while the women kept house and gathered such additions to the daily fare as wild shoots, berries and fruits, and edible snails. Pottery-making was probably then, as it is today, the woman's task, although presumably there was no full-time specialization in this work. Among the men, a few of the more erratic or gifted may have served as part-time shamans, but there is no evidence of an organized religious cult or priesthood.

Since each little band was largely, if not wholly, self-sufficient, intercommunication throughout the valley was probably of the most casual and informal sort. From all indications, trade with outside regions was practically non-existent. Obsidian, it is true, does not occur in the Copan valley, but it might well have been gathered by the Copanecos themselves from outcrops not far away. The presumably imported figurines may have been brought back as curiosities by occasional far-ranging hunters or travelers.

This reconstruction of Archaic Copan society places these people at a rather low level of cultural complexity, but nothing in the archeological record indicates that it was higher. Indeed, many isolated Indian groups in the hills surrounding the valley would lead much the same life today, if we removed from them such European conveniences as the machete and the mule.

From where did these Archaic people come, and how long did they occupy the Copan valley before the advent of the Maya? Neither of these questions can be answered at present with any high degree of assurance. The pottery of the Copan Archaic resembles most closely that of similarly early levels in the Comayagua Valley of Honduras. It is probable, then, that the Copan migrants arrived from, or at least by way of, the Comayagua region. It is not, perhaps, too far-fetched to imagine that the Copanecos found their new home by chance, having been driven from the populous Comayagua by war or famine and, appreciating the qualities of this pleasant intervale, settled there to enjoy the peace and self-sufficiency that isolation often brings.

All this must have come about quite late in the Archaic Period. The Copan deposits of this age are characterized, from top to bottom, by the presence of decoration in Usulutan technique and are, besides, markedly uniform as regards wares and vessel forms. Thus, they cannot span a long period of time. Furthermore, not only in the Comayagua, but also in other Middle American regions,

Archaic deposits have been found which are divisible into two or three sub-periods.[2] In every instance, pottery with Usulutan technique is found only in the latest levels. The people represented by the Archaic pottery at Copan, then, could not have migrated into the valley until they had reached the latest, or Usulutan stage of this period. Considering the above facts; i.e., the uniformity of the Copan deposits and their domination by the Usulutan technique, I find it hard to believe that much over 100 years, if that long, elapsed between the beginning of Copan's Archaic Period and the start of the next, or Early Classic Period.

EARLY CLASSIC PERIOD

Architecture.—Beginning of construction in the Acropolis.

Dated monuments.—Several, ranging from 9.1.10.0.0 (A.D. 465) to 9.6.10.0.0 (A.D. 564).[3]

Pottery.—Old wares and forms continue, with burnished ware falling off toward the end. New wares and forms appear, including especially polychrome basal-flange bowls and tripod vases, and red on brown and burnished ware bowls with hollow mammiform legs.

Stone.—Obsidian blades very numerous. Metates and manos.

Domestic refuse.—Animal bones and snail shells less frequent than in Archaic Period.

Burials.—Extended, with furniture, in graves or slab cists.

Sometime about the beginning of the ninth cycle of the Maya era, a band of priests or devotees of the Maya hierarchic cult came to Copan and assumed leadership there. How they happened to find this little valley we do not know—certainly they had wandered far from the Guatemalan Peten, which at that time was not only the nucleus but practically the only stronghold of the Maya civilization.

However they reached the Copan valley, the Maya influenced life there very little at first, to judge from material remains. A few additions to pottery, especially the polychrome basal-flange bowls and the tripod vases, are the only sure evidences of the new cult at this time. Perhaps, also, the Maya introduced the mammiform vessel support, since it appears early on polychrome pottery in the Peten. But at first, the invaders had to consolidate their conquest. Lines of communication with the homeland had to be established, a site for the local ceremonial center selected, and experienced masons and sculptors brought in for its construction. The close of this phase of the conquest may have been marked by the erection of the first stela at Copan in 9.1.10.0.0 (A.D. 465).

Preliminaries out of the way, work could begin in earnest, and now the life of the common people no doubt underwent a marked change. The men probably

2. Joel Canby, Peabody Museum of Harvard, personal communication; see Shook (310).

3. All Christian dates in this paper conform to the Goodman-Thompson-Martinez 11.16.0.0.0 correlation.

had to spend a certain portion of their time quarrying and hauling stone for the Acropolis. Time for hunting and fishing, consequently, was curtailed, and they had to place greater dependence on agriculture for their food. The women, too, spent longer hours at the pottery kilns, turning out the new wares required for the Maya ceremonial observances.

The knowledge of the calendar, the attributes of the many gods, the proper times and paraphernalia of the rituals—all these concerned the common people little, if at all, for they were not admitted to the mysteries of the Maya cult. This civilization did, however, affect the lives of the people in other ways.

Specialization increased as the men became more expert at quarrying and masonry, and the best potters among the women doubtless found much of their time occupied in the manufacture of ceremonial vessels alone. Some of the younger members of the community also, presumably, engaged in new activities, a few participating in the sacred ball games, while others may have been chosen for training in the priesthood. At times, all the inhabitants of the valley were probably summoned to witness an important ritual at the Acropolis. These occasions brought large numbers of people together, and considerably heightened their emotional life. Finally, the life of the valley was stabilized through the priestly government, which by no means regulated all activity, but did set times for planting and harvesting, collected crops, assigned men to work gangs, and fixed periods of ceremony or festival.

Trade with the outside world now became frequent and regular, but most, if not all of the imports were of a ceremonial or luxury nature. This trade, apparently, was confined almost entirely to commerce with classic Maya centers to the north and west of Copan.

Maya civilization, therefore, brought to Copan a considerable increase in the complexity of society. The people engaged in more activities, with considerable part-time specialization as a result, they were controlled by a central government, and had contact with the outside world. This situation was to continue as long as the Maya priests and their cult dominated the valley.

FULL CLASSIC PERIOD

Architecture.—Completion of Acropolis; construction of outlying groups.

Dated monuments.—Many, ranging from 9.9.0.0.0 (A.D. 613) to 9.18.10.0.0 (A.D. 800).

Pottery.—All wares except coarse and polychrome decline in frequency, and diagnostic Early Classic vessel forms disappear. Copador ware is the dominant polychrome pottery. Numerous polychrome imports indicate wide trade.

Stone.—Much work in obsidian and jade.

Domestic refuse.—Continued decline in frequency of animal bones. Snail shells practically absent.

Burials.—Flexed, with furniture, in graves or cut stone tombs.

We do not know exactly when the transition from Early Classic to Full

Classic took place at Copan, but the change is clearly marked, especially in the pottery deposits. Polychrome basal-flange bowls and black tripod vases, so diagnostic of Early Classic refuse, suddenly disappear, to be replaced by an equally distinctive type of local pottery called Copador ware. This same change —from the wide-spread flanged bowls and tripod vases of the Early Classic to Full Classic local styles—took place at most other Maya centers, and our present evidence indicates that it occurred everywhere sometime between the Maya dates 9.6.0.0.0 and 9.9.0.0.0. This transition to local styles may indicate the breakdown of centralized control over all the Maya area, and the rise of independent city-states.

Life in the Copan valley was probably not too different from that of Early Classic times. Heightened building activity on the Acropolis no doubt kept the men busier than ever, and our evidence shows that the smaller outlying groups in the valley were also constructed at this time. These latter, which appear to have been secondary ceremonial centers, suggest that religion was becoming a more integral part of the people's daily life.

The emergence of a local ceremonial pottery—Copador ware—also kept the women busy. Although they still shaped and fired these vessels, the highly stylized and symbolic decoration appears to have been dictated by a special school of artists, probably drawn from the priestly class. Copan potters produced Copador vessels not only for local use, but also for export to other centers in the southeastern frontier region. Trade, however, was not confined to these nearby sites. Articles, especially of pottery, from British Honduras, the Peten, and the Guatemala highlands show that Copan's contacts with the central Maya area were frequent and intimate.

The latter half of the Full Classic Period saw the greatest development of Copan's culture, exemplified particularly in the Acropolis. In the last half-century of Maya occupation the great Hieroglyphic Stairway, the Ball Court, and at least three large temples were completed, and several elaborate monuments were dedicated. Then, at almost the zenith of this activity, just before the end of the ninth cycle, the Maya suddenly abandoned Copan.

POST-CLASSIC PERIOD

Architecture.—None known.

Dated monuments.—None known.

Pottery.—An almost complete break in the ceramic sequence occurs. Wares are predominantly coarse, with little decoration. All fine wares appear to be imported, and include plumbate, Nicoya polychrome and other effigy and polychrome types.

Stone.—None definitely assignable to this period.

Domestic refuse.—None found.

Burials.—Flexed, with furniture, in abandoned temple rooms, or in crude tombs built of re-used stones.

The abandonment of Copan by the Maya marks a great break in the historic sequence at this site. At one moment, the valley bustles with the activity engendered by the pursuit of a complicated theocratic civilization; in the next, the great center is deserted by priests and commoners alike, and the magnificent buildings and monuments are given over to the elements and the jungle.

What caused this sudden move we do not know, but it does not seem to have been accompanied by violence or disaster. The priests appear simply to have packed up and left, and, with their going, the whole elaborate culture-structure of the valley collapsed. There was nothing, now, to keep the common people in the vicinity of the Acropolis, and the absence of Post-Classic occupational debris in this area indicates that they removed to the surrounding hills. Their cornfields were probably already located there, and wild game would be more plentiful away from the buildings and the flat lands which had been kept cleared for so many years. In small, isolated clusters, the thatched huts sprang up, and the Copanecos settled back into their Archaic routine of tending fields, hunting, and fishing. Life in the Copan valley had come full circle.

A few vestiges of their former existence remained. Archeological evidence shows that small parties occasionally camped for short periods of time in the deserted Acropolis, possibly to practice certain simple rites in honor of some still-remembered deity. From time to time, persons of note, perhaps local chieftains, were buried in tombs formed by small rooms in outlying buildings, or built up of masonry and broken sculpture quarried from a convenient mound. With these personages were interred pottery vessels of exotic types, showing that Copan was still in contact with the outside world. Apparently, a trade route between the Guatemala highlands and the Chorotegan area passed through, or near, the Copan valley, for the burial pieces consist of plumbate ware and Alta Verapaz forms, together with Nicoya polychrome and other effigy vessels having a definite southern feeling.

Aside from these few holdovers from the Classic era, however, the Maya civilization appears to have left not the slightest lasting impression on the inhabitants of the Copan valley. The cultural reversal which followed the abandonment of the Acropolis shows clearly the veneer-like character of a hieratic cult which, despite its magnificent outward show, utterly failed to create a lasting society because the common people, on whom it depended for labor and livelihood, could neither understand nor appreciate its values.

THE PRESENT STATUS OF RESEARCH ON THE PRE-CLASSIC HORIZONS IN GUATEMALA

Edwin M. Shook

There are few areas within the Western Hemisphere as strategically situated geographically as is Guatemala, where evidence may be found bearing on such fundamental Americanists' problems as the diffusion of the earliest inhabitants, the evaluation of indigenous cultures, the domestication and spread of cultivated plants, and the rise of advanced civilizations. Guatemala is a land bridge, so to speak, across which early man made his way, as did subsequent people from time to time up through the ages to the Spanish Conquest in 1524. Topographically the country divides into three zones of prime importance: the Pacific Coast plain, the Southern Highlands, and the Atlantic Lowlands. The first is a narrow, fertile, alluvial plain crossed every few miles by swift-flowing streams from the chain of lofty and geologically recent volcanoes paralleling the coast. The Southern Highlands just north of the volcanic chain consist largely of upland valleys and ash-filled basins between three and eight thousand feet elevation. The Atlantic Lowlands of Northern Guatemala are separated from the second zone by a great mass of geologically older mountains, running east-west. In the tropical rain forests of Northern Guatemala and the adjacent areas, there developed one of the most brilliant of American civilizations—that of the Lowland Maya.

Knowledge is woefully lacking on early man and the early sedentary cultures in Guatemala. However, Dr. Barnum Brown has given us, perhaps, the first clue to man's association with Upper Pleistocene fauna. Recently he discovered on bars and beaches of the Pasion river in southern Peten petrified bones of the camel, mastodon, megatherium and glypdodon. Among them was one fragment, apparently from a sloth, bearing three sharp V-shaped cuts on the unbroken external surface. The cuts were made in fresh bone, according to Dr. Brown, an observation with which Dr. Kidder and I agree, after close examination of the specimen.

Similar fauna remains have been uncovered elsewhere. A particularly rich deposit occurs near Zacapa in the Motagua Valley. Sporadic finds have been made in the Departments of Santa Rosa, Guatemala, Quetzaltenango, and Huehuetenango. Dr. Brown excavated bones of glypdodon, elephas, and mastodon in Tivoli, a suburban district of Guatemala City. The bones were found only six feet below the present surface, under the brown clay layer which blankets most of the valley, and on top of the latest volcanic ash bed. This discovery is of considerable importance because it directs search for early man and subsequent

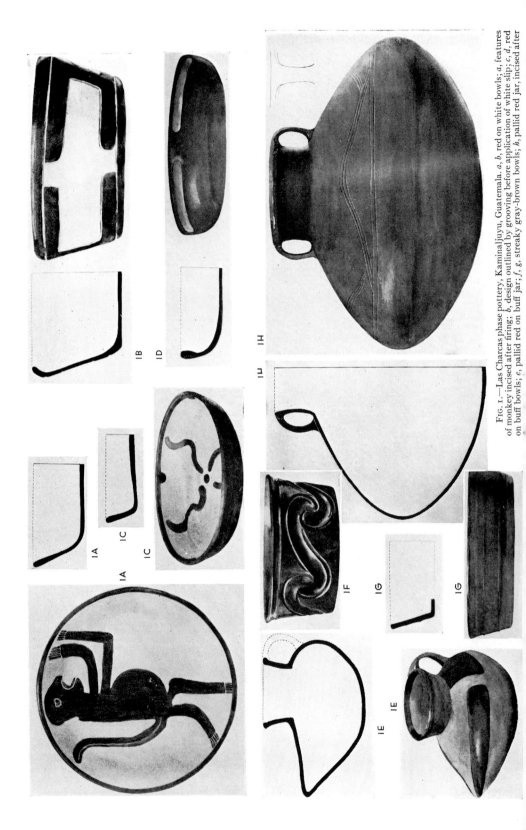

FIG. 1.—Las Charcas phase pottery, Kaminaljuyu, Guatemala. *a, b,* red on white bowls; *a,* features of monkey incised after firing; *b,* design outlined by grooving before application of white slip; *c, d,* red on buff bowls; *e,* pallid red on buff jar; *f, g,* streaky gray-brown bowls; *h,* pallid red jar, incised after

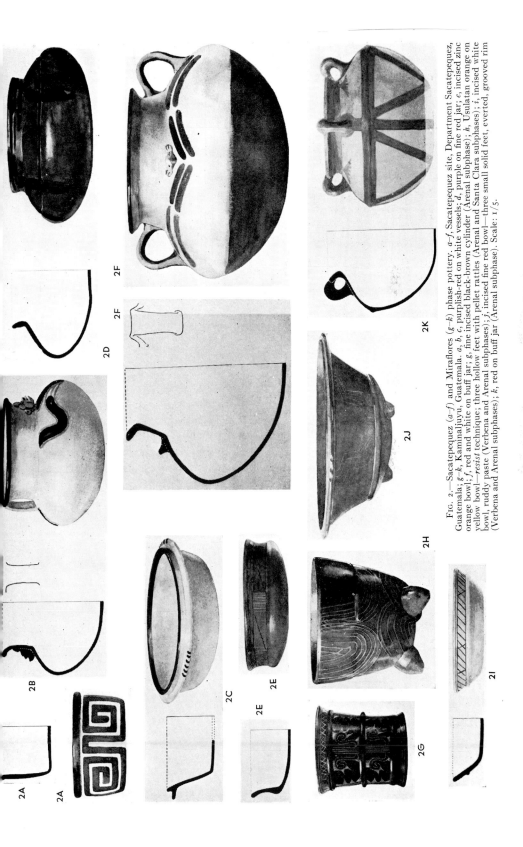

FIG. 2.—Sacatepequez (*a–f*) and Miraflores (*g–k*) phase pottery. *a–f*, Sacatepequez site, Department Sacatepequez, Guatemala; *g–k*, Kaminaljuyu, Guatemala. *a, b, c*, purplish-red on white vessels; *d*, purple on fine red jar; *e*, incised zinc orange bowl; *f*, red and white on buff jar; *g*, fine incised black-brown cylinder (Arenal subphase); *h*, Usulatan orange on yellow bowl—*resist* technique; three hollow feet with pellet rattles (Arenal and Santa Clara subphases); *i*, incised white bowl, ruddy paste (Verbena and Arenal subphases); *j*, incised fine red bowl—three small solid feet, everted, grooved rim (Verbena and Arenal subphases); *k*, red on buff jar (Arenal subphase). Scale: 1/5.

cultural remains to the uppermost strata instead of the deeply buried levels be-low hundreds of feet of volcanic eruptives. All Pre-Classic remains in the Guate-mala Valley so far brought to light have overlain or been intrusive into the brown clay.

Remains of early man are assuredly in Guatemala and will be found even-tually as in Mexico, the United States, and South America when specific search is made and more detailed studies are available on the Upper Pleistocene and Recent geology. Important as this portion of man's history may be to Ameri-canists, it seems to me of even greater significance to discover the transitional period from a hunting-gathering economy to the sedentary life presumably brought about by the domestication of food plants. In Meso-America this im-mensely important transitional stage still eludes us and the earliest remains we can now report are those of a people already living in communities with a well established society and a secure economy based on agriculture with corn as the staple food. These conditions are not too far removed from those which prevailed up to the Spanish Conquest. The Pre-Classic horizon with which we are here concerned encompasses all the known pottery-making cultures throughout Meso-America up to A.D. 200, the approximate date based on the Goodman-Martinez-Thompson correlation for the beginning of the extraordinary burst of intellectual achievement of the Classic period. The Pre-Classic has previously been termed Archaic, Middle, Formative, Developmental, Pre-Maya, etc. None of these designations fits the general picture in Meso-America quite so well and allows as much latitude for hemispherical correlation as Pre-Classic. In the Southern Highlands, especially at the great site of Kaminaljuyu, near Guate-mala City, there have been defined three Pre-Classic phases—Las Charcas, Sacatepequez, and Miraflores, the latter divisible into the Providencia, Verbena, Arenal, and Santa Clara sub-phases.

Las Charcas—the oldest phase identified at present—is represented by a large body of household debris from deep pits sunk through the surface layer of sterile brown clay into the underlying white volcanic ash. Some pits were left empty, their openings sealed with stone slabs; others contained burials, but the majority were filled with rubbish. It is thought that the wide-mouthed pits were dug primarily to obtain material for house foundations and other purposes and secondarily were used as trash dumps. However, this does not explain the care-fully made rectangular and bottle-shaped ones with small, round orifices. These may have served as sweat baths, storage, weaving, or ritual chambers. What-ever their true function may have been, these pits were dug throughout a wide area in the Highlands in Pre-Classic times. The chultuns found in Uaxactun, some below the black earth containing the most ancient ceramic material of the Mamom period, compare in shape, size, and perhaps function with the bottle-shaped pits of the Highlands.

The Las Charcas Phase, as well as the whole Pre-Classic Horizon, is char-acterized by excellent pottery. The principal slipped and polished wares are White, Red-on-White (Fig. 1, a, b), Red-on-Buff (Fig. 1, c, d), Pallid Red (Fig.

1, *e*, *h*), and Streaky Gray-Brown (Fig. 1, *f*, *g*). Some of the forms in these wares are incurved rim, flat-based bowls (Fig. 1, *b*); effigy, spouted, shoe-shaped vessels (Fig. 1, *e*); and large jars with heavy bolstered rims (Fig. 1, *h*). The coarse, unslipped, and unpolished wares are generally ruddy-brown. They include simple silhouette, bowl-shaped comales; heavily scored "graters"; three-pronged incensarios, and a specialized vessel—a small cup set on three tall, slender feet. This form continues, with slight modification, through the Pre-Classic, Classic, and Post-Classic in certain regions of Meso-America. It is the only pottery vessel with secondary supports found in either the Las Charcas or Sacatepequez Phase.

Other cultural features first seen in Las Charcas are cylindrical and stemmed clay stamps; solid, hand-modeled human and monkey figurines; and a variety of small effigy whistles representing birds and animals. Stone material consists of metates and manos; obsidian flake-blades and scrapers; and green-stone celts. Simple sculpture probably begins in this phase with the fashioning of effigy mushroom-like stones.

Perishable materials have been identified through the accidental preservation of forms in ashes, and casts in burned adobe. There were seeds of several fruits—one possibly an avocado; corn husks and cobs; and woven goods—probably textiles; baskets, and surely mats and rope.

The Sacatepequez Phase follows Las Charcas in time and appears to be a direct growth from the latter (Fig. 2, *a–f*). Many of the earlier wares continue in different forms, and several new ones appear. The diagnostic pottery of this phase is a fine white ware often with simple decoration in purplish paint, which constitutes in excavated lots from 25 per cent to 55 per cent of all pottery (Fig. 2, *a–c*). Less common, fine wares occurring for the first time are Purple-on-Fine Red (Fig. 2, *d*); Incised Zinc Orange (Fig. 2, *e*); and a glossy Gray-Brown Ware. New features are labial flanged bowls (Fig. 2, *c*), bowls and jars with faceted shoulder (Fig. 2, *d*), and flattish plate-like comales. A few fragments of solid, hand-modeled human figurines have been found but they are exceedingly rare.

No Las Charcas or Sacatepequez mounds have yet been found. However, it is known that the people lived in settled communities and had houses of pole and thatch with walls partially daubed with adobe.

The evidently very long Miraflores phase is distinguished from the older ones by the institution of religious and civic architecture of a permanent nature. Platforms and pyramids of earth surfaced with adobe plaster which supported perishable structures were formally arranged around elongated rectangular plazas. This type of city planning may have developed into that seen at Teotihuacan where the plaza became so long in comparison to its width that it is called an avenue.

The first sub-phase, Providencia, seems to have developed directly from Sacatepequez. Ceramic innovations were Coarse Incised Black-Brown, and Usulutan wares; and an abundance of solid, hand-modeled figurines in the so-called Archaic style. The Black-Brown is a distinctive, polished ware which continues with changes of form and decoration through the Verbena and Arenal sub-phases (Fig. 2, g). Usulutan ware, an important Meso-American pottery found only in small amounts in the Las Charcas and Sacatepequez phases, becomes relatively abundant in Providencia sub-phase and continues with style and form changes through the remainder of the Pre-Classic and well into the Classic period (Fig. 2, h).

The earliest use, with the exception of the tall-footed tripod cup, of secondary supports on pottery vessels occurs in Providencia. These are small, solid nubbins, and solid conical feet—their use is rare.

In the next sub-phase, Verbena, the amount of mound building at Kaminaljuyu staggers the imagination. Str. E-III-3, largest of the some two hundred at the site, was built mostly in this phase. It developed from a small, semicircular, adobe unit about 2.0 meters high, through many minor and six major architectural additions, to a massive, flat-topped rectangular pyramid over 20 meters in height. In this great pyramid two richly stocked tombs were discovered and excavated during the past two years. Each had been cut through the top of a pyramid in a serits of terraces stepping in on all four sides toward the spacious, rectangular burial chamber. Four wood posts were set, one in each corner of the chamber to support heavy longitudinal timbers on which rested transverse roof beams. Prior to roofing, the principal body was laid extended on a low wooden platform in the center of the tomb floor and offerings lavishly heaped around it. After roofing, more offerings were placed on the terraces. The remaining open space from the tomb roof to the pyramid top was then filled and floored over. This permitted the use of the pyramid, temporarily, while a successive one was being constructed.

The location of these tombs in the principal structure of the site, the labor involved in their construction, and the wealth of mortuary furnishings give ample evidence of the position of great honor and esteem held by the deceased. The offerings included over four hundred pottery vessels; finely wrought ones of jade, marble, and greenstone; carved "mushroom" stones and mortars; a life-sized mask or headdress heavily encrusted with jade elements; ornaments of jade, bone, and shell; and a pyrite mosaic plaque or mirror.

Only a few of the more outstanding ceramic features of the Verbena and Arenal sub-phases will be mentioned here. Verbena is characterized by the first appearance of Fine Incised Black-Brown (Fig. 2, g) and Incised Fine Red wares (Fig. 2, j); the standard everted grooved-rim bowl; shallow dishes with open or gutter spouts; specially made pot covers; and painted stucco decoration. This is a clay stucco, not lime as found in the Classic Period.

The Arenal sub-phase shows continuation of architectural activities, progressive enrichment and variation of earlier ceramic forms (Fig. 2, g–k), the widest trade relations, and perhaps the cultural peak of Kaminaljuyu as a great center.

Pottery diagnostics are Usulutan (Fig. 2, h) and a few Black-Brown tripod vessels with hollow feet; one whistling vessel; and the appearance of a fine ivory-white pottery in very small amounts and unusual forms. Among thousands of whole or restorable vessels of Arenal wares, there are several bowls of ivory-white with four hollow mammiform feet. The feet are not the greatly swollen mammiform of the Early Classic Period, as found in Holmul I and Monte Alban II.

Santa Clara, the final sub-phase of Miraflores, from the comparatively small amount of material on hand, suggests degeneration. Many earlier wares remain in vogue, though they are noticeably coarser.

Santa Clara abruptly ends the Pre-Classic Horizon in the Southern Highlands and the Pacific Coastal Plain, as does the Chicanel Period in Uaxactun in the Peten Lowlands. In most areas of Meso-America, stratigraphy shows radical changes in cultural material from Pre-Classic to Early Classic.

The Pre-Classic horizon in the Southern Highland region of Guatemala was an integral part of a similar cultural development throughout Meso-America. Within the time range from Las Charcas through Miraflores occur the Playa de los Muertos and Ulua Bichrome phases in Honduras, the Mamom and Chicanel phases at Uaxactun, and the Archaic or Middle Cultures of the Gulf Coast and Highlands of Mexico. Not previously emphasized is the Pacific coastal plain of Chiapas and Guatemala. Manifestations of the Pre-Classic Horizon are, I believe, greater in this region than perhaps anywhere else in Meso-America. Here, archeological sites of enormous size are situated along the banks of live streams from the foot of the volcanoes almost to the beach. Many of these were constructed entirely in Pre-Classic times. I think it probable that in such areas as the hot Pacific coast and the Atlantic lowlands of Mexico, Guatemala, and Honduras there may have taken place the first steps from a nomadic existence to a sedentary one based on agriculture. Carrying this hypothesis further, the increased population brought about by a stable food supply eventually caused the coastal peoples to push up the valley heads into the Highlands in search of further cultivatable land. Here, however, new problems were encountered. The productivity of the land was not so great as that of the lowlands. Proteins for a balanced diet were not so readily available, unless they had already obtained the bean. Only one corn crop was harvestable each year instead of the two and occasionally three in the lowlands, thus providing bare subsistence rather than a surplus. These conditions may have led to the development of industries, the products of which were exchangeable for food from the coast. Such industries as the manufacture of metates, manos, jade ornaments, tools of obsidian; the weaving of baskets, mats, and textiles, and the production of pottery perhaps became largely centralized in the highlands, while the coastal regions produced the cotton, cacao, fruits and surplus corn, as well as salt, dried fish, and marine shells.

To return from theory to fact, we know that as early as Las Charcas, the people lived in communities with an advanced economy based on agriculture, industry and commerce. A stratified society with a religious hierarchy is suggested by the incensarios recovered. From this base may be seen a continual growth of religious and civic authority culminating in the great centers of the Pacific coast; of Kaminaljuyu and other sites in the Southern Highlands; E group at Uaxactun; Cuicuilco, and perhaps the pyramids of the Sun and the Moon at Teotihuacan.

In other words, our oldest known ceramic cultures already show regional specialization and crystallization which stemmed from a still older basic horizon in Meso-America. The Pre-Classic seems to have been a peaceful period during which there was free interchange of products, techniques, and ideas. Evidences of nationalism, inter-group quarrels, and open warfare are not apparent. However, in the first centuries after Christ, according to the correlation previously mentioned, forces became active throughout Meso-America which ultimately brought to a close this period of stability and prosperity. The first recognizable widespread disturbance, accompanied perhaps by wars, conquests, and migrations, seems to have begun at this time. Many great and long established civic centers and many areas were temporarily abandoned; others were immediately utilized by the bearers of new cultures. The local people, if they remained, were so dominated by the new arrivals that their culture suffered a complete breakdown. Pottery, both ceremonial and domestic, underwent radical changes. I would postulate that the widespread collapse of the Pre-Classic cultures was due to a chain reaction of pressure exerted from north to south which may have originated in northern Mexico or even farther north resulting in a general north to south movement. The pressure affecting the Pacific coast and Southern Highlands of Guatemala emanated from Mexico, perhaps the central highland area. Whatever the basic causes may be, it is certain that in the subsequent Early Classic period a strong Mexican influence may be seen in the ceramics of the Pacific Coast, Zaculeu, and Kaminaljuyu. As a working hypothesis, it is suggested that the Pre-Classic Guatemalans were forced southeastward and that they in turn either pushed the inhabitants of those areas still further south or were accepted into southern groups of similar culture.

The persistence into Classic and Post-Classic times of many only slightly modified, Pre-Classic elements through Central America to Northern South America gives substance to the above theory and further suggests a strong cultural diffusion southward just prior to the rise of the highly specialized Classic cultures of Meso-America.

THE DENSITY OF POPULATION IN THE SOUTHERN AND NORTHERN MAYA EMPIRES AS AN ARCHEO-LOGICAL AND GEOGRAPHICAL PROBLEM

Franz Termer

The attention of Americanists has been directed in recent years to the consideration of the problem of the density of population among the indigenous peoples of America. Kroeber has made a study of the indigenous population of North America (168), which includes population estimates for Mexico. There have been no corresponding researches on South America, although such studies have been undertaken by Sapper, for Central America, with regard to recent Indians. Above all, investigations on selected districts of small area are lacking, and for this reason I am here considering the problem with regard to the Maya district, which—now sparsely populated in wide areas, in strong contrast to its former high level of civilization—shows plainly the problematic character of the former density of population.

It has been suggested that archeological evidence be employed in attempting to estimate the former density of population. Such evidence is found in the number of settlements, and of settlement traces in general, in archeologically defined areas of homogeneous civilization. There is a propensity to infer from the relative number of objects brought to light in a certain area of habitation that the area was densely, or sparsely, populated. Here, the quantitative criterion is applied. Wherever there are large buildings which reveal a technically complicated method of construction and therefore presuppose a differentiated working order —large-scale haulage of materials over great distances, the handling of tremendous loads, and the need for the services of technical experts for special tasks— the facts are subsumed under a qualitative criterion. It is assumed that such undertakings could have been carried out only by organized groups of multitudes of men. This line of reasoning leads to variable results in estimating former population density. It becomes a matter of the inclination of the particular scholar, as well as of his appreciation for the imposing, highly artistic buildings of the Mayas, whether he populates these remnants of settlements with cities of hundreds or thousands or even sees the Maya territory crowded with millions of inhabitants.

Density of population is a geographical function, formed by the interrelation between a definite area of settlement and the number of people living in it. The geographic environment is a given factor, providing the physical and biological living conditions for the inhabitants. The extent to which the inhabitants improve and expand their possibilities depends upon their physical ability, their social structure, and their intelligence. Thus, a technological increase of efficiency may influence the density of population. However, the "efficiency" of a whole tribe or a people is an incommensurable quantity and cannot be exactly ranged in the functional interrelation between area and population. Nevertheless, ethnologists must stress the point that cultural ability may exercise a determining influence on the density of population. The development of Maya civilization to its fullest bloom during the time of the Southern Empire stimulates thought along these lines.

Unfortunately, acquaintance with creative Maya productivity is exclusively derived from the material remains of their civilization. Of the three factors—physical ability, social structure, and intellectual endowments—we may judge only the first and the third, by describing both as highly developed. The second factor—social structure—remains unknown. To accomplish technical achievements of so high an order in a climate of tropical rain forests, in hot and damp lowlands situated at less than three hundred meters above sea level, could have been possible only through an excellent adaptation of mind and body to climatic conditions.

To the statement that the density of population beyond being a purely geographical function, is also connected with cultural ability; that is, with the intellectual gifts of man, it must be added that the latter also sets its limits. Certain stages of civilization limit the ability of a people to better living conditions, and thereby limit the density of population in a certain area of settlement to that which is the optimum for the particular stage of civilization. This line is crossed when man succeeds in taking the most crucial step in civilization, the step from food gathering to systematic tillage of the soil. This step the Mayas, or their ancestors, must have taken a very long time ago.

I shall now discuss the problem of population density in the pre-Columbian Maya Empires in the light of the above considerations. In this discussion, acquaintance, on the part of the reader, with the elements of the physical geography of the Yucatan peninsula and northern Guatemala is assumed. Most important among these elements, so far as the problem of population density is concerned, are geological structure, climate, and vegetation.

Although the flat peninsula of Yucatan is in the zone of the wet trade winds so that a relatively uniform distribution of rainfall might be expected, there are, nevertheless, regional differences which become apparent through the grouping of vegetative formation. This is true particularly in the area of tropical forest in the northeastern part of the peninsula, in distinct contrast to the growth of North Yucatan. The cause of this is unknown and merits investigation. The vegetation map drawn by R. L. Roys shows dry and low bush forests for the West, the Northwest, and the major part of the interior. According to information made available to me by Mr. H. E. D. Pollock after his journey there in 1948, the west coast from Campeche to Celestun is skirted by a strip of tall rain forest from one to three kilometers wide. South of the northeast sector (which is apparently subject to more abundant rainfalls) there is along the east coast a zone of tall dry forest traversing diagonally to the West through South Yucatan to Campeche, and penetrating like a wedge far into the South as far as Petén. In the East (British Honduras) and West (Tabasco, Chiapas), this zone or wedge of tall dry forest merges into the tropical rain forest. Unfortunately, I have had no opportunity to consult Roys's study, and so do not know the criteria he used to distinguish between a tall dry forest and a tropical rain forest. However, these two different forest formations point to the fact that we are not so much concerned with different geological formations, but that the cause for the coexistence of these forest formations is rather to be found in varying conditions of humidity.

The question now arises as to whether these different conditions of climate and vegetation were influential on pre-Columbian density of population and location of settlements. No answer to this question may be given as yet. Prerequisite to this would be a detailed ruin map of the entire peninsula, which would also show vegetation formations. However, according to present archeological understanding, it is a striking fact that those inhabitants of the Southern Empire who migrated to the peninsula in the fifth century, passed through the zone of tall dry forest up to the northeastern sector which is covered with rain forest. The province of Ziyancaan Bakhalal, the temple city of Tulum, that of Yaxuna, and the first settlement of Chichen Itza are situated, it is true, within the region of dry bush forest, but still adjacent to the borders of the tropical rain forests in the northeastern sector. Thus, immigration into the eastern part of the peninsula passed through the zone of tall dry forest; i.e., through a countryside corresponding to that of the Southern Empire and offering the same type of living conditions. In this connection it is also interesting to note by what route the first colonists of Chichen Itza departed. On their way to Chakanputun (at the end of the seventh century) they moved southwest. It would be important to investigate archeologically whether they crossed the zone of dry scrub in a westerly direction, or whether they did not, indeed, first move south from Chichen Itza and then turn west on the edge of the tall dry forest. Later they decided to settle in the timber forest area of Champoton instead of on the west coast in the dry scrub region. In addition to the eastward migration there was a westward migration of some of the Mayas of the Southern Empire to Yucatan, who proceeded in several migratory waves from northern Petén and perhaps also from the Usumacinta valley (228). It is remarkable that this westward migration went from the timber forest into the dry scrub, but, judging from present-day archeological finds, brought about the establishment of settlements in only five places (Edzna, Oxkintok, Xtampak, Holactun, and on the island of Jaina), of which Edzna is close to the edge of the tall dry forest.

The sparse settlements in Yucatan from the fifth to the tenth centuries indicate a low density of population. Older sources point to the populousness of Yucatan, but they concern a later period, principally the fifteenth century; even so, these estimates must be regarded with some reserve. A more intensified set-tlement of the peninsula, in the dry bush forest area, began in the period when the Younger Empire was in full bloom. Indians coming from the open country in Mexico had a part in it. The number of small village settlements increased rap-idly, but only a few important places of worship, which at the same time devel-oped into centers of political and secular power, grew into cities.

It would be a mistake to use temple cities such as Chichen Itza, Uxmal, and others as a starting-point for theoretical calculation of the population density of the Younger Empire. If these were, in fact, cities as we understand them today, then it would be necessary to prove archeologically how the mass of inhabitants was distributed over the city area. Now there is a city in Yucatan for which there exists a statement on the amount of population: Mayapan. This is also, besides Tulum, the only city so far known, surrounded by a wall which is suf-ficiently preserved so that the extension of the city area can be calculated. In *Relaciones de Yucatan* (274, p. 254), it is estimated that there were approxi-mately 60,000 houses. Morley in 1938 (236) specified the length of the city wall to be 8.8 kilometers; that is, 5.5 miles, which equals a city area of 5.2 square kilometers or 2 square miles. The number 60,000 seems to be governed by the vigesimal system of the Mayas, or it might have been given as a general term for "great number." Moreover, we know from Landa that the center of the city was occupied by cult buildings and was also encircled by a wall. The extent of this inner wall has not yet been archeologically determined, so the area covered by the temple structures may not as yet be subtracted from the total area. If it be assumed that there were 60,000 huts, an area of 87 square meters would have been available for each. Specifications of the area covered by present-day Yuca-tecan huts are not known to me. If hut areas for the region inhabited by the highland Maya, as given by Sapper for the Kekchi and Pokomchi, are used, the average area is 44 to 45 square meters per hut. The result is that at Mayapan there would have been, apart from the house, an area of from 40 to 45 square meters available as a courtyard. If the area required for buildings of worship is taken into consideration, there would have been hardly enough room in the re-maining space for 60,000 huts, even if it be assumed that the buildings were con-tiguous, in an entirely un-Indian way. Even this is apt to prove that the quoted figure is too big. Arguments of a different nature, which I can only summarize here, yielded the same result. Using the observations made by Redfield and Villa, I calculated the total number of inhabitants of 60,000 huts and obtained a population of 480,000 for Mayapan. This number surpasses the present total of the population of the state of Yucatan by approximately 100,000 and almost equals the aggregate population of the modern states of Yucatan, Campeche, and Quintana Roo. If the area required for feeding the population be taken as a starting-point, once more making use of the observations of Redfield and Villa, according to whom the per capita share of the population was 42 mecates of farming land, then 510,000 hectares or 5,100 square kilometers of cultivated land would have been required even if allowance is made for only 300,000 inhabitants at Mayapan. This is more than one-seventh of the area of modern Yucatan. Neither as to quality nor as to area is there enough arable land in the peninsula to make such great spaces available for a single city, if the primitive method of cultivation of the Mayas is properly taken into account.

If we draw on the present graduation of settlement types in Yucatan, as it is disclosed for thirty settlements, according to observations made by Steggerda, we find only three settlements representing cities of more than 5,000 inhabitants. Six others show figures of from 3,000 to 5,000 and four from 1,000 to 3,000. The majority has only a population of from 100 to 1,000. Thus, the small village is the predominant type of settlement, and in all likelihood this was true in the pre-Spanish period. Taking into consideration a decrease of the population of Yucatan by 50 per cent since the Conquest, we would get average figures for the pre-Spanish period of between 200 and 2,000 persons for the majority of settlements, and from 4,000 to 8,000 for those of a city-like character. It should be ascertained how many settlements existed in Yucatan during the Younger Empire. This requires reliable maps of the ruins; the *Atlas arqueológico de la República Mexicana* (19) has room for improvement in this respect. Nevertheless, I have based my calculations upon it, obtaining a figure of 200,000 for the old population total of the modern state of Yucatan, and 100,000 persons for Campeche and Quintana Roo taken together, resulting in an aggregate population for the entire Younger Empire of approximately 300,000. It must be taken into consideration that some of the population lived in individual settlements or small hamlets, as is typical of the Indian type of settlement. I estimate this part of the population to have numbered 200,000. Thus we arrive at approximately 500,000 inhabitants as the total population of the peninsula in the pre-Spanish period. The area of the Younger Empire having been roughly 135,000 square kilometers, this would equal a population density of just under 4 (3.7).

I have estimated the population of the Southern Empire in a similar way. On this, too, I can only submit a summary report. The question, whether the temple centers in the virgin forests were cities in our meaning of the term, arises even more emphatically with regard to the Southern Empire. I have opposed this view for a considerable time, and I have emphasized that these centers were probably places of worship only and solely occupied by persons connected with ritual functions. All the information we possess so far points to the fact that the Southern Empire was a theocracy which appears to parallel the Tibetan sacerdotal state. The situation in the Southern Empire seems to have been similar to that in Tibet, where city-like settlements were monasterial or temple centers, in which almost one-sixth, or, according to other estimates, one-fourth of the population was connected with the functions of worship. Dr. Eric Thompson a short time ago also considered the nature of the cities in the Southern Empire. I am pleased to find that his statements, which came to my knowledge only a short time ago, are entirely in accord with my own. These cities were centers of worship in which there lived from 3,000 to 5,000 people. If we proceed from a total number of 150 worship centers in the Southern Empire, which were all inhabited in the same period, and take an average number of 500 sacerdotal persons, since the majority of the ritual centers were small, we obtain roughly 75,000 persons connected with the functions of worship. If we presume that one-fourth of the population was connected with sacerdotal functions, we arrive at a number of approximately 300,000 to represent the total population of the Southern Empire. In case we proceed from only 100 simultaneously inhabited cities, the corresponding figures would be 50,000 priestly persons and 200,000 members of the masses.

I have used scanty statements on settlement figures in the forests of Chiapas during the Spanish colonial period, dating back to Alvárez de Miranda, Villagutierre, and Ximénez, and found the population of hamlets to be 150 inhabitants in from eight to ten huts and villages of 1,625 inhabitants in sixty-five huts. Geographical considerations would show that this type of settlement must also have existed anciently in the forest regions of Northern Guatemala. The mass of the population was scattered in small settlements of this type. If we accept an average number of 100 inhabitants for these stray settlements, and if it be recalled that we rated the population unconnected with the cult at 225,000, there would remain 225 settlements in the Southern Empire which were distributed throughout the region of rain forests. Taking a planimetrically defined area of the Southern Empire of 45,000 square kilometers, which approximately equals the area of Belgium and Holland, there would have been enough scope for farming ground to warrant a settlement period of some length.

If the objection be raised that our estimates are not consistent with the great technical achievements in the temple centers, then the following may be replied. It is obvious that such achievements were possible only in a firmly organized community, and only through well planned labor, and that a sufficient number of working men must always have been available. Therefore we must distinguish between unskilled mass labor and skilled special labor. The former handled earth work, transportation of big loads, preparation of building material, and the coarse part of masonry; the skilled work—ornamental decoration of the façades, the sculpture, the hieroglyphic inscriptions, mural paintings, wooden sculpture, etc.—was executed by the members of the worship centers themselves.

Taking an area calculated at 45,000 square kilometers, and a total population of 300,000 in the Southern Empire, a density of population of 6.6 is obtained. From a geographical point of view, this is an acceptable figure for a native civilization with digging stick tillage, and wood and stone techniques, a figure which may for a period of some length be regarded as an optimum in the interrelation between man and his *Lebensraum* ("living space") in the tropical lowlands of Central America. We need not assume a climatic change in order to explain the decrease in population. For conditions will change for the worse as soon as one of the factors in the functional interrelation—climate, soil, plant, and man—undergoes a change. In accordance with the opinions of other Maya students I consider the soil to be the most unstable factor. A decrease in the quality of the soil upset the equilibrium between man and his natural environment. Man was the movable factor. Thus he looked for new land outside the hitherto occupied area of settlement. The religious notions of the Mayas, among the masses, were of the animistic kind, with belief in demonism and magic. This was overlaid by an esoteric cult of deities and chthonic and astral beliefs, coupled with astrology. If people became conscious of obnoxious influences emanating from nature—from soil, water, or plant—which were felt to be dangerous to their subsistence, then this was interpreted as the agency of demonic and magical forces. It was easy for learned priests, as astrologers and interpreters of the will of divine powers, to make themselves the mouthpieces of these powers. They communicated to the believing multitude the commands of the gods to leave their native grounds and to depart for a new land which was at the same time a land of promise. Thus the shifting and finally the complete vacation of the settlements of the Southern Empire may be sufficiently explained by the concurrence of physiographic, cultural-technical, and religious elements.

With this I conclude a condensation of my reflections on the population density of the Maya Empires; I have no doubt but that they will elicit criticism. Estimations, however, will always be criticized.

SOME NON-CLASSIC TRAITS IN THE SCULPTURE
OF YUCATAN

Tatiana Proskouriakoff

It is more than twenty years since Dr. Tozzer presented before this congress a paper on the Maya and Toltec figures at Chichen Itza (380). His clear identification of the conquering Toltec warriors has since been confirmed by excavations carried on by the government of Mexico at Tula, Hidalgo, where very similar figures are typical. A different complex of traits equally clearly identifies other figures as the Maya whom the Toltec encountered on their arrival in Yucatan. Even now, however, the history and the cultural affiliations of these pre-Toltec Yucatan Maya remain obscure. At the time when Tozzer presented his study, they were regarded as late immigrants from the Petén, and differences between their culture and that of the earlier Petén Maya were explained as historical changes, and were strongly imbued with chronological significance. The entire period covering the architectural remains of the Puuc, Chenes, and Rio-Bec regions was interpolated between the close of the Maya Old Empire in 10.3.0.0.0 and the period of Toltec invasion. With the discovery that high civilization had its own long history in Yucatan, this view was rejected by most students, and as it became increasingly clear that much of the architecture and sculpture of Yucatan must have been contemporary with that of the "Old Empire" sites, there was a growing tendency to regard the earlier Yucatan cultures as merely variants of a larger Classic Maya Culture.

Accepting the chronological implications of the new discoveries, I nevertheless wish to call attention to the fact that the stylistic differences between Yucatan sculpture and the sculpture formerly designated as Old Empire are such that the former cannot be regarded as derivative of the latter. The artistic styles of the Peten, the Usumacinta, and the Copan-Quirigua regions, in spite of certain local differences, show a single coherent development over a period of at least five centuries. The sculpture of Yucatan does not constitute a comparably uniform group which can be thought of as the product of a single tradition, even if we exclude all monuments showing traits that can be traced to Tula, and all the cruder types which can be attributed to post-architectural periods. In Yucatan, sculpture is essentially heterogeneous and seems to represent an imperfect fusion of several independent styles. I would therefore urge that we disassociate the term "Classic Maya" from the Puuc, Chenes, and Rio-Bec remains and reserve it exclusively for those cultures in which the stela cult was clearly dominant, and which habitually used Initial Series and Period Ending notations in their inscriptions. If we do this, the Classic Maya tradition will appear as a more coherent entity, with a definite artistic style as its chief vehicle of expression. In most of the sites of Yucatan and northern Campeche, we will find it as one of the components of cultures of mixed type, and we can then proceed more readily to identify other traditions which enter into their composition.

There is a considerable group of stelae in Yucatan, perhaps the largest, which can be regarded as essentially Classic. By the presence of Initial Series and Period Ending dates alone, such monuments can be identified at Tulum, Coba, Oxkintok, Jaina, Etzna, and Santa Rosa Xtampak. Others, at Sayil and Uxmal, for example, though with shortened inscriptions, undoubtedly carry on the same tradition and can be regarded as derivative in style. Although some of the characteristic aspects of the Classic development are missing in Yucatan, as, for instance, the regular succession of scroll forms, by and large this group of monuments not only conforms to the typical Classic arrangement and depicts a similar costume, but also reflects the general stylistic trends of the successive periods of Classic Maya art.

The costume of the Maya portrayed in the sculpture of Chichen Itza is very different from the costumes that appear on these Classic monuments. Its characteristic elements occur rarely, if at all, on stelae with Initial Series, and virtually never in northern Petén, which seems to have been the center of the Classic culture. Figure 1 illustrates three types of figures from Yucatan. The first is Toltec, identified by the spearthrower and darts, the pointed headdress, the puff anklets and garters, and the button and pendant nose bead. None of these elements occurs in Classic sculpture except the last, which is depicted on one of the lintels of Yaxchilan. The second figure (Fig. 1, b) is a Maya of the Toltec period at Chichen Itza. He carries a long rectangular shield with a fringe, and wears spirally wound gaiters and a tubular nose bead. The third (Fig. 1, c) is an earlier Maya from Xcalumkin. His is a typical Classic costume, which includes sandals with a fringed ankle guard, a round shield, and a long necklace with a bead ornament like those worn at Coba.

The elements of dress which characterize the Maya figures at Chichen Itza occur only rarely and sporadically in Classic art. The long rectangular shield, for example, is carried by warriors on some of the Yaxchilan lintels and on the murals at Bonampak, though stela figures at both sites hold a smaller round or squarish shield with a mask design on its face, which is the typical Classic form. Earlier warriors at Piedras Negras have a smaller rectangular shield, but as this site comes under the influence of northeastern Petén, we find this form on Stela 8 modified by rounded corners and the addition of tassels. The long form apparently occurs on the Usumacinta only in late times, and probably originates outside the area. Similarly, the tubular nose bead, a common form at Tula and in other parts of Mexico, occurs on a Cycle 10 monument at Seibal. Here we also find a headdress similar to that of the Chichen Itza Maya figure and a number of other traits which suggest very late Mexican, or in any case exotic influences. In every case that such rare and scattered similarities can be cited, there is reason

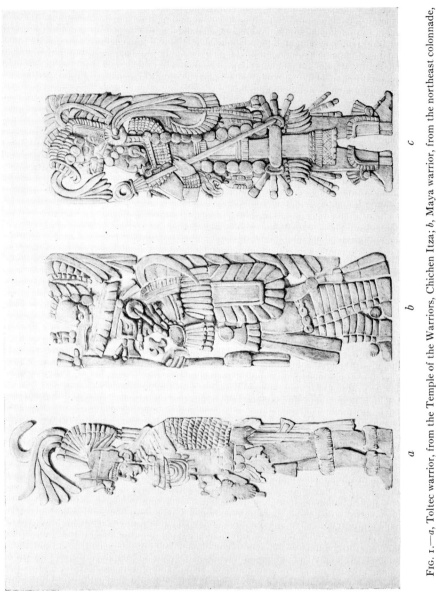

a   *b*   *c*

Fig. 1.—*a*, Toltec warrior, from the Temple of the Warriors, Chichen Itza; *b*, Maya warrior, from the northeast colonnade, Chichen Itza; *c*, Classic figure, from the Temple of the Initial Series, Xcalumkin, Campeche.

to think that the elements are intrusive in the Classic style. It is therefore a fair inference that the Chichen Itza Maya were a group distinct from the Classic Maya. There is no evidence that they derived their culture from that of north-eastern Petén, or even that they ever came into contact with people of this region.

That they were not Toltec, however, is at least suggested by the fact that there are similar figures at sites in Yucatan where there is no clear evidence of Toltec occupation. Figure 2 shows a Maya figure from the Temple of the Chac-mool at Chichen Itza, another from Oxkintok, and a third from Halal. The similarity of these figures is apparent. None of them wears the Classic fringed ankle guard, and all three have a tubular nose bead. The Oxkintok figure carries a long rectangular shield and a spear with a triangular blade different in form from those carried by the Classic Maya. Its girdle is like that of the Chacmool Temple figure, and the form of its headdress is one common at Chichen Itza. On the Halal figure we see the high gaiters and the unhafted blade held in the hand, again as on the Chacmool Temple figure. The circle around the eye is an-other trait intrusive in Classic sculpture, occurring at Piedras Negras and at Copan, but not in the central area. The facial features, with their sharp nose and chin, are quite un-Maya, and the head is not deformed.

Etzna, which, judging by its inscriptions, was a Classic site until 9.18.0.0.0, furnishes perhaps the best example of contrast between such figures and those of the Classic style. Here, however, another type apparently intervenes. The latest of the dated Classic figures of Etzna, carved in 9.18.0.0.0, is shown in Figure 3, *a*. The manikin sceptre, the serpent-fret apron and the fringed ankle guard of the sandals are all familiar Petén traits. A katun later in 9.19.0.0.0, if we accept Thompson's reading, Stela 9 was erected, and Stela 8, shown in Figure 3, *b*, is so similar that it can be safely referred to the same period. No feature of these monuments can be derived from the earlier Classic style at the site. The motif, the arrangement, and the artistic manner and detail are all new. There is no precedent in Maya art for the hunchbacked dwarf figures carrying human heads, and their position at the corners of the stela is incongruent with the Classic preference for a single dominant figure.

Stelae 15 and 16 (Fig. 3, *c*, *d*) are, unfortunately, undated. They show another type of composition fairly common in Yucatan, in which the figures are pre-sented in panels. Although there appear to be some Maya glyphs on Stela 15, they are not legible. The main figure is certainly that of the pre-Toltec Maya previously described, with the rectangular shield and the blade held in the hand. Stela 16, which has no glyphic inscription, shows some similarities to the Toltec style. The arrangement of the featherwork on the figure holding a severed hu-man head is extremely reminiscent of some Chichen Itza designs. Except for its stela form, this monument has almost nothing in common with Classic representa-tions.

The relation between the style of Stelae 8 and 9, on the one hand, and that of

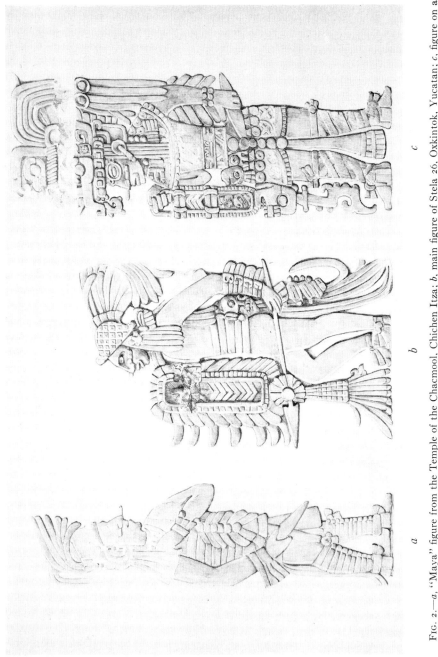

FIG. 2.—*a*, "Maya" figure from the Temple of the Chacmool, Chichen Itza; *b*, main figure of Stela 26, Oxkintok, Yucatan; *c*, figure on a lintel from Halal, Yucatan.

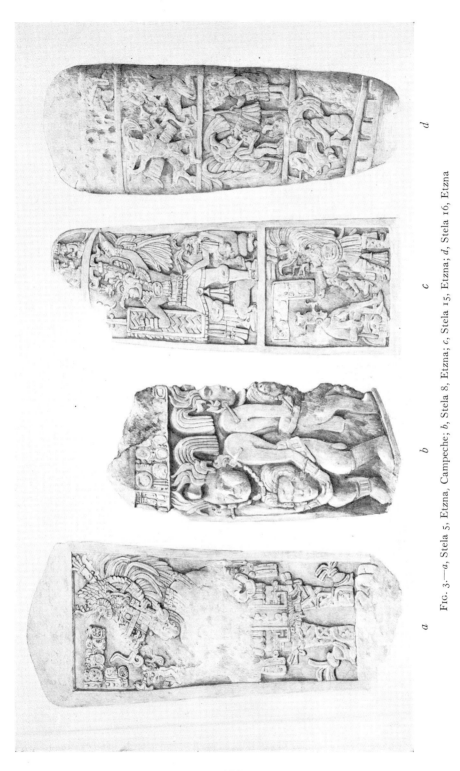

FIG. 3.—a, Stela 5, Etzna, Campeche; b, Stela 8, Etzna; c, Stela 15, Etzna; d, Stela 16, Etzna

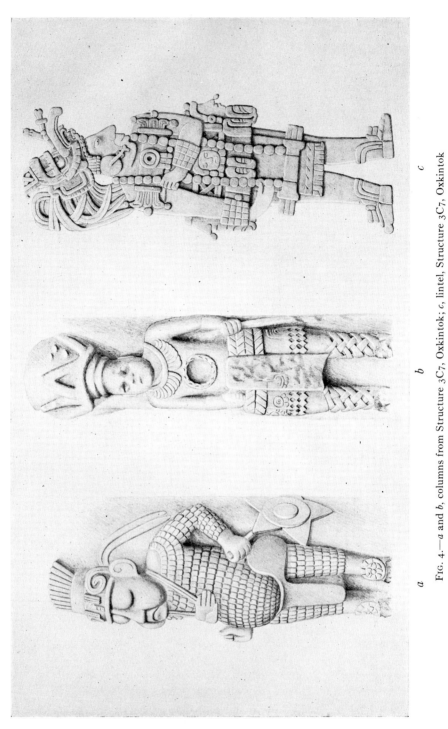

a   *b*   *c*

Fig. 4.—*a* and *b*, columns from Structure 3C7, Oxkintok; *c*, lintel, Structure 3C7, Oxkintok

Stelae 15 and 16 is not entirely clear. I believe Stelae 8 and 9 may be classed with some high relief sculptures on buildings of typical Puuc construction at Oxkintok, Xcochkax, San Pedro Dzitbalche and Dsecilna. They have similar relief, share costume traits with the Classic style in about equal degree, and similarly differ from the Classic style in the manner of depicting the human face and figure. Among the figures portrayed on columns of this type is a stout little individual dressed like a bird in a tight-fitting garment of feathers. At Xculoc he is shown as a small atlantean, and a similar figure seems to have been a banner holder in the building of the High Priest's Grave at Chichen Itza. He is also represented in pottery both in·Yucatan and in Alta Vera Paz. Some of the sculpture from Structure 3C7 at Oxkintok is shown in Figure 4. Here the bird figure holds a star-shaped club, which is also carried by some atlantean figures at Chichen Itza. Associated with the bird figure is a disk depressed into the body. At Desecilna this occurs on the bird figure itself, but at Oxkintok it is worn by another figure, and it occurs also on low relief columns at Xculoc and Sayil. It is somewhat surprising to find in the same building with these representations a purely Classic lintel, related to the Coba style (Fig. 4, c). If this lintel is contemporary with the columns, of which we cannot be sure, for it is in another part of the building, then the complex of non-Classic traits must have been present in Yucatan long before the close of the Classic era. The date of Stela 9 at Etzna (9.19.0.0.0) suggests the time when such ideas may have been introduced.

Another stylistic variant of Yucatan is represented by a column from Chilib, Campeche (Fig. 5, a). The rendering of such figures is extremely simple, but it is characterized by distinctive anatomica distortions and peculiarities of pose. The sharp ridge of the brow is a minor but revealing mannerism. Another is a tendency to reduce the size of the foot and to simplify its outline. Disregard of realism in the poses on Stela 19 at Oxkintok (Fig. 5, b) exemplifies another characteristic. I believe that the Comalcalco style, which in other ways resembles that of Palenque, is somehow related to this Yucatecan type, for the general feeling expressed in the tomb figures (Fig. 5, c) is very similar.

These three Yucatan types: The Chichen Itza Maya, the Oxkintok high relief columns, and the Chilib stylistic variant appear to be contemporary with the Puuc style of masonry construction. It is not known, however, if the three types are sequent or contemporaneous, or even if any of them has specific ceramic or architectural associations. Since the Chilib style is defined by generalized traits and its influence can be felt on both Classic and non-Classic monuments, it is probably a local stylistic variant which may have considerable antiquity. The other two types are more clearly differentiated and have no apparent local history of development. They may represent two aspects of a single cultural influence or may stem from two entirely different sources.

In any case, it is clear that Yucatan before the coming of the Toltec already contained more than one independent tradition. Until recently there has been a

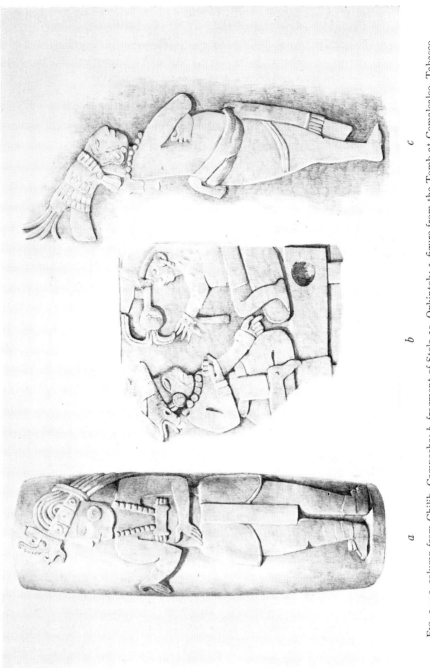

FIG. 5.—*a*, column from Chilib, Campeche; *b*, fragment of Stela 19, Oxkintok; *c*, figure from the Tomb at Comalcalco, Tabasco

a

b

c

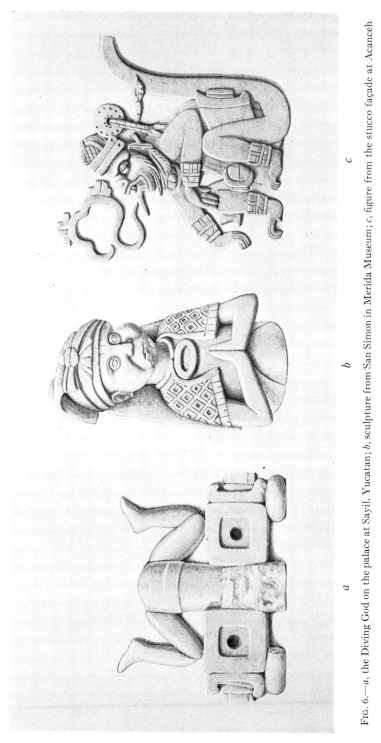

a

b

c

Fig. 6.—a, the Diving God on the palace at Sayil, Yucatan; b, sculpture from San Simon in Merida Museum; c, figure from the stucco façade at Acanceh

tendency to attribute all non-Classic traits in the north, particularly if they could be linked with Mexico, to the Toltec or later horizons. Repeatedly, however, so-called "Mexican" traits turn up in association with various remains. During the past season, Dr. Brainerd discovered at Dzibilnocac a mask with gouged out or extruded eyeballs, a motif common in Mexico and at Santa Lucia Cotzumalhuapa but not previously reported from the Maya area. I believe it is also shown on the carving at the cave of Loltun in Yucatan, which in my opinion is of very early date. The stucco façade at Acanceh, which depicts speech scrolls (Fig. 6, c), also probably pre-dates the Puuc period, although certain proof is lacking. In the Puuc period we have the diving god on the palace at Sayil (Fig. 6, a), which is a feature also of late East Coast architecture. Finally, the strange figure from San Simon (Fig. 6, b), although of unknown period, is interesting because the design on its cape also occurs on Costa Rican sculptures. This figure may be extremely late, but it suggests a wider range of influences than is usually given consideration.

These isolated examples of single traits apparently of foreign origin do not in themselves define particular styles. They hint, however, that outside influences in Yucatan were not confined to one period or to one source. In order to determine if specific influences were concentrated in particular periods, we need a basic chronology of pre-Toltec remains and a correlation of sculptural, ceramic, and architectural types which would permit us to identify definite cultural complexes. Until recently the contrast between Toltec and Maya remains has tended to overshadow the contrast between the Classic component in Yucatan cultures and other stylistic variants. These variants cannot be derived one from another in a chronological sequence such as can be worked out for the Classic style. They clearly show independent origins and indicate that even before the period of Toltec dominance Yucatan was culturally less stable than the Southern Lowlands, and was probably subjected to more than one significant wave of immigration.

LA HISTORIA DE LOS MAYAS DE YUCATÁN A TRAVÉS DE SUS PROPIAS CRÓNICAS

Alfredo Barrera Vásquez

Bajo los auspicios de varias instituciones científicas de los Estados Unidos y de México, he realizado desde 1932 diversos estudios e investigaciones en el campo de la lingüística y filología mayances especialmente para contribuir al esclarecimiento de los problemas que ofrecen los Libros de Chilam Balam. Me dí cuenta de que había dos clases de textos en estos manuscritos, a saber: (I) los que tenían varias versiones susceptibles de cotejo y reconstrucción y (II) los que sólo aparecen en una versión, por lo tanto singulares, sin posibilidad de reconstrucción. En vista de este hecho, deseché mi propósitio original de traducir aisladamente El Libro de Chilam Balam de Tizimín y cualquier otro que contuviera textos con versiones en otros libros o en el mismo.

Procedí entonces a recoger todas las versiones de cada texto de la clase I para cotejarlas, reconstruir el texto original y traducir la reconstrucción, dejando aparte los textos de la clase II, para traducirlos con las reservas debidas, porque pudieran descubrirse otras versiones posteriormente que vinieran a rectificar su forma y significado.

El trabajo realizado con los textos de la clase I está prácticamente listo para su publicación total en forma académica. En el momento en que se escriben estas líneas está en prensa sólo una parte—*Las Crónicas Mayas*—en inglés que publica Carnegie Institution of Washington con un amplio comentario del finado Dr. Sylvanus G. Morley (22a). Sin embargo, en forma resumida para divulgación se publicaron únicamente las traducciones en español, de todos los textos reconstruídos, inclusive las Crónicas, en un tomo, con la colaboración de la Sra. Silvia Rendón (22).

Como este informe se refiere con especialidad a las Crónicas de la Clase II, quiero hacer notar que además de que difieren las dos ediciones por lo que toca a la lengua utilizada en la traducción en cada caso y por lo que concierne a la inclusión y exclusión en cada una de ellas de los textos en maya, difieren igualmente por lo que respecta a su denominación y a su forma de presentación. Mientras que en la edición académica en inglés se presentan en forma corrida de líneas numeradas por su correspondencia con las líneas en que se dividieron las versiones originales para su cotejo y reconstrucción, en la edición popular en español se evitó la ya innecesaria subdivisión en líneas. Por otra parte, en la edición inglesa se sigue la forma tradicional de nominar como Crónica I, Crónica II y Crónica III a las tres versiones de un mismo texto porque aparecen en tres libros distintos, a saber: (*a*) el de Maní, (*b*) el de Tizimín, y (*c*) el de Chumayel.

Pero en la edición española las tres versiones o Crónicas I, II y III de la inglesa quedaron convertidas de nuevo en un solo texto al reconstruirse, con una sola traducción que fué la publicada. A esta traducción de la reconstrucción de las tres versiones se le llama en la edición española Crónica I y está dividida en tres partes, por un descuido, pues deberían ser cuatro partes como se indica en la Nota Introductoria correspondiente (22, pp. 43–45).

Esta Crónica I de la edición española (o sea la reconstrucción de las Crónicas I, II y III de la edición inglesa), es el más importante de los documentos históricos mayas existentes, pues abarca en serie contínua, aunque a veces repitiendo algunos lapsos, un período que parte de un 8 Ahau (9.0.0.0.0.: 415–435), hasta un 3 Ahau (12.1.0.0.0.: 1618–1638), es decir, más de doce siglos.

La importancia de mi contribución a la ciencia americanista en lo referente a las Crónicas Mayas, estriba en lo siguiente: (1) Por la primera vez se presentan los textos colacionados y reconstruidos en los pasajes paralelos. (2) Se ha descubierto que las primeras trienta y seis líneas de la reconstrucción (edición inglesa, Crónicas I, II y III o sea la Primera Parte de la Crónica I de la edición española) de la más importante, es la historia de la emigración Xiu desde Tula hasta Chacnabitón. (3) Que a partir de las siguientes líneas 37–102 o sea la Segunda Parte de la edición española, se transcribe la historia Itzá. (4) Que las líneas que siguen, 103–250, se refieren al Nuevo Imperio y su desbaratamiento hasta la llegada de los españoles y las últimas líneas, 251–89, se refieren a primeros hechos de la Colonia. Estas dos secciones quedaron incluídas en la Tercera Parte de la edición española. (5) Que el nuevo ajuste cronológico coloca a la emigración Xiu entre los años 849–869 (3 Ahau) hasta la veintena 1086–1106 (5 Ahau). La historia Itzá queda cubriendo el período a partir del 8 Ahau (9.0.0.0.0: 415–435) hasta el 4 Ahau (10.8.0.0.0: 968–987). Este período incluye la aparición de los Itzáes en Bacalar (Bakhalal), su establecimiento en Chichen Itzá la primera vez después de su "descubrimiento," su primera salida de esa ciudad para el sur hasta su establecimiento en Chakanputún y por último su salida de Chakanputún y su reestablecimiento en Chichen Itzá. La historia del Nuevo Imperio comienza en el 2 Ahau (10.9.0.0.0: 987–1007) hasta el siguiente 2 Ahau (11.15.0.0.0: 1500–1520) cuando llegan los europeos. La Liga de Mayapán queda incluída aquí, lo mismo que el segundo abandono de Chichen Itzá acaecido precisamente el año tun 10 de la veintena 8 Ahau (10.19.0.0.0: 1185–1204) o sea en 1149. Las represalias entre Itzáes y "náhuas" de Mayapán y el final de esta última ciudad, ocurrido entre la veintena 8 Ahau (11.12.0.0.0: 1441–1461). Por último, los siguientes katunes se refieren a epidemias y pestes, a la muerte del Ofrendador del Agua, Napot Xiu; a la llegada y establecimiento de los blancos y a varios acontecimientos iniciales de la colonia.

Esta historia pinta el panorama en lo que respecta a los factores culturales de la siguiente manera: Los Itzáes, portadores de la civilización técnicamente llamada Maya, aparecen en la península en el siglo V de la era cristiana; en el siglo VII siguiente abandonan Chichen Itzá y se establecen en Chakanputún al sur de Campeche de donde parten para regresar a Chichen Itzá en el siglo X. Al regresar los Itzáes seguramente ya habían cambiado su habla maya del norte por el chontal del sur por una parte y por la otra su propia cultura estaría influenciada por otras civilizaciones ("tolteca," etc.) Al final del propio siglo X los Xíues aparecen en Uxmal procedentes de Tula de donde habían partido el siglo anterior, perdiendo por su parte mucho de su influencia "tolteca" en el camino. Al final de siglo XII capitanes "náhuas" de Mayapán arrojan a los Itzáes de Chichen Itzá. Esto hace suponer que los "náhuas" estaban en Mayapán desde el comienzo de la Liga al final del siglo X. En efecto, por otras fuentes documentales (Landa) y por evidencias arqueológicas se sabe que un Quetzalcoatl-Kukulcan penetró Yucatán, vivió en Chichen Itzá y fundó Mayapán (y otras ciudades posiblemente) alrededor del siglo X. Entonces este siglo es de gran importancia en la historia maya de Yucatán ya que se mueven tres grupos para señorear la península: Itzáes (mayas) ya influenciados por culturas de fuera de la península; Xíues procedentes de Tula pero aparentemente remayanizados, si ellos fueron a Tula procedentes de tierras mayas y regresaron; "náhuas" de Quetzalcoatl-Kukulcan (de civilización "tolteca-chichimeca"). ¿Qué fué de todos éstos? ¿Por qué acaban súbitamente? ¿Por qué sus descendientes no continuaron la tradición cultural? Cuando aparecen los hispanos en el siglo XVI (cuarto factor cultural de invasión), ya no quedaban sino vestigios intermezclados de las civilizaciones monumentales entre algunos descendientes de los antiguos caudillos de los que los frailes extrajeron las noticias que conocemos. Entre estos vestigios afortunadamente se contó el hábito de registrar la historia de la región por los mismos nativos. Ahora bien, el factor cultural más importante, el quinto en esta cuenta, explico como corolario, es el grupo que estaba antes de los Itzáes, antes del siglo V, permaneció como soporte de las civilizaciones prehispánicas americanas invasoras, contribuyó a su muerte, recibió sobre sus espaldas el peso de la civilización moderna y permanece aún, con una cultura que en ciertos rasgos fundamentales es la misma que tuvo hace más de doce siglos, pero que en varios grados está teñida por el color de las otras que ha soportado y soporta. Me refiero a los nativos mayas actuales de cultura milpera, "los de atrás de la muralla" que dicen las *Crónicas*, con choza, ritos en relación con la agricultura y una identificación ecológica con la tierra que los sustenta tan compenetrada, que se bastan a sí mismos para ver morir a su vera cualquier civilización. Son el cañamazo sobre el que se han bordado varios dramas culturales. Entre la trama de su cultura quedan hilos de los bordados, pero la trama sigue incólume aún. No han tenido nada que ver directamente con el desenvolvimiento de las civilizaciones que han alimentado si no es pasivamente; cuando han sido activos ha sido para sacudir su yugo y absorver posteriormente a los supervivientes. Esto responde a la pregunta hecha poco antes, de porqué los supervivientes Itzáes y Xíues y aún los de tradición "náhua" como los Cocomes no continuaron alimentando la civilización de sus antepasados, y explica los movimientos rebeldes de los mayas milperos como la llamada Guerra de Castas de Yucatán de 1847.

Hay que tener cuidado pues en el uso del término *maya* cuando se investiga la cultura de los grupos mayances actuales, que aún cuando lingüística y somáticamente son mayas, culturalmente son otra cosa.

Este cuidado debe extenderse en el estudio de otros grupos nativos actuales de México, en donde posiblemente el mismo fenómeno aconteció: que las civilizaciones han sido sólo incidentes en la historia de los grupos mayoritarios. La civilización llamada técnicamente maya fué un incidente en la vida del maya milpero, del premaya que aun subsiste.

THE MAYA SUPPLEMENTARY SERIES

E. Wyllys Andrews

The tables accompanying the present paper attempt to summarize for the student of Maya epigraphy all known Maya hieroglyphic texts containing Initial Series in association with the stylized presentation of lunar astronomical data commonly known as the "Supplementary Series." No attempt has previously been made to present this considerable body of data in condensed graphic form. It is believed that such a presentation will save the new student considerable time in assembling the basic data now scattered through scores of different publications, many rare and difficult of access. It should also be useful to the specialized scholar as a check list in laying out approaches to new inquiries in the field. Finally, progress in the study of Maya glyphs has been such in recent years that many of the original descriptions and translations of basic texts have become obsolete. The time seemed ripe to undertake a complete reexamination of this material in the light of today's knowledge.

The translations in the attached tables (unless noted specifically to the contrary) are based upon direct study of the original monuments or photographs thereof, and have been compared with all published drawings and interpretations of the texts in question. The Initial Series positions listed in the tables are usually those suggested in the published material in the bibliography; an attempt has been made to choose the most recent or valid reading available. Wherever latest published readings are rejected or new readings suggested by the present author, this is indicated on the tables. This has not been done in the case of the Supplementary Series glyphs. Changes from previously published incomplete or incorrect readings were so numerous, particularly in the case of glyphs of partially or wholly unknown meaning, that detailed reference to earlier studies would have overburdened the tables to the point of destroying their intended simplicity. Where such changes bear direct known relationship to the reading of the Initial Series, or affect published ideas based on their earlier interpretations (often the case with recordings of Moon Number and Moon Age) an attempt has been made to note this fact in the "Remarks" column of the tables. An exception to this has been made in the case of the synoptic tables in Teeple (340). This work has been used and will continue for so long to be used as a basis of astronomical studies that it seems well worth while to indicate each of the 30-odd corrections to Teeple's readings in the present tables. His readings of Uaxactun, Stela 16 (Table 3, No. 1); Pusilha, Stela M (Table 3, No. 66), and Copan, Stela 16 (Table 4, No. 2) have been dropped in view of our belief that they were not Supplementary Series.

One cannot stress too strongly the danger in the use of such tables as these of the reader failing to take into account the inevitably strong element of subjective interpretation, strongest in the choice of glyph forms (as versus coefficients) where the range and circumstances of variation remain wholly or partially unknown. Our frequent use of the question mark after individual readings offers only a partial solution to this problem. It should further be borne in mind that in a table containing several thousand glyph interpretations and mathematical entries there will inevitably be errors of a mechanical or typographical nature. Beyer (51, P. 1) in referring to the synoptic tables of Teeple (340), stressed the pitfalls of assuming such compilations to be 100 per cent correct. If the present paper is honored by even a fraction of the use made of Teeple's shorter and restricted tables during the last eighteen years, it will be more than worthwhile to urge those who may consult it to re-examine the original texts in the light of newly published readings before final use of this material is made in published form.

BACKGROUND

The clearest and most readable exposition of the Maya calendar and its expression in the inscriptions is still to be found in Morley (235). To this need be added only two short but important contributions by Beyer (53) and Thompson (367) to complete our present understanding of the Initial Series mechanism. A short but readable account of the Maya calendar appears in Teeple (338, 340). An excellent basic text by Palacios (257) is also available in Spanish. Finally, attention should be called to Thompson's new book (372).

The existence of the Supplementary Series as a group of glyphs consistently following the Initial Series on Maya monuments was first noted by Goodman (129, pp. 117–18) who later (130, p. 647) suggested they recorded dates from the foundation of the city in which the monument was erected. The name "Supplementary Series" was assigned the glyphs by Bowditch (63, p. 5; 64, p. 224) on the basis that they "supplemented" the meaning of the Initial Series, but his final publication listed these glyphs among "points to be investigated" (64, p. 224). It remained for Morley (235, p. 152, n. 1) to suggest that the Supplementary Series embodied a lunar calendar, a thesis he later expanded (237, 233). Morley's 1916 publication (237), including complete and accurate drawings of the entire 80 texts known at that time, remained our basic reference on the subject for a decade and a half.

The outstanding contribution to our knowledge of Maya lunar inscriptions, however, is that of Teeple, whose untimely death in 1935 deprived the field prematurely of one of its greatest scholars. His researches on the Supplementary Series appear in five papers (341, 344, 342, 343, 339) culminating in his book, *Maya Astronomy* (340; Spanish ed., 338), which will long serve as the foundation for further study. Teeple's work on the inscriptions, coordinated with that of Guthe (137, 135, 136) and Willson (415) on the codices, proved definitely that Glyphs E and D expressed the Moon Age on the date of the related Initial

Series, that Glyph C defined the position of lunations in a series of lunar semesters of varying length, and that Glyph A defined patterns of 29- and 30-day lunations within these semesters.

Further development of our knowledge of the mechanics of the Maya lunar count may be traced in publications of the following authors: Beyer (55, 45, 54, 50); Berlin (42); Roys (283); Merrill (224); Satterthwaite (289, 290, 291); Thompson (365, 370), and Weitzel (410).

One of the more important discoveries regarding the Supplementary Series was the explanation of Glyph G by Thompson (371) who proved this glyph to be in reality a series of nine glyphs representing the Maya counterpart of the Nine Lords of the Night of the Aztec. One form of this glyph, unidentified by Thompson, was published by Beyer (52), and further minor contributions appear in Andrews (9), Morley (232), and Thompson (369).

The meanings of five of the Supplementary Series glyphs (F, Z, Y, X, and B) remain to be either partially or entirely explained. Suggestions regarding Glyphs Z and Y were made by Andrews (8). Based upon Lawrence Roys' definition of six forms of Glyph X and their correlation with the coefficient of Glyph C, an attempt was made by Andrews (7) to establish the meaning of the former glyph. The solution offered now appears to its author to be highly doubtful. A suggestion by Belmont (31) that Glyphs F, X, and B represented 177, 178, and 144 day Maya lunar groupings must be regarded as having little basis in fact. Interesting suggestions regarding the interpretation of Glyph B were made by Lizardi Ramos (192). And mention should also be made of Beyer's taxonomic studies of Glyphs E and D (46, 56), as well as Whorf's phonetic interpretation of Glyph C (411), regarded by the present author as highly improbable (10).

Finally, mention should be made of a group of contributions attempting to apply the evidence of the astronomical inscriptions to the correlation problem: Andrews (6), Beyer (57, 55, 47), Escalona Ramos (117), Kreichgauer (161, 162),[1] Lizardi Ramos (192), Ludendorff (205, 204, 206), Makemson (210, 211), Noll-Husum (250), Palacios (259), Roys (282), Schulz (299, 300, 301, 302), Spinden (316, 317), Thompson (357, 366).

It should be stressed that a number of the works referred to above contain valid and important contributions to topics in our outline other than those under which they are listed above. This is particularly true of the papers by Beyer, Guthe, Satterthwaite, and Thompson.

SOURCE MATERIAL

The late Dr. Morley's monumental *The Inscriptions of Peten* (234) offered a firm foundation for interpretation of hieroglyphic texts in this area, and along the adjacent Usumacintla and Motagua drainages. Many of the original photo-

1. Peabody Museum, Harvard University, possesses manuscript English translations prepared by the present author of all German papers listed in the above section, with the exception of Kreichgauer (162).

graphs in Maler's studies (212, 213, 214, 215) and in Maudslay's *Archaeology* (221), as well as Miss Annie Hunter's drawings in the latter work, were so excellent as to make further reproduction in Morley's survey unnecessary. Other original material may be found in the paper on Pusilha by Joyce, Gann, Gruning, and Long (155), Lundell's paper on Polol (208), Thompson's paper on Hatzcab Ceel (355), and Tozzer's monograph on Tikal (381). Use has also been made of a number of later corrections and emendations to interpretations in Morley's . . . *Peten:* Beyer (50, 51), F. R. and S. G. Morley (227), Morley (231, 232), Satterthwaite (292), and Thompson (355, 365, 353, 369, 362, 363, 359). Readings of the texts on Stela 9 at La Florida and Stela 7 at La Milpa are reproduced as furnished by Thompson from unpublished notes. Studies of many of the texts at Yaxchilan and Piedras Negras were made by the present author in 1939.

Morley's *The Inscriptions at Copan* (233), often referring to earlier photographs and drawings in Gordon (131, 132) and Maudslay (221), served as a basis of our interpretations at that site and at Los Higos, modified by subsequent emendations by Satterthwaite (290), Teeple (340), Thompson (361), and Morley himself (232). Examination of the Copan texts by the present author in 1934 served as a basis for further suggested changes.

The present readings of Coba inscriptions follow closely those of Thompson, Pollock, and Charlot (376), with minor corrections and additions suggested as a result of the author's study at the site in 1937 (8). Other texts from the northern part of the Yucatan peninsula (Chichen Itza, Holactun, Ichpaatun) follow the Initial Series readings of Morley (234), Thompson (355, Appendix V), and Gann (121). Corrections to the readings of Stelae 18 and 19 at Etzna were kindly furnished the author in a letter from Thompson, supplementing partial readings in Proskouriakoff and Thompson (271), and Ruz Lhuillier's drawings of the texts (286)

The large body of inscriptions from Calakmul, Oxpemul, and other sites in southern Campeche is the least satisfactory material in the present tables. This most badly eroded group of Maya texts has been treated only by Denison (Ruppert and Denison, 285), who, unfortunately, made little effort to transcribe the Supplementary Series except as an occasional aid in fixing the position of Initial Series dates. The published report contains almost no descriptions or drawings of individual glyphs, and photographs of only five monuments with Supplementary Series. Denison's renditions of the Initial Series dates have been accepted in the attached tables. Thanks are due the Carnegie Institution of Washington for unpublished photographs of many of the Campeche inscriptions, which have been used as the basis for the present readings. Notation has been made in the tables wherever it has been necessary to present unchecked readings from Denison's study.

The reading of Stela 1 at Moral, Tabasco, follows that published with the original description of this monument (Andrews, 5). That of Stela 2 at this site was furnished by Thompson, based on a photograph by Pavon Abreu which the author has not examined.

The Palenque readings are based on Maudslay's photographic record (221), as deciphered and augmented by Beyer (47, 48, 54), Berlin (41, 42, 43), Teeple (340), and notes made by the present author at the site in 1939. Readings of the three lunar series on the newly discovered Palenque tablet were obtained from the manuscript of J. E. S. Thompson's discussion of the inscription, as a part of Ruz Lhuillier's report on the first season's excavations at Palenque. For other sites in Chiapas, we have drawn on the publications of Beyer (49, 54), Blom (61), Palacios (257, 258), Teeple (340), and Thompson (370). Published photographs of many Chiapas texts are so poor that it has been necessary to accept almost completely unchecked Supplementary Series readings for the present tables. Such cases are noted. The reading of Lacanha follows the photo and drawing by Pavon Abreu.[2] That at Chinkultic was furnished by Thompson, from as yet unpublished notes.

Morley's *Check List of Maya Inscriptions* (230) and the lists in Appendix VI of his *Inscriptions of the Peten* were extensively used in this paper. Thanks are due Mr. Linton Satterthwaite, at whose suggestion a smaller series of tables prepared before the war were revised and supplemented to form the present work. Finally, sincere gratitude is expressed to Mr. J. Eric S. Thompson, who patiently assisted the author in the original preparation of these tables, contributed several unpublished decipherments listed above, and generously loaned other manuscripts which enabled the author to correct a number of errors which would otherwise have reached print.

DESCRIPTION OF THE TABLES

The present tables are arranged by site and monument, because of our belief that they must essentially be regarded as a check list of available data, and because a sampling and rearrangement of texts would be necessary in any case before any chronological arrangement would be effective for research purposes.

The question also arose of the desirability of attempting to classify in the tables only partially understood variations in the form of several of the Supplementary Series Glyphs (e.g., the "Full-" as versus "New-moon" variants of the moon sign in Glyphs E, D, C, and A; the variable element accompanying the hand and the moon sign in the body of Glyph C; etc.). It was decided that in view of our present lack of established classifications of such variations presentable in symbolic form, such attempts would overburden the "Remarks" column and tend to destroy the simplicity of presentation. Let us hope, rather, that the present tabulation will serve as a framework which will aid the future student in working out the precise nature of these variations.

An exception was made in the case of the distinctive glyph form referred to by Teeple as the glyph for "Same Moon Age or New Moon Day" (340, p. 69, Fig. 15), also discussed by Beyer (56), and Thompson (361). Occurrence of this

---

[2] R. Pavon Abreu, "Nuevas fechas mayas" (no date).

glyph, used as a substitute for or an element of Glyphs F, E, and D, is noted in the "Remarks" column with the abbreviation "NMG."

Data considered will be outlined below under the titles given at the top of the columns in the tables themselves:

No. Order of texts in the tables, for reference purposes.

Site. Inscriptions arranged by site in alphabetical order.

Monument. Most recently published nomenclature of texts.

Date. Initial Series position of the Supplementary Series.

G. Numbers refer to variants of Glyph G as outlined in Thompson (371) and Beyer (52). The symbol "√" indicates Glyph G definitely absent; "+?" indicates glyph probably present but form not identifiable; "?" indicates presence or absence of glyph uncertain.

F. The symbols "√," "?," and "+," indicate that Glyph F is, respectively, absent, doubtful, or present.

Z. Glyph Z as defined in Andrews (8). "√" denotes absence. If present, a numeral denotes coefficient attached, or a "+" indicates coefficient is present. "?" indicates presence or absence uncertain.

Y. Same as Glyph Z.

E. Glyph E. Same as Glyph Z.

D. Same as Glyph E.

C. Glyph C. "√" denotes absence. "?" denotes uncertainty as to presence of glyph. "+" indicates glyph present, but coefficient, in any, illegible. The number "1" indicates certain absence of numerical coefficient. The numbers 2 to 6 denote numerical coefficients.

X. Glyph X. "√" denotes absence. "?" denotes uncertainty as to presence or absence of glyph. Numerals (1 to 6) indicate form as classified in Andrews (7). "+" indicates present, but not identifiable.

B. Same as Glyph F.

A. Glyph A. "√," "?," and "+" are used in the same sense as with Glyph G. The numbers 29 and 30, respectively, refer to numerical coefficients of 9 and 10.

M.N. Moon Number corresponding to Initial Series date as calculated by the even 6-lunation semester pattern used during the "Period of Uniformity" as described by Teeple (340). If Moon Number is "uniform," this is indicated by an asterisk.

M.A. "Actual Moon Age" corresponding to the Initial Series position, presuming a New Moon at 9.17.0.0.0. Calculated by tables in Roys (283).

Remarks. In this column are listed:

    a) Irregularities and transpositions in sequence

    b) Anomalies and apparent contradictions in form and coefficient

    c) Disagreement of present reading with previously published versions.

Photo. ⎫ These columns list references to the most generally available published photo-
Draw. ⎭ graphs and drawings of the texts, or indicated by "—" that none are known to the author. Effort has been made to use the minimum possible number of references. Reference symbols are equated below to the Bibliography:

    AC—Andrews, (11)

    AS—Andrews, (5)

    B—Blom and La Farge, (61)

    BO—Berlin, (43)

    BP—Berlin, (42)

    BT—Beyer, (49)

    C—Morley, (233)

ET—E. H. Thompson, (352)
G-24—Gann, (122)
G-26—Gann, (121)
H—Morley, (237)
I—Morley, (235)
L—Lundell, (208)
LR—Lizardi Ramos (MS. read at XXIX ICA)
MA—Morley, (232)
M-I, M-II, etc.—Maudslay, (221) (Rom Num.—Volume No.)
NL—Nottebohm, (254)
P-I, P-II, etc.—Peabody Museum Memoirs (Rom. Num.—Volume No.)
PA—Pavon Abreu, (262)
PC—Palacios, (257)
PM—Pavon Abreu, (261)
PS—Palacios, (258)
RD—Ruppert and Denison, (285)
RL—Ruz, (286)
RP—Ruz, (287)
SGM—Morley, (234)
SP—Satterthwaite, (292)
T—Thompson, Pollock, and Charlot, (376)
TC—J. E. S. Thompson, (364)
TG—J. E. S. Thompson, (372)
TQ—J. E. S. Thompson, (363)

No.	Site	Monument	Date	G	F	Z	Y	E	D	C	X	B	A	M.N.	M.A.	Remarks	Photo	Draw
1	Alt. Sacrificios	Stela 4	9.10.3.17.0. - 4Ahau 8Muan	7?	+	✓	✓	✓	11	4	✓	✓	29	6	11.2	G-F Combined	P-1V 2	H. 1
2	Alt. Sacrificios	Stela 5	9.10.11.12.17 - 6Caban 5Chen	5?	+	✓	✓	✓	3	5	✓?	✓?	✓?	*	2.9		M.A. 1	—
3	Alt. Sacrificios	Stela 8	9.9.15.0.0. - 8Ahau 13Cumhu	✓	+	✓	✓	✓	10	+	✓	✓	29	—	10.1	Month between G-F	—	SGM Fig 32 / SGM
4	Alt. Sacrificios	Stela 9	Uncertain	?	?	?	?	?	?	5	✓	✓	30	—	—		—	Fig 33
5	Alt. Sacrificios	Stela 10	9.7.0.0.0. - 6Ahau 13Zac (2?)	?	?	?	?	?	?	5 or 6	✓	✓	29	—	22.4	Coeff. 9 under A not inverted / Unconfirmed Morley (1938) reading	—	SGM Fig 51
6	Alt. Sacrificios	Stela 11	9.7.10.0.0. - 6Ahau 13Zac (2?)	?	+	✓	✓	✓	✓	4	✓	✓	29	—	22.4	Coeff. 9 under A not inverted / Unconfirmed Morley (1938) reading	—	SGM Fig 51 / SG3I
7	Alt. Sacrificios	Stela 12	9.4.10.0.0. - 12Ahau 8Mol	O	+	✓	✓	✓	8	3	4	✓	29	—	9.3	Month between G-F	—	Fig 50
8	Balakbal	Stela 5	9.18.9.17.18 - 9Eznab 16Pop	?	?	✓	✓	✓	9	4?	✓	✓	✓	—	10.6		RD 57	SGM Fig 11
9	Calakmul	Stela 1	9.10.0.?.5.	?	?	?	?	?	11	?	?	?	?	—	—	Unchecked RD reading	—	—
10	Calakmul	Stela 8	9.14.10.0.0. - 5Ahau 3Mac	?	+	✓	✓	✓	11	4 or 5	5	+	29	5	13.7		—	—
11	Calakmul	Stela 9	9.11.10.0.0. - 11Ahau 18Chen	O	+	?	✓	+	1	5	?	+?	29	6	0.6		—	—
12	Calakmul	Stela 13	9.12.0.0.0. - 10Ahau 8Yaxkin	?	?	?	?	?	?	?	?	+	29	1	27.3	Unchecked RD reading	—	—
13	Calakmul	Stela 16	9.19.0.0.0. - 9Ahau 18Mol (?)	+	?	✓	✓	✓	19	?	+	+	29	4	18.6	"	—	—
14	Calakmul	Stela 24	9.13.10.0.0. - 7Ahau 3Cumhu	✓	+	?	✓	?	?	?	?	?	29	1	19.1	"	—	—
15	Calakmul	Stela 25	9.15.10.0.0. - 3Ahau 3Mol	+?	+	✓	✓	✓	9	+	5?	+	30	3	8.2	"	—	—
16	Calakmul	Stela 26	9.15.5.0.0. - 10Ahau 8Chen	?	+	✓	✓	?	9?	?	?	?	?	2	9.6	"	—	—
17	Calakmul	Stela 27	9.15.10.0.0. - 3Ahau 3Mol	?	?	?	✓	?	?	?	?	?	29	3	8.2	Unchecked RD reading	—	—
18	Calakmul	Stela 28	9.9.10.0.0. - 2Ahau 13Pop	O?	?	✓	✓	✓	9	3	?	?	30	—	11.5	Stela 29 records 9A	—	—
19	Calakmul	Stela 29	9.9.10.0.0. - 2Ahau 13Pop	?	?	✓	✓	✓	9	3	?	?	29	—	11.5	Stela 28 records 10A	—	—
20	Calakmul	Stela 35	9.11.10.0.0. - 11Ahau 18Chen	?	+	?	✓	?	?	+	5	+	30	6	0.6		—	—
21	Calakmul	Stela 35,1	9.11.8.10.8. - 6Lamat 11Uo (?)	?	?	?	?	?	?	?	?	?	+	6	20.1	Unchecked RD reading	—	—
22	Calakmul	Stela 41	9.13.10.0.0. - 7Ahau 3Cumhu (2?)	?	+	?	?	8 or	8	3	?	?	?	1	19.1	"	—	—

No.	Site	Monument	Initial Series — Date										Value	Notes	Ref.
24	Calakmul	Stela 51	9.14.19.5.0. - 4Ahau 18Muan	+	+	v	+	14	4	+	29	*	16.7	:	H 1
25	Calakmul	Stela 52	9.15.0.0.0. - 4Ahau 13Yax	O	+	v	+	8	+	+	30	1	10.9	G-F Combined	—
26	Calakmul	Stela 54	9.15.0.0.0. - 4Ahau 13Yax	v	+	v	+	8	+	+	+	1	10.9	Unchecked RD reading	—
27	Calakmul	Stela 57	9.17.0.0.0. - 13Ahau 18Cumhu	+?	+	v	+	?	+	+	+	3	0.0	Denison reads 9E 5C. 2 glyphs without coeff. between F and C	—
28	Calakmul	Stela 58	9.17.0.0.0. - 13Ahau 18Cumhu	O	+	v	+	3	3	+	29	*	0.0	3 eroded glyphs without coeff. between F and C	RD 52
29	Calakmul	Stela 64	9.19.0.0.0. - 9Ahau 18Mol	?	+	v	?	+?	?	+?	?	4	18.6	Unchecked RD reading	—
30	Calakmul	Stela 67	9.18.10.0.0. - 10Ahau 8Zac	O	+	v	?	5?	?	+	29	2	21.3		—
31	Calakmul	Stela 69	9.18.10.0.0. - 10Ahau 8Zac	O	+	v	?	?	?	?	?	2	21.3		—
32	Calakmul	Stela 70	9.12.8.9.9. - 11Muluc 17Kankin	O?	+	v	3?	2 or 3	?	+	+	3	25.2		—
33	Calakmul	Stela 71	9.14.0.0.0. - 6Ahau 13Muan	?	?	v	?	15	?	+	+	3	16.4	Unchecked RD reading	—
34	Calakmul	Stela 73	9.14.0.0.0. - 6Ahau 13Muan	+?	+?	v	v	15?	?	+?	+?	3	16.4	Unchecked RD reading	—
35	Calakmul	Stela 75	9.12.0.0.0. - 10Ahau 8Yaxkin	O?	+	v	?	?	?	+	29	1	27.3		—
36	Calakmul	Stela 76	9.12.5.0.0. - 3Ahau 3Xul	+?	?	v	v	8	?	+	+?	2	26.0	Unchecked RD reading	—
37	Calakmul	Stela 80	9.18.0.0.0. - 11Ahau 18Mac	?	+	v	6?	+	5?	+	30	6	24.1		—
38	Calakmul	Stela 86	9.12.0.0.0. - 10Ahau 8Yaxkin	?	+	v	?	?	?	?	?	1	27.3		—
39	Calakmul	Stela 89	9.15.0.0.14. - 5Ix 7Zac	5	+	v	v	15	1	+	30	*	24.9	G-F combined. 15D clear. Note C-X combination	RD 53
40	Calakmul	Stela 94	9.12.10.0.0. - 9Ahau 18Zotz	?	+	v	4	+?	?	v	30?	3	24.6	Denison reads 2C	—
41	Chichen Itza	T of I.S.	10.2.9.1.9. 9Muluc 7Zac	2	+	v	5	v	5	+	v	—	22.9	Info. from J. E. Thompson	E.T. Fig. 2
42	Chinkultic	Stela 10	9.9.?.?.?.	?	?	v	?	8	2	3	10	—	—		—
43	Coba	Stela 1, E#1	9.11.0.5.9. - 4Muluc 17Kayab	1	?	v	?	+	2?	22?	30	*	23.7		T 1
44	Coba	Stela 1, E#2	9.12.10.5.12. 4Eb 10Yax	?	?	v	?	19	+	+	30	6	18.5	This I.S. occurs twice at Naranjo	T 1
45	Coba	Stela 1, W#1	13.0.0.0.0. - 4Ahau 8Cumhu	O	+	v	v	v	1	2	30	—	—		T 2
46	Coba	Stela 1, W#2	9.12.0.0.0. - 10Ahau 8Yaxkin	O	+	v	v	5	5?	+	30	1	27.3	Thompson (1932) reads "1C"	T 2

No.	Site	Monument	Date	G	F	Z	Y	E	D	C	X	B	A	M.N.	M.A.	Remarks	Photo	Draw
47	Coba	Stela 3	9.10.0.0.0 1Ahau 8Kayab	?	?	v	v	?	?	?	?	+	30	6	8.7		T 4	—
48	Coba	Stela 5	9.11.10.0.0 - 11Ahau 18Chen	O	+	v	v	?	?	1	?	+	29	6	0.6		T 5	—
49	Coba	Stela 6	9.9.10.0.0 - 2Ahau 13Pop	O	+	v	v	?	9	2	?	+	30	—	11.5		T 6	—
50	Coba	Stela 15	Uncertain	O	+	v	v	3?	v	+?	+?	+?	?	—	—		T 8	—
51	Coba	Stela 16	Uncertain	?	?	v	v	v	7	2	3	+	30	—	—		T 10	—
52	Coba	Stela 20	Uncertain	?	?	?	?	v	+	4	4	+	29	—	—	Coeff. of D missing	T⁻ᴵ	12
53	Copan	Stela 1	9.11.15.14.0 - 11Ahau 8Zotz	1	+	v	v	v	12	5	5	?	?	4	13.4	Note C-X Combination	—	M-I 100
54	Copan	Stela 2	9.10.15.0.0 - 6Ahau 13Mac (??)	+	+	v	v	v	v	1	3	+	30	3	4.6	Central Element of F is N.M.G. Teeple reads 9.10.0.10.0	C 18	M-I 102
55	Copan	Stela 3,e	9.10.19.5.0 - 12Ahau 13Kayab	v	v	v	v	v	10?	3	3	+	30	1	9.0	Teeple reads 9.11.0.0.0,	TC 1	C 19
56	Copan	Stela 3,w	9.10.19.5.11 - 10Chuen 4Cumhu	?	?	v	v	+	+	+	3	+	30	1	20.0	Teeple reads 9.0.0.0.0. and 1D-1C	TC 1	C 19
57	Copan	Stela 5	9.13.15.1.0 - 7Ahau 18Kayab	?	?	?	?	?	8	3	3	+	29	*	8.3		—	C 19
58	Copan	Stela 6	9.12.10.0.0 - 9Ahau 18Zotz	O	+	v	v	2	+	3	3	+	30	3	24.6		M-I 105	M-I 107
59	Copan	Stela 7	9.9.0.0.0 3Ahau 3Zotz	O	+	v	v	v	13	?	4	+	30	—	14.2	Teeple reads 4C	C 13	M-I 108
60	Copan	Stela 9	9.6.10.0.0 - 8Ahau 13Pox	?	+	v	v	5	v	5	5	v	30	—	27.9	"E" consists of North Star God face and Ahau sign	P-VI 20	M-I 110
61	Copan	Stela 10	9.10.19.13.0 - 3Ahau 8Yaxkin	8	+	v	v	3	+	6	?	+	29	*	21.4	G-F Combined	—	M-I 111
62	Copan	Stela 12	9.10.14.1.15 - 6Men 13Muan	8	+	v	v	v	3	+	2	+	30	4	4.5	Teeple reads 9.10.15.0.0	C 17	C 17
63	Copan	Stela 13	9.11.0.0.0 - 12Ahau 8Ceh	v	+	v	v	v	5	3	3	+	29	4	3.3		—	C 15
64	Copan	Stela 19	9.10.19.15.0 - 4Ahau 8Chen	3	+	v	v	v	4	2	2	+	29	*	2.3		C 16	C 16
65	Copan	Stela 20	9.1.10.0.0. 5Ahau 3Tzec (?)	O	?	v	v	over 6	+	+	3	v	+	—	25.7	Teeple reads "5E-2C"	C 9	C Fig. 9
66	Copan	Stela 23	9.10.18.12.8 8Lamat 1Yaxkin (?)	?	?	?	?	?	5	1	2	+	30	6	3.8		—	C Fig 26
67	Copan	Stela A	9.14.19.8.0 12Ahau 18Cumhu	7	+	v	+	v	15	6	6 or 1	+	29	*	17.7	Unknown glyph follows Y Form of A unusual	M-I 27	M-I 30
68	Copan	Stela D	9.15.5.0.0 - 10Ahau 8Chen	O	+	v	v	v	9	2	?	?	?	*	9.6	All in full figure glyphs	M-I 47	M-I 48
69	Copan	Stela F	9.9.2.17.0 - 10Ahau 8Uo (?)	?	?	v	?	v	?	4	4	+	30	—	11.1	13 blocks after I.S. with C.R. date. Teeple reads 9.5.10.0.0		M-I

No.	Site	Monument	Long Count	Calendar Round														Moon day	Notes	Ref	Ref
																			New Moon day expressed by N.M.G. & E. without coeff. G-1 and F repeated on side		
70	Copan	Stela I	9.12.3.14.0. -	5Ahau 8Uo	1	+	√	√	√	+	√	18	√	4	5	+	29	5	28.9		M-I 61	M-I 65
71	Copan	Stela J	9.13.10.0.0 -	7Ahau 3Cumhu	O	+	√	+	√	5	1	5	1	1	+	30	*	19.1	Y follows 2 glyphs after A	M-I 66	M-I 71
72	Copan	Stela M	9.16.5.0.0 -	8Ahau 8Zotz	√	+	√	√	+	5	5	5	6	+	30	6		4.1		C 28	M-I 71
73	Copan	Stela N	9.16.10.0.0	1Ahau 3Zip	O	+	√	√	√	1	1	1	2	+	30	1		2.7	"D" is North Star God. Form of A unusual	M-I 79	M-I 78
74	Copan	Stela P	9.9.10.0.0	2Ahau 13Pop	√	+	√	√	√	9	3	3	+	30	—			11.5		M-I 88	M-I 89
75	Copan	Altar H'	9.12.8.3.9.	8Muluc 17Mol	6	+	√	√	2	+	5	V	+	29	*			23.3		—	C 23
76	Copan	Altar K	9.12.16.7.8	3Lamat 16Yax	4	+	√	√	?	2?	2?	V	29	3				29.2		—	M-I 73
77	Copan	E. Altar, Stela 5	9.11.15.0.0	4Ahau 13Mol	?	?	√	√	8	+	3	3	+	29	6			28.7		—	C 20 Fig. 29
78	Copan	W. Altar, Stela 5	9.7.19.17.11	9Chuen 14Mol	O	?	?	?	?	?	?	?	29	—				10.7		—	C 20
79	Copan	Mound 2	9.15.17.0.0 -	1Ahau 8Xul (?)	O	√	√	√	1-5	+	5	+	30	4				18.1	With C.R. dates, IS position doubtful. G follows A	P-I 6	C 26
80	Copan	Temple 11 #1	9.16.12.5.17	6Caban 10Mol	?	+	√	√	?	6	?	?	30	5				12.9	F between day and month	C 28	C 23
81	Copan	Temple 11 #2	9.14.15.0.0 -	11Ahau 8Zac (??)	O	+	√	√	?	5	3	+	30	6				12.3	G-F combined. Teeple read 9.17.7.13.0	—	C 29
82	Copan	Frog Y1	uncertain		?	?	?	?	?	?	?	?	—						Fragment contains only C	—	C Fig. 35
83	Copan	H S. Date 1	9.5.19.3.0	8Ahau 3Zotz	?	+	√	√	5	+	5	?	29	—				26.0	Teeple reads 9.5.19.13.0	P-I 6	—
84	Copan	H S. Date 3	9.7.5.0.8	8Lamat 6Mac	?	+?	√	√	5	2?	2?	+?	29?	—				2.3		P-I 6	—
85	Copan	H S. Date 5	9.9.14.17.5	6Chicchan 18Kayab	8	+	√	√	3	4	4	+	30	—				24.7		P-I 6	—
86	Copan	H S. Date 10	9.13.18.17.9	12Muluc 7Muan	7	√	√	√	7	1 or 2	2	+	30	2				29.3	F-V coeff on E. Month between G and E	P-I 6	C 26
87	Copan	H S. Date 24	uncertain		3	?	?	√	√	9	4	?	—						Full figure glyphs. Morley & Teeple reading (9.13.3.7.8.) by G3 and 4C.	C 27	C 27
88	El Cayo	Lintel 1	9.16.2.2.16	6Cib 9Mol	2?	+?	√	√	3	8	1	2	+	30	*			2.5	2C drawn by Morley	P-II 35	H 2
89	El Pabellon	Stela 1	9.10.0.0.0 -	1Ahau 8Kayab	O	+	√	√	√	8	5	5	V	30	6			8.7		SGM 98	SGM 17
90	Etzna	Stela 18	9.12.0.0.0.10Ahau 7Yaxkin		√	+	√	√	6-8	+	5	5?	+	10?	1			27.3	Thompson suggests "6-8E". Drawn as 5E in reference	—	RL p.6
91	Etzna	Stela 19	9.13.0.0.0 -	8Ahau 7Uo	√	+	√	√	1	+	6	1?	+	?	5			21.9	Unidentified glyph between F and E	—	RL 1.6

No. Site	Monument	Date	G	F	Z	Y	E	D	C	X	B	A	M.N.	M.A.	Remarks	Photo	Draw
92 Hatzcab Ceel	Altar 2	9.19.0.0.0. - 9Ahau 18Mol	O?	+?	✓	✓	?	?	?	?	+	29	4	18.6		SGM 95	—
93 Holactun	T of I. S.	9.15.12.6.9. - 7Muluc 2Kankin	3	+	+	+	✓	2	2	2	+	30	*	0.9	Extraneous Kin glyph between Muluc and G Thompson (1937) reading. Teeple read 9.16.14.0.9.	G-24 p.156	H I
94 Ichpaatun	Stela 7	9.8.0.0.0. - 5Ahau 3Chen	O	+?	✓	✓	+	19	3	?	?	?	—	19.7	D precedes E	G-26 p.48	G-26 p.48
95 Itsimte	Stela 2	9.15.10.0.0. - 3Ahau 3Mol	O	+	✓	✓	✓	10	6	6 or 1	✓	✓	3	8.2	Non-Uniform	SGM 155	SGM 43
96 Itsimte	Stela 5	9.15.0.0.0. - 4Ahau 13Yax	O	+?	✓	✓	✓	10	1?	2?	+	29	*	10.9		SGM 155	SGM 43
97 Ikkun	Stela 1	9.18.0.0.0. - 11Ahau 18Mac	O	✓	✓	✓	4	+	6	6	+	29	*	24.1	2 unknown glyphs between G and E. Not Z or Y	SGM 93	SGM 16
98 Ikkun	Stela 2	9.17.9.0.13. - 3Ben 6Kayab	4	+	✓	✓	✓	5	3	3	+	30	5	4.6	3 unknown glyphs between F and D	SGM 93	SGM 16
99 Locanha	Stela 1	9.8.0.0.0. - 5Ahau 3Chen	O	+	✓	6	✓	17	4	✓	✓	9?	—	19.7		PA 2	PA 1
100 La Florida	Stela 9	9.15.0.0.0. - 4Ahau 13Yax	O	+	✓	✓	✓	11	3	3	+	10	1	10.9	Info. from J. E. Thompson	TG Fig.43	—
101 La Hondradez	Stela 7	9.17.0.0.0. - 13Ahau 18Cumhu	?	?	✓	✓	?	?	3?	3?	+	30	*	0.0	No coeff. on eroded MA glyph	SGM 83	SGM 12
102 La Milpa	Stela 7	9.17.10.0.0. - 12Ahau 8Pax	?	+	✓	✓	?	?	4	4?	+	10	*	26.8	Info. from J. E. Thompson	—	—
103 La Muneca	Stela 4	9.18.0.0.0. - 11Ahau 18Mac	O	+	✓	✓	3	✓	4	+	+	?	6	24.1		—	—
104 La Muneca	Stela 5	9.17.10.0.0. - 12Ahau 8Pax (?)	O	+?	✓	✓	7	✓	+	+	+	29?	4	26.8	Denison reads 4C	—	—
105 Leyden Plate	—	8.14.3.1.12. - 1Eb 5Yaxkin	5	✓	✓	✓	✓?	+?	1?	6 or 1?	+?	?	—		Only G5 clear. Reminder very doubtful Reading after Nottebohm (1944)	—	NL 3
106 Los Higos	Stela 1	9.17.10.7.0. - 9Ahau 3Tzec	5	+	✓	✓	✓	18	3	3	?	30?	2	19.2	If A present, coeff. is at left	—	C Fig.62

No. / Site	Stela	Long Count										29	6 / *	4.1	Central element of F is N.M.G.	(26)	(13)
107 Moral	Stela 1	9.16.5.0.0. - 8Ahau 8Zotz	O	+	✓	✓	5	?	4	+		29	6	4.1			PM fig.
108 Moral	Stela 2	9.13.19.8.1. - 21mix 14Tzec	8	+	✓	2	+	2	3	+		29	*	24.2			PM fig.
109 Naachtun	Stela 1	9.9.10.0.0. - 2Ahau 13Pop	O	✓	✓	9?	✓	2 or 3	3?	✓		30	—	11.5	9E or 9D	SGM 149	SGM 40
110 Naachtun	Stela 2	9.10.10.0.0. - 13Ahau 18Kankin	O	+	✓	?	?	5	?	+		30	2	6.0		SGM 149	SGM 41
111 Naachtun	Stela 8	9.16.0.0.0. - 2Ahau 13Tzec	✓	+	?	?	7?	?	?	?		29?	5	5.5	Glyph with coeff. 7 unfamiliar	SGM 151	SGM 42
112 Naachtun	Stela 9	9.15.0.0.0. - 4Ahau 13Yox	✓	+	?	?	7?	?	?	?		30	1	10.9	:	SGM 151	SGM 42
113 Naachtun	Stela 10	9.16.10.0.0. - 1Ahau 3Zip	O	?	?	?	?	?	?	?		30	1	2.7		SGM 151	SGM 41
114 Naachtun	Stela 21	9.12.16.17.12 - 12Eb 15Uo (??)	+	+	✓	4	+	5	✓	✓		30	4	26.5	Might be 4D	SGM 153	Fig. 12?
115 Naranjo	Stela 2	9.14.1.3.19. - 3Cauac 2Pop	?	?	✓	✓	13	5?	5?	+		29?	6	12.5		SGM 88	—
116 Naranjo	Stela 6	9.18.5.5.17. - 4Caban 10Cumhu (??)	+	+	✓	3	+	5	+	+		30	*	21.6		SGM 92	—
117 Naranjo	Stela 8	9.18.10.0.0. - 10Ahau 8Zac	0	✓	✓	1	+	2	2	+		29	*	21.3		P-IV 23	H 6
118 Naranjo	Stela 13	9.17.10.0.0. - 12Ahau 8Pax	0	+	✓	7	+	4	4	+		29	*	26.8		P-IV 22	I 5
119 Naranjo	Stela 14	9.17.13.4.3. - 5Akbal 11Pop	2 or 3	+	✓	✓	7	2	3	+		29	*	8.6	Teeple reads 3C / G-F follow 9A	P-IV 33	H 5
120 Naranjo	Stela 18	9.14.15.0.0. - 11Ahau 18Zac	O	+	✓	✓	11	6	?	+		+	*	12.3		SGM 89	SGM 15
121 Naranjo	Stela 22	9.12.15.13.7 - 9Manik O Kayab	?	✓	2?	2?	+	1	✓	+?		?	*	24.4	Doubtful reading. Unfamiliar glyph, coeff. 9 between Manik and E	P-IV 36	I 6
122 Naranjo	Stela 23	9.13.18.4.18. - 8Eznab 13Uo	✓	✓	✓	✓	15	5 or 1	5?	+		30	6	14.6		P-IV 37	H 5
123 Naranjo	Stela 24	9.12.10.5.12. - 4Eb 10Yox	4	+	✓	✓	18	1	✓	✓		30	*	18.5	Uniform MN, as vs. Stela 29 Same I.S. on Stela 1, Coba	P-IV 39	I 6
124 Naranjo	Stela 28	9.11.4.10.2. - 3Ik 52Zip (?)	4	+	✓	2	✓	5	5	+		+	*	21.1	Morley (1938) reads: 9.12.4.10.2.	SGM 90	—
125 Naranjo	Stela 29	9.12.10.5.12. - 4Eb 10 Yox	4	+	✓	✓	19	6	1?	+		30	1	18.5	A and B in inverted order NonUniform MN, aa vs Stela 24	P-IV 41	H 5
126 Naranjo	Stela 30	9.14.3.0.0. - 7Ahau 18Kankin	✓	✓	✓	✓	4	4	5	+		?	*	3.8		P-IV 42	I 5
127 Naranjo	Stela 31	9.14.4.12.7. - 3Manik 15Mol	4	+	?	?	?	5 or 6	?	+		+	6	20.2		SGM 90	—
128 Oxpemul	Stela 2	9.17.0.0.0. - 13Ahau 18Cumhu	O	+?	?	?	?	?	?	?		?	3	0.0		—	—
129 Oxpemul	Stela 7	10.0.0.0.0. - 7Ahau 18Zip	+	+	✓	✓	13	6	+	+		29	2	13.1		—	—

No.	Site	Monument	Date	G	F	Z	Y	E	D	C	X	B	A	M.N.	M.A.	Remarks	Photo	Draw
130	Oxpemul	Stela 9	9.16.0.0.0. - 2Ahau 13Tzec	O?	+	v	v	v	v	4	5	+	29	5	5.5	E-D definitely absent C not uniform. Text clear	—	—
131	Oxpemul	Stela 12	9.15.0.0.0. - 4Ahau 13Yax	O?	v?	v	v	v	9 or 10	1	1	v	29	*	10.9		—	—
132	Oxpemul	Stela 18	9.16.5.0.0. - 8Ahau 8Zotz	O	+	v	v	v	5	5	6	+	30	6	4.1		—	—
133	Oxpemul	Stela 19	9.16.5.0.0. - 8Ahau 8Zotz	O	+	v	v	v	5?	5	6	+	30	6	4.1		—	—
134	Palenque	Tablet 1	9.12.6.5.8 - 3Lamat 6Zac	O	+	v	v	v	19	5	5	+	30	6	21.5	N.M.G. follows D	—	M-IV 78
135	Palenque	T. of Cross	12.19.13.4.0. - 8Ahau 18Tzec	8	+	v	v	5	+	2	3	+	29	—	—	G-F combined. D is N.M.G. Y used for E	M-IV 74	M-IV 75
136	Palenque	T. of F. Cross	1.18.5.4.0. - 1Ahau 13Mac	8	+	v	v	v	10	5	6	+	30	—	—	G-F Combined Moon-age glyph is N.M.G.	M-IV 80	M-IV 82
137	Palenque	T. of Sun	1.18.5.3.6. - 13Cimi 19Ceh	3	+	v	v	6	+	4	4	+	30	—	—	Month between G-F D is N.M.G.	M-IV 81	M-IV 89
138	Palenque	T. of Sun (Basement)	9.12.19.14.12. - 5Eb 5Kayab (??)	3	+	v	v	v	11	3	4	?	?	*	12.9	Doubtful date after Berlin (1943) G-F combined between day and month	—	BP 1
139	Palenque	Palace, House A	9.8.?.?.?	?	+	v	?	?	+	?	?	?	30	—	—	D is N.M.G.	M-IV 8	M-IV 9
140	Palenque	T. "Olividado"	9.10.14.5.10. - 30c 3Pop	?	+	?	?	?	?	6	?	?	?	*	20.4	C has. F.V. coeff.	BO 15	—
141	Palenque	New Tablet #1	9.10.11.17.0. - 11Ahau 8Mac	7	+	v	v	v	v	2	2	+	29	—	—	G-F Combined. Face of God "C" between F and C.	RP fig.	RP fig.
142	Palenque	New Tablet #2	9.13.10.6.8. - 5Lamat 6Mol	2	+	v	v	+	v	6	?	?	?	—	—	G-F Comb. God "C" between F and C. Not with I.S.	RP fig.	RP fig.
143	Palenque	New Tablet #3	9.14.8.14.15. - 9Men 3Yax	7	+	v	v	v	+	3	4	+	29	—	—	G-F Combined. Not with I.S.	RP fig.	RP fig.
144	Piedras Negras	Stela 1, b	9.12.2.0.16. - 5Cib 14Yaxkin	+	+	v	v	v	8	3	4	+	30	2	25.1		P-II 12	SGM 32
145	Piedras Negras	Stela 1, I	9.13.15.0.0. - 13Ahau 18Pax	O	+	v	v	16-18	+?	2	3?	+	29	*	17.8		SGM 129	SGM 32
146	Piedras Negras	Stela 2	9.13.5.0.0. - 1Ahau 3Pop	+	+	v	v	1	+	6	+	v	+	*	20.5		SGM 128	SGM 32
147	Piedras Negras	Stela 3, b	9.12.2.0.16. - 5Cib 14 Yaxkin	7	+?	v	v	7	v	2	2	v	29	*	25.1	F form unfamiliar. E repeated	P-II 13	SGM 33
148	Piedras Negras	Stela 3, 1	9.14.0.0.0. - 6Ahau 13Muan	O	+	v	v	7	17	3	3?	+?	30	*	16.4		SGM 129	SGM 33
149	Piedras Negras	Stela 4	9.13.10.0.0. - 7Ahau 3Cumhu	O	+	v	v	+	+	1?	2	+	30	*	19.1		SGM 128	SGM 33
150	Piedras Negras	Stela 5	9.14.5.0.0. - 12Ahau 8Kankin	O	+	v	v	v	16?	4	4	+	29	*	15.0		SGM 131	SGM 33
151	Piedras Negras	Stela 6	9.12.15.0.0. - 2Ahau 13Zip	O	+	v	v	5	+	4	5	+	29	*	23.2		P-II 16	SGM 33

															%	Notes		
152	Piedras Negras	Stela	7	9.14.10.0.0. - 5Ahau 3Mac	?	+	✓	✓	14	5	5	5	30	*	13.7		SGM 131	SGM 33
153	Piedras Negras	Stela	8	9.11.12.7.2 - 2Ik 10Pax	7?	+	✓	✓	6	5	5	5	30	*	6.2		SGM 127	SGM 31
154	Piedras Negras	Stela	9	9.15.5.0.0 - 10Ahau 8Chen	0	+	✓	✓ over 5	✓	2	+	+	+	*	9.6	Thompson (1937) and Beyer (1937) read "9D?" Teeple reads 10D	134	34
155	Piedras Negras	Stela	10	9.15.10.0.0 - 3Ahau 3Mol	O	+	✓	9	✓	3	4	+	30	*	8.2	G-F Combined	SGM 133	SGM 35
156	Piedras Negras	Stela	11	9.15.0.0.0 - 4Ahau 13Yax	O	+	✓	✓	10	1	+	+	30	1	10.9		SGM 133	SGM 34
157	Piedras Negras	Stela	12	9.18.5.0.0 - 4Ahau 13Ceh	O	?	✓	3	✓	6	1	+	30	3	22.7	E is repeated	SGM 142	SGM 39
158	Piedras Negras	Stela	13	9.17.0.0. - 13Ahau 18Cumhu	?	+?	?	+	✓	+	3	+?	+	3	0.0	E repeated without coeff.	SGM 138	SGM 37
159	Piedras Negras	Stela	14	9.16.17.1 - 7Imix 19Uo (?)	8	+	✓	6 or 8	+	4	5	+	30	5	25.9	Thompson (1942) reading, Morley (1938) and Teeple read 9.18.0.3.1 and 2C	SP 1.2	SGM 39
160	Piedras Negras	Stela	16	9.16.15.0.0 - 7Ahau 18Pop	V?	+	✓	3 or 4?	✓	2	2	+	29	*	1.4	Thompson (1937) reads 4E Beyer (1937) reads 2E Teeple reads 1E	SGM 138	SGM 37
161	Piedras Negras	Stela	23	9.14 15.0.0. - 11Ahau 18Zac (?)	O	+	✓	✓	13	6	?	?	?	*	12.3		SGM 132	SGM 34
162	Piedras Negras	Stela	25	9.8.10.6.16. - 10Cib 9Cumhu	1	+	✓	✓	3	3	3	+	29	—	5.3	A expressed as coeff. of 9 to right of C	SGM 120	SGM 28
163	Piedras Negras	Stela	26	9.9.15.0.0 - 8Ahau 13Cumhu	O	+	✓	✓	13	5	5?	+?	29	—	10.1	A expressed as coeff. of 9 to right of C	SGM 121	SGM 28
164	Piedras Negras	Stela	30	9.5.0.0.0 - 11Ahau 18Tzec	?	?	✓	✓	5	5	+	✓	30	—	6.6		SGM 120	SGM 27
165	Piedras Negras	Stela	31	9.10.5.0.0 - 7Ahau 3Pox (?)	?	+	✓	?	?	3	✓	+	30	1	7.4		P-II 25	SGM 27
166	Piedras Negras	Stela	35	9.11.9.8.6 - 12Cimi 9Cumhu	?	?	✓	✓	14	?	5	✓	?	5	13.3		SGM 124	SGM 29
?67	Piedras Negras	Stela	36	9.10.6.5.9. - 8Muluc 2Zip	1	+	✓	✓	4	4	5	✓	29	5	3.9		P-II 36	SGM 30
168	Piedras Negras	Stela	37	9.12.0.0.0. - 10Ahau 8Yaxkin	O?	+	✓	6 or 7	+	5	5	+	29	1	27.3	Teeple reads 8E	SGM 125	SGM 20
169	Piedras Negras	Stela	38	9.12.10.0.0. - 9Ahau 18Zotz	?	?	✓	?	?	2	2	?	+	3	24.6		SGM 125	SGM 31
170	Piedras Negras	Stela	39	9.12.5.0.0. - 3Ahau 3Xul	O	+	✓	7	+	4	+	+	30	2	26.0	Thompson (1937) and Teeple read 1C	SGM 125	SGM 31
171	Piedras Negras	Stela	40	9.15.14.9.13. - 11Ben 16Pax	4?	+	✓	11-15	✓	5	4	✓	+	*	17.0		SGM 135	SGM 35
172	Piedras Negras	Lintel	2	9.11.6.2.1 - 3Imix 14Ceh	5	+	✓	19	+	1	5	6?	29	6	19.0		P-II 31	SGM 38
173	Piedras Negras	Lintel	3	9.15.18.3.13. - 5Ben 16Chen	1	+	✓	9	✓	2	1	✓	30	*	8.1		SGM 146	SGM 37
174	Piedras Negras	Lintel	7	9.9.8.0.?.	?	?	?	?	?	?	2	3	29	—	—		SGM 128	—
175	Piedras Negras	Lintel	12	9.3.19.12.12. - 9Eb 10Tzec	8	+	✓	+?	+	?	?	?	?	—	22.2	G8-F combined. Should be G0. Month follows G-F M.A. Coeff. missing	SGM 119	SGM Fig. 90

No. Site	Monument	Date	G	F	Z	Y	E	D	C	X	B	A	M.N.	M.A.	Remarks	Photo	Draw
176 Piedras Negras	Lintel 13	uncertain	?	+	✓	✓	?	?	2?	3?	+	29	—	—	Possibly 3C	SGM 132	—
177 Piedras Negras	Lintel 2	9.16.0.0.0 - 2Ahau 13Tzec	?	?	?	?	?	?	5?	?	+	+	*	5.5	Doubtful reading	SGM 136	SGM 36
178 Piedras Negras	Altar 4	9.18.0.0.0 - 11Ahau 18Mac (?)	O?	?	?	?	?	?	?	?	+?	30?	6	24.1		SGM 111	SGM 39
179 Piedras Negras	Misc. Sc. Stone 13	uncertain	?	?	?	?	?	?	?	?	?	29	—	—		SGM 178G	—
180 Poco Uinic	Stela 3	9.18.0.0.0 - 11Ahau 18Mac	?	?	✓	✓	2	✓	1?	2?	+	29	6	24.1		PS 93	PC 11
181 Polol	Stela 1	9.18.0.0.0 - 11Ahau 18Mac	?	?	?	?	+?	✓	1?	✓	?	?	6	24.1		L 2	—
182 Polol	Stela 4	9.17.7.0.4 - 2Kan 7Kayab (?)	?	+	?	?	+?	✓	3	4	+	30	*	14.0		L 4	SGM Fig. 135
183 Pusilha	Stela D #1	9.8.0.0.0 - 5Ahau 3Chen (?)	✓	✓	✓	✓	✓	12 or 17	4	✓	✓	30	—	19.7	Teeple reads 9.3.0.0.0.	SGM 163	SGM 47
184 Pusilha	Stela D #2	9.10.15.0.0 - 6Ahau 13Mac	0	+	✓	✓	3	+	3	✓	✓	+	*	4.6	3E quite clear	SGM 163	SGM 47
185 Pusilha	Stela E	9.15.0.0.0 - 4Ahau 13Yax	✓	✓	✓	✓	✓	11	1?	2	+	29	*	10.9	Teeple reads 9.10.0.0.0. and 4C	SGM 165	SGM 46
186 Pusilha	Stela H#1	9.11.0.0.0 - 12Ahau 8Ceh	✓	✓	✓	✓	4	✓	4	+	+	29	*	3.3	4E quite clear / Teeple reads 3C	SGM 164	SGM 47
187 Pusilha	Stela H#2	9.7.12.6.7 - 8Manik 10Kayab	O	✓	✓	✓	✓	4	5	5	+	30	—	13.1	GO, 4D do not correspond to clear I.S.	SGM 164	SGM 47
188 Pusilha	Stela K	9.12.0.0.0 - 10Ahau 8Yaxkin	✓	✓	✓	✓	✓	1	3	+	+	29	1	27.3	X clear but unfamiliar	SGM 164	SGM 46
189 Pusilha	Stela N	uncertain	?	?	?	?	?	?	5?	+?	+	+?	—	—	Only B clear	SGM 165	—
190 Pusilha	Stela O	9.7.0.0.0 - 7Ahau 3Kankin	O	+	✓	✓	5	+	6	6 or 1	+	29	—	25.1	X-B-A combined in 1 glyph	SGM 163	SGM 46
191 Pusilha	Stela P #1	9.7.0.0.0 - 7Ahau 3Kankin	0	+	✓	✓	3	✓	3	✓	✓	29	—	25.1	Compare 6C. Stela O same date: both MN's clear	SGM 163	SGM 47
192 Pusilha	Stela P #2	9.10.15.0.0 - 6Ahau 13Mac	O	✓	✓	✓	✓	3	3	✓	✓	29	3	4.6	Listed in Teeple as Stela Y	SGM 163	SGM 47
193 Pusilha	Stela U	uncertain	?	?	?	?	?	6?	+	3?	+	29	—	—	Very doubtful readings / Coef. of A on right side	SGM 165	—
194 Quirigua	Stela A	9.17.5.0.0 - 6Ahau 13Kayab	O	+	✓	✓	6	+	2	2	✓	30	3	28.2	Teeple reads 8E	M-II 5	M-II 7
195 Quirigua	Zoom B	9.17.10.0.0 - 12Ahau 8Pax	O	+	✓	✓	7	+	1 or 2	2	+	29	4	26.8	Full figure glyphs	M-II 15	M-II 15
196 Quirigua	Stela D (e)	9.16.15.0.0 - 7Ahau 18Pop	O	+	✓	✓	✓	1	1	2	+	30	2	1.4	D combined wwith N.M.G. Coef. of 1 in cartouche Beyer (1936) reads M.A. O.0d	M-II 15	M-II 2?

No.	Site	Monument	Long Count – Date	G	F	E	D	C	X	B	A	Len	N	Age	Notes	Ref. 1	Ref. 2
197	Quirigua	Stela D (w)	9.16.13.4.17. - 8Caban 5Yaxkin	7	+	>	4	>		5	4	5	+	29	*	28.0		M-II 21	M-II 26
198	Quirigua	Stela E (e)	9.17.0.0.0. - 13Ahau 18Cumhu	O	+	>	>	2	3	3	+	29	3	0.0	Day and two unidentified glyphs between F and C.	M-II 29	M-II 22
199	Quirigua	Stela E (w)	9.14.13.4.17. - 12Caban 5Kayab	7	+	>	7	3	3	+	30	*	9.5		G-F combined	M-II 30	M-II 31
200	Quirigua	Stela F	9.16.10.0.0. - 1Ahau 3Zip	O	+	>	>	6	1?	>	30	1	2.7		Unidentified f.v. and N.M.G. between F and C, read by Teeple as "3d"	M-II 33	M-II 40
201	Quirigua	Zoom G	9.17.15.0.0. - 5Ahau 3Muan	O	+	3	+	5	5	5	+	30	*	25.4	B presented as two glyphs	M-II 43	M-II 44
202	Quirigua	Stela H	9.16.0.0.0. - 2Ahau 13Tzec	?	+	>	5	5	?	+	30	*	5.5		SGM 169	SGM Fig. I / Fig. 71
203	Quirigua	Stela I	9.18.10.0.0. - 10Ahau 8Zac	O	>	>	16	2	3	+	29	*	21.3	Coeff. above A. Teeple reads "11D" Beyer (1936) reads "18B"	SGM 172	H 7
204	Quirigua	Stela J	9.16.5.0.0. - 8Ahau 8Zotz	O	+	>	4	6	1	+	29	*	4.1		SGM 171	M-II 46
205	Quirigua	Stela K	9.18.15.0.0. - 3Ahau 3Yax	O	+	>	>	13 or 18	3	4	+	30	*	20.0	Read by Teeple as Od. Coeff. above A. 7 "parenthetical" glyphs between F & D. (Cf. Thompson, 1931)	M-II 47-48	M-II 49
206	Quirigua	Zoom O	9.18.0.0.0. - 11Ahau 18Mac	O	+	>	+	6	5	4	+	30	*	24.1	Beyer (1936) reads "3 or 8E"	SGM 173	H 7
207	Quirigua	Zoom O, Altar	9.17.14.16.18. - 9Eznab 1Kankin	O?	+	>	+	over 10	4	5	+	30	*	3.4	Doubtful glyph and D without coeff. Thompson ,1945) reads as "1 day"	TQ 1	SGM Fig.110
208	Quirigua	Zoom P	9.18.5.0.0. - 4Ahau 13Ceh	O?	+	>	3	4	4	+	29	1	22.7	E intended here?	M-II 51	M-II 59
209	Quirigua	Zoom P, Altar	9.18.5.0.0. - 4Ahau 13Ceh	O	+	>	3	+	4	5	+	29	1	22.7	A misdrawn in reference F.V. Coeff. inside moon glyph	SGM Vol. III frontis	SGM Fig.143
210	Quirigua	Stela S	9.15.15.0.0. - 9Ahau 18Xul	?	+	>	5		4	4	+	30	*	6.8		SGM 170	SGM 48
211	Quirigua	Stela T	9.13.0.0.0. - 8Ahau 8Uo (??)	?	+?	>	+?	+?	?	?	+?	30	5	21.9	Badly eroded	SGM 169	—
212	Quirigua	Structure 1	9.19.0.0.0. - 9Ahau 18Mol	?	+	>	+	over 10	4	5	+	?	*	18.6	Teeple reads M.A. - 2d	SGM 174	SGM 174
213	Tikal	Stela 3	9.2.13.0.0. - 4Ahau 13Kayab	O	+	>	17	3	4	>	29	—	2.2		P-V 15	II 1
214	Tikal	Stela 6	9.4.0.0.0. - 13Ahau 18Yax	O	>	>	13	5	>	>	?	—	12.0	A apparently present without coeff.	SGM 70	SGM 8
215	Tikal	Stela 11	10.2.0.0.0. - 3Ahau 3Ceh	?	?	?	?	?	?	+	?	—	2.2		SGM 72	SGM 8
216	Tikal	Stela 17	9.6.3.9.15. - 10Men 18Chen	?	+	>	+	4	?	>	?	—	6.3		SGM 68	—
217	Tila	Stela B	9.12.13.0.0. - 10Ahau 3Zotz	O	+	+	>	9 or 14	3	4	+	30	4	12.0		—	BT 10
218	Tonina	Stela 1 (T3)	9.15.3.0.0. - 5Ahau 18Chen (??)	?	?	?	>	+	5	?	?	30	1	27.8		B 217	B 218

No.	Site	Monument	Date	G	F	Z	Y	E	D	C	X	B	A	M.N.	M.A.	Remarks	Photo	Draw
219	Tonina	Stela Base 1 (T8)	9.12.10.0.0 - 9Ahau 18Zotz	O	v	v	v	1 or 2	+	+	+	+	30	3	24.6	Month follows G. B (?) follows A	B 227	B 228
220	Tonina	Stela 4 (T-9)	9.17.0.0.0 - 15Ahau 18Cumhu (??)	?	?	?	?	?	+	3	4	+	30	*	0.0	Teeple I.S. reading	B 230	H 4
221	Tonina	Stela 9 (T20)	9.18.0.0.0 - 11Ahau 18Mac	?	?	?	?	5?	?	1?	?	?	30	6	24.1	After Thompson (1944)	TJ 1	B 243
222	Tonina	Stela 13 (T28)	9.11.5.0.0 - 5Ahau 3Zac	?	?	v	v	1?	+	5	5	+	30	*	1.9	Teeple reads 9.17.15.0.0.	B 252	B 254
223	Uaxactun	Stela 1	9.14.0.0.0 - 6Ahau 13Muan (???)	v	v	v	v	v	17	3	?	?	?	*	16.4	Very doubtful reading	SGM 63	SGM 4
224	Uaxactun	Stela 3	9.3.13.0.0 - 2Ahau 13Ceh	O?	+?	v	v	v	2	5	v	v	30	—	2.2		SGM 60	SGM 4
225	Uaxactun	Stela 18	8.16.0.0.0 - 3Ahau 8Kankin	O	+	v	v	5	v	1	?	?	29	—	26.2		SGM 54	SGM 1
226	Uaxactun	Stela 22	9.3.10.0.0 - 1Ahau 8Mac	O?	+	v	v	v	14	4	5?	v	29	—	14.8	Dots above bar on Coeff. below A.	SGM 59	SGM 2
227	Uaxactun	Polychrome Vase	8.5.0.0.0 - 12Ahau 13Kankin	O	+	v	v	v	3	3	+	v	29	—	—		SGM 55	SGM 2
228	Uxul	Stela 2	9.9.?.?.?	?	v	v	v	v	10 or 15	5?	5	?	?	—	—		RD 58	—
229	Uxul	Stela 11	9.15.?.0.0	?	?	?	?	?	?	?	?	?	30	—	—	Unchecked RD reading	—	—
230	Uxul	Stela 12	9.11.10.0.0 - 11Ahau 18Chen	?	?	?	?	?	?	?	?	+	30	6	0.6	" "	—	—
231	Uxul	Stela 13	9.11.10.0.0 - 11Ahau 18Chen	?	?	?	?	?	9	?	?	?	29	6	0.6	" "	—	—
232	Uxul	Altar 2 #1	9.9.9.9.18 - 9Eznab 16Zac	O?	+	v	v	3-5	+	5?	5?	+	30?	—	26.6		RD 59	—
233	Uxul	Altar 2 #2	9.10.9.17.0 - 6Ahau 18Mac	?	+	v	v	over 10	+	2 or 3	3	+	30	1	15.6		RD 59	—
234	Uxul	Altar 2 #3	9.10.10.0.0 - 13Ahau 18Kankin	?	+	v	v	v	6-10	3	3	+	30	2	6.0		RD 59	—
235	Xultun	Stela 4	9.11.0.0.0 - 12Ahau 8Ceh	?	?	v	v	?	?	+	+	+	30	4	3.3		SGM 76	—
236	Xultun	Stela 6	9.3.17.0.0 - 12Ahau 13Zac	O	+	v	?	5	+	4	?	?	?	—	24.7	Teeple reads 9.3.0.0.0. G-F Combined	SGM 74	SGM 9
237	Xultun	Stela 15	9.14.0.0.0 - 6Ahau 13Muan	?	?	?	?	?	3 or 4	?	+	+z	29	3	16.4		SGM 77	—
238	Yaxchilan	Stela 1	9.16.10.0.0 - 1Ahau 3Zip	?	?	?	+	3	v	1	2	+	30	*	2.7		P-II 69	SGM 19
239	Yaxchilan	Stela 4	uncertain	?	?	?	+	?	?	?	?	?	?	—	—	Only Z and Y remain	SGM 101	SGM 19

No.	Site	Monument	Long Count												D.N.	Remarks	Ref. 1	Ref. 2
240	Yaxchilan	Stela 6	9.11.3.10.13. - 5Ben	1Zotz (??)	✓	+	✓	9?	6	✓	2	3	+	29	5	26.5	9Y precedes F Thompson (1937) reads I.S. - 9.11.16.10.3.	P-II 71	SGM 19
241	Yaxchilan	Stela 10	9.16.15.0.0. - 7Ahau	18Pop (??)	O	+	?	?	?	?	?	?	?	30	2	1.4	G misdrawn in reference	SGM 102	SGM 19
242	Yaxchilan	Stela 11, f.	9.16.1.0.0. - 11Ahau	8Tzec	O	+	+	+	12	✓	4	5	+	29	5	11.1		P-II 75	SGM 20
243	Yaxchilan	Stela 11, s	9.16.1.0.0. - 11Ahau	8Tzec	O	+	✓	6	12	✓	5	+	+	30	*	11.1	G-F Combined X-unfamiliar	SGM 102	SGM 20
244	Yaxchilan	Lintel 20	uncertain		?	+	✓	✓	3	?	?	?	?	?	—	—	E might be N.M.G.	SGM 112	SGM 21
245	Yaxchilan	Lintel 21	9.0.19.2.4. - 2Kan	2Yax	8	+	+	5	7	✓	3	4	>	29	*	7.8	G-F Combined. Y repeated as part of E. Thompson (1937) reading. Teeple reads 9.14.17.12.0. - 8E	P-II 56	SGM 21
246	Yaxchilan	Lintel 26	9.14.8.12.5. - 11Chicchan	13Yaxkin	2?	+	+	✓	13	✓	4	>	+	30	1	11.2	F is N.M.G.	P-II 59	SGM 22
247	Yaxchilan	Lintel 29	9.13.17.12.10. - 8Oc	13Yax	✓	+	+	5	15	+	2 or 3	4	+	30	5	13.3	Thompson prefers 3C / F is N.M.G.	SGM 112	SGM 22
248	Yaxchilan	Lintel 46	9.12.9.8.14. - 5Ix	17Mac (??)	3	+	+	2?	14	✓	3	4	+	30	*	15.9	C-2 drawn in reference. Thompson (1946) reads I.S. 9.11.17.14. Teeple reads 9.15.14.8.14. and 9C	P-II 68	SGM 25
249	Yaxchilan	Lintel 47	9.4.11.8.16. - 2Cib	19Yax	See Lintel 48				✓	13	2	2	✓	29	—	13.8	13D clear - misdrawn in reference	SGM 113	SGM 24
250	Yaxchilan	Lintel 48	9.4.11.8.16. - 2Cib	19Yox	5	+	+?	48	+?	—	See Lintel 47			—	—	—		SGM 113	SGM 23
251	Yaxchilan	Lintel 56	9.15.6.13.1 - 7Imix	19Zip	O	+	5	✓	✓	11	5	5	+	30	*	10.5	F is N.M.G.	M-II 98	SGM 26
252	Yaxchilan	Altar 3	9.16.1.9.3. - 12Akbal	11Kankin	3	+	✓	3	17	✓	5	5	+	30	*	17.0	Coeff. of A on left	P-II 80	SGM 26
253	Yaxchilan	Altar 6	9.16.15.0.0. - 7Ahau	18Pop (??)	?	?	?	6 or 8	3?	v?	4?	?	+	?	2	1.4	Morley (1938) reading - very doubtful	SGM 105	—
254	Yaxchilan	Altar 9	9.16.0.0.0. - 2Ahau	13Tzec	?	?	V	6 or 8	6	?	5	✓	+	30	*	5.5		SGM 105	SGM 26
255	Yaxchilan	Structure 44	9.12.8.14.1. - 12Imix	4Pop	2?	+	✓	6	7 or 8	✓	5	5	+	29	6	28.6	F is N.M.G. E repeated twice. Teeple and Thompson (1946) read "4C"	P-II 79	SGM 25

MOON AGES OF THE MAYA INSCRIPTIONS: THE PROBLEM
OF THEIR SEVEN-DAY RANGE OF DEVIATION
FROM CALCULATED MEAN AGES

LINTON SATTERTHWAITE

As has been known since the time of Teeple's important contributions, reliably read moon ages of the Maya inscriptions deviate from calculated mean ages through a range or "spread" of about seven days of time-distance. This range appears if we take some one recorded Maya age and its Long Count date as a base, calculate the ages at the other dates with the mean value of the lunation (29.53059 days), and compare the results with what is recorded. The deviations will be all plus, plus and minus, or all minus, depending on the Maya base chosen. Choosing a particular Maya age, which is expressed as a number of whole days, as the base of calculation, is an arbitrary procedure. We may, instead, choose an arbitrary age, expressed accurately with fractions of a day, and assign it to any Long Count day, the procedure adopted here. The range remains the same.

If the recorded ages were all counted by the Maya from days of some single moon-phase, then the seven-day range appears to be excessive whether we take all the recorded ages as counted from the days when the phase was last observed ("observed ages"), or as calculated by the Maya from some one zero day as a base ("calculated ages"). If this range could be explained by analysis of the moon record itself, that record would afford a more precise test for proposed correlations of Maya and European chronology.

This paper is intended primarily to place on record data and results of calculations pertinent to hypotheses discussed in a paper presented to the last Congress (290), and to avoid needless repetition, familiarity with that paper is assumed.

One way out of the difficulty of the seemingly excessive deviation range is to assume that incorrect ages were sometimes recorded for esoteric reasons. The differing theory being further investigated here is twofold. First, we are dealing with a mixed record of calculated and observed ages. Since we have reason to believe the Maya calculated a group of several days, any one of which might turn out to be the correct zero day, a mixed record, in which the first or last calculated day was selected as the recorded representative of the group, would tend to extend the range of deviations beyond that expectable with an unmixed record. For a given sample there would be a greater chance of encountering ages showing the extreme range of deviation called for by the calculating system as a whole, though in any instance, only one of the days of the predicted group was recorded. Second, it is postulated that in early Long Count times, the day of visible new moon was the only zero-day of the Maya lunation, but eventually a developing efficiency in predicting solar eclipses led to interest in predicting visible old-moon day and conjunction-day. As a result, at some times and places, there were shifts to old-moon day and/or to conjunction-day as the lunation-zero and, probably, occasional shifts back in the other direction.

The second, or shift postulate, requires not only that deviations of all recorded ages be calculated from a single base, as has been done before, but that they be arranged by sites and in the chronological order of the contemporaneous dates of the monuments, which sometimes differ from the dates for which the ages are given. Thus arranged, the deviation values should reveal a pattern, if there have been shifts in the lunation-zero. Tables 2 to 7 provide the data in this way for six sites, the arrangement being the same as in Table I of my prior paper, which dealt with the deviations at Copan. Included now are all sites with "double dates" (two differing lunar statements as of the same Long Count date) and, I think, all sites for which more than a half-dozen reliable deviations can be calculated. As in the tables for Copan, the deviations in Column G of these tables reflect an arbitrarily assumed age of 13.26 days at 4 Ahau 8 Cumhu, the base date for Initial Series at 13.0.0.0.0, resulting in the arbitrary mean ages of Column E (from which the recorded ages of Column F are subtracted).

The recorded ages, their Long Count dates (and bracketed contemporary dates when these differ) are mostly according to Morley (233), and, for Calakmul, according to Denison's presentation of Morley's data in Ruppert and Denison (285). However I have considered and generally followed subsequent criticism of certain Morley readings by Thompson,[1] and I have made use of manuscript lists supplied by him and also by Andrews. Criticism of the basic statements of Columns C and F is invited, and changes might affect reasoning. However I do not think they will be greatly modified. A few question marks indicate mild degrees of doubt, while Table 9 lists dates excluded because of serious doubt as to correctness of readings, as to proper contemporaneous dates, or because the recorded age may have been calculated at a considerable time-distance. The propriety of some of these exclusions may be questioned, and again criticism is invited.

COMPARISONS OF THE DEVIATIONS AT THE SEVEN SITES

The deviation data of Tables 2 to 7 are combined with those previously published for Copan in the summary provided by Table 1. As indicated at the bottom, the total range for 79 deviations at the seven sites is 6.98 days, so our extensive sample fairly represents the extreme range allowed by Teeple. It may be noted that we should subtract .51 days from the arbitrary 13.26 at 4 Ahau 8

1. See Thompson (362, 358, 363, 359); Satterthwaite (292). Published photographs have usually been consulted, but judgments must often be based on text only; no useful photographs or drawings are available for the Calakmul inscriptions.

Cumhu, and hence from all mean ages of Column E of the deviations tables, if we desire the deviations in the form of equal plus and minus maximum amounts. On the scale used and reflected in Columns 3 and 6 of Table 1, a deviation of .51 is midway in the total spread for the seven sites.

Columns 5, 6 and 7 of Table 1 correspond to Columns 2, 3 and 4, after excluding the indicated nine deviations for as many dates at three sites. This exclusion is not arbitrary. The six Copan deviations eliminated are those considered in the previous paper to be surely on an earlier lunation-zero base than the others at that site (group 2a of that paper). The eliminations for Piedras Negras and Yaxchilan not only effect the most extreme deviations in the plus direction at those sites; they apply to the earliest inscriptions there, dating from a time when we have assumed that only the visible new moon base was in use.

TABLE 1

DEVIATION RANGES AT SEVEN SITES*

SITE	ALL DEVIATIONS			EXCLUDING COPAN B–G, PIEDRAS NEGRAS 1–2, YAX. 1		
	No. of Dates	Extreme Deviations	Ranges	No. of Dates	Extreme Deviations	Ranges
(1)	(2)	(3)	(4)	(5)	(6)	(7)
Copan............	19	− 1.79 to 2.60	4.39	13	− .66 to 2.60	3.26
Quirigua.........	13	− .34 to 4.00	4.34	13	− .34 to 4.00	4.34
Pusilha..........	5	− .79 to 2.07	2.86	5	− .79 to 2.07	2.86
Naranjo.........	8	− .57 to 1.26	1.83	8	− .57 to 1.26	1.83
Calakmul........	8	− .84 to 2.89	3.73	8	− .84 to 2.89	3.73
Piedras Negras...	18	−2.98 to 2.22	5.20	16	−2.98 to .89	3.87
Yaxchilan.......	8	−1.59 to 1.65	3.24	7	−1.79 to .93	2.72
Combined sites.	79	−2.98 to 4.00	6.98	70	−2.98 to 4.00	6.98

* Data for Copan based on Table I of Satterthwaite (1948); for other sites, on Tables 2–7 of this paper.

The result of these excisions *of chronologically contiguous records only* yields a pattern in Columns 6 and 7 which seems strongly to suggest that after a time the two Usumacinta sites shifted their lunation-zero back in the lunation, that Copan did so for a time only, but that the other sites did not, or if they did, the shift was in lesser amount. We are dealing here in part with the same data which led Beyer to assign the old-moon zero day to the Piedras Negras inscriptions of the Period of Uniformity, and apparently to all Maya inscriptions (50). Our hypothesis of shifts, unlike his proposal of the old-moon zero day, does not result from analysis after first assuming a correlation constant, and it is based on a large sample.

Column 7 as well as Column 4 of Table 1 show the greatest range for a single site to be that for Quirigua, and Table 2, giving the individual deviations for this site, shows a rather consistent oscillation in the amounts and directions of devia-

TABLE 2
DEVIATIONS AT QUIRIGUA

A	B	C	D	E	F	G	H
1	St. S	9.15.15. o. o	1,409,400 1,800	6.79	− 5	1.79	U*
2	St. H	9.16. o. o. o	1,411,200 1,800	5.43	− 5	.43	U*
3	St. J	9.16. 5. o. o	1,413,000 1,800	4.06	− 4	.06	U*
4	St. F	9.16.10. o. o	1,414,800 1,177	2.69	− o	2.69	N
5	St. D, west	9.16.13. 4.17 (9.16.15. o. o)**	1,415,977 623	28.00	−24	4.00	u
6	St. D, east	9.16.15. o. o	1,416,600 − 15,023	1.33	− o	1.33	?
7	St. E, west	9.14.13. 4.17 (9.17. o. o. o)**	1,401,577 16,823	9.40	− 7	2.40	N
8	St. E, east	9.17. o. o. o	1,418,400 1,800	29.49	− o	− .04	N
9	St. A	9.17. 5. o. o	1,420,200 3,600	28.12	−26	2.12	N
10	Zo. G	9.17.15. o. o	1,423,800 − 22	25.39	−23	2.39	u
11	Alt. of Zo. O	9.17.14.16.18 (9.18. o. o. o)	1,423,778 3,622	3.37	− o	3.37	N
12	Zo. P & Alt.	9.18. 5. o. o	1,427,400 3,600	22.66	−23?	− .34?	N
13	St. K	9.18.15. o. o	1,431,000	19.13	−18?	1.13?	u

TABLE 3
DEVIATIONS AT PUSILHA

A	B	C	D	E	F	G	H
1	St. O	9. 7. o. o. o	1,346,400 o	25.07	−25	.07	u
2	St. P, 1st	9. 7. o. o. o (9.10.15. o. o)**	1,346.400 27,000	25.07	−23	2.07	N
3	St. P, 2nd & D 2nd	9.10.15. o. o	1,373,400 1,800	4.58	− 3	1.58	u
4	St. H, 1st	9.11. o. o. o	1,375,200 28,800	3.21	− 4	− .79	?
5	St. E	9.15. o. o. o	1,404,000	10.89	−11	− .11	?

TABLE 4

DEVIATIONS AT NARANJO

A	B	C	D	E	F	G	H
1	St. 24	9.12.10.5.12 (9.13.10.0. 0)**	1,386,112 10,066	18.43	−18	.43	U*
2	St. 23	9.13.18.4.18	1,396,178 1,061	14.50	−15	− .50	U*
3	St. 2	9.14. 1.3.19	1,397,239 − 11,127	12.39	−13	− .61	?
4	St. 29	9.12.10.5.12 (9.14. 3.0. 0)**	1,386,112 11,768	18.43	−19	− .57	N
5	St. 30	9.14. 3.0. 0	1,397,880 4,320	3.72	− 4	− .28	U*
6	St. 18	9.14.15.0. 0	1,402,200 19,800	12.26	−11	1.26	U*
7	St. 13	9.17.10.0. 0	1,422,000 7,200	26.76	−27	− .24	u
8	St. 8	9.18.10.0. 0	1,429,200	21.30	−21	.30	u

TABLE 5

DEVIATIONS AT CALAKMUL

A	B	C	D	E	F	G	H
1	St. 70	9.12. 8.9.9	1,385,469 531	25.10	−23	2.10	?
2	St. 94	9.12.10.0.0	1,386,000 10,800	24.55	−24	.55	N
3	St. 73	9.14. 0.0.0	1,396,800 6,940	16.35	−15	1.35	?
4	St. 51	9.14.19.5.0 (9.15. 0.0.0)	1,403,740 260	16.66	−14	2.66	U*
5	St. 52 & 54	9.15. 0.0.0	1,404,000 1,800	10.89	− 8	2.89	U*
6	St. 26	9.15. 5.0.0	1,405,800 1,800	9.52	− 9	.52	?
7	St. 25	9.15.10.0.0	1,407,600 10,800	8.16	− 9	− .84	?
8	St. 58	9.17. 0.0.0	1,418,400	29.49	− 0?	− .04?	u

TABLE 6

DEVIATIONS AT PIEDRAS NEGRAS

A	B	C	D	E	F	G	H
1	St. 30	9. 5. 0.0. 0	1,332,000 25,336	6.47	− 5	1.47	u
2	St. 25	9. 8.10.6.16 (9. 8.15.0. 0)**	1,357,336 21,270	5.22	− 3	2.22	N
3	St. 35	9.11. 9.8. 6 (9.11.10.0. 0)?	1,378,606 − 8,337	13.21	−14	− .79	?
4	St. 36	9.10. 6.5. 9 (9.11.15.0. 0)**	1,370,269 7,132	3.82	− 4	− .18	N
5	L 2	9.11. 6.2. 1 (9.11.15.0. 0)**	1,377,401 6,799	18.95	−19	− .05	N
6	St. 39	9.12. 5.0. 0	1,384,200 3,600	25.91	−27	−1.09	N
7	St. 6	9.12.15.0. 0	1,387,800 3,600	23.18	−25	−1.81	U*
8	St. 2	9.13. 5.0. 0	1,391,400 1,800	20.45	−21	− .55	U*
9	St. 4	9.13.10.0 .0	1,393,200 − 10,064	19.08	−20	− .92	U*
10	St. 1	9.12. 2.0.16 (9.13.15.0. 0)**	1,383,136 0	25.02	−28	−2.98	N
11	St. 3	9.12. 2.0.16 (9.14. 0.0. 0)**	1,383,136 13,664	23.02	−27	−1.98	U*
12	St. 3	9.14. 0.0. 0	1,396,800 3,600	16.35	−17	− .65	U*
13	St. 7	9.14.10.0. 0	1,400,400 − 20,738	13.62	−14	− .38	U*
14	St. 8	9.11.12.7. 2 (9.14.15.0. 0)?	1,379,662 24,338	6.10	− 6	.10	U*
15	St. 11	9.15. 0.0. 0	1,404,000 3,600	0.89	−10	.89	U*
16	St. 10	9.15.10.0. 0	1,407,600 2,953	8.16	− 9	− .84	U*
17	L. 3	9.15.18.3.13 (9.17.15.0. 0)?	1,410,553 16,847	8.10	− 9	− .90	U*
18	St. 12	9.18. 5.0. 0	1,427,400	22.66	−25	− .34	N

tion as we pass down Column G and forward in time. The latter fact suggests that only one zero day is involved at Quirigua, and that the range for a single base in the lunation may be well over four days, rather than "something more than three days" as suggested in the prior paper. Unfortunately the inclusion of Date 12 at Quirigua is subject to some question. If we eliminate it, the indicated range for one base is still over four days, but very little.

On our arbitrary scale the Quirigua range, supposed to be for a base after old-moon day, would start at least by −.04. This deviation would apply to a cal-

TABLE 7

DEVIATIONS AT YAXCHILAN

A	B	C	D	E	F	G	H
1	L. 48	9. 4.11. 8.16	1,328,936 47,557	13.65	−12	1.65	N
2	St. 6	9.11. 3.10.13 (9.11.10. 0. 0)??	1,376,493 29,928	26.93	−26	.93	N
3	L. 56	9.15. 6.13. 1 (9.15.10 .0. 0)??	1,406,421 4,779	10.38	−11	− .62	U*
4	Alt. 9	9.16. 0. 0. 0	1,411,200 360	5.43	− 6	− .57	U*
5	St. 11, front	9.16. 1. 0. 0	1,411,560 0	11.06	−12	− .94	N
6	St. 11, side	9.16. 1. 0. 0	1,411,560 183	11.06	−12	− .94	U*
7	Alt. 3	9.16. 1. 9. 3	1,411,743 − 15,773	16.08	−17	− .92	u
8	Ls. 29– 31	9.13.17.12.10 (9.17. 0. 0. 0)**	1,395,970	13.21	−15	−1.79	u

culated age, if the first of the predicted group of days was recorded. It is interesting to compare this with the deviation for the apparent base for long-distance age calculations at Palenque. The deviation for 9.12.6.5.8 of Stela 1 comes out as 2.43 days (21.43 less a recorded age of 19 days). Unless Palenque was recording the *last* of a prediced group of days we have a hint that Palenque used a zero day later than that of Quirigua. This possibility will be disregarded here, since the evidence is so uncertain.

DEVIATIONS AND THE DRESDEN ECLIPSE TABLE

The pattern of the table of pages 51–58 of the Dresden Codex guarantees that it deals in intervals of complete lunations, and the eclipse nature of the pattern shows that it was not set to visible new- or old-moon days. If our shift hypothesis is correct, it must have been set to conjunction-day, rather than to full-moon day. If we could be sure of the Maya date which was the epoch when the table was first valid as a predicting mechanism, the problem of fully understanding our deviation tables would be vastly simplified. Table 8 gives deviations for alternative epochs, and for the same arbitrary 13.26 age at 4 Ahau 8 Cumhu as was used for the other tables. Date 1 appears in the "Introduction" (89, pp. 51a–

TABLE 8

DEVIATIONS FOR RECORDED AND DERIVED DATES, INTRO-
DUCTION TO ECLIPSE TABLE OF DRESDEN CODEX

A	B	C	D	G	Range of Group	
1	Dr. 52, Bl	9.16. 4.10. 8	1,412,848 6,409	− .29	(−1.29 to	.71)
1x	Derived	9.17. 2. 6.17	1,419,257 3,483	.57	(− .43 to	1.57)
1y	Derived	9.17.12. 1. 0	1,422,740	−1.04	(−2.04 to −	.04)
2	Dr. 51, red	10. 9.10. 6. 8?	1,508,528 6,409	.60	(− .40 to	1.60)?
2x	Derived	10.10. 8. 2.17?	1,514,937 3,483	1.46	(.46 to	2.46)?
2y	Derived	10.10.17.15. 0?	1,518,420	− .15	(−1.15 to	.85)?
3	Dr. 51, red	10.19. 6. 1. 8?	1,578,988 6,409	.61	(− .39 to	1.61)?
3x	Derived	11. 0. 3.15.17?	1,585,397 3,483	1.47	(.47 to	2.47)?
3y	Derived	11. 0.13.10. 0?	1,588,880	− .14	(−1.14 to	.86)?
4	Derived*	11. 6. 2.10. 8	1,628,128 6,409	1.71	(.71 to	2.71)
4x	Derived	11. 7. 0. 6.17	1,634,537 3,483	2.51	(1.57 to	3.57)
4y	Derived	11. 7.10. 1. 0	1,638,020	.96	(− .04 to	1.96)

* From Date 1.

52a). There is no question about its reading, and it is the orothodox epoch for the sixty-nine entries of the table proper. Dates 2 and 3 are alternative readings for another date in the Introduction, which requires correction of some sort. The first interpretation was proposed by Makemson, and from it she advanced 2 × 11960 days to a supposed epoch, but she has since gone back to the orthodox date (210, 211). Date 3, the alternative reading, I get from Schulz. Though I do not think it has been proposed as a base for the table, it is perhaps a possibility.

It is interesting to note that the two dates, both at 12 Lamat but nearly ten katuns apart, show almost identical deviations. Either of these would permit "late" Maya datings for both Eclipse and Venus tables, a possibility suggested by Teeple.

Date 4 of Table 8 is a still later hypothetical epoch, here suggested for the first time, and for what it may be worth. The argument for it is as follows: To obtain the necessary late datings of both Venus and Eclipse tables (necessary if either is to be late) (340, p. 98) for the Venus table a particular number, given in its Introduction (89, p. 24), must be added to a given Long Count number, 9.9.9.16.0. The particular added number, 1.5.14.4.0, is understandable as a distance number but not otherwise, so late datings are most likely, and a similar method of locating the epoch of the Eclipse table is expectable. In the Introduction to the Eclipse table there is a considerable number of multiples or near-multiples of 11960. One of these, 1.9.18.0.0, would be come upon first in left to right reading, and it is the only multiple given special visual prominence by not being interwritten with another of different color in the same column. It is the highest of the black multiples and corresponds to Date 1 in color. These circumstances might be sufficient to indicate to an informed Maya priest which multiple was to be added to Date 1 to find the epoch. It must be admitted that in the manuscript Date 1 is close to the beginning of the table proper, and our supposed distance-number is as far from it as possible.

Further, it might not be accidental that this number, the eighteenth multiple of 11960 days, has a property possessed by none of the others, and this might in time be discovered by the Maya and have usefulness in calculating epochs for their table (or for similar ones of equal period) at considerable distances. From epochs separated by this interval the table will predict two series of same-tzolkin and same-age days which are spaced almost precisely two days apart in the mean lunation, those calculated from the later of two such epochs being the later in the lunation. Thus the prominence accorded this number and a special property suggest a hypothesis for testing: that the 12 Lamat of Date 1 (9.16.4.10.8) was a proper epoch from which to calculate the central one of three possible old-moon days with an 11960-day formula, while the 12 Lamat of Date 4, eighteen periods later, was a proper epoch for calculating "central" conjunction-days.

To facilitate reasoning and the bringing of other evidence to bear on the question of the true Maya epoch, including the age-records of the monuments, the full range for each of the dates, considering all three of the sequent days predicted by the table, is given in brackets, after the deviations for the central day only, that is, for a 12 Lamat. The deviations are also given, in each case, for derived "x" and "y" dates, these being two of the sixty-nine dates the table will predict from the epoch in question. While the range of deviation at the ends or beginnings of three sequent days is only two days, the range for combined "x" and "y" groups is 3.61 days, the maximum for one use of the table.

DEVIATIONS OF DOUBLE DATES AND THE PROBABLE AMOUNTS OF SHIFTS

Four pairs of double dates appear in our tables of deviations (Piedras Negras, 10 and 11; Yaxchilan, 5 and 6; Naranjo, 1 and 4; Pusilha, 1 and 2). The very nature of such dates, which change the lunar record for the same Long Count day, implies that at least one of a pair, if not both, is in agreement with calculation. Assuming that one may not be, those showing a Uniformity Period moon number for only one of the pair would seem to be the most probably calculated ones. At Pusilha both members of the pair precede the Period of Uniformity, neither shows a moon number in agreement with the Uniformity system, and we can at least guess that the later to be carved is the calculated one, since it changes an old record. After selecting the most probably calculated age from each site on these principles, if we compare the deviations of those dates with the same accompanying Glyph A values, we can expect a minimum of differences in deviations, if all apply to ages counted from the same base in the lunation.

We compare, then, Yaxchilan Date 11 with Naranjo Date 1, Glyph A10 applying to each. The respective deviations, −.94 and .43, yield a difference well within the 1.61-day range we should get with the Eclipse Table, for single-day rather than group record, and at the 3483-day interval which gives the maximum known amount of deviation of the formula used. So we have no reason to suspect difference in the lunation-zero from this difference of deviation alone.

The case is otherwise with Piedras Negras Date 11 and Pusilha Date 2, each with Glyph A9. The deviations, −1.98 and 2.07 respectively, show a difference of 4.05 days. If we are correct in ruling out the possibility of observed ages here, the indication is that lunation-zeros were used which were spaced more than two days apart. Since the other member of the Piedras Negras pair, Date 10, gives the extreme negative deviation for our whole sample and would increase the gap to 5.05 days, it is unlikely that Piedras Negras Date 11 is too far forward in the lunation, with an adjustment about to take place. Rather one supposes an error in the formula has just been allowed for, and both Piedras Negras ages are calculated ones. The first recorded of the two Pusilha ages is two days, not one day, less than the age shown by the later inscription, so its deviation falls about midway between, and we are still dealing with Glyph A9 values only. Thus it seems to me that we have some evidence for two-day spreads between calculated visible old-moon and conjunction-day zeros, and between the latter and calculated visible new-moon day zeros, and this tends in some measure to confirm our speculations concerning the epoch for the Eclipse Table.

The case is better for seeing only a single gap of two days between two lunar bases not needing adjustment because of accumulated error in the formula. The two deviations for Pusilha stand respectively near the beginning and near the middle of the total spread for Quirigua, while that range probably applies to a system on one lunation-zero. The two Pusilha ages are then explainable according to the first part of the thesis. We can believe that the earlier Pusilha age record, indicating a two-day gap with respect to Piedras Negras, is the calculated one. Later, the Pusilha observed age, corresponding to the third day of the group of days actually predicted for it, was set down in stone for some reason. This might be connected with the fact that the katun-end in question bore the same tzolkin-day name as would the katun which would end the current baktun.

TENTATIVE CONCLUSIONS

With an extensive sample of lunar inscriptions to consider, the site patterns of deviations at Piedras Negras and Yaxchilan indicate backward shifts in the zero day of the lunation. This confirms the evidence for Copan, discussed in the prior paper. There seems to be no clear evidence that shifts occurred at four other sites during the periods represented in our tables; such evidence as there is suggests no shifts, or else shifts in lesser amounts at certain of these sites.

The deviations at Quirigua repeatedly approach or reach the plus and minus extremes for the site as we proceed forward among the contemporary dates, indicating that here a deviation range of over four days reflects only one zero day for the lunation. Since this site provides the two most extreme deviations on the plus side, this is the latest zero day we have to consider, hence it is either visible new-moon or conjunction-day. Granting that shifts occurred elsewhere, as evidenced above, Piedras Negras and Yaxchilan used visible old-moon and/or conjunction-day, after initial periods at those sites. That is, they used a zero-day or days differing from that at Quirigua. Copan seems to have done likewise during a middle period.

When compared, the deviations of the double dates at Piedras Negras and Pusilha confirm the presence of shifts in the zero-day as evidenced by complete site ranges, and they indicate an intentional 4-day or 2-day gap, probably the latter, between the Piedras Negras lunation-zero (after the backward shift there) and the zero-day at Pusilha. The term "intentional gap" is used in the sense that on calculating the first of a group of several days for the actual observation of the phase-day taken as zero at Piedras Negras, the priests there would have counted forward two complete days to the first day of a second group of days expected to cover the phase-day taken as zero-day at Pusilha; and at Pusilha the phase-day taken as zero-day at Piedras Negras would have been allowed for in a reverse manner. If at one site the priests decided to shift the base of the calculating mechanism so that the zero day applied to the other phase, they would shift two whole days. The difference between the deviations in two systems on the two different zero-day bases, when found for two widely separated lunations, would not ordinarily be precisely 2.00 days, though Glyph A values were the same; but if both systems were giving good results, with the same Glyph A values the intended two-day difference would be closely reflected in the deviation difference.

Thus far I believe we have not gone beyond what is highly probable on the basis of an extensive sample. I pass on to what may be useful speculation. It has been necessary to allow for possible presence of three lunation-zeros in the inscriptions, that is, conjunction-day as well as visible old- and new-moon days. However, if we are correct in ascribing all Quirigua deviations to a mixed system of calculation and observation for a single zero-day, the temptation is strong to extend the Quirigua range for this base so as.to include all the deviations of Column 6 of Table 1 except those for the two Usumacinta sites, Piedras and Yaxchilan. If we do this, the deviations for a single base, producing the most extreme deviations on the plus side, extend (on our arbitrary scale) from −.84 at Calakmul to 4.00 at Quirigua. The resulting range of 4.84 days is roughly

TABLE 9

INSCRIPTIONS EXCLUDED FOR REASONS NOTED IN TEXT

Quirigua	Pusilha	Naranjo	Calakmul
Alt. of Zo. O	St. D, 1st	St. 6	St. 1
St. I	St. H, 2nd	St. 14	St. 8
St. T	St. K	St. 22	St. 9
Zo. B	St. N	St. 28	St. 13
Zo. O		St. 31	St. 16
Str. 1			St. 24
			St. 27
Piedras Negras	Yaxchilan		St. 28
			St. 29
Alt. 2	L. 20		St. 35 rt.
Alt. 4	L. 21		St. 35 lft.
L. 7	L. 26		St. 41
L. 12	L. 46		St. 43
L. 13	St. 1		St. 57
M.S.S. 13	St. 4		St. 64
St. 1, lft.	St. 10		St. 67
St. 5	Str. 44 mid.		St. 71
St. 9			St. 75
St. 13			St. 76
St. 14			St. 80
St. 16			St. 86
St. 23			St. 89
St. 26			
St. 31			
St. 37			
St. 38			
St. 40			

comparable with a 3-day group range of 4.61 for the Eclipse Table, after it has been repeated nine times, has accumulated a full day of error in the formula, and first theoretically requires an adjustment of one day. Moreover, visible old- and new-moon days might seem to the Maya to sometimes occur a day earlier or later (respectively) than they should have, but eclipses would be observed, if at all, on the correct day. Therefore a three-day predicted group for possible eclipse days (conjunction-days) does not guarantee that groups for visible old-and/or new-moon days did not contain four days. Nine uses of the lunar formula of the Eclipse Table, set to one of the other zero-days, 4-day instead of 3-day groups being implied, would extend the maximum group deviation range to 5.61 days.

Thus a 4.84-day range for a single base applicable to the first five rows of Column 6 of Table 1 does not appear to be excessive, especially if the zero-day is visible new-moon day. Even if it is conjunction-day, since the maximum range for the Eclipse Table lunar formula may have been somewhat more than is shown by the 69 entries selected by the Maya, we may, I think, properly entertain the hypothesis that only two zero-days are represented in the deviations of the inscriptions covered by our tables.

The further question arises, which two of the three possible zero-days should we postulate as separated by the two-day gap of which we have evidence? The answer depends in part on what epoch one accepts for the Eclipse Table. For this reason, four alternative epochs have been listed in Table 8, with resulting different plus and minus deviations. Without reference to the latter it has been argued that the hypothetical Date 4 is most probably the correct epoch. This suggested very late dating of the Eclipse Table may or may not withstand criticism. If we accept it provisionally, I think at the same time we must postulate only two zero days in the inscriptions here considered, visible old-moon and conjunction-days. With 11.6.2.10.8 as the epoch, nine repetitions of the table produce a maximum range extending from $-.04$ to 4.57 on our scale, the extreme on the plus side exceeding that for Quirigua and our sample as a whole. Therefore, with this dating for the Eclipse Table, surely on a conjunction-day zero, we have only the visible old-moon zero to explain the apparent backward shift at Piedras Negras, Yaxchilan and Copan.

We started with the hypothesis that visible new-moon day was the universal lunation-zero during an early part of the Long Count or Initial Series period. To accommodate the notion that only visible old-moon and conjunction-days determined the zero-days of the sample we may add the alternative postulate that, at some sites at least, visible new-moon day was abandoned in favor of conjunction-day in pre-monuments times, with the implication that solar eclipses were being successfully predicted in this Pre-Classical or Pre-Initial Series period.

THE CALENDAR OF THE TZOTZIL INDIANS

HEINRICH BERLIN

One of the most characteristic features of the Meso-American cultures was the use of a special calendar, dividing the year into 18 months of 20 days with an additional month of only 5 days to make up the 365 days of the solar year. Each month and day had a name, the days also being numbered progressively from 1 to 13, then starting again from 1.

From the days of the Conquest, the more enlightened of the newcomers were aware of this calendar, and ever since attempts have been made to establish a correlation between our Christian calendar and the Indian one. This was not an easy task because of the gradual dying out of the latter, of preconceived ideas of the European-minded investigators, and of the shift in our own calendar from Julian to Gregorian in the second half of the sixteenth century.

In addition to the general division of the year as outlined above, the Mayas were using a long count, connecting their dates with a zero point of their own, and "position numbers" for each day of a month. This connection is clear and definite during the apogee of the Maya culture but gets vaguer and vaguer in later times, as can be seen from the last Pre-Spanish inscriptions, and then in Colonial entries, where Maya calendar dates are recorded. Different approaches have been advanced to establish a clear cut correlation between the Maya calendar and our own, but so far none of these has been able to win the support of all students.

In order to elaborate the final solution, it is evident that all new source possibilities should be investigated. For this it is particularly fortunate that many of the tribes speaking languages related to Maya are still using part of the old calendar. The present use of such calendars has been reported during the last years by J. S. Lincoln (187), D. S. Byers and O. la Farge (177) for Guatemala, and M. E. Becerra (30) and R. P. C. Schultz (298) for Chiapas. However, the existence of a calendar among the tribes of Chiapas has been mentioned before by Bishop Francisco Núñez de la Vega, who, as early as 1702, published in his famous *Constituciones Diocesanas* (255) the day names of the Tzeltals(?), now apparently no longer in use. During the past century, two local scholars, Emeterio Pineda (266) and Vicente Pineda (267) published the names of the months which they had obtained from the Tzotzil and Tzeltal speaking Indians, but without giving any correlation.

The Tzeltal Indians are living close to such important old Maya ruins as Ocosingo-Tonina, and the Tzotzils, immediate neighbors of the Tzeltals, speak a Maya dialect and live in a region where authentic Old Maya specimens have been found. Therefore it is very likely that the Tzotzils are true descendants of the great Old Maya people, as are also the present Mayas of Yucatan and other tribes.

There exists an interesting manuscript which throws additional light on the use of the calendar among the Tzotzil Indians and which, as far as I know, has never been analyzed by any student of the correlation problem, despite the fact that its calendric contents had been published as early as 1885 by Charency (80). The title of this manuscript is *"Arte de la lengua Tzotzlem ó Tzinacanteca con explicación de Año solar y un Tratado de las quentas de los Indios en Lengua Tzotzlem."*[1]

Before analyzing the calendric part of the manuscript, I shall briefly describe it in a general way. The original was written as early as 1688 by a Franciscan Friar Juan de Rodaz, who at that time was parson of the village and convent of Nuestra Señora de la Asunción de Gueytiupan, situated in the northern part of the Tzotzil region, near Simojovel. Mr. Kenneth Weathers of the Summer Institute of Linguists, who is an expert on the Tzotzil language, revised the manuscript and considers the language in which it is written as akin to the Tzotzil dialect as spoken at San Juan del Bosque, also located in the neighborhood of Simojovel. The document as we possess it today is an early copy made by a Dominican friar (Dionycio Pereyra) in 1723. Including the title page, the manuscript consists of thirty-one leaves, written generally on both sides. The first twenty leaves contain a grammar of the Tzotzil language. Leaf 20 reverse gives a list of kinship terms, showing that the Tzotzils, like so many other American Indians, differentiated very sharply between relatives of the husband's side and those of the wife's side. On leaf 21 we find a kind of vocabulary of the nouns related to the human body. Leaf 22 contains a list of names of months with their equivalent in our own calendaric system, and then follows, up to and including leaf 27, a complete list of numbers and time-counting terms. The last four leaves contain some Spanish sentences with their translation into Tzotzil. Father Rodaz seems also to have written a special Spanish-Tzotzil (or Tzotzil-Spanish?) vocabulary, as several times in the text reference is made to pages of a Thesaurus Verborum.

Let us now consider the list of months contained on leaf 22 of the manuscript. To facilitate working I have arranged them in a table (Fig. 1), showing at the same time the data gathered in three Tzotzil villages by Becerra, Schultz, and also myself during my stay in the Tzotzil region in August, 1948. I obtained my information by asking the Indians the date in their own calendar of the current day. The rapidity of their reply was amazing. According to them, everybody keeps personal count, no written references or patterns exist, nor are there special persons in charge of the calendar who might be approached in case of doubt.

In the chart the names of the months are spelled as in the manuscript; varia-

---

1. I am indebted to the Bibliothèque Nationale in Paris for the use of this manuscript, classified there as Manuscrit Mexicain 411.

	Ms. 411		Chenalho						San Andrés					Santa Marta					Landa-	
	Ms. 411		Becerra[1]		Schultz		Berlin		Becerra		Schultz	Berlin		Becerra	Schultz	Berlin			Landa-	
Batzul	17-I	5-II	14-I	2-II	16-I	4-II	9-I	28-I	15-I	3-II	The same as his table for Chenalho	15-I	3-II	The same as table of Ms. 411-	The same as his table for Chenalho	15-I	3-II	Yax	12-I	31-I
Cicac	6-II	25-II	3-II	22-II	5-II	24-II	29-I	17-II	4-II	23-II		4-II	23-II			4-II	23-II	Zac	1-II	20-II
Chaiquin	26-II	2-III	23-II	27-II	25-II	7-III	18-II	22-II	(2)			24-II	28-II			(3)		Ceh	21-II	12-III
Muctacac	3-III	22-III	28-II	19-III	2-III	21-III	23-II	14-III				1-III	20-III					Mac	13-III	1-IV
Moc	23-III	11-IV	20-III	8-IV	22-III	10-IV	15-III	3-IV	21-III	9-IV		21-III	9-IV			21-III	9-IV	Kankin	2-IV	21-IV
Olalti	12-IV	1-V	9-IV	28-IV	11-IV	30-IV	4-IV	23-IV	10-IV	29-IV		10-IV	29-IV			10-IV	29-IV	Muan	22-IV	11-V
Ulol (Hoyoh)	2-V	21-V	29-IV	18-V	7-V	20-V	24-IV	13-V	30-IV	19-V		30-IV	19-V			30-IV	19-V	Pax	12-V	31-V
Oquin Aghual	22-V	10-VI	19-V	7-VI	21-V	9-VI	14-V	2-VI	20-V	8-VI		20-V	8-VI			20-V	8-VI	Kayab	1-VI	20-VI
Uch	11-VI	30-VI	8-VI	27-VI	10-VI	29-VI	3-VI	22-VI	9-VI	28-VI		9-VI	28-VI			9-VI	28-VI	Cumhu	21-VI	10-VII
Elech	1-VII	20-VII	28-VI	17-VII	30-VI	19-VII	23-VI	12-VII	29-VI	18-VII		29-VI	18-VII			29-VI	18-VII	Uayeb	11-VII	15-VII
Nichilquin	21-VII	9-VIII	18-VII	6-VIII	20-VII	8-VIII	13-VII	1-VIII	19-VII	7-VIII		19-VII	7-VIII			19-VII	7-VIII	Pop	16-VII	4-VIII
Ghunvinquil	10-VIII	29-VIII	7-VIII	26-VIII	9-VIII	28-VIII	2-VIII	21-VIII	8-VIII	27-VIII		8-VIII	27-VIII			8-VIII	27-VIII	Uo	5-VIII	24-VIII
Xchibalvinquil.	30-VIII	18-IX	27-VIII	15-IX	29-VIII	17-IX	22-VIII	10-IX	28-VIII	16-IX		28-VIII	16-IX			28-VIII	16-IX	Zip	25-VIII	13-IX
Yoxibalvinquil	19-IX	8-X	16-IX	5-X	18-IX	7-X	11-IX	30-IX	17-IX	6-X		17-IX	6-X			17-IX	6-X	Tzoz	14-IX	3-X
Xchanibalvinquil	9-X	28-X	6-X	25-X	8-X	27-X	1-X	20-X	7-X	26-X		7-X	26-X			7-X	26-X	Tzec	4-X	23-X
Porm	29-X	17-XI	26-X	14-XI	28-X	16-XI	21-X	9-XI	27-X	15-XI		27-X	15-XI			27-X	15-XI	Xul	24-X	12-XI
Yaxquin	18-XI	7-XII	15-XI	4-XII	17-XI	6-XII	10-XI	29-XI	16-XI	5-XII		16-XI	5-XII			16-XI	5-XII	Yaxkin	13-XI	2-XII
Muy	8-XII	27-XII	5-XII	24-XII	7-XII	26-XII	30-XI	19-XII	6-XII	25-XII		6-XII	25-XII			6-XII	25-XII	Mol	3-XII	22-XII
Tzun	28-XII	16-I	25-XII	13-I	27-XII	15-I	20-XII	8-I	26-XII	14-I		26-XII	14-I			26-XII	14-I	Chen	23-XII	11-I

1-A Typographical error in the Becerra publication is here properly corrected

2 — Here Becerra reads: { Muctacac: 24-II-15-III; Chaiquin: 16-III-20-III }

3 — My informants of Santa Marta { Muctacac: 24-II-15-III; Chaiquin: 16-III-20-III }

FIG. 1

tions can be found in the original publications of Becerra, Schultz, and the Pinedas. It will be noted that the position of the 5-day month, the Chaiquin, varies with the different informants. For two other villages not given in the chart, San Miguel Mitontic and Santa Catarina Pantelhó, Schultz reports the position of the Chaiquin between Muctacac and Moc, with the same correlation as given by our manuscript. On the other hand, for San Miguel Mitontic, Becerra gives the sequence Cicac-Chaiquin-Muctacac. These differences may originate from a temporary lapse of memory of the informants. They should be checked thoroughly in the field.

All data as to the correlation coincide almost completely, with the exception of my own for Chenalhó. But there my informants confessed that they were not altogether sure and told me that Saint Peter's day (June 29) corresponded to the second day of Elech, which would make their calendar run as given by Becerra. Others at Chenalhó gave the first day of Elech, or even the last day of Uch, as Saint Peter's day. If the latter were true, there would only be a difference of two days when compared with the Becerra data, but never five as actually given during my visit. Under these circumstances I would rather consider the San Andrés and Santa Marta data as the more correct traditional figures. The tradition at Chenalhó may have been somewhat blurred through more frequent communication with Spanish people.[2]

Furthermore, all my informants of Chenalhó, San Andrés, and Santa Marta agreed that the Fiesta de Animas (All Souls' Day) always fell on the fifth or sixth day of Pom. At San Andrés the fifth day of Pom was specified as vísperas (eve) and the sixth as the real feast. At Santa Marta I was told that the festival was on the afternoon of the fifth of Pom, which seems to indicate the same customs as at San Andrés. These statements coincide with the San Andrés and Santa Marta data of Schultz, as there November 1 (All Saints' Day) corresponds to the fifth of Pom and November 2 (All Souls' Day) to the sixth of Pom. As I gathered my data in August, and as I do not believe that the Tzotzils reckon in advance, the correlation fifth/sixth of Pom to All Souls' Day seems to be a fixed landmark, at least in modern times. Thus, on arriving at All Souls' Day in 1948, the Indians of Santa Marta and San Andrés must have noted that it fell on the seventh of Pom, due to the fact that 1948 was a leap year, and they apparently had not made any leap year corrections since All Souls' Day of 1947.

To confuse matters further, the same Indians of San Andrés maintained (as they had done many years ago to Becerra, who built up his calendar in accordance with the correlation existing between the Indian month day and the saint's day, in the Christian calendar, of the local patron saint of the church) that Saint Andrew's day (November 30) always fell on the fifteenth of Yaxquin. But if the second of November is really a landmark equaling the sixth of Pom, then it is

---

2. On the other hand, it was at Chenalhó that I was told that on the afternoon of the last day of Oquinaghual, a special festival for the following month was held. This, I suspect, dates back to Pre-Spanish customs.

impossible that Saint Andrew's day is another landmark equaling the fifteenth of Yaxquin, for from the second to the thirtieth of November there are twenty-eight days as against the twenty-nine days between the sixth of Pom and the fifteenth of Yaxquin. Even in the Indian calendar, days are (according to my informants) counted at present from midnight to midnight, and the fourteenth of Yaxquin was specially mentioned as the eve of Saint Andrew's day. I therefore cannot see any possibility of reconciling both dates as landmarks.

Schultz clearly states that he gathered his data in 1941. Becerra is not as clear, but as his publication bears the date of March–April, 1933, it is evident that he obtained his data no later than 1932.

Comparing the data, one sees at once that they have remained essentially the same in all details through a period of at least 250 years. It is therefore evident that the Indians must have adopted a system of leap years. If they had not done so, the first day of a given month could not fall on the same Christian day 250 years later, as it actually does; it would have moved back by about sixty days, e.g., the first day of Elech, which according to our manuscript of 1688 fell on the first of July would have fallen on approximately the first of May in 1932. But for Santa Marta, Becerra reports exactly the same Christian dates as does the manuscript.

It is held by most of the present scholars that the Indians who used the Meso-American calendar did not use leap years in Pre-Spanish times, despite the fact that many old chroniclers assure us of the contrary. However, it is probable that the Mayas had methods of their own for always knowing the exact position of the sun in a strict 365-day year. Unfortunately, neither Becerra nor Schultz investigated this particular problem.

At first glance one might think that at present the Tzotzils do not use leap years either, since the 1941 Schultz data are one day behind the Becerra data for Santa Marta. But, as mentioned above, the Becerra data must have been collected in 1932 at the latest, and between 1932 and 1941 there were two leap years: 1936 and 1940. If the Indians had not counted leap years then in 1941 they ought to have been at least two days behind the Becerra data, but Schultz reports only one day's difference. Moreover, as stated already, for two villages even Schultz reports in 1941 the same correspondence between Indian and Christian dates as do our manuscript and Becerra for Santa Marta. Again, my own data are one day behind those of Schultz. But here, too, if no leap years were used, the difference should be two days, because of the leap years 1944 and 1948.

The total shift of only two days, from 1688 to 1948, clearly shows that at least since 1688 the Tzotzils are in fact using a correction equivalent to a leap year count, although they are not aware of it. In spite of my questioning them, I failed to find out how they manage their leap years. All informants agreed that (1) they never used a Chaiquin of six days or a month of 21 days (which would certainly be the easiest way), (2) that they never failed to register a day, and

(3) that they never made any adjustment, but that the correspondence of their calendar to the Christian one always turned out right. But the facts as given by the Indians themselves prove that in one way or another they must make adjustments. Local differences in the way of making these adjustments may account for the differences of one or two days from one village to another. It is also possible that the adjustments are not made strictly every four years, but only when people are aware that their calendar is not any longer in strict harmony with traditional landmarks; then they return to a fixed landmark pattern.

Spinden (318) has already advanced the belief that "originally Chen of the Mayas and Tzun of the Tzentals and Tzotzils must have been close together and may have coincided exactly." This belief seems highly plausible.[3]

For comparison let us use the month Yaxquin, as this occurs equally in all three calendars, thus proving its common origin, while other month names differ widely in the various calendars. In our manuscript (which practically coincides with the customs of the present), the first of Yaxquin corresponds to the eighteenth of November in a frozen calendar. It is not unreasonable to suppose that the Indians did not take into consideration the Gregorian 10-day correction in their own calendar at the very time this correction was introduced in our calendar. Now the Tzotzil Chaiquin is inserted at another place in the sequence of months than the corresponding Maya Uayeb. The Chaiquin is, at present, roughly speaking, at the end of February. This seems suspicious and might indicate that it was moved to this place in post-Conquest times under the influence of the friars. We can imagine the shift as follows: originally the Chaiquin was placed in the same position as the Maya Uayeb, that it was omitted for one year and then moved to the present position. This shift may have taken place about 1582 and the Indians, perhaps advised by the friars, may have considered it as an equivalent for the Gregorian correction. The process therefore would have been as shown in the accompanying tabulation.

1581 jul.	Chaiquin 11.VII–15.VII	1581 jul.	Yaxquin 13.XI–2.XII
1582 "	" 11.VII–15.VII	1582 greg.	" 23.XI–12.XII
1583 greg.	" omitted	1583 "	" 18.XI–7.XII
1584 "	" 26.II–2.III	1584 "	" 18.XI–7.XII

Another solution would be to suppose that the Tzotzil Indians, having had the same starting point as the Mayas in 1553 and with the first of Yaxquin on

3. But Spinden is certainly incorrect when, speaking of the Tzeltal and Tzotzil calendars, he asserts (*ibid.*, p. 88), "This calendar is still maintained, but the first of Chen or Tzun is in constant conformity with January 1." According to all information available, the first of Tzun never coincides with January 1, at least not among the Tzotzils. At Chenalhó it is believed that January 1 corresponds to the tenth of Tzun, whereas at San Andrés it is taken to correspond to the fifth or sixth of Tzun. If at San Andrés the correlation fifth of Tzun = January 1 were really a landmark, then the calendar there would conform exactly to the pattern of our manuscript and All Souls' Day would fall on the fifth of Pom, but Saint Andrew's Day would fall on the thirteenth of Yaxquin and not on the fifteenth as given by Becerra's and my own informants.

November 13, went on using their old time count of 365 days without leap year corrections until 1572. By doing so, the first of Yaxquin would have moved back from November 13 to November 8 in the Julian calendar. Then their calendar might have been frozen into the Christian one and they may not have interrupted their counting of days when the Gregorian correction was introduced. This supposition assumes that the Landa calendar (104) was not already frozen, a point which would first need to be clarified. These are, of course, only speculations and other equally plausible explanations may be found.

But whatever the reason for the discrepancy between the Tzotzil and the Landa Maya calendars may be, I think all available material shows that they are intimately related. In a recent publication Maud Makemson (211) has suggested a new Maya/Christian correlation which, in 1552, makes the first of Yaxquin fall on March 21, thus frankly contradicting Landa's typical year, which even she believes to correspond to 1553. Without discussing here the points on which Makemson depends for suggesting the change, this change does not seem admissible from what I should like to call the Tzotzil point of view. I can see no explanation to justify the destruction of an almost day for day harmony between the Tzotzil calendar and the Landa Maya one. To assume that the Tzotzils, who depend entirely on oral tradition, had made a parallel "mistake" to the one Makemson accuses the Landa copyist of having made would certainly be taxing credulity.

INTERMEDIATE

LAS CIVILIZACIONES DEL SUR DE CENTRO AMÉRICA Y EL NOROESTE DE SUD AMÉRICA

Jacinto Jijon y Caamaño[1]

Cooper propuso la división etnográfica cuadripartita de la América Meridional (99), si bien la cuarta, la que nos interesa especialmente, sólo fue vagamente enunciada al señalar que las Antillas y el sur de Centro América desde el Istmo de Panama hasta Honduras, formaban una región especial.

Esta clasificación cuadripartita ha sido adoptada por el monumental *Handbook of South American Indians* (325), pero cuando Steward planeó la obra, la división de los pueblos del Circuito Caribeano parece haber sido un simple concepto geográfico, no étnico. Por lo tanto, las diversas monografías pertinentes a los pueblos que vivieron en lo que hoy es la república de Colombia aparecen lamentablemente dispersas entre el segundo y el cuarto volumen del *Handbook*, como lo ha reconocido su editor (326, p. xv).

Más el grupo etnográfico homogeneo, diverso del constituído por los pueblos andinos del Perú, Bolivia, el Noroeste de la Argentina y Chile setentrional y central, no sólo lo constituyen los pueblos que moraron desde Honduras hasta Colombia, inclusivo, sino también los aborígines del Ecuador.

El territorio Interandino de esta república, y parte del Litoral fué conquistado por los Incas, y hoy la población indígena de la Sierra y hasta algunos tribus de la Región oriental, habla Quechua, por obra de los Incas y de los misioneros españoles; pero las culturas aborígenes pertenecen al mismo ciclo que las de Colombia, no existiendo mayores diferencias entre las del país Quimbaya en Colombia y la del Pasto en el Ecuador, que entre la de éste y la del Cañari-Ecuador, por ejemplo.

Ya en 1920 habíamos reconocido y escribamos: "... del Carchi al Macará, más visible en unas provincias etnológicas, menos en otras y en todo el Ecuador Occidental ... el arte prehistórico tiene el mismo sello Sur Centroamericano que en Imbabura" (146, p. 169).

El límite meridional de este territorio en el cual las civilizaciones prehistóricas tienen marcada afinidad, puede fijarse, provisionalmente, para la última época precolombiana en el Desierto de Tumbes; pero es seguro que en tiempos más antiguos llegaba hasta el callejón de Huaylas en el Perú. La civilización llamada de Recuay si bien contiene muchas formas y decoraciones Andinas en sus raices, pertenece al círculo de que venimos hablando; se observa también en el Norte en

---

[1]. The author's untimely death interrupted the final editing of his manuscript. He did not, therefore, see the final version of this paper. The editor hopes that the appearance of his essay is faithful to his vision of it.

donde, por ejemplo, el estilo policromo del Valle del Ulua, está lleno de aportes Mayas. En cambio parécenos que las civilizaciones de las Antillas y la mayor parte de Venezuela pertenecen a otro grupo, en el que deben incluirse las de bajo Amazonas (Marajo, Santarem) y el alto Napo.

El nombre que se ha dado de Circum-caribeano, nos parece, pues, poco exacto, y como la designación geográfica Sur de Centro América y Noroeste de la Meridional, aún cuando tiene la ventaja de no prejuzgar nada es demasiado larga, preferimos llamar a esta división cultural "Zona Chibcha," en efecto en este inmenso territorio a la época de la Conquista Española habían tribus que hablaban idiomas pertenecientes a la familia lingüística Chibcha o al Phylum Macro-Chibcha y hay razones de mucho peso para creer que en tiempos más antiguos casi ocupaban sin interrupción toda esta bastísima zona.

Creemos haber demostrado que existe parentesco entre las lenguas del Phylum Macro-Chibcha y las de Hokan y hemos constituído el Super Phylum Macro-Chibcha-Hokan (145, pp. 239–477).

El inmenso territorio de los pueblos Chibchas, propiamente tales, dejó de ser continuo en virtud de movimientos de pueblos que se pueden comprobar en virtud de fuentes históricos aún prescindiendo de las arqueológicas. En el Norte tenemos las penetraciones Nahuas y Nahuatles, que van dejando una cadena de colonias hasta el mismo Istmo de Panama; los Cholutecas de Honduras, los Mangues de Nicaragua y los Orotiñas de Nicoya, demuestran otra invasión del Norte al Sur de los Otomangues (185, II, 789 ff.).

En Colombia se puede constatar otra invasión que duró siglos y estaba aún verificándose cuando Andagoya exploró, por vez primera en 1829, la Costa, la de los Caribes, que penetrando por el Oriente, especialmente por la abra que queda entre el extremo septentrional de la Cordillera Oriental de los Andes y la Sierra Nevada de Santa Marta fueron paulatinamente ocupando la parte baja de los Valles del Cauca y el Magdalena, hasta que desbordándose sobre la Cordillera Occidental y desparramándose por la Hoya de Atrato, llegaron al Pacífico. La antigüedad relativa de estas varias invasiones se mide por el grado en que las lenguas se han diversificado.

Esta invasión Caribe afectó profundamente la etnografía de Colombia, rompiendo la unidad de los pueblos Chibchas, pero como fué muy lenta y el pueblo invasor que era el de cultura más rudimentaria, adoptó muchos de los elementos de la civilización de los conquistados. Una civilización Caribe con débiles influencias Chibchas es la que nos muestran los hallazgos del Valle del Magdalena (278, pp. 210–11; 151); en cambio ciertos artefactos de la región Quimbaya corresponden a una cultura Chibcha con influencias Caribes.

Otra invasión Caribe, mas reciente y de menos envergadura, es aquella a que se debe la presencia de los Patagoenes en Jaén (145, III, 845). Los Jíbaros pueblo cuya cultura tiene mucho que ver con la Chibcha, pero cuya lengua, hasta hoy, no clasificada en ninguna de las grandes familias lingüísticas, pero que tiene un vocabulario fuertemente Arawaquisado, rompiendo la unidad de los pueblos

Muratos, penetraron desde el Oriente en las Hoyas del Pastaza, el Morona y Santiago, arrinconando a los Muratos y Shapras en ciertos afluentes del Pastaza y el Tigre a los Chirinos y Sacatas en Jaén y por Zamora penetraron en el Callejón Interandino, donde son conocidos con el nombre de Paltas.

Sería incompleta esta enumeración si no mencionamos la invasión Quechua, hecho histórico bien conocido, que, llevó el Imperio Incaico, la organización Cuzqueña hasta el Sur de Colombia.

El conocimiento científico del desarrollo de las civilizaciones Andinas, basado no en tradiciones ni leyendas, sino en estudios arqueológicos cuyos fundamentos estableció Uhle en 1903, puede decirse que, en líneas generales, estuvo ya precisado entre 1904 y 1908, aún cuando los fundamentos de sus deducciones sólo los diera a conocer, si bien someramente, en 1912 y 1913, por los cuales la Universidad de California revisó las colecciones hechas por el arqueólogo Alemán, confirmándose así su esquema cronológico, al cual los últimos estudios han añadido nuevos períodos más remotos.

Para 1921 habíamos nosotros establecido el cuadro general de la cronología de las civilizaciones prehistóricas del Ecuador.

En cambio, si los monumentos arquitectónicos del País Maya y México y las tradiciones mesoamericanas habían sido estudiados por grandes arqueólogos, el conocimiento del desarrollo histórico de las viejas civilizaciones, puede decirse, se inicia sólo en 1912 y tenemos que esperar hasta 1930 para conocer, en algún detalle, las más antiguas culturas del Valle de México (400) y a 1936 para obtener información acerca del historia de la alfarería Maya (311 y 312).

Desde que en 1914 publicamos nuestro segundo escrito sobre arqueología ecuatoriana, advertimos las claras afinidades que hay entre las culturas del Ecuador y las del Sur de Centro-America (144, pp. 328–30).

El Dr. Max Uhle desde que inició sus exploraciones arqueológicas en el Ecuador, advirtió las grandes conecciones que existían entre las culturas ecuatorianas y las de América Central, lo que le llevó a postular una serie de migraciones Mayas y Toltecas, que habrán sido también las productoras de las civilizaciones más antiguas del Perú y Bolivia (387, 389, 390).

Nosotros, al advertir que las tres más antiguas culturas del Ecuador estaban caracterizadas por elementos que, encontrándose en las civilizaciones del Sur de Centro-América son extraños a las Andinas, en donde, cuando se hallan, se ve claramente que representan influencias e irradiaciones partidas de la Sierra o la Costa ecuatoriana. Al observar que esos mismos elementos, generalmente en una forma muy elaborada, se encuentran también en las culturas de Mesoamérica, pensamos que eran originarios de éstas últimas. Más el ser ellas mejor conocidas en la profundidad de su desarrollo histórico, apareció claramente que muchos eran tan exóticos en las civilizaciones mesoamericanas como en las Andinas, por lo cual hemos llegado a la conclusión lógica de que siendo oriundos de el territorio Chibcha, se propagaron hacia el Norte y el Sur, más intensamente al septentrión, siendo elementos fecundantes de las culturas de Mesoamérica.

Pero antes de seguir adelante queremos poner en claro nuestro modo de pensar:

1. La población del Nuevo Mundo se verificó del Norte hacia el Sur y, como prueba de ello, quedan en el extremo meridional del continente y en algunos otros parajes, especialmente en el Chaco, ciertos elementos culturales que también se encuentran en el septentrional, que, por su naturaleza y por las tribus en que se ocurren, se ve que datan de una época muy remota, anterior al conocimiento de la agricultura (253, pp. 1–15).

2. Los pueblos Chibchas, principales pobladores del Sur de Centro-América y el Noroeste de Sud América, debieron, en un tiempo, atravesar México, como lo comprueba la afinidad del Phylum Macro-Chibcha con el Hokan, produciéndose la separación de los unos de los otros cuando ya conocían el maíz, cultivado, o salvaje (145, IV, 339 y 342).

3. La agricultura no ha tenido un origen único y unitario en América; diversas plantas fueron domesticadas, independientemente, en distintos parajes. La agricultura de la zona de las civilizaciones Andinas se inicia sin el conocimiento del maíz (60, pp. 23 y 24).

4. Existen en el Norte, Centro- y Sud América una serie de elementos comunes, propios de una civilización agrícola, basada especialmente en el cultivo del maíz. Estos, de los que no nos ocuparemos y que sólo nos limitaremos a enumerar unos pocos, son comunes a Mesoamérica, el Noroeste de Sud América, las Antillas, el Este de los Estados Unidos, y la zona Andina de la América Meridional. Mencionaremos: (a) el cultivo del maíz; (b) la construcción de pirámides para fines de culto; (c) la existencia de centros ceremoniales.

Cual sea el centro donde se originó y desde el cual se propagó esta cultura, lo desconocemos, pero debe ser aquel en que se domesticó el maíz. Dos teoras principales se han enunciado: según la una, sería oriundo de las serranías, occidentales de Guatemala; según la otra, de Sud América, específicamente del Paraguay, la que debe ser excluída, pues repugna a todo lo que se conoce del desarrollo histórico de los aborígines americanos. Ultimamente, basándose especialmente en razones lingüísticas, Birket-Smith ha postulado que el origen del maíz debe buscarse en Colombia (28).

5. Una diversificación de esta cultura se produjo en el Sur de la América Central y en el Noroeste de la Meridional, la que influye en el desarrollo de las vecinas del Norte y del Sur, la Mesoamericana y la Andina.

6. Las culturas propias de los pueblos Chibcha recibieron, a su vez, en distintos tiempos aportes de Mesoamérica.

Para presentar algunas pruebas de las dos últimas afirmaciones es preciso fijar la posición cronológica de las civilizaciones del Sur de la América Central y el Noroeste de la Meridional; desgraciadamente sólo tenemos datos estratigráficos para hacerlo, relativos a la extremidad septentrional y Sur del area en cuestión, e indicios fundados, para, en Colombia, considerar como las civilizaciones más antiguas la de San Augustín de Timana, en donde hay que distinguir dos etapas: primero, la de la cerámica más profunda del montículo Noroeste de la Meseta B (264, pp. 72–81), a la que deben pertenecer las clásicas estatuas de piedra; y segundo, la de Tierra Adentro, en cuanto está caracterizada por las "tumbas pintadas" y la alfarería con ornamentos grabados rellenos de pintura blanca. Estas dos civilizaciones deben haber sido coetáneas, como lo demuestran el mascarón de oro de Inzá (265, Lam. XII), y un vaso del estilo de Tierra Adentro de una tumba del Alto de Lavapatas, en San Augustín (264, p. 103, Fig. 108).

Entre las estatuas de San Augustín, el mascaron de Inzá y las esculturas de Chavín, hay indudable semejanza que sugiere, por lo menos, relativa coetaneidad.

Las otras culturas colombianas pueden datarse, con probabilidad, en comparación con la cronología de las del Ecuador.

En el extremo Norte del área que nos interesa, tenemos tres cerámicas de la época "formativa," a saber, "Yojoa Monocromo," "Playa de los Muertos," y "Ulua Bicromo," seguidas en el tiempo por "Ulua Yoja Policromo," "Ulua, estilo geométrico fuerte," "Ulua Mayoide" que son más o menos coetanos, a los que sustituyen "Ulua-Comayagua Policromo" y por último "Naco," que es el contemporáneo con la Conquista. Con el "Ulua Bicromo" se asocia la cerámica más antigua del Salvador la de "Usulatán" (196, pp. 391–92; 331, cuadro; 330, pp. 87–99).

Presentamos el cuadro cronológico de las culturas ecuatorianas, tal cual resulta de nuestras estudios a la fecha.

En Babahoyo el Profesor Huerta Rendón encontró, con alfarería Chaullabamba, un fragmento Cupisnique y otro de Chavín de la Sierra. En Loja, Uhle excavó un templo, el de Chinguilanchi, que contiene alfarería Chaullabamba, en el que se encontró una estatuilla de animal de puro estilo Chavín. La alfarería de las "Sillas de Barro" de Narrío que Collier y Murra llaman grupo "Intrusivo X," y que está representada en Alausí y Macas (96, Lams. 5, Figs. 1–13; 6; 7; 31; 32; 33; 34, Figs. 3–14) presenta una casi perfecta identidad con la que en el Valle de Huallaga se encontró mezclada con clásica cerámica Chavín (346, Lam. 19). Algunos de los dibujos de la alfarería del período de los "Sellos cilíndricos de Manabí" son malas copias de motivos de Chavín (389, Lam. 7, Figs. 2 y 2a).

Con la cerámica de Ilumán hay un vaso muy parecido a los de Salinar.

La alfarería del período de Tuncahuán pertenece al mismo estilo horizonte que la de Recuay y la Proto-Lima "Interlocking." En Manta extrajimos en la última capa del período de Tuncahuán, un fragmento "Cajamarquilla." Hace Años publicamos una lista de artefactos Tiahuanaquenses encontrados en el Ecuador (144, pp. 333–34 n.) y después probamos la contemporaneidad del período de Guano con Tiahuanaco (144, Lams. 40, Fig. 1; 47; 48, Figs. 1–3).

Cronología Prehistórica del Ecuador

	SIERRA					COSTA			AMAZONIA		
PASTO	CARANQUI	PANZALEO	PURUHA	CAÑAR	PALTA	ESMERALDE-ÑOS	MANABITAS	HUANCAVIL-CAS	QUIJOS	JIBAROS	PERU, COSTA N.
?	?	Proto-Panzaleo I A / Proto-Panzaleo I B	Proto-Panzaleo I A	Proto-Pan zaleo I A	Proto-Pan zaleo I A	?	Proto-Pan zaleo I	Proto-Pan zaleo I	?	?	Agricultores pre-ceramista — Huaca—Prieta
?	?	Proto-Panzaleo II	Proto-Panzaleo II / Chaullabamba	(Uchucay, Monjas-huaico) / Narrio antiguo	Proto-Pan zaleo II / Chaullabamba / Chinguilanchi	?	Proto-Pan zaleo II / Chaullabamba (Manta)	Chaullabamba (Babahoyo)	?	Chaullabamba (Sillas de barro)	Chavin / Cupisnique
		PROTO-PANZALEO II	PROTO-PANZALEO II	SILLAS DE BARRO	PALTA	SILLOS CILINDRICOS	SELLOS CILINDRICOS	?	?		
Alfarería campos distintos colores, grabada	Ilumán							?			Salinar
Tuncahuán	?	Panzaleo I	Tuncahuán	Tuncahuán		Tuncahuán	Tuncahuán				Gallinazo / Pro Lima / Interlocking
Negativa	Negativa	Panzaleo II	Guano	Tacalshapa				Guagalá			Proto-Chimú
											Tiahuanaco
Cuashmal I	Cuashmal		Elen-Pata					Engoroy	Panzaleo II		
Cuashmal II	Tolas					TOLITA	MANTEÑO			PALTA	Chimú
		Panzaleo III	Huavalac	Cañari moderno				Manteño	Panzaleo III		
				Incaico	Incaico						
Incaico	Incaico	Incaico	Incaico				Incaico	Incaico	Incaico		Incaico

El haberse encontrado en Imbabura un vaso "Thin Orange" permite establecer relaciones entre el período Negativo del Carchi e Imbabura, con la época "Esperanza" de Guatemala (149, pp. 226-28).

A base, pues, de las edades establecidas para las culturas del Sur de Centro América y Noroeste de la Meridional podemos señalar la influencia que éstas ejercen en las de Mesoamérica.

La civilización de Proto-Panzaleo I-A nos ofrece de los doce elementos que se estiman como característicos de lo que Lothrop y Vaillant llaman el complejo "Q" (394, p. 90) los siguientes: (2°) vasos efigies sea modelados o con extremidades pastilladas (147, Lam. 6, Figs. 1-4); (4°) vasos decorados por pastillaje (147, Lam. 6, Figs. 1, 3, 5, 7, 10), modelado (147, Lam. 6, Fig. 4), incisiones (147, Lams. 7-10), pulimento (Proto-Panzaleo I-B) a la virtual exclusión de la pintura (147, pp. 16-19); (6°) vasijas trébedes de pies alargados (147, Lam. 5, Fig. 10); (7°) platos sobre altas bases anulares cilíndricas—compoteras (147, Lam. 5, Fig. 9).

Creemos que se puede demostrar como de los doce elementos constitutivos del Complejo "Q," diez se encuentran en las más viejas culturas del Ecuador, y que en ellas se asocian con otros, que igualmente parecen oriundos del país Chibcha, por lo cual creemos poder afirmar que aquel conjunto que Vaillant y Lothrop llamaron "Q" y que tanto influye en la formación de las culturas de México y el país Maya, es originario del Sur de Centro América y del Noroeste de la Meridional.

Al mismo tiempo hemos aportado pruebas de influencias Mesoamericanas en el Ecuador, éstas, para épocas más tardías, podríamos multiplicarlas, encontrando especialmente, que corresponden en buena parte, a un tiempo en que ya se habían mezclado elementos Teotihuanacos y Mayas.

A PRELIMINARY REPORT ON THE MONAGRILLO CULTURE OF PANAMA

Gordon R. Willey

INTRODUCTORY STATEMENT

In recent years archeologists studying the problems of prehistoric American civilizations in Middle and South America have become increasingly interested in the earlier, simpler cultures which underlie the more spectacular and later developments. Presumably, these underlying, less specialized cultures formed the bases out of which grew such regional florescences as the Maya or Mochica. The earlier, basic cultures have been referred to, both in Central America and the Andean area, as the Formative Periods.[1] It is evident that, no matter where they occur, they bear a close functional-developmental similarity to each other. It remains to be demonstrated whether these similarities between Middle and South American Formative Periods are no more than developmental parallelisms or whether they are the result of historical interconnections. Future field researches should eventually clarify this point of historical relationships. Certainly, one of the most important immediate objectives for this research is the continued exploration of the vast territory intervening between the Maya frontier and northern Peru. The present paper is concerned with this interlying region, specifically with Panama. It is offered to place upon record a newly discovered archeological complex that appears to be Formative in type.

In 1948 a series of archeological excavations were conducted in western Panama under the sponsorship of a joint Smithsonian Institution–National Geographic expedition. The field party was headed by Dr. M. W. Stirling, Director of the Bureau of American Ethnology, who was assisted by the writer. In a three month period exploratory and strati-pit diggings were made at four sites in the vicinity of Parita near the base of the Azuero Peninsula (Fig. 1). The country around Parita, except for the immediate coast, is tropical hill terrain under the one thousand foot elevation mark. Today it is semi-open and used for cattle grazing although agriculture is extensively practiced, particularly along the numerous rivers. There is a marked seasonal variation in the climate with the months from January to May being warm, windy, and dry while the remainder of the year is rainy and hot. The site with which we are particularly concerned is located near the sea in the coastal strip of desert-like wastes, salt flats, and mangrove swamps.

1. This term has been used by several writers. See Thompson (373, 374); Larco (179); Armillas (17); Strong (332); Steward (324); and Willey (413). Larco uses the name "Evolutiva," but the concept is much the same.

173

THE SITE AND EXCAVATIONS

The Monagrillo shell mound, near the modern town of the same name, lies on the edge of a saline flat a little over a kilometer from the sea near the mouth of the Parita River (Fig. 1). The salt flats that surround the site were wet and muddy at the time of our visit, although they are subject to tidal fluctuation and during parts of the dry season are dry and sun-baked. They are devoid of any vegetation except for a mangrove fringe which follows along the coast and borders the Parita River. About 200 meters south and west of the mound is the dry ground of the mainland. Rising only a meter or so higher than the salt flats, it is connected to the mound by a natural ridge. The mainland here is flat and semiarid, sustaining largely xerophytic trees and cactus. This type of landscape prevails for two or three kilometers as one goes inland before it is replaced by the more fertile clay hills and potreros.

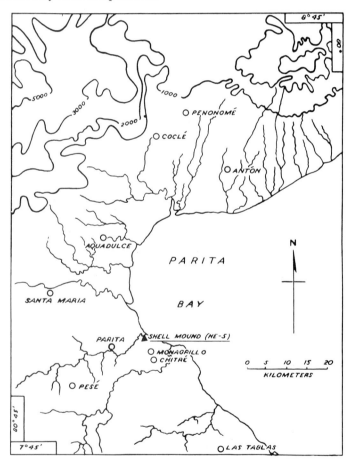

Fig. 1.—Map of the Parita region at the base of the Azuero peninsula, Panama. The Monagrillo shell mound site is indicated by the black triangle.

The appearance of the shell mound site suggests that there has been ecological change since aboriginal occupancy. Today, the closest source of shellfish is the ocean, over a kilometer distant. It seems likely that the site was originally selected as a shellfishing station, probably as a conveniently located small spur jutting out from the mainland, or as a periodically connected island. If this were the case, the surrounding salt flats must have once been a marsh or lagoon in which shellfish were obtainable. Their nearly dry condition at the present time would, thus, argue for a filling in of the marsh, a land rise, or a sea subsidence. Competent geological opinion[2] offers the first interpretation, that of filling as the result of alluvial action by the Parita River.

The shell mound rises between 1.5 and 2.00 meters above the surrounding flats, and the midden refuse has an extent of about 170 meters east-west by 50 meters north-south. Two principal refuse deposits form parallel ridges running along the long axis of the site. Eight stratigraphic pits were opened on the south ridge, and another series of tests was run at right angles to these, cutting across the north refuse ridge. Additional pits were also put down at random.

In general, excavation profiles presented, from the surface down, the following physical stratification: 40 cm. of compact shell; 80 cm. of shell and sand with scattered shell lenses; 40 cm. of virtually sterile brown sand; 30 cm. of shells, sand, and rocks partially solidified into a sort of coquina; and the sterile grey clay or basic subsoil.[3] In some places the deposits were deeper than 2.00 meters, in others shallower. Water was encountered at varying depths, depending upon the height of the mound, and the coquina-like or conglomeritic condition of the shells, rocks, and sand in the lowest refuse layer was undoubtedly due to the seasonal fluctuation of the water table.

Potsherds were, in all pits, more numerous in the upper 50 to 75 cm. In these levels the shell was also more abundant, more tightly packed, and mixed with blacker, heavier refuse earth. The brown sand stratum, beneath the upper midden layer, was almost, but not completely, sterile of cultural material. Its appearance and consistency are alluvial. Water-worn sherds were found in the shell and rock stratum underlying the brown sand, and numerous pebbles and small boulders in this layer look like river material. Apparently an early, thin midden layer had been disturbed by flooding and then silted over.

In all of the excavations at the Monagrillo site, most of which were carried

2. Dr. W. P. Woodring, U.S. Geological Survey, as of April, 1949.

3. Whole and crushed shell was found at all levels but, as stated, was more common toward the top of the refuse. A great number of species were recovered. Among the more common were *Ostrea chilensis*, *Anadara grandis*, *Scapharca concinna*, *Melongena patula*, *Tivela gracilior*, and *Chione asperrima*. These and other shells found in the site have been identified as to species by Dr. Tucker Abbott, of the Division of Mollusks, U.S. National Museum. Dr. Abbott is of the opinion that all species are still found today in Panamanian waters. This conflicts with Dr. Nils Ohdner's statement (see Linne, 190, p. 129) to the effect that *Ostrea chilensis*, as found in archeological sites on the Pearl Islands, were no longer native to waters north of Ecuador. Animal bones were scattered through the refuse at all depths although they were not numerous. Most of these were deer and peccary bones.

down to the underlying subsoil, no definite house features such as floors or fire basins were encountered. Occasional lenses of ash and charcoal did, however, indicate fires. No burials were located nor was any scrap of human bone found in the midden.

CERAMIC TYPES AND ARTIFACTS

The predominant ware at the shell mound I have called the Monagrillo. It consists of three types: Plain, Incised, and Red Painted. All three are closely related in features of rim and vessel form and in paste, temper, and firing. The ware is coiled. The paste texture is homogeneous and sandy. In many specimens medium to coarse sand was the principal tempering material, but crushed quartz was also used as an aplastic.[4] The firing is uneven and the most common surface color is a mottled buff; however, some sherds are brick-red while others are grey-black. Ware thickness averages 8 mm. and hardness is 4.5 to 5 on the Moh scale. Surfaces are usually well-smoothed, particularly the exteriors. There are three principal rim silhouettes. The most common is a very slightly incurved form from a wide-mouthed jar or deep bowl (Fig. 2, *a–g*). Less common is a markedly incurved type, obviously from a sub-globular bowl (Fig. 2, *h–k*). Also present is an outslanted rim shape from an open bowl or shallow bowl (Fig. 2, *l–q*). Only one recurved or flared rim was found in several thousand sherds. Most rims are unmodified at the lip (Fig. 3, *i*), but there are some with exterior folds (Fig. 2, *r–w;* Fig. 3, *j*). Folds occur on all three of the main rim forms.

The type Monagrillo Incised is decorated with both broad and fine lines. Deep pits or punctuations effect terminations of lines (Fig. 3, *a, c*). Incisions appear to have been made after the paste was extremely dry but before firing. Designs are predominantly curvilinear and rather intricate. The spiral and scroll are the most common motives (Fig. 3, *a, b*). Horizontal parallel lines serve as background fields to other designs. Occasional areas of the vessel surface have been carved out (Fig. 3, *e*). There are also complex motives, not fully comprehended, which combine bars, triangles, and series of curved parallel lines (Fig. 3, *c, d*). There is one example of a series of close-spaced, short incisions lying transversely within a deep groove (Fig. 3, *f*). All incised decoration is placed on the vessel exteriors and was, probably, arranged in a band below the rim. Execution of designs is neither perfect nor slovenly.

The type Monagrillo Red is decorated with a carmine pigment which has been set by firing although, in some instances, it has partially weathered away. The pigment was applied to the complete vessel exterior, to portions of the exterior, to all or portions of the interior, and in vertical and horizontal bands on either surface (Fig. 3, *h*).

Although complete stratigraphic analysis of types is not yet available, we know that Monagrillo Incised is found consistently in the upper levels. Monagrillo Red, on the other hand, seems to have had an earlier inception. Mo-

4. Identified by Dr. E. P. Henderson, Department of Geology, U.S. National Museum.

nagrillo Plain, which makes up over 95 per cent of the pottery from the site, runs from top to bottom, including the lowest shell midden layer lying beneath the alluvial sand.

As opposed to the several thousand Monagrillo sherds, there were found at the site about 100 plain fragments of a quite different ware. This has been called El Tigre Plain (Fig. 3, *k*). It is a heavier, coarser ceramic than the Monagrillo, and the paste is often contorted and less compact. Temper particles of heavy sand extrude through on the vessel surfaces which are poorly smoothed. It is unevenly fired and the color of both surface and core ranges from brick-red to grey-black. Average thickness is 11 mm. The vessels are consistently larger than those of the Monagrillo series. Large collared jars or ollas (Fig. 2, *x*), deep

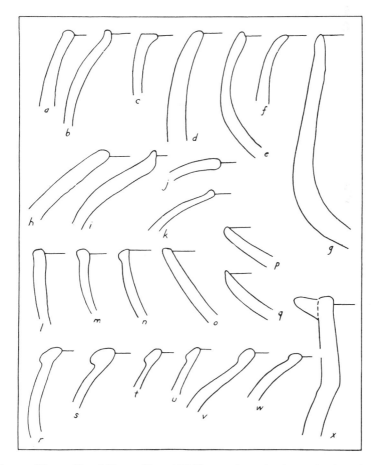

Fig. 2.—Rim profiles of Monagrillo and El Tigre style potsherds. *a–f*, bowls with slightly inturned rims (Monagrillo); *h–k*, sub-globular bowls (Monagrillo); *l–p*, open bowls or bowls with outslanting rims (Monagrillo); *r–w*, folded or thickened rims (Monagrillo); *x*, large collared jar with rim lug (El Tigre).

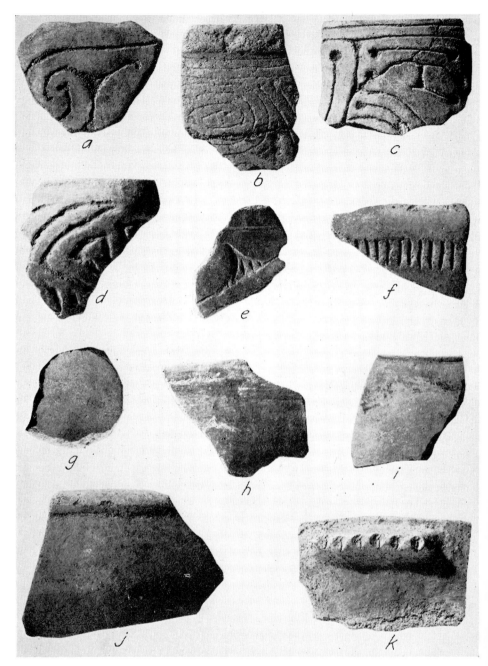

FIG. 3.—Monagrillo and El Tigre pottery sherds. *a–f,* Monagrillo incised, sherd *d* is red-slipped; *g,* Monagrillo plain jar base or coiling pat; *h,* Monagrillo red; this sherd has a rim with an attached vertical band; *i, j,* Monagrillo plain rim sherds; *k,* El Tigre plain rim sherd and lug.

bowls or pots with straight or incurved rims, and deep open bowls are the typical vessel forms. Rims are unmodified but appendages are present in the form of heavy horizontal lugs placed at or just below the level of the lip. These lugs are usually fluted or indented (Fig. 3, k). One large loop handle of this ware type was also found.

The El Tigre Plain sherds were found in only two or three of the excavations, and in these they were confined to the top 25 cm. of the refuse. Aside from this, the remainder of El Tigre Plain from the Monagrillo site came from the surface collections.[5] From its stratigraphic position it is clear that El Tigre Plain is a later type than those of the Monagrillo series. Its radically different appearance suggests that El Tigre did not develop out of Monagrillo but is the result of a later and briefer reoccupation of the shell mound.

A few chipped and ground stone artifacts were found both on the surface of the shell heap and at varying depths in the rubbish. This distribution in the site implies an association with the Monagrillo rather than the El Tigre ware. The only definite flint implement was an end and side-scraper. These are an unspecialized, plano-convex form, made of chert and jasper and ranging from 3.5 to 6 cm. in length. The chipping is largely primary and may be percussion. Ground stone tools include a slab-shaped pounder, spherical pebble hammers, and some simple pestles. The latter are relatively short and four- or five-sided in cross-section. They are made of dioritic and volcanic rocks.[6] Two large worked stones were found on the surface. One of these had a deep concavity on one face and must have been a mortar or "saddle-stone."

COMPARISONS

The most striking thing about the Monagrillo assemblage is its typological isolation from known Panamanian cultures. It stands in sharp contrast to Coclé, Veraguas, and Chiriquí with their ornate ceramics, stone carving, and metallurgy.[7] In southern Panama, in Darien and on the Pearl Islands, Linne reports incised pottery styles associated with various stone artifacts (190). Some of these sites resemble the Monagrillo complex in the presence of stone mortars, pestles, and stone ball hammers (Linne, 190, see Saboga, Site 2 and Casaya, Site 3, pp. 80–81 and 89); however, the Darien and island sites also possess the stone celt, an artifact type not found at Monagrillo. Moreover, the Darien and early Pearl Island pottery, although incised, differs significantly

5. It should be mentioned in this connection that El Tigre Plain was found at another, smaller shell refuse deposit in the salt flats. This site, He-13, located 300 meters northeast of the Monagrillo heap, covers an equal area but appears to be much more superficial. In the surface collection from He-13 El Tigre Plain was the only type represented.

6. Identification by Dr. E. P. Henderson, Department of Geology, U.S. National Museum.

7. This contrast is, perhaps, emphasized by the fact that no grave materials were found at Monagrillo; yet, even so, it is difficult to imagine that even the hypothetical special manufactures of the Monagrillo culture would have approached any of the above-named three in excellence.

from Monagrillo in the presence of relief modelling, ring bases, handles, and compound silhouette forms. Nor are the Monagrillo decorative motives duplicated in the materials illustrated from Darien.

Going further afield, I know of no pottery style that could be said to be closely related to the Monagrillo; however, there are some general similarities to early incised ceramics of the Chavín horizon in Peru (Bennett, 37, pp. 81–87; Strong, 334, Pl. 48). These are seen in both simplicity of vessel forms and in decorative techniques, although not in elements of design. Vaguely suggestive similarities are also seen in the early bold-line incised potteries of Honduras (Strong, Kidder, and Paul, 335, Pls. 9, 10), Mexico (Ekholm, 114, Fig. 28), and even the southeastern United States; but again it is largely a matter of constructional simplicity and decorative technique rather than specific style. Perhaps the closest similarities in actual designs are seen in the Los Barrancos incised ware of the earliest horizon on the Lower Orinoco in Venezuela (Osgood and Howard, 256, pp. 99 and 106; also personal communication, C. Osgood and I. Rouse, April, 1949). The Monagrillo scroll or hook designs, the lines ending in deep punctations, and the carved-out triangular areas are all matched in Los Barrancos; but Los Barrancos pottery features modelled effigy adornos, handles, and ring bases, none of which are seen in the relatively simpler Monagrillo style.

SUMMARY

A shell heap in western Panama, near the mouth of the Parita River, has disclosed a cultural complex heretofore unknown in the Isthmian region. From the ecological setting of the site it is believed that it was once a fishing station in a marsh, and that it was occupied by a people who depended to a large extent upon marine foods. The complex, here named the "Monagrillo," is characterized by simple flint scrapers, stone mortars and pestles, stone ball hammers, and plain, incised, and red painted pottery of a very simple sort. On the surface and in the upper levels of the site is a ware named "El Tigre." This is a different ceramic tradition than the Monagrillo, and it seems likely that the El Tigre material represents a later reoccupation of the site. The Monagrillo culture complex is significantly unlike any other previously discovered in Panama. Its typological uniqueness, together with the environmental situation of the site, imply antiquity. Quite probably Monagrillo is the earliest ceramic complex known for the region. Monagrillo pottery has general technological similarities to Formative Period ware in Peru, Honduras, Mexico, and the southeastern United States. It has somewhat greater, although not close, resemblances to some of the incised pottery of an early Venezuelan pottery horizon. It appears to represent another regional expression of Formative Period ceramics in the Americas.

LA REPRESENTACIÓN AVE, SÍMBOLO DEL DIOS SUA: EL DIOS SOL ENTRE LOS CHIBCHA DE COLOMBIA

Edith Jiménez de Muñoz

Convencida como estoy de la complejidad del problema, sólo aspiro a dar a conocer el resultado de algunas observaciones hechas en colecciones de objetos de la cultura material de los Chibcha que habitaron los departamentos de Cundinamarca, Boyacá y Santander.

PRIMERA PARTE

I. ARTE REPRESENTATIVO DE LOS CHIBCHA

Los utensilios y armas, tejidos y adornos, presentan un material ornamental, abundante más que en formas, en composiciones bellas. Sobre las superficies aparecen los temas iconográficos pintados, grabados o modelados, con rasgos naturalistas los unos, esquemáticos y estilizados los otros. La distribución es sencilla y elegante.

A primera vista se puede juzgar que las imágenes fueron creadas con una intención ornamental. Reunen condiciones suficientes para producir una sensación de belleza. En este sentido cumplen su papel de temas decorativos.

Pero si observamos los detalles de las composiciones ornamentales, nos damos cuenta de que el valor decorativo no es el único que tienen. Su mérito no está solamente en la forma de las representaciones, ni en la combinación de los temas en la superficie que decoran. Está principalmente en el contenido emocional que poseen, vertido en formas·tangibles, simples y poco realistas Las imágenes son verdaderos estímulos que provocan reacciones de tipo espiritual. Los detalles que nos ofrecen los objetos mismos, asociados a otros que se relacionan con su uso en determinadas ocasiones, nos hablan con evidencia de este carácter de las representaciones chibchas. La frecuencia de una imagen en especiales objetos, la presencia de estos objetos en unas determinadas ceremonias, dedicadas a una conocida divinidad, y la relación etimológica del nombre de la divinidad con el nombre del tema representado, nos llevan a la conclusión de que las imágenes plásticas o pintadas corresponden a un ser superior, a quien se rinde un culto. Ellas ponen de presente una gran sensibilidad espiritual que subordina, a la vida mágico-religiosa, las demás manifestaciones de la conducta humana. Son, pues, símbolos de valores espirituales, expresados en formas muy simples.

Además de tener un contenido representativo, las imágenes chibchas presentan otras características cuyo conocimiento puede ayudar a la identificación de los temas autóctonos. Por ejemplo:

1. Las imágenes son símbolos de conceptos abstractos. La mitología ha sido la fuente inagotable de estas imágenes. Crea sus personajes y al mismo tiempo escoge los símbolos representativos, en las formas reales de la naturaleza. Es esta la razón por la cual, aparecen representaciones de animales como símbolos de sus creaciones. Crea un dios con atributos variados que lo hacen superior a los seres humanos y a los animales. La imagen simbólica que para él ha escogido, a pesar de que se inspire en formas naturalistas, aparece irreal por cuanto que en ella se hacen visibles atributos de varios seres, por ejemplo, en la representación de un gato montés, coronado con plumas. Si juzgamos esta imagen con un criterio de naturalismo la encontramos monstruosa y sin explicación. Pero si tenemos en cuenta que es el símbolo de una divinidad del panteón chibcha, nos explicamos en seguida el significado de las plumas que lleva en la cabeza. No se trata de un gato montés común. Se trata de la representación simbólica de una divinidad resplandeciente y es por esto por lo que se ha agregado, a la representación simbólica gato montés, el símbolo de la luz (plumas de ave). Esta clase de imágenes se presentan con frecuencia como símbolos de las divinidades que amparan y protegen al pueblo.

2. La estilización de los símbolos se lleva hasta los simples esquemas y sencillos esbozos. Mas frecuentemente en formas geometrizadas.

Las composiciones decorativas impresionan como asociaciones de elementos geométricos. Las espirales alternan con los triángulos, con las circunferencias y las paralelas. Las unidades temáticas se pueden identificar mediante el reconocimiento de determinados elementos, asociados de la misma manera. El tema ⟨⟨ puede servir de ejemplo. Dos triángulos y una espiral lo caracterizan en seguida. Así se repite centenares de veces. El hallazgo de la figura que le dió origen ⟨⟨ ha permitido su identificación, como de un esquema simple de un símbolo del ave.

Las imágenes desprovistas de los rasgos naturalistas son las que predominan en la iconografía chibcha. En ellas solamente se conservan elementos, que a juicio del artista, son los necesarios para identificar el tema, con todo su significado emotivo. De esta manera, las representaciones reducidas a formas mínimas conservan todo el valor de la representación naturalista. El efecto puramente formal cede el campo al efecto emotivo, logrado con símbolos de una máxima simplicidad.

3. Abundan las imágenes de perfil: Cuando se trata de representar figuras zoomorfas, bien en su forma naturalista, o bien con símbolos desprovistos de rasgos realistas, la iconografía es rica en representaciones de los seres vistos de perfil. Las imágenes del ave y del gato montés pueden servir de ejemplo. Las de este último lo presentan en actitud de saltar, en el momento en que dobla sus extremidades y arquea el cuerpo para lograr un mayor impulso en el salto.

II. FUENTES DE LOS MOTIVOS DECORATIVOS

La naturaleza fué, sin duda, la inspiradora de los motivos decorativos. Especialmente en lo que dice relación con las formas iconográficas; porque comprobado está que los chibchas no representaron los seres de la naturaleza sino como símbolos de otros y sus representaciones las utilizaron en las composiciones ornamentales como temas representativos.

Teniendo en cuenta lo anteriormente enunciado, pueden agruparse los temas tratados en tres grandes grupos: zoomorfos, fitomorfos y antropomorfos.

Zoomorfos.—Son los más numerosos y preferidos de los aborígenes. Entre los Chibcha esta tendencia tiene sus raíces en una primitiva organización totémica.

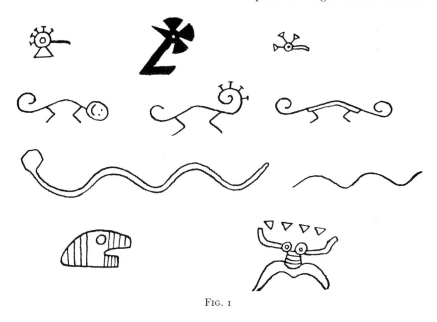

FIG. I

En la representación de los dioses y semidioses, los temas zoomorfos tienen una gran importancia. Ellos expresan la figura de las deidades y proporcionan los recursos suficientes para expresar los atributos que la mitología crea para sus fantásticos personajes.

Con el tema ave, el central de la mitología chibcha, alternan otros temas entre los cuales están: rana, serpiente, lagarto, pez, y gato montés.

Fitomorfos.—Son los menos comunes en las representaciones gráficas y plásticas. En algunas piezas de orfebrería pueden reconocerse formas de flores campanulares. La ausencia de formas fitomorfas posiblemente obedece a la costumbre de aprovechar los frutos y las flores en su estado natural, para adornos en las fiestas y ceremonias.

Antropomorfos.—De preferencia la cara humana. Estos temas son menos frecuentes que los zoomorfos, pero sí en mayor número que los fitomorfos. Algunas representaciones aparecen con todos los rasgos naturalistas; en otras, el artista juzgó que podía suprimirlos hasta el punto de representar la cara con un triángulo isóceles, cuyo vértice se encuentra hacia arriba.

SEGUNDA PARTE

EL AVE EN SUS REPRESENTACIONES MÁS FRECUENTES, DESDE LA FORMA NATURALISTA HASTA LA SIMPLE ESTILIZACIÓN

El tema más importante de la iconografía chibcha es, sin duda, el ave. Aparece en las formas más variadas, en combinación con la representación de otros seres preferentemente de la figura humana.

Con las imágenes del ave, identificadas hasta hoy, se han formado ocho series que muestran el proceso de desnaturalización de la representación realista.

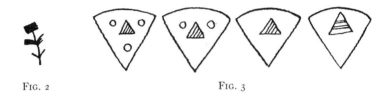

Fig. 2   Fig. 3

Las figuras que inician las series reproducen con claridad el motivo ave. Solamente la que inicia la serie N° 7 no es naturalista, pero ha sido tomada de la serie N° 6.

Las series mencionadas se inician y terminan en la forma siguiente:

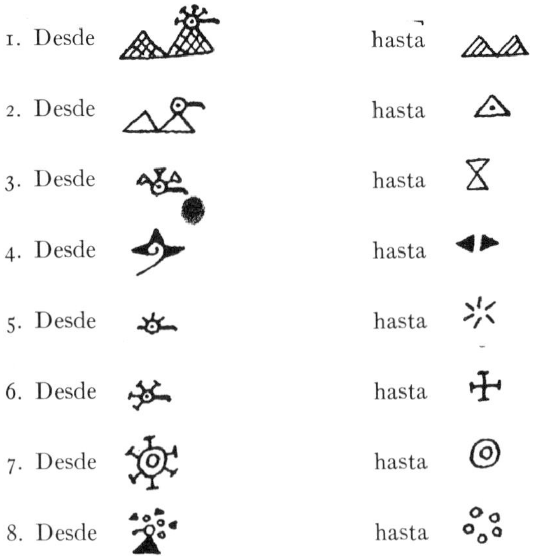

1. Desde ... hasta ...
2. Desde ... hasta ...
3. Desde ... hasta ...
4. Desde ... hasta ...
5. Desde ... hasta ...
6. Desde ... hasta ...
7. Desde ... hasta ...
8. Desde ... hasta ...

Fig. 4

Las figuras intermedias constituyen los pasos entre la representación naturalista y la esquematizada. En cada una de ellas se puede reconocer la idea expresada en la inmediatamente anterior, cada vez con menos elementos y más simplificados, pero con los necesarios para conservar el carácter de símbolos representativos.

En este tema, la geometrización de las figuras alcanza su máxima expresión.

TERCERA PARTE
LAS IMÁGENES ORNITOMORFAS APLICADAS EN LA DECORACIÓN DE DIFERENTES ESPACIOS

Los signos representativos del ave se presentan en profusión sobre distintas superficies. Las imágenes aparecen con el tamaño y la forma apropiados para cada espacio y para cada superficie.

El espacio fué cuidadosamente estudiado para repartirlo simétricamente, precisamente, en las partes necesarias para estampar un número determinado de imágenes. Las superficies planas, esféricas y de tronco de cono; los espacios triangulares, rectangulares y circulares, muestran composiciones ornamentales que revelan una intención definida en la distribución de los espacios y de los elementos decorativos.

Unos cuantos ejemplos pueden dar idea del hecho enunciado:

FIG. 5

Definidas normas de equilibrio se ponen de presente en la distribución de los espacios en las superficies circulares (Fig. 6).

CUARTA PARTE
IDENTIFICACIÓN DEL AVE COMO SÍMBOLO DE SUA

1. *Relación entre el ave y el sol.*—El nombre de la divinidad principal de los chibcha es Sua, Dios Sol.

Etimológicamente Sua significa ave.

Los caciques se consideran hijos del Sol. Los emblemas que aparecen en sus coronas, pectorales, narigueras, y vestidos, son aves.

La religión practica ceremonias especiales para enviar mensajeros al Sol: hombres puros y aves.

Las aves son portadoras de la luz en uno de los principales mitos: el mito de Chiminigagua o de la creación del mundo.

2. *Mito de Bochica: Identificación del Sol con Bochica, héroe civilizador de los chibcha.*—Después de que Bochica moraliza al pueblo y le enseña a tejer algodón y a pintar las mantas, se va al sol y se identifica con él. Antes había convertido a su mujer en luna.

Desde el momento en que se verifica la identificación de Bochica con el Sol, el símbolo del Sol debe ser el mismo de Bochica.

Así nos explicamos por qué aparece la imagen del Sol en casi la totalidad de los volantes de huso. El origen divino de la industria de tejidos está expresado en esta forma.

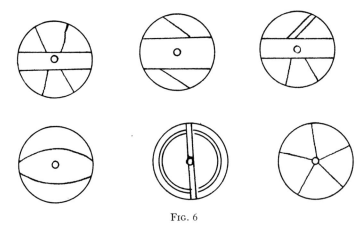

FIG. 6

3. *Presencia de las imágenes de Sua en los objetos vinculados con ceremonias religiosas; con actividades de origen divino, como insignias de superioridad social.*— Los vestidos de los caciques y gente privilegiada presentan imágenes de Sua.

En las vasijas ceremoniales aparecen imágenes de Sua. En las armas y adornos se observan los símbolos de Sua, como emblemas heráldicos.

En las pinturas rupestres como símbolos de la divinidad en lugares sagrados. Sobre las piedras come el sol las víctimas humanas que le inmolan.

En los volantes de huso como símbolos del personaje divino que les enseñó a tejer.

CONCLUSIONES

I. UNA BASE TOTÉMICA EN LA RELIGIÓN DE LOS CHIBCHA

Hechos especiales me han llevado a la conclusión de que, originariamente, existió en el pueblo chibcha una organización totémica que sirvió de base a su religión. La frecuencia con que se repiten y las circunstancias que los rodean hacen que estos hechos sean concluyentes. Algunos de ellos expresan con evidencia la trascendencia que tuvieron en la vida social-religiosa y la importancia que aún se les reconoce en la época de la conquista española.

En esta parte final de mi trabajo trato de analizar algunos de estos hechos, de los cuales anoto los principales a continuación:

1. *Un precavido uso del nombre del tótem.*—Un solo ejemplo nos da idea del hecho que enuncio. En el idioma chibcha existe la palabra *güia* para designar al oso. Existe, además, la palabra *chijizaba* para nombrar el mismo animal. Estudiando la etimología de ambas palabras encontramos que, para la primera, *güia*, no hay más significado que el de oso. Es por lo tanto el nombre con que se le distingue de los demás animales. Para *chijizaba* existe el siguiente significado:

> *chi* = nuestro
> *ji* = arriba
> *za* = varón
> *ba* = digno, merecedor.
> = Nuestro digno varón arriba (arriba en el sentido de progenitor).
> Nuestro digno varón progenitor.

Como se ve, *chijizaba* es la palabra que se usa para designar a un animal que se considera como progenitor.

Hasta el presente momento he logrado reunir setenta y dos palabras de la zoonimia chibcha, sesenta y seis de las cuales hacen referencia a un ser bueno, un varón fuerte, un progenitor. Esto, naturalmente significa que se trata de animales considerados como animales totémicos o antepasados míticos.

2. *Trasmisión del tótem en el mismo momento en que se genera la vida.*—Es el caso de Goranchacha engendrado por el dios Sol en el vientre de una virgen. Como hijo del Sol hereda los atributos de su padre. Los caciques que le suceden son considerados como Hijos del Sol. Con ellos se observan tabús por su condición especialísima. Por esto los súbditos no pueden mirar la cara de su cacique. Solamente cuando han cometido una falta y el soberano quiere que sobre ellos caigan los castigos que acarrea la violación de tabús, la faz del cacique es contemplada de frente.

3. *Animales en cautiverio.*—Los chibchas mantienen en cautividad tigrillos, papagayos y otros animales y estos son objeto de consideraciones especiales. La proximidad de estos animales es esquivada por el común del pueblo y este hecho es aprovechado por los caciques para lograr que los deudores morosos paguen los tributos.

4. *Las imágenes del tótem son usadas como símbolos heráldicos.*—Es esta la razón por la cual aparecen las representaciones del ave y de otros animales en los pectorales, coronas, narigueras y otros adornos.

5. *La presencia de nombres de parcialidades y de personas aprovechando el nombre del tótem.*—Tal es el caso de Soacha o Suacha (Varón Sol) y de Nemgatá (gato montés resplandeciente), nombres de parcialidad y de persona, respectivamente.

6. *Algunos animales son enterrados con las mismas consideraciones que una persona.*—Se han encontrado venados enterrados en urnas funerarias y como si se tratara de un ser humano.

7. *Prohibición de matar y comer ciertos animales.*—Solamente los caciques, sus familiares y personas privilegiadas pueden matar y comer el venado. Ellos poseen los poderes superiores que les ponen a cubierto de los males que acarrea el "asesinato" del tótem.

8. *Llantos y lamentaciones por el sacrificio del tótem. Fiestas y regocijos posteriores a los lamentos y llantos.*—Cada año y cada veinticinco años se celebran fiestas que tienen este carácter.

9. *Máscaras y vestidos de pieles de animales.*—En las fiestas que se realizan en Sogamoso, Guatavita y otros sitios del imperio, los individuos van cubiertos con las pieles de animales y en sus meneos imitan al animal cuya piel llevan.

10. *En la pintura facial aparecen figuras emblémicas del tótem.*

11. *Los animales predicen hechos futuros.*—Consideran el canto de ciertas aves, las voces de determinados animales como anuncios de hechos que van a suceder.

12. *Los miembros de un clan totémico se sienten vinculados con el tótem en un origen común.*—Es el caso de los caciques tenidos como hijos del Sol.

13. *El tótem protege y defiende la vida de sus afiliados.*—El portar partes del tótem evita peligros y cura enfermedades tales como la patita del venado, el ojo de venado y los trece huesitos de guala. La sangre y el estiércol de cóndor sirve para curar algunas enfermedades.

14. *Existen tótemes particulares para grupos de personas que se distinguen por cualidades señaladas o se dedican a ocupaciones especiales.*—Los corredores, los que se distinguen por su fuerza física en eventos públicos, entran a ser protegidos por un ser cuyo símbolo es el tigre. Los tejedores tienen por tótem el ave.

15. *Prohibición del incesto: Caso de Hunzahua.*—Al llamarse hermanos todos los afiliados a un tótem, y siendo prohibido el matrimonio entre hermanos, tuvo, necesariamente, que exister la exogamia.

Los anteriores hechos enunciados y otros no menos interesantes, ponen en evidencia la existencia de un totemismo originario.

En una etapa avanzada, cuando el ánimal totémico es tenido por el antepasado del grupo, se le diviniza y se convierte en el objeto de un culto. Adquiere una personalidad, a semejanza de la humana, pero conserva los atributos del tótem en un grado superior. Por esto se hace generalmente temible. Nacen así los semidioses chibcha: Nemcatacoa, Tomagata, Chaquén y Nemterequeteba. Llegan a ser rivales unos de otros, a vencerse y a establecer una jerarquía de dioses y semidioses.

Se presenta entonces la superposición de tótemes y de sus correspondientes tabús. Este hecho interesa en cuanto puede explicar los tabús que deben guardar determinados miembros de la sociedad, en relación con el venado y otros animales.

Cuando la divinización del tótem se ha consumado, el dios se interpreta siempre como padre. A veces es diáfana la ambivalencia de los sentimientos en relación con el padre (ser divinizado) y por esta razón, en el momento en que se le ofrecen sacrificios como reconocimiento a mercedes recibidas, se le ofrenda para aplacar su cólera o para asegurar sus beneficios. Es bien claro este hecho en la intención que tienen cuando hacen sacrificios humanos al sol. Unas veces son adolescentes puros que han de interceder por el pueblo. Otras, niños inocentes que han de aplacar la cólera divina.

II. SÍMBOLOS ZOOMORFOS PARA DIVINIDADES CHIBCHAS

Infructuosa ha sido la búsqueda de las representaciones de los dioses del panteón chibcha. Nadie hasta hoy ha encontrado objeto en donde aparezca Bochica con su barba larga y su vestido talar. Ninguna figura nos ofrece la imagen de Tomagata, el genio del mal, monstruoso y temible, con cuatro orejas y un solo ojo.

Es cierto que algunos cronistas nos dicen que los indios nunca hicieron imágenes de sus dioses. Pero otros, de la autoridad de Pedro Simón, nos hablan de las figuras de sus dioses, a quienes adoraban.

Los hechos anotados podrían tener una explicación: es posible que los indios hubieran tratado de ocultar la existencia de sus ídolos para defenderlos de la implacable obra de destrucción realizada por los extirpadores de herejías. Los indios sí hicieron figuras de sus dioses, pero las convirtieron en formas simbólicas. Con el ave representaron al dios Sol; con el gato montés, al dios Nemcatacoa. Y seguramente los españoles no entendieron las figuras de la iconografía chibcha, porque las imágenes son bien esquemáticas y geometrizadas. Si ellos las hubieran reconocido, no habría quedado ni una sola *múcura* (vasija para guardar la chicha).

Las figuras que se han identificado hasta hoy nos permiten creer que los chibcha ornamentaron sus objetos con temas simbólicos, zoomorfos, representativos de sus dioses.

NOTE ON ANDEAN GLACIATION AND PRE-COLOMBIAN MAN

Victor Oppenheim

At the request of the International Commission on Snow and Glaciers the writer outlined in 1948 some of his observations on the movements of glaciers and the snow line in the Colombian Andes.

Field observations with graphic records were made by the writer particularly on the Nevado del Cocuy in the Cordillera Oriental of Colombia at intervals between December 1939 and December 1947. The retreat of the ice or deglaciation of the snow cap of Nevado del Cocuy could thus be established as taking place at a rate of about one meter per year.

The process of deglaciation of the South American Andes since historic times is quite evident and widespread. The intensity of deglaciation can, however, vary with the local climatic and topographic conditions in different parts of the high Andes.

The deglaciation process is not a recent phenomenon and can be clearly traced throughout the Pleistocene epoch in the Andean geology. Thus, unmistakable evidences of past glaciations are clearly visible in the Andes of Colombia, Ecuador, Peru, and Bolivia down to an elevation of about twenty-seven hundred meters above sea level. Considering that the present-day line of perpetual ice and snow or line of *nevé* in the high Andes of these countries is at about forty-seven hundred meters above sea level, we have unmistakable evidence of a retreat of ice in the Andes of about two thousand meters during the last Wisconsin stage of glaciation including the present-day glacial period.

Although research data are almost completely lacking on the different climatic fluctuations in the high Andes and their causal relation to phenomena of glaciation in different parts of the Andes, the writer's observations express a numeric criterium which, being true of present-day deglaciation, could reasonably be applied to the same phenomena within historic times.

The dating of different Andean cultures has been mostly left to the vague and arbitrary judgment of the individual archeologists concerned with the local problems. Climatic or paleo-climatic conditions have rarely been considered by the Andean anthropologists. Cultures and human remains found in different parts of the high Andes, often close to the present-day snow line, have been attributed an antiquity of thousands of years. This would be the case of the Tiahuanaco culture in the Altiplano of Bolivia or the monolithic San Augustin culture in Colombia.

If the present rate of deglaciation in the case of Colombia would be extended to the immediate past, as it has been observed to be taking place, then the San Augustin area, which has an elevation of about three thousand meters and shows evidences of an intense recent glaciation, must have been covered with glaciers only about seventeen hundred years ago. Thus, the age determination of thousands of years attributed to this culture by some archeologists becomes quite untenable.

The migrations of the living or extinct forms of mammals of the highlands, as well as of the primitive man of South America, were greatly influenced by the glacier movements in the Andes.

Thus paleo-climatic conditions become essential in anthropological investigations in the Andes, and the dating of human skeletal remains or archeological materials, when dealing with Andean regions, must necessarily bear on the glacial geology of the high Andes.

CENTRAL ANDES

PERUVIAN SETTLEMENT AND SOCIO-ECONOMIC PATTERNS

Gordon R. Willey

A comprehension of the structure and function of past social institutions lies at the heart of an understanding of Peru-Bolivian[1] prehistory. In this essay, it is my assumption that in settlement patternings as revealed by archeology we have a guide-line of evidence that is most directly reflective of institutional development. The concept "settlement pattern" implies more than a study of site situation, building plans, or architectural detail. It is all of these, but it is also more. It is a consideration of total community integration, ecologically and culturally. The relation of man to his natural environment, the nature of population groupings, and the shifts of both of these through time—these are the bases of inference concerning the socio-economic orientations of ancient societies. And from these basic data and inferences, supplemented by other aspects of the archeological record, we may go a step further and advance some interpretations as to the coexisting political and religious institutions.

A trial survey of Peruvian settlement patterns has been made feasible by two recent events in Andean archeology. The first of these was the intensive research program of the Institute of Andean Research (Willey, 414) in the Virú Valley. Settlement studies in this one valley have provided a pilot developmental sequence that may, with proper caution, be extended to other parts of the area.[2] The second event has been the establishment of a functional-developmental classification for Central Andean cultures. This classification is grounded in time-space systematics in that it is an outgrowth of the Uhle-Kroeber scheme of horizon-markers; however, it goes beyond pure temporal-spatial formulations in that it recognizes functional characteristics of the successive cultural horizons. Larco Hoyle (179) was the first to apply such a classification to the north coast. Bennett (38), Strong (332), Willey (413), and Steward (324) have used similar functional-developmental schemes for the Peru-Bolivian area as a whole. Nomenclature has varied somewhat with all of these authors, but the major outlines and implications are the same. In the present discussion I will refer to such a sequential-classificatory scheme. It is given below with equivalent explanations and estimated dates.[3]

---

1. This is the Central Andean culture area or "co-tradition." It consists of the Peruvian highlands and coast and the Bolivian altiplano (see Bennett, 38; Bennett and Bird, 40).

2. Supplemented to some extent by Bird's work (60) in the Chicama Valley.

3. Compare with Bennett and Bird (40, pp. 111–14).

Early Agricultural (3000–1000 B.C.): Pre-maize horticulture, fishing-gathering important, no ceramics, small villages near coast. North Coast region.

Early Formative (1000 B.C.–0): Maize, some dependence on fishing-gathering, ceramics, villages near coast and in marginal lands of interior, beginnings of ceremonial centers, Chavín style. Chavín, Cupisnique, Nepena, Casma, Ancon-Supe.

Late Formative (A.D. 0–500): Developing craft technologies, marked population expansion, full agriculture, numerous villages, ceremonial centers, beginnings of fortifications. Salinar, related White-on-red cultures, Paracas Cavernas, Chanapata, Chiripa.

Florescent (A.D. 500–1000): Full technological and esthetic control attained, great religious centers, larger villages. Mochica, Recuay, Gallinazo, Interlocking, Early Lima, Nazca, Pucara, Early Tiahuanaco.

Early Expansionist (A.D. 1000–1200): Political and/or religious expansion, beginnings of larger communities. The Tiahuanaco horizon.

Late Expansionist (A.D. 1200–1532): Political expansionism continues, rise of urban centers. Late Chimu, Late Chancay, Ica-Chincha, Inca conquest after A.D. 1450.

Settlements of the Early Agricultural stage are small, compact villages located along the ocean shore at favorable shell-fishing stations. This site ecology, as well as the refuse contents, attests to a subsistence economy divided between fishing and horticulture. Houses were simple semi-subterranean affairs of one or two small rooms lined with stone and mortar or hand-made adobes. They were arranged at random in the village area. In only one site of the period, Aspero near Supe, is there a building which might be considered a temple or ceremonial structure. These small Early Agricultural populations with their minimum surplus economy had only a limited craft technology which was confined mainly to twined cotton textiles, basketry, and tools of stone. Burials, placed in stone-lined or plain pits were accompanied by only a few such manufactures. The socio-political picture is one of simplicity, of little autonomous villages without differentiated craft workers or social classes. Religious rites or controls appear to have been equally uncomplicated.

Early Formative settlement patterns are similar to those of the preceding stage in that the small, unplanned village remained as the basic unit. These, however, became more numerous, and this reflects the intensification of the agricultural economy with the appearance of maize which in turn is responsible for increased population. The village dwelling sites were clusters of irregularly arranged above-ground houses of one to five room construction. Both stone and conical hand-made adobes were used as building materials. An important innovation of this stage is the religious structure. It varies from the crude rectangular stone foundations excavated in Virú to the famous dressed-stone castillo at Chavín de Huantar. Stone sculpture, in connection with the temple, flourished at Chavín while architectural sculpture in clay is seen at the coastal temples of Nepeña and Casma. It is obvious that these temples were constructed and supported by a considerable population so that we know more than a single village group was involved. Undoubtedly, the temple served as a politico-religious nucleus for several surrounding villages. Skillful and esthetically sophisticated work in small stone, bone, and ceramics during this period indicates a degree of craft specialization, but there is little evidence, aside from differentiation in the amounts and quality of burial goods, to suggest class stratification. During the latter half of the period a single religious theme, represented by the Chavín feline deity, dominates the artistic tradition. This, together with the clearly recognizable importance of the temple centers, argues for the supremacy of sacred rather than secular ideology and control. In spite of stylistic similarity of the feline art motif throughout much of the Peruvian area at this time, it is most likely that this religious or theocratic control was independently invoked in the several temple centers rather than directed from a common source of sovereignty (Willey, 413, p. 10).

A full agricultural economy was achieved during the Late Formative stage, and in response to this, population showed a marked increase. This is seen to advantage in Virú where the shell-fishing stations, so popular during the earlier periods, now form but a small part of the total Valley occupation. Sites have spread inland to all parts of the valley, and this expansion is explained best by irrigation as it is likely that the canal systems were put into operation during the Late Formative. Although the number of sites greatly increases, the small village pattern persists. House size and arrangement similar to those of the Early Formative continue, but somewhat larger and more compact room aggregates also appear. These last are found on the hillslopes overlooking the valley floor in Virú. They are constructed on successive step-terraces, and the rooms are contiguous though without over-all plan. That there was some general idea of community arrangement at this time is revealed in the Chiripa culture of the Bolivian altiplano. Here individual houses were found grouped around a common courtyard. The impressive temples of the Early Formative do not seem to be duplicated in the Late Formative although there is considerable evidence for religious sites. In Virú there are pyramids of conical adobes, earth, or rocks that date from the later period, and it seems likely that these must have served as bases for temples or governmental structures. There are no outstanding sites in Virú from this era that could be interpreted as politico-religious capitals, but there are two or three hilltop redoubts of impressive size. These rock-walled inclosures contain multi-room dwellings and small flat-topped earth-rock pyramids. During attack they could have served as places of refuge for several hundred people, presumably drawing from a number of the small, scattered villages. This is the first appearance of fortifications in the Peruvian sequence, and the nature of warfare at this time is an important point. Although the lack of large ceremonial centers makes it doubtful if the single valleys had complete political unity within themselves, the valley irrigation systems do imply a degree of internal co-ordination and centralized authority. Such co-ordination would preclude intra-valley warfare and suggests that the hilltop forts were built against raiders from outside the valley unit. A prevailing motif of the Late Formative is technological experimentation. Craft work is competent and in some cases excellent. Ceramics show a technological improvement over the preceding stage although with the disappearance of the Chavín art style there is a corresponding esthetic decline. In the south, in the Paracas Cavernas culture, loom-weaving shows great advances over the previous periods. In general, burial practices are somewhat more elaborate than formerly. The Late Formative can, as a whole, be summed up as that stage in Peru-Bolivian development when large populations came into being, technology made rapid strides, but society was still decentralized into autonomous politico-religious groups. Nevertheless, the institution of inter-valley or inter-regional warfare was beginning. This and the necessity for centralized control of the all-important irrigation systems were inevitably compressing the social order into more formalized and cohesive forms.

As the name implies, technological and esthetic excellence is the hallmark of the Florescent stage of Peru-Bolivian culture. The centuries-long traditions in ceramics, other handicrafts, and architecture finally came to fulfillment. In the Virú Valley settlements reach their maximum number at this time. The increase over Late Formative times is, however, relatively small as compared with the rapid expansion of settlements and populations that was noted between the Early and Late Formative stages. The basic unit of the Virú settlement pattern during the Florescent is still the small or medium-sized village, but many of these are larger than in previous periods. Contiguous rooms, numbering up to 50 or more, are found in irregularly arranged compounds which give the appearance of having been built partially according to plan but largely by haphazard accretion. The big politico-religious capitals of Gallinazo and Huancaco, Florescent sites in Virú, are exceptions to the small village clusters. At Gallinazo, in conjunction with great pyramids and presumed palace or temple quarters, there are hundreds or even thousands of small adobe-walled rooms placed in irregularly arranged groups on the summits of large adobe platforms. These small rooms appear to be dwellings of great masses of the population, not just sacred or governmental precincts. On the north and central coasts Florescent stage architecture is massive and impressive, and the construction unit is the mold-made rectangular adobe. North highland architecture is of dressed stone and equally impressive if not as mammoth. The artistic representations of the stage are wellknown from the ceramics, bone, stone, shell, and metalwork of the Mochica and the ceramics and textiles of Paracas Necropolis and Nazca. These are the finest in Peruvian prehistory. Metallurgy takes a great spurt during these periods, and all techniques and materials ever known to the aboriginal area, with the exception of bronze, are competently used and commonly possessed. Copper weapons and tools are the rule for Mochica, and from this time on the north coast was in a true metal age. Craft specialization is obvious. Religion and its significance are attested to by the great pyramids and by the representations in Mochica pottery. On the north coast there is abundant evidence that secular and military power were contesting with purely religious authority. Total valley or multiple valley states came into being. Military fortifications or great castillos were constructed at strategic points in each valley. War scenes are common on Mochica pottery as are representations of enthroned dignitaries inspecting captives or giving auditions to vassals. The implications of class stratification are clear in this as also in the marked differentiation of grave goods placed with individuals.

The Early Expansionist stage is that characterized by the widespread diffusion of Tiahuanaco-like art. This inundation seems to have swept over much of Peru-Bolivia, terminating the Florescent cultures, and to have come as the climax to the first upsurge of Peruvian empire attempts. We know that on the north coast the Mochica were military expansionists and that they were pressing southward on the valleys adjacent to their original homeland. Similar events may have been taking place in other regions of Peru. The Tiahuanaco stylistic wave may or may not have been a centrally directed empire attempt; but whatever its over-all organization we can be sure that it moved into the north Coast in the wake of military force. The obliteration of all of the Mochica war and state symbols is too complete and too sudden to be explained by peaceful processes. In Virú many of the settlements of this Early Expansionist stage are identical with those of the Florescent stage. In fact, many of the small and medium-sized room clusters were continuously occupied through both periods. This, together with the fact that utilitarian pottery remains much the same while ceremonial ware undergoes violent change, would indicate a continuity of much of the population. Some dwelling sites of the period are, however, significantly different. These are planned compound structures of many rooms, regularly arranged and inclosed within an outer wall. It is questionable if many big pyramids or fortifications were built during this time, but those of the Florescent were occupied, used, and probably added to. The level of technology of the Florescent is maintained in the Early Expansionist stage, but there is a general esthetic decline which is noted for all parts of Peru. The period is one of flux and change, but, judging from both preceding and succeeding periods, it is almost certain that large-scale warfare, military states, and class differentiated societies were continued.

The Late Expansionist stage saw the culmination of the settlement and empire trends begun in the latter part of the Florescent and carried through the Early Expansionist period. After the disappearance of the Tiahuanaco horizon influence, a number of large but not pan-Peruvian kingdoms were formed. The Chimu, Late Chancay, Ica, and Chincha styles denote some of these on the coast; others were undubtedly in existence in the highlands. The characteristic settlement of the stage is the planned community. On the north coast the first of these were seen in Early Expansionist times, but in the later stage they became the rule. The great group of gigantic walled compounds, containing symmetrical arrangements of rooms of all sizes, courtyards, basins, and pyramids, that is found at Chanchan is the classic example. There are similar groups in other north coast, central coastal, and even south coastal valleys. In Virú, a small valley, there are no such huge centers, but there are several quadrangular compounds of the Late Expansionist period which are miniatures of the large compounds of Chanchan. It seems unlikely that absolute population was any greater then than it was in Florescent times. These Late Expansionist sites are considerably larger than earlier communities, but they are also much fewer. Peoples were concentrated into a city type existence Such communities continue up to and after the Inca conquest which seems to have effected little change on the north coast except in the matter of political consolidation. In general, the technology of the Late Expansionist stage is that which was achieved in Florescent times with the exception of the invention and distribution of bronze. Art forms of the period lack the richness and painstaking care of earlier times. Craft goods are extremely plentiful, however. In some places they give the appearance of being hastily turned out, mass-produced articles in which the maker took little pride. Religious concepts are much rarer in the art of the period than previously. Temples and pyramids are constructed but usually as a part of an urban concentration. And, from the early Colonial documents, we know that religion had become an adjunct and an implement to the all-powerful state under the Inca. Constant large-scale, long-distance warfare with empire incorporation of territories and peoples as its objective was the guiding force in Late Expansionist society. Both archeologic and ethno-historic sources tell us that class differentiation was marked and governmental control all-pervading. Peruvian society, which had begun with simple farming villages oriented toward a sacred temple-shrine, had finally become as well-organized and tightly constructed as one of the symmetrically planned cities of its final phase.

NECESIDADES DE LA ARQUEOLOGÍA PERUANA

Jorge C. Muelle

La fotografía adjunta es de una botella zoomorfa que calificamos de espécimen único. Aunque pudiera considerarse como una originalidad individual sin trascendencia evolutiva, es decir, como esfuerzo frustrado para crear una rama estilística, otros ejemplares relacionados que el autor conoce hacen pensar en todo un estilo desconocido, o por lo menos una escuela ceramista cuya procedencia debemos buscar.

Fig. 1

Fué comprado en Lima en una de las muchas tiendas del jirón de la Unión que trafican en antigüedades. El vendedor sostenía que el objeto era del Norte, pero fué incapaz de dar más precisos detalles porque también él compró el *huaco* a un extraño. Tiene una altura de 18 cm. y el color actual de la arcilla es ocre naranja como el típico de algunos ceramios de Nievería. La base es aplanada, pero el recipiente tiene poca estabilidad. En la base hay un relieve longitudinal que representa la *huara* o pañete de los antiguos peruanos, la cual pasa entre las piernas y se sujeta por detrás y por delante al cinturón, que es un rudón semejante. Este pañete en relieve, la pintura en el dorso del animal, que evidentemente significa una prenda de vestir, y la actitud de éste, que bebe del tazón

201

sostenido entre sus manos, le dan características antropomorfas aunque se trata de un cuadrúpedo. Se parece mucho a un *ucumari* (*spectacle bear*). Pese a que el autor no recuerda haber visto nunca esculturas de osos entre las representaciones del Perú antiguo, son reveladoras unas líneas blancas en la cara, y dos pequeñas circunferencias negras en la parte alta de la frente que representan las manchas supraorbitales.

Se diría que el artista conocía soluciones tradicionales para todos los problemas que tuvo que afrontar. Modelado en parte, el ejemplar presenta un conjunto proporcionado. El tronco parece haberse conseguido por la unión de dos pedazos que pueden deberse a la estampa en molde bivalvo (unidos cuando el barro estaba todavía fresco) pues a los costados puede apreciarse irregularidades en la pega. La cabeza se hizo por separado de manera análoga, pero quizás el hocico se modeló aparte, lo mismo que las orejas, que fueron colocadas después. La boca, los ojos, las fosas nasales, así como la separación de los dedos de manos y pies hubieron de ser retocados con el esteque. Lo más notable en el ejemplar es la técnica del modelado de los brazos: desde los hombros parten arcos tubulares que van a unirse a las rodillas; a la mitad de estos arcos se ha insertado tubos, que van a desembocar en la tacita semiesférica, modelada por separado, que la figura sostiene con las dos manos. De modo que las únicas aberturas del recipiente son estos "golletes" que comunican la taza con el interior de la figura, y que como son dos, permiten fácilmente la salida del contenido líquido por uno de ellos mientras el aire penetra por el otro.

El acabado se ha obtenido por el conocido método de pulimento en oreado, con chinas que han dejado sus rayaduras a lo largo de las superficies exteriores. La pintura es blanca, margosa en los detalles del pelaje de la cabeza, de un negro tenue que parece de origen orgánico porque ha desaparecido en parte, y un gris-violeta de Marte que dibuja un aspa en la espalda. Los escaques de la prenda de vestir, que parece una *lliclla* o una manteleta, así como las mangas del *uncu*, las manos y la decoración losangeada en el borde de la tacita, están hechos con ese negro.

Los ya aludidos especímenes semejantes al descrito eran dos, iguales; existían en los antiguos fondos del Museo Nacional de Arqueología de Lima y habían sido adquiridos por Don Víctor Larco Herrera. La mayor parte de los *huacos* entre los que se encontraban venía de Virú y Chicama, y éstos diferían tanto del grupo, que fueron supuestos como procedentes de Venezuela o Colombia. Representaban un hombre en cuclillas sosteniendo una taza entre las manos en la misma forma que el oso que nos ocupa. Aunque los ejemplares eran monocromos, con un engobe blanco, la postura de los brazos y, sobre todo, la técnica de unir codos y rodillas con la taza en que "bebe" la figura, no deja duda del parentesco de estos tres ceramios.

El caso presentado no es único y nos mueve a consideraciones más generales: ¿Hay todavía en la arqueología peruana culturas originales que no conocemos? ¿estilos originales que no conocemos? ¿O se trata aquí de simples desviaciones individuales esporádicas? La conexión de los codos con las rodillas y con la tacita que sirve de salida al contenido forma, prácticamente, dos golletes de los llamados "estribos." Esta constatación nos lleva a una reconsideración de los factores técnicos como manifestaciones fortuitas en un espécimen arqueológico. En los factores estilísticos hay siempre una mayor cantidad de rasgos deliberados.

Al estudiar un objeto artificia' se hace mucho hincapié en su aspecto estético. Pero hay más de una razón etnocéntrica que impide a un grupo copiar el estilo de otros: por ejemplo, razones religiosas, de xenofobia o simplemente de valoración artística. Es idea corriente dar por cierto que cuando dos estilos artísticos se ponen en contacto, han de influenciarse mútuamente, o que la aceptación de rasgos extraños al lugar ha de realizarse inevitable y conscientemente sólo ante la presencia de esos rasgos. En realidad, el fenómeno es más complejo, y surge muy a menudo un rechazo completo. Sin embargo, involuntariamente, puede quedar testimonio de dicho contacto. Es muy curioso que en los bordados de Paracas (Necropolis) (403, Lam. 1, Fig. 1; 420, Fig. 14e) y en la tapicería Tiahuanacoide de la Costa, haya la costumbre de juntar figuras de animales, aves o peces, para formar con ellas la ilusión de una cara humana, digamos, que ha de verse mirando el conjunto a la distancia. También en los grabados líticos de Chavín encontramos que, por ejemplo, dos perfiles felínicos se unen para formar una cara antropoide de frente (239, p. 142 A). Asimismo, la cerámica mochica y la de Cupisnique (40, p. 127, Fig. 23) tienen cabezas monstruos que observadas de perfil representan un animal, y de frente, o del otro perfil, un ser completamente diferente. Esta costumbre es rasgo común en los citados estilos.

Una mayor elaboración de la teoría general del estilo es necesaria, por supuesto, y cualquier cosa que se haga en este terreno ha de repercutir en la arqueología peruana, aunque no podemos decir que toca obligadamente a los peruanistas esa tarea.

Ante la repetición de formas en la cerámica del Perú antiguo, nos sentimos inclinados a creer que la originalidad del hombre precolombino agotó sus posibilidades y que tenemos ya una muestra, por lo menos, de todas sus creaciones. Sin embargo, si pensamos en los estilos como unidades trascendentes, supraindividuales, unidades orgánicas que no pueden haber salido de la nada sino que cada una cuenta con una historia detrás de sí, hemos de aceptar que el pasado evolutivo de muchos estilos peruanos está trunco todavía en nuestro conocimiento. Esta es una consideración universal pero señala una necesidad de la arqueología peruana. ¿Cuál es el criterio definitivo de organicidad de los estilos? ¿Qué cosa es una fase estilística? ¿Cuándo se considera completo el ciclo vital de un estilo? Me parece que aún la cuestión de definición de provincias artísticas está supeditada al previo acuerdo sobre lo que debe considerarse estilo, moda o modo. Los factores de idiosincracia, de tiempo, de lugar, etc., no han sido todavía definitivamente establecidos, y las consecuencias están en las reacomodaciones continuas que debe hacer la arqueología peruana. Es verdad innegable que nos faltan datos y que los trabajos de campo son los únicos que pueden conseguirlos; pero es asimismo verdad que para fertilizar las prácticas características de la arqueología peruana falta una teoría general del estilo y que mientras no la tengamos continuaremos con la derrotista actitud de sostener que el método tipológico es estéril.

Por supuesto que el trabajo estratigráfico es la primera necesidad; este método, préstamo de la geología, nos da únicamente la *historia del sitio*, es decir, una secuencia desorganizada dentro de un orden aparente. Únicamente cuando ponemos tipológicamente en relación el material de todos los yacimientos conocidos podemos separar y reconstruír aquellas unidades orgánicas y trascendentes. Si el criterio de los *préstamos geográficos* puede darse por conclusivo, no podemos decir lo mismo del criterio de los *préstamos tecnológicos*, que todavía no ha sido bien elaborado. Parecemos reincidentes en los viejos pecados de la arqueología peruana, pero ya el Prof. A. L. Kroeber, hablando de *Los Métodos de la Arqueología Peruana* (170), señaló sus peculiaridades. No solamente porque hay en las colecciones una enorme cantidad de material sin procedencia, que no podemos ignorar o desechar, debemos insistir sobre los métodos tipológicos, sino precisamente porque es gracias a esa enorme cantidad que el método puede ser de utilidad. Desde su introducción por el Prof. Max Uhle, que usó y abusó de él, el método tipológico se dió por malogrado. Y sin embargo muchos de los derroteros que Uhle señaló son válidos todavía. Lo que pasa es que no tenemos estudios tecnológicos suficientes para fundamentar nuestros supuestos. Es por eso que nos toca aquí rendir sentido homenaje a la memoria de Lila Morris O'Neale, que trabajó efectivamente en este descuidado terreno. Para los peruanos, los estudios tecnológicos, que se menosprecian tan frecuentemente como *armchair-archaeology*, son estudios factibles por lo poco costosos, y no deben ser descuidados.

No se trata de tipología versus estratigrafía. Quizás la necesidad mayor de la arqueología peruana es completar un catálogo de sitios, de la bondad del que comenzó en el Cuzco John Rowe; y después explorar metódicamente como en Virú, si es posible, los valles desconocidos o con pocos datos válidos. Con todo, es innegable que las crecidas sumas que una buena excavación de esta clase requiere, colocan, lógicamente, fuera del alcance de las instituciones y personas del Perú, un buen *valley-survey*.

La secuencia cronológica de un lugar es importante; continúa siendo, empero, un paso descriptivo, de igual valor que un buen estudio tecnológico. Al lado del corte cronológico, debemos reconstruír la vida completa de cada estilo; mientras no lo consigamos, habráse de considerar incompleta la labor. He leído últimamente que esto no concierne al arqueólogo. Creo que sí y que cada arqueólogo, de manera más o menos consciente, lo está haciendo. El trabajo del arqueólogo comienza con la pala; mas no debe concluír con ella. Si en la interpretación de los datos el arqueólogo se transforma en "historiador," etnólogo o algo más, hay que admitir que lo importante está en los finales.

Cuando Winkelmann trasladó el concepto de *estilo* de las artes literarias a las plásticas, esbozó la teoría de un método que todavía hoy no ha ganado completa aceptación. Es, simplemente, lástima que los tropiezos de los evolucionistas condujesen a descuidar un instrumento de trabajo que puede y debe ser perfeccionado. Hace algunos años se dijo en un congreso que el concepto "biológico" era falaz y que no tenía utilidad alguna y se trajo a colación ejemplos de ceramistas indígenas actuales que habían copiado la ornamentación de tiestos desenterrados de un yacimiento arqueológico.[1] El ejemplo citado era, sin embargo, uno muy típico de epígonos, es decir, de resurrección de un estilo. Es claro que poco puede servir un arreglo *post-facto* para la construcción de una cronología—insisto que tiene cierta utilidad hasta para eso—pero no se debe ir tan lejos como para negarle todo valor. El método evolucionista deja mucho margen para consideraciones subjetivas, aunque cada vez menos y es esto, justamente, lo que alienta nuestras esperanzas sobre el perfeccionamiento de una herramienta siempre de utilidad práctica, aún ahora, pese a las controversias teóricas.

Cuando conceptos como *crecimiento orgánico, margen de difusión, superposición histórica, survivals* o *vestigios* se reconcilien, entonces una de las necesidades de la Teoría del Estilo se verá satisfecha.

Todos los estilos tienen orígenes balbucientes muy semejantes. Según los recursos que ofrecen los materiales, se ha venido nombrando *arcaica* a esta etapa. Posteriormente se hace evidente una *voluntad de forma*, para usar del viejo concepto de Alois Riegl, aunque los recursos técnicos no se dominan todavía: llamemos *básica* a esta etapa, que es distinta para cada estilo. Cuando se alcanza un equilibrio de *forma* y *fondo*, la definición de Hegel nos dice que estamos ante un período *clásico*. Maneras *derivadas, decadentes* o *degenerativas* pueden suceder-lo. El estilo puede morir; si renace alguna vez, tenemos los *epígonos*.

El ejemplo que he presentado al comienzo no puede ser arcaico; tiene antecedentes que no conocemos y ubicarlo en su contexto histórico es revelar su proceso interno de crecimiento y su proceso externo de difusión y contactos. Una de las necesidades de la arqueología peruana es comparar, con sus peculiares métodos, las formas conocidas y señalar los eslabones que nos faltan. No cabe duda que el Dr. Bennett realizó un magnífico trabajo estratigráfico en Tiahuanaco (35), pero la génesis del estilo propio del Altiplano no pudo ser explicada: su *Tiahuanaco Clásico* y *Tiahuanaco Decadente* no tienen etapa *básica* ni *arcaica* y las otras espléndidas excavaciones del Dr. Bennett en Bolivia (36) tampoco nos exhumaron la solución. Pero el mismo Dr. Bennett tocó el punto álgido cuando dijo en una de sus publicaciones que las ornamentaciones típicas del gran monolito tiahuanaquense antropomórfico que descubrió parecían reproducciones de

---

1. "Nampeyo, un maestro alfarero Hopi que había visto las vasijas exhumadas de las ruinas de Sityatki, se interesó en ellas, las copió, aunque con muchas modificaciones. Otros alfareros siguieron su ejemplo, y así se estableció un escuela artística nueva cuyo estilo no estaba emparentado con el de la precedente" (Gladys A. Reichard, 273).

ornamentaciones textiles del vestido. Creo que debería trabajarse más con la idea. El profesor Kroeber tiene razón cuando insinúa que muchas de las formas de la costa peruana llamadas *Epigonal Tiahuanaco* pueden ser pre-Tiahuanaco Clásico (172*a*, pp. 118 y 120). Un examen comparativo de la ornamentación tecnomorfa de la tapicería tiahuanacoide de la costa, muy en especial del departamento de Ica, nos traería la solución. El Prof. Uhle, en el Congreso de Americanistas de Sevilla, aceptó que el Epigonal Tiahuanaco era simplemente un *Tiahuanaco* impuro (386, p. 45). Habiendo introducido él la palabra *epigonal* en la terminología arqueológica, tomándola de la literaria, su confesión tiene el valor de una revelación.

Menos podemos esperar de las conexiones inmediatas con la cerámica de Pucara. Con las comparaciones estilísticas dentro de un mismo material o una misma técnica pasa lo que con la comparación de los estilos de un solo yacimiento: la reconstrucción no puede ser orgánica. Pucara puede significar una ramificación divergente, aunque anterior a la fase clásica de las piedras de Tiahuanaco. Pucara nos recuerda temas mochicas, y no sólo por el tigrillo con dogal (37, p. 116, Fig. 10*b*), que se traslada con el mismo tratamiento a las representaciones de alpacas, al cambiar de medio físico. El dogal de Tiahuanaco termina en circulitos concéntricos, convencionalizados a través de una deformación en reproducciones de tapicería. Recordemos los contornos escalonados de ese motivo mochica mal llamado *raya*, monstruo imaginario que una aberración tecnógena creó en el estilo mochica (275, p. 282, Figs. *a, b, c*); pues bien, aparece copiado en piedras como la estela ("El Suche") que el Dr. Luis E. Valcárcel nos ha dado a conocer (40, Fig. 32). Lo que decimos del estilo Tiahuanaco puede aplicarse a otros conjuntos estilísticos peruanos. La meta últ'ma de los estudios arqueológicos es la reconstrucción de la cultura del pasado. Pretender la exhumación total de esa cultura es utópico, pero esa cultura está simbolizada en uno de sus aspectos: la obra material de hombre. Y no es el aspecto individual de esta obra lo importante sino aquello que la rebasa para alcanzar categorías inmateriales más amplias: como estilo, ciclo cultural, tipo, familia morfológica, etc. Cronología, función, estratigrafía o historia del sitio son medios y no deben considerarse como fines en sí.

Perdóneseme la insistencia sobre puntos obvios para muchos arqueólogos, pero para los peruanos, una de las necesidades de su arqueología es la comparación exhaustiva de los materiales depositados en los museos y la consideración orgánica de sus principales estilos artísticos. Si no podemos estructurarlos, no es únicamente porque falta escarbar sino porque estamos abandonando una técnica de análisis cuya defensa pretendemos aquí.

GREAT ART STYLES OF ANCIENT SOUTH AMERICA

Alfred L. Kroeber

This essay is an endeavor to characterize the typical values of the principal forms of visual art developed in ancient native South America. Chronological relations are assumed, without citation of their supporting archeological evidence. The consideration is aesthetic: it is directed at qualities of style.

In Peru, the art of the type site of Chavín, at Huantar, is lithic, and is possessed of grandeur in the sense that it is charged with strong feeling, both symbolic and decorative. Its lines are at once heavy and flowing, with an effect of massiveness even in small areas; and most objects look larger and heavier than they are. Curves predominate, generally within an implicit rectangular contour. Straight lines are not altogether avoided, especially in relief, but are employed to achieve secondary contrast with the curves, or as part of the frame. The total effect is one of slow motion, often intricate but never flamboyant, without lightness of touch, every detail seemingly significant, and impressive rather than pleasing. In fact, the monstrous is not avoided. Both the type of line and the load of symbolism carry a suggestion of Maya art, though there is no evidence of historical connection.

The freest specimens of Chavín sculpture are heads in the round. Most of these have the faces furrowed, and in some the furrows or hair are converted into snakes. A second type of stone-carving is constituted by monoliths with surface carving. A third type consists of incised or relief carvings on slabs. Feline figures are perhaps most characteristic among these, the full-spread condor most readily appreciated on first approach to the art. There are some jaguar representations whose heaviness of line and monstrosity of concept put them among the least attractive Chavín pieces. A dominant trait is the fangs or tusks projecting beyond the lips.

The type site of Chavín has yielded little besides this sculpture, which fortunately is nearly all preserved, either as originals or in casts, at the Museo de Antropología at Magdalena. The entire range of Chavín style art, in metals, cloth, and clay modeling as well as in stone, is recoverable from the remains occurring, more often on the Coast than in the Highland, from Chiclayo to Paracas. Here there are included: embossed gold from Chongoyape; incised trumpet shells and carved stone jars from Chiclayo; Cupisnique type modeled and incised pottery from Chicama; a modeled monstrous clay idol at Puncurí and a decorative adobe relief at Cerro Blanco, both in Nepeña Valley; in Casma, more clay modeling in pure Chavín type at Mojeque, and at Cerro Sechín incised slabs somewhat deviant from the classic manner but still Chavinoid; at

Supe and Ancon, Chavín-like pottery, also bone-carvings; at Paracas, in the Cavernas part of the cemetery, pottery modeled, incised, or inlaid under Chavín influence, along with pyrographic designs on gourds. The variety of materials and technologies in which the Chavín manner is expressed evidence the strength of the style.

The Chavín style may be considered the greatest art style evolved in Peru and in South America. Also, it appears to be one of the earliest. Above all, it possesses a line that is unique in its assurance of form, its true dignity, in the inevitability of its curves. Hardly less extraordinary is the slow plastic flow of the surfaces produced by this art. Consistently symbolic, the art is saturated with feeling equally in its themes and its forms. At its best it possesses grandeur, at its worst it becomes obsessed with the monstrous.

By contrast, on the north coast of Peru, Mochica or Early Chimú art, famous for its sculptural ceramic modeling, was oriented toward representation rather than symbolism, and excelled in painting almost as much as in modeling. This pottery is extraordinarily mature and supple in style. Very few fundamental vessel shapes underlie an endlessly exuberant variety of modeling and painting, executed with high technological competence.

The peak of Mochica art was attained by the so-called portrait heads. Whether these are individual portraits in our sense is uncertain. The Mochica may have been like the Greeks, Egyptians, and Chinese, in being more inter- ested in the type. However, they made the type astonishingly lifelike and often ideal as well. They were equally successful in depicting deformities, mutilations, paralysis and other diseases, the abjectness of prisoners, punishments, ironical as well as macabre caricatures, and erotic scenes. They had the gift of seizing and reproducing salient features and posture. Strict anatomical realism is often violated: many heads are disproportionately large for the body, or eyes for the face; but this becomes evident only on analytic reflection. There is little Mochica representation of the fantastic or chimerically symbolic, as there is in Chavín art. Preference is for a single, free-standing head, body, or animal; less com- monly for two or three figures; groups of five or six small figures occur rather rarely, chiefly in scenes of religious sacrifice, and may represent an influence from Recuay scene-modeling. The Mochica showed themselves thoroughly pos- sessed of true sculptural feeling in preferring permanent form at rest to "story." Certainly their aesthetically best modeling, as well as the bulk of their work, ex- presses form rather than event.

The Mochica were scarcely less successful as painters, both in monochrome red or brown on the cream slip of their pottery, and in larger flat-color mural frescoes. They preferred depicting couples, groups, or processions. Representa- tion is almost wholly in profile. In sharp contrast with the modeling, it is action, not rest that is painted; and the action is generally rapid, often vehement. Background is confined to essential indications. Animals, imaginary and fantas- tic as well as free-realistic, are also represented; and from these there is a transi- tion to merely decorative and geometric figures. The painting stroke was firm, swift, and sure—indicative of a control parallel to that of the modeler. The fresco painter outlined his figures with long, sweeping incisions, then filled in areas with flat-color masses in several hues.

Mochica ceramic art was preceded in its own territory not only by the Cupisnique form of Chavín, but also by Salinar and then by Negative or Gallinazo. Negative has highland affiliations, especially with Recuay, in vessel shapes and in small-figure modeling, as well as in use of resist or negative painting. But the Salinar white-on-red pottery, a coastal product, seems to be the principal parent of Mochica. It is a formative, fumbling, experimenting style, attempting many subjects and shapes, but always in a modeler's manner, as distinct from the stone carver's. Like Mochica it is secular, not stylized symbolically, oriented toward representational likeness, even though crude in achievement. Mochica appears to have grown out of Salinar by the double process of learning to increase patterned control and to eliminate random efforts. Salinar explored new paths, Mochica channeled and traversed them to a culmination.

On the southern coast, the ceramics of Nazca rival Mochica in quality, and are generally considered more or less contemporary, though Nazca metallurgy, brick-molding, and construction are considerably retarded in comparison. Nazca attempts only minimal modeling, but specializes on polychrome designs, varying from pictorial to symbolic, though never genuinely realistic even in the Mochica sense. The ware is fine-grained, thin, metallic, highly polished, and carries many colors in definitely harmonious combinations. An earlier phase has fewer forms, fewer and more somber colors, and a narrower range of designs. The later Nazca phase adds more specialized shapes; more colors, tending toward pastel tints; and a whole series of new designs, such as anthropomorphic deities and rows of women's yellow faces with almond eyes. The designs of this later phase tend toward the flamboyant and exaggerated, as in the multiplication of faces on demons, and in providing them with tentacle-like rays. While the earlier Nazca has been found only in Nazca and Ica Valleys, the later phase has a much wider distribution, and in the Sierra it blends into other manners, such as Tello's Huari or Huanca, Chanca, and Rucana.

The famous Paracas Necropolis embroidered textiles are obviously allied in theme and line to the painted ceramic designs of Nazca. It is not known which is derivative from the other. The most sumptuous of the embroideries, unsurpassed anywhere in fineness and richness of design and color, are rectangular mantles, bearing alignments of figures of gods, masked impersonators, demons, warriors, or animals, either in a wide border surrounding an empty panel, or in the panel itself. The embroideries are in wool, their sheer background is of cotton. Other fabrics have wool weft on cotton warp. The embroidered figures attempt any and every curve, in most untextile-like manner—and successfully. There is known one Paracas mantle which is painted instead of embroidered, but otherwise in the typical style; also a Nazca canvas fragment painted with hummingbirds like those frequent on jars.

Necropolis pottery looks as if it might be a development out of Nazca, though in the direction of having lost former designs. It is a plain ivory-color ware, favoring the double-spout jar, but in a flattened form, with long slender spouts: the effect is one of refined, specialized, weak elegance, a dead end of stylistic development.

The Tiahuanaco style is very well defined. It is named after a famous architectural and sculptural ruin with associated pottery, near Lake Titicaca in the Bolivian Highlands. The distribution in the Sierra is restricted, except southward into Bolivia. But from Arequipa to Trujillo the Peruvian Coast almost everywhere shows a period of specific Tiahuanaco influences, in pottery, textiles, and metals. This Coastal Tiahuanaco manner gathered into itself certain new shapes and traits unknown at Tiahuanaco, such as the flaring-double-spout; and the resultant hybrid style then flowed northward along the coast, picking up additional local features on the way. It was this "Tiahuanacoid" art of the northern coast, with only a minor proportion of indubitably Tiahuanaco-derived features left in it, that largely displaced Mochica art. Out of it in turn there subsequently grew, along with some resurgence of Mochica forms and manner, the Late Chimú style. Similarly, the ceramics of Huari at present seem a blend of Nazca and Tiahuanaco.

For ceramics, Bennett has worked out stratigraphically a sequence of Early, Classic, and Decadent Tiahuanaco pottery phases at the type site, which is stylistically convincing. The Classic phase has its design elements arranged significantly, and the Decadent meaninglessly, on the whole. Yet a new problem is posed, since Bennett's Early Tiahuanaco examples are far from expressing formative stages, either of representative or of geometric designs, but look like the broken-down complex end-product of some previous style.

Tiahuanaco sculpture rivals that of Chavín. These two are the only South American styles in stone which have achieved thorough control and a degree of grandeur. Tiahuanaco is a severe style, but it avoids the representation of the monstrous and the impression of terror which lurks in Chavín sculpture. With all its condors, cats, serpents, and chimeras composed of them, the Tiahuanaco figures remain decoratively interesting and are never shocking or repulsive, though they may seem barbaric. Allied to the psychological severity of the art is its stiffness, its fondness for straight lines, for chords rather than arcs. It will round its corners, but the implicit design remains rectilinear—in contrast to the flowing curve which still is basic in Chavín even when actual outlines approach the rectangular. This emphasis on the severely straight line in Tiahuanaco may derive from specialties of masonry technique, such as appear in the strangely elaborate stereometric cut stones found at Tiahuanaco itself. The design of most the relief sculpture, as in the famous monolithic gateway, is so angular as to be easily transferable to tapestry; there is even considerable suggestion of its own derivation from woven tapestry patterns.

Along with the architectural severity of line, Tiahuanaco sculpture has architectonic organization. This is evident on comparison. In Chavín, the strength is in the form of the detail—the curved lid of an eye, its eccentric pupil, the bend of a fang or claw, the roll of a lip; whereas the total composition may be intricate or bewildering to grasp. The corresponding elements in a Tiahuanaco relief or statue are likely to be insipid in their schematic simplicity. The eye, for instance, is an even square, octagon, or circle; tusks are two opposite-pointing right triangles; a claw is indicated by a square at the end of a rectangular digit or toe. Nevertheless, these vapid geometric units are pulled together in Tiahuanaco art by a strong sense of organization into a composition which is almost always impressive and often interesting. Tiahuanaco sculpture remains attached to the quarry block—even more than that of Chavín, on the whole; but it has made the most of this attachment in developing its peculiar and highly specific stylistic quality of surface treatment.

The Pucara style of the northern Titicaca Basin is less impressive, less abundant, more localized, and possibly somewhat earlier than that of Tiahuanaco. Stelae or slabs are carved in relief with representations of fish, occasionally of men, and sometimes geometrically. These last are the best, aesthetically; curves are handled with skill and imagination. Pucara pottery combines modeling, incising, painting, and burnishing even more strikingly than Paracas-Cavernas. There are positive though not close Tiahuanaco affinities in modeling, themes, and details. It is a well-controlled, original ceramic not dependent on or imitative of its southern sister.

The Recuay style of the Callejón de Huaylas is most fully expressed in high-grade pottery with negatively painted linear designs of highly stylized felines in panels. These cats come in rampant or sitting position, angular, open-mouthed, long-tailed, with serpent-like head appendages, almost resembling dragons. The vessels are frequently modeled, carrying not only spouts, stirrups, and bridges, but figures of men and animals. These modeled figures are smaller, clumsier, and stiffer than Mochica ones, but tend to appear in groups illustrating genre scenes. There are no sure Chavín influences in Recuay, in spite of the close geographical proximity of the two type sites.

Callejón and Aija sculpture consists of stone lintels and of statues. The lintels bear relief carving of a squatting or spread-leg human figure flanked by profile felines whose conspicuously eared faces may be turned front. The style of execution is not highly characterized. Statues are little more than blocks, slightly shaped from a boulder with a main cut into the stone made between head and trunk. The head constitutes about two-fifths of the total length, the nose is long, the eye without expression, the mouth thin and rudimentary; the execution is without either skill of line or feeling for planes; it is stylistically meager, almost inept. Accessories in some of the surface relief suggest time connection with Recuay pottery.

The highland north of the Callejón is little known. Huamachuco has yielded some sculpture, especially fairly life-like, full-round, human heads on tenons, presumably for wall insertion; also tenoned, squarish, serpent-horned cat heads.

There are similar pieces from Santiago de Chuco and Cabana, not far south. The handling of the carving is skilful and definite. The human heads come nearer to successful plastic depiction of actual human heads than can be found in any other South American stone sculpture. Chavín is too interested in the monstrous, Tiahuanaco in the schematic, San Agustín in both, ever to be life-like.

The Inca style of Cuzco is the latest of the Highland styles. Exemplars occur from Ecuador to Argentina. This wide spread is believed to have occurred within the century preceding the Spanish Conquest. Although little Developmental Inca has yet been found, the style is well characterized in a number of media, emphasizes technological control, and possesses a set of firm patterns.

The Cuzco people found satisfaction in the fine working of stone, from gigantic masonry blocks as at Sacsahuamán and bedrock cuttings of intihuatana down to utilitarian vessels. All these show a feeling for mass and for planes, for exact fit if they are joined, for surface texture, and for functional form.

The best plastic work consists of miniature figures, mostly of llamas or human beings, carved of fine-grained stone or cast in bronze, silver, or gold. These figures are very simple, not too realistic, but extremely expressive of tactile effect in their curving planes.

Inca pottery is marked by chaste classic form and sobriety of design and color. The number of shapes is limited; so is the range of patterns, which are executed within a channel of good taste but without either strong interest or slovenliness. Representation is chiefly of small animals, like flies, or of highly conventionalized birds. Colors tend to the somber; if they are bright, it is without vivid hues. It is the quality of intended and achieved control that the Cuzco ceramics share with Cuzco stonework, rather than an outright transfer to plastic clay of qualities of form (in contrast with the relationship of Chavín lithic and ceramic design). Inca textiles are again different in manner. They favor over-all ornament, with the surface broken into many small panels containing diverse designs, sometimes repeated diagonally. The aim is to fill the frame of the cloth pleasingly, evenly, and with variety, not to organize it.

All in all, Cuzco art is well directed, steadily controlled, unexuberant, rather deficient in imagination or ambition and in objectives other than technological ones. It keeps a consistent level without falling into weaknesses; but it has none of the smouldering drive of Chavín, the imaginative skill of Mochica, the primitive taste of Nazca, or the compositional ability of Tiahuanaco.

In the post-Tiahuanaco Period of the last two or three centuries before the Spanish Conquest, a considerable degree of assimilation of culture occurred along the Peruvian Coast, even anterior to the Inca Conquest. Metal had become fairly abundant and metallurgical processes were skilful and uniform. The designs were stiff even when representative. Similar "arabesques" of more or less geometrically patterned adobes, or cut into sun-dried stucco, decorated the walls of public buildings. Textile decoration everywhere tended to geometric regularity, and especially to borders and corner fillings of small repetitive elements—geometric cats, birds, or fish. The over-all, large, human-figure or divine feline designs of Tiahuanaco were on the way out, the over-all paneling of Cuzco not yet well developed. Wood carving was neat, angular, repetitive, and without much feeling for plane surfaces—certainly not for curved ones. Against the relative uniformity of this generalized Late Coast technology, several local variations in ceramic styles stand out: Chimú, Chancay, Chincha-Ica.

Of these, Chimú pottery is a resurgence of Mochica, with many losses, with the addition of shapes and ornament derived through Coast Tiahuanacoid, and with prevalence of blackware imitative of metal. The portrait heads of Mochica are replaced by stiff, stereotyped faces and figures. The art has the facility of long repetition and some degree of conscious elegance. But it is eclectic, shallow, done without feeling, and superficial in taste. In the mudbrick architecture, geometric relief friezes replace the Mochica naturalistic frescos.

Chancay is a black-and-white ceramic, technically poor, hastily made, with embellishments either crude or florid; but showing an original feeling for design disposition in panels including balanced asymmetry—unlike right and left halves.

Chincha-Ica ceramics have shapes partly influenced by metal vessels; the painting is obviously stimulated by textile patterns; technology and finish are competent.

These variants typify the condition of Peruvian art on the Coast in the last pre-Conquest Period. This late art possessed diversity, facility, reasonable skill, occasional taste, but only mild interests and no feeling. In the Highlands, Inca art retained a measure of severity, and therewith a certain self-respect; but it evinced little more emotion. The drives were gone which in earlier priods had led to the originality and creativeness of Chavín, Mochica, Nazca, Paracas, and Tiahuanaco.

In ancient Ecuador, which had little intimate connection with Peru, art was most developed in the north coast provinces of Manabí and Esmeraldas, with some overlap into adjacent Colombia. In stone, there were chairs and low-relief slabs. The chairs or thrones, without backs, are executed in a single graceful sweep of seat and arms, resting on an Atlantean pedestal of a crouching human figure. The reliefs are, partly, geometric; in part they represent stylized insects or lizards or human figures of about the naïveté of those in Peruvian sculpture from Pucara or the Callejón.

Most interesting is a secular, informal, lively art of modeling and molding small pottery heads and figurines, sometimes grotesque, more often naturalistic, varied in feature, posture, and expression. Technology and finish are only mediocre, execution is rather careless, but it is marked by verve, dash, imaginative seizure of characteristic form and attitude. Compared with Mochica, this art is unchanneled, playful, unfinished. It is both more trivial and more humorous. But it is comparable in quality.

Colombian goldwork suffers aesthetically from an indecision between three and two dimensional treatment, due perhaps to a desire to spread the glitter, even though in flat form. Executed in a baser material, few would linger over this jewelry.

The famous San Agustín sculpture is limited to a small area of occurrence east of the Magdalena headwaters. Compared with Chavín and Tiahuanaco, San Agustín is crude in conception and execution. Everything wavers in this art. Eyes may be circles, semicircles, crescents, almonds, or commas. Mouths may have tusks or be miniature narrow slits. Noses vary from triangles to inverted T's. Proportion of width to height of the total statue range from three-tenths to three-fourths. The figures are if anything even less extricated from the block than in Highland Peruvian sculpture. At any rate they seem less channeled into a coherent style. Each piece begins all over again to express its own idea in its own way. The size of the statues—up to several meters and some tons—results in an effect of monumentality, of stolid weight, of labored feeling, of barbaric strangeness verging on the monstrous, of minimal organization and almost no beauty of line or flow of surface; and yet, an effect of indubitable impressiveness.

A remarkable ceramic art once flourished on Marajó Island in the mouth of the Amazon. Decorative devices include modeling, cutting away, incising, painting, often several of these in combination. The art is weakest in figure modeling, strongest when it riots in rich decoration of surface, sometimes suggesting the effects of Shang bronzes. In this pattern ornament, representation is often no longer discernible: stylization has been carried far; it is intricate and continuous; blank spaces are rare. The fundamental motive varies from a fret or rectangular spiral at its fullest, to an E, L, or H figure at its simplest. Angles are skilfully staggered to oppose or interlock. Design lines are frequently double, or accompanied by shadow counterparts: a heavy line or stripe is paralleled by a fine line or one of lighter value or color. Thin lines may be used as a frame for repetitions of heavier motives, and at the same time as a net to draw these heavier masses together. These many devices add up to a rich and imaginative decorative style, varied in its expressions and yet unified in feeling, successful in element detail as well as in over-all effect.

Marajó proves to be the local expression of a widespread style which at one time extended along the Atlantic coast and especially up the Amazon drainage, and of which descendants have survived among backward tropical forest culture tribes at the eastern foot of the Andes. Upstream, ancient pottery from about the mouth of the Madeira, and again from the Napo in Ecuador, skilfully utilize relief, incision, and polychrome painting with intricacy and control and in the generic manner of Marajó. Wares once made to the south on the Gurupi river, and to the north at Cunany in Brazil and in Surinam, also seem stylistically related to Marajó.

In modern times, pottery painted in a manner allied to that of Marajó has been characteristic of the lower Ucayali and Huallaga affluents of the Amazon in the Peruvian montaña, especially among the Pano-speaking Conibo, Shipibo, and Panobo tribes, but also among the Arawak Piro and Tupian Cocama. In three-color ware, brightened by a resinous coating, a similar design scheme is maintained, two thousand miles from Marajó and perhaps five hundred years later. There are complete and incomplete spirals; engagement or interlocking of the figures into an over-all pattern; and paralleling or shadowing of lines. At least among the Shipibo, patterns in this style are also painted on human faces and limbs, on the blades of paddles, and are woven into textiles. Inferior qualita- tively, but perhaps also related historically, is the pottery painting of the Aguano, Chayamite, and neighboring tribes, who paint the corners of their suc- cessions of zigzags or diamond figures with tiny black rhomboids. Farther north, the styles of pottery painting of the Baniva and of the Arawak-speaking tribes of the Isana River, and that of the Guianan Carib of Maroni River, show simi- larities which suggest that they too may be recent local variations of the wide- flung basic Marajó-related tradition.

On review of these major art styles of native South America, it is evident that successful naturalism was attained only twice: by the Mochica and in Manabí- Esmeraldas—both times in clay. Far more often the South American Indians achieved aesthetic success by subordinating representation to decoration, to stylized expression of form as such. This holds true equally of their efforts in stone sculpture, in metal casting, in pottery modeling and painting, and in weaving. It holds true equally, also, whether interest was directed primarily to strength of line, to organization of elements, or to over-all continuity of pattern. And finally, where the record of sequence is complete enough to allow of judg- ment, there is evident a general sequential drift from strongly-experienced styles of a certain grandeur to manners that are less imaginative and flatter in meaning and feeling.

A RARE PERUVIAN SQUARE BONNET

H. Newell Wardle

The small square bonnets, which are among the choicest treasures of Ancient Peruvian collections, are characterized by their knotted structure and the four points or cylinders, which rise from their corners. There are two recognized classes: the handsome pile-knot, or *simili-velours*, structure, and the unadorned, knotted fabric, self-patterned by manipulation of the knots.

Fig. 1.—Peruvian tapestry hat with needle-knitted birds

The University Museum of Philadelphia recently acquired a unique hat of square form, woven in tapestry technique, and bearing upon each corner, in place of the point, a needle-knitted bird. A flowering plant, in the latter technique, rises from the center of the crown. The height of the hat proper is 6.5 cm., and the circumference, 48 cm. (Fig. 1).

Closer study reveals certain peculiarities. The vertical band is not woven in a single piece, but constructed of two, the larger forming three sides, and joined by

216

sewing to the piece which forms the fourth side. The seam is neat and the pattern matched at the first joining. The second seam has a cut edge. Contrary to the usual custom of weaving a tapestry band with wefts laid in the shorter direction, the wefting was done lengthwise of the band. The count is fifteen or sixteen wool wefts to eight or nine cotton warps per centimeter. The diagonal interlocking fish design, in white, amber and rose, is outlined in olive on a red ground. The rose is lacking in the shorter piece.

The crown of the hat appears to have been made from a tapestry strip. It is a square, 7 × 7 cm., and thus of less dimensions than the upright band might

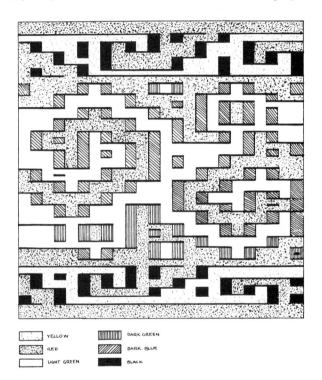

Fig. 2.—Interlocking bird design; double-bird in cruciform arrangement

require. The smaller crown is normal to these square bonnets. The slack of the sides, which, in the hats of knotted structure, forms a loop at each corner, from which rises the point or cylinder, is here pinched and sewed together to support the applied bird.

A double-bird design appears on the crown in cruciform, or pinwheel arrangement, blue-green, and outlined in ultramarine, and with greyed green replacing the latter in some spots. Above and below the central figure, a narrow border, with bird-derived pattern in amber yellow, lies on the red ground, which is more orange than the ground of the hat-band (Fig. 2). The ends of the strip used for the crown have no border, and were evidently cut and neatly sewed in.

The lower edge of the hat is thickened by needle-knitting in red, olive, yellow, and white, grouped; the colored threads, when not in use, are carried under the rest, until again required, thus thickening the marginal roll.

The bonnet's interior shows the reverse of the tapestry to be a mass of floated colors, which condition, while not unknown, is not characteristic of good Peruvian weaving.

The vari-colored, needle-knitted humming-birds are not identical in form or color; two have their bills inserted in striped flowers; one has lost its bill. Three face the center of the hat, one looks outward, though it is doubtful if that is the original position. The central flowering plant is delightful, with two blooms and a bud, supported by a stem of knitted red and white cotton threads. These ornaments give the impression of having been taken from a garment fringe.

Thus, this hat, charming as it is, presents many inconsistencies:

a) The tapestry technique has not been recorded previously in any Peruvian square bonnet, although tapestry head-bands and stiffeners for a bonnet are known.

b) The cut and pieced band: a tapestry strip should be woven to desired dimensions, and usually with the wefts crossing in the narrower direction.

c) The numerous floated wefts on the interior, suggesting a single-faced warp-pattern weave, while the face is definitely tapestry weave.

d) The different, though not incongruous, color schemes of band and crown.

e) The distinct design styles, though probably not widely separated in time, are apparently unrelated.

f) The superposition of the Early Nazcu birds and flowers.

It is regrettable that this bonnet, handsome as it is, should ever have been created to beguile the textile student.[1]

---

1. Since writing the above, the attention of the author has been called to several Peruvian bonnets, apparently made from textile fragments put together with modern thread. In one instance, the maker has not hesitated to combine material from cultures widely separated in time.

PERUVIAN METALLURGY

Samuel K. Lothrop

At the time of the Discovery, most American Indians who had access to metals also had some knowledge of metals. But the higher skills, based on casting rather than hammering, became widespread only about a thousand years ago.

There is a certain uniformity in the spread of metallurgy. Excavations have shown that the Maya became acquainted with metal near the end of their Classic period. The inhabitants of central Mexico began to hammer gold and to cast copper bells in Tula-Toltec times before 1000 A.D., and this knowledge of casting spread to the southwestern United States before 1100 A.D., as is established by tree-ring dating. In Costa Rica and Panama, all kinds of metals are associated with the historic tribes, but earlier cultures, recently discovered, had no metals. At present we can say nothing about dating in Colombia. In most of Bolivia, in Chile, and in Argentina no metals earlier than the Tiahuanaco horizon are on record.

In several parts of Peru, however, metal was worked perhaps more than two thousand years ago. There are two principal regions where the development of metallurgical techniques can be followed in considerable detail and over this long period of time. One is on the south coast, embracing the valleys from Chincha to Acarí, approximately the area covered by the Nazca culture. The other is on the north-central coast, including the region between Lambayeque and Virú. Professor W. C. Root (280) has recently published a detailed study of the southern area.

The archeological knowledge of north-central Peru extends back to about 3000 B.C. At that time, there were villages near the mouths of the Chicama and Virú rivers. The natives had developed agriculture, basketry, and weaving. Pottery seems to have been introduced about 1800 B.C. and the complex culture known as Chavín was developed over a thousand years later. These dates are estimates of Mr. Junius Bird, based on geological data and on a carbon 14 test. The earliest metal now known comes from three Chavín tombs, two found near Chongoyape and the third in the interior. The objects recovered include crowns, circlets, ear spools, finger rings, necklaces, nose pendants, gorgets, pins, spoons, and tweezers. They are of a sheet gold, except two specimens which are partly of gold and partly of silver. Designs follow the classical sculpture of Chavín de Huántar (200, 201).

As there are no known antecedents to Chavín metallurgy in either style or technique, the presumption is strong that we are confronted with new inventions. After noting the presence of gold and silver nuggets, the natives must have learned that they were malleable and could be hammered in sheets, which they found could be cut in various shapes. Then followed the discovery of decorative techniques: embossing or making raised patterns, champlevé or driving in the background of a design, incising, and various combinations of these.

In addition there followed the discovery of certain effects of heat. This resulted in annealing, which made it possible to soften metal and thus to hammer it into more elaborate forms, and in the use of solder, which made it possible to join sheets of the same or different metals. Molds and the art of casting remained unknown.

This is a formidable list of inventions, but there were many basic processes left for future discovery. Chavín craftsmen could make hollow beads or hollow figurines by soldering together the parts. They were ignorant, however, of copper, tin, lead, the use of alloys, open and closed molds, gilding, and silvering. Although objects of great artistic merit were produced, the Chavín workmanship, apart from soldering and annealing, is definitely primitive.

Turning now to the south coast, the Necropolis culture discovered at Paracas was in part contemporaneous with Chavín, as established by certain art motives shared in common. Paracas produced beaten gold ornaments which were embossed. Root (280, p. 12) has shown that the process of annealing, or recrystallization of metal which had become brittle from hammering, was understood at that time. The other techniques of Chavín were not practiced.

The Nazca culture on the south coast of Peru also produced articles of sheet gold at an early period. These include masks, head ornaments, huge nose pendants, plumes, belts, cut-out figures to be sewn on clothing, and hollow beads (199). Comparison with pottery designs suggests that the gold dates from the latter portion of the period. The beads were made in two parts which were soldered together.

It is possible that casting in molds became known in late Nazca times. The evidence is based on some graves opened by my wife at Chaviña between Nazca and Chala. Typical late Nazca pottery was found together with spear throwers tipped with solid copper pegs in the form of animals. Analysis will show whether these were cast or hammered from nuggets. Casting never became common in the subsequent periods on the south coast of Peru.

The Nazca period was followed by Early Ica. The only metal object found by Uhle in twelve graves of this date was a copper earplug. Root suggests that this specimen was imported and that all knowledge of metallurgy may have been lost throughout the Early Ica and the subsequent Middle Ica I periods, a span of several centuries.

In the Middle Ica II period, metalwork again became common on the south coast of Peru. New artifacts such as cuffs, earplugs, tweezers, bowls, and jars were introduced, as well as new designs. In earlier times, most objects were of high grade native gold, but this later was replaced by gold-silver and silver-copper alloys. The latter became predominant in Late Ica times. Tumbaga, a gold-copper alloy, apparently never was employed on the south coast.

Turning again to the north-central coast of Peru, we find that the history of metallurgy partly parallels the evolution we have described in the south. While metalwork was rare in the Chavín period, it became almost extinct in the subsequent Salinar period. Only a few crude objects of sheet gold were manufactured, and technical processes were limited to simple embossing and occasional cut-out patterns (182, Fig. 203; 33, Pl. 68). Why the metal industry should have been almost completely obliterated in both northern and southern Peru we cannot say. The facts now known, however, indicate that few if any metal objects were manufactured over a period of centuries.

The renaissance of metallury in north central Peru took place in the Gallinazo period. Some of the old Chavín techniques were revived, and new metals and processes came into use. Occasional embossed ornaments of sheet gold continued to be manufactured, and silver again appeared. The great technical advance, however, was represented by simple castings of copper in closed molds. The oldest New World bells now known date from this epoch. Soldering also reappeared, gilding was discovered, as well as the use of metal sheets for overlays.

Technically, Gallinazo produced a great advance in metalworking. These growing skills, however, did not reach a high esthetic level until the Mochica period, an epoch when all the arts flourished. Delicate castings, probably by the *cire perdue* method, were produced. Bimetallic objects again appeared. Tumbaga, a copper-gold alloy, was discovered. Both gilding and silvering were mastered. Although bronze did not come into use until later (171, Appendix C), tools and weapons were now manufactured and became progressively more common and more complex.

The Early Tiahuanaco period in the Lake Titicaca basin differs from other Peruvian cultures because copper rather than gold was the first metal to be utilized. In the Classic Tiahuanaco period, gold and silver objects were manufactured and a copper-tin alloy, or bronze, came into use. Tiahuanaco influence, as is well known, later spread over most of Peru. In spite of its proximity, however, Tiahuanaco had practically no effect on south-coast metallurgy, notwithstanding the introduction of Tiahuanaco pottery and weaving styles. It seems probable, though, that the use of bronze on the north coast was the result of Tiahuanaco penetration.

In the Chimu period, shortly before the Conquest, the north-central coast enjoyed all known Peruvian metals, alloys, and technical processes, except the inlaying of one metal in another. This was practiced only in the mountains of southern Peru during the Inca period.

In this discussion we have said little about the influence of one region on another. Root has suggested that the renaissance of metals on the south coast was due to the influence of the central coast. This seems quite possible. Although

TABLE 1

DEVELOPMENT OF METALLURGY IN NORTHERN PERU

Period	Metals	Techniques	
Chavín	Gold Silver (rare)	Hammering Embossing Champlevé Incising Cut-out designs	Annealing Welding Soldering Strap joining Bimetallic objects
Salinar	Gold (rare)	Hammering Embossing Cut-out designs (rare)	
Gallinazo	Copper Gold (rare) Silver (rare)	Hammering Embossing Simple casting	Soldering Gilding Overlays
Mochica	Gold Copper Silver (rare) Tumbaga?	Hammering Embossing Cut-out designs Casting Soldering	Gilding Silvering Bimetallic objects Tools
Tiahuanaco	Gold Silver Copper Tin ?	Mochica techniques, plus bronze?	
Chimu	Gold Silver Copper Tin Lead (rare)	All Peruvian metals, techniques and processes except metal in metal inlays	

TABLE 2

DEVELOPMENT OF METALLURGY IN SOUTHERN PERU
(After Root, 1949)

	Paracas	Nazca	Early Ica	Middle Ica I	Middle Ica II	Late Ica I	Late Ica II	Inca
Gold	✕	✕			✕	✕	✕	✕
Silver					✕	✕	✕	✕
Copper		?	?		✕	✕	✕	✕
Gold-silver					✕	✕	✕	✕
Silver-copper					✕	✕	✕	✕
Bronze							✕	✕
Hammering	✕	✕			✕	✕	✕	✕
Embossing	✕	✕			✕	✕	✕	✕
Engraving	✕	✕			✕	✕	✕	✕
Annealing	✕	✕			✕	✕	✕	✕
Casting		?			?		✕	✕
Soldering		✕			✕	✕	✕	✕
Welding							?	✕
Gilding								

the sequence of metallurgical development in the Lima region is uncertain, it is known that objects of Classic Tiahuanaco style have been found at Pachacamac (297, p. 370). This indicates that metal either was imported or manufactured on the central coast precisely during the period when it was not produced in the south.

The discovery of tin and the invention of bronze cannot yet be definitely placed. Obviously a stanniferous region was involved (251). Data now available indicate that the use of bronze was confined largely to the Inca period.

Peruvian metallurgy probably contributed to the metalwork of Ecuador but the reverse is not true. On the other hand, it seems that a gold-copper alloy, mis-en-couler gilding and complex cire perdue casting were developed first in Colombia, and later influenced Peru, perhaps as early as the end of the Mochica period. In the Lambayeque region during the Late Chimu period, delicate filigree castings became very popular (12).

Finally, a brief word should be said about possible Peruvian influence on Mexican metallurgy. It has been suggested that the entire Mexican knowledge of metals was acquired as a unit from Peru by sea. The chief arguments in favor of this hypothesis are that silver and bronze were used commonly in both countries but rarely or not at all in intervening regions. Against this theory we may point out that no silver alloys are known in Mexico, although they are common in Peru. Bronze was used only for tools in Mexico, but its value in making sharp castings for ornaments was understood in Peru. Objects of pure lead were cast in Peru, but in Mexico lead was alloyed with copper. Thus it appears to me that both countries had discovered the same five basic metals and shared many of the same techniques, but each used them in ways suited to their own needs.

CERAMIC COMPARISONS OF TWO NORTH COAST PERUVIAN VALLEYS

Heinrich Ubbelohde Doering

In the past few years, the American archeologists have published many important monographs on Peruvian pre-history, including excellent accounts of excavations.[1] In this paper I would like to present some of the ideas which have resulted from my reading of these publications and comparing the results with my as yet unpublished field work in Pacasmayo (Jequetepeque) Valley in northern Peru.

To approach the coastal archeological problems on the basis of excavation evidence, we must consider the following significant accounts:

1. Uhle's work at the Huaca de la Luna, Moche.

2. Uhle's work at Pachacamac, perhaps his best field account.

3. Notes, although not complete reports, on Tello's work at Paracas, Nepeña, and Chavín.

4. Preliminary accounts of the work in Virú Valley by Bennett, Strong, Bird, and others.

5. The excavations and collections of Larco from Chicama Valley.

6. Uhle's and Kroeber's work in Nazca Valley, as well as my own which will soon be published.

7. The excavation of pre-ceramic sites in Chicama Valley by Bird.

8. The excavations by Disselhoff and myself in Jequetepeque Valley soon to be published.

For a scientifically sound chronological chart we should limit ourselves to such field excavation reports. The resulting chart would admittedly be fragmentary and incomplete, like an ancient mosaic, but what it contained would be based on sound facts and it would serve as a framework to be filled in by future excavators.

On the excavation evidence now available we can establish chronologies for specific valleys, but not a general one which covers all of them. In fact, one of my purposes in this paper is to point out some of the difficulties which arise from assuming that the chronology of one valley will apply to another. For example, the preliminary reports on Virú Valley place the Mochica culture in the tenth century A.D., while the coast Chavín culture is assigned to the beginning of the Christian era, or even earlier. Let us consider this in the light of our excavations in Jequetepeque Valley, less than 200 kilometers to the north.

1. The bibliographic references here and elsewhere in this paper can be found in the articles and bibliography in *A Reappraisal of Peruvian Archaeology* (39).

Our excavations in Jequetepeque were concentrated at the site called Pacat-namú or La Barranca which is composed of over sixty pyramids near the ocean shore. The pit described here was in a cemetery to one side of the largest pyramid. We encountered first a grave, at two meters' depth, which contained a disintegrated coffin of cane and a modeled owl vessel, with incised designs and a Chavinoid ring spout. Below this grave, at about four meters' depth, were three others (Field numbers, E-I, M-XI, M-XII).

The first grave (E-I) had a chamber at the base of a shaft, and was closed by an adobe wall supported by posts. In the chamber were several intact cane

FIG. 1

coffins and many vessels (Fig. 1). The coffins were brittle and decayed, but it was possible to remove them and examine their contents. One had a mummy with a folded turban around its head. The decoration on this cloth was of pure Mochica style. There was a central house or temple with a roof of snakelike beams surmounted by clubs. A fox-demon figure with sceptre is depicted within the temple. Another fabric was folded on the breast of the mummy. The design presents a snakelike scolopendra forming an arc over some mythological figures (Fig. 2). Similar designs are found on a Mochica vessel in the Berlin Museum. Other proof of the Mochica affiliation of this grave is presented by the designs on engraved calabashes and by the tattooed figures on a mummy's arms.

The textiles, calabashes, and tattooed designs thus identify the grave as Mochica, but the fifty ceramic vessels found with it are, with few exceptions (Fig. 4), non-Mochica. These present various styles. A flat black bottle with a relief design could be assigned to the coast Chavín culture (Fig. 3). A black vessel with bird relief and another with relief lizards might represent a peripheral Mochica style, although next to them was a gray owl jar with inlaid shell eyes, and another with crude incision. There are grayish-black jars with small relief figures of animals or warriors which seem archaic in syle. Exceptional, too, is a modeled head of a jaguar, almost thirty centimeters in height. There

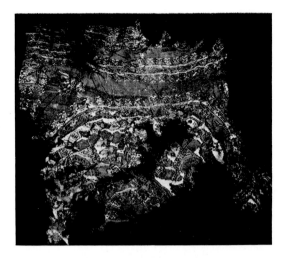

FIG. 2

FIG. 3

were several large jars with face collars, similar to Mochica, but with hands painted on the body of the vessel in broad brush strokes, reminiscent of Nazca style. The combination of plastic heads and rough painted body designs occurs in several vessels (Fig. 4). Finally, there were a series of quite primitive vessels which presented such details as the representation of a man with a hand over one eye, eyes made by a row of impressed circles (Fig. 5), and mouth-shaped reliefs. In brief, our Mochica grave contains many ceramic styles, including Chavinoid types.

FIG. 4

In the second grave (M-XI), we found more than twenty non-Mochica style vessels, including a fruit shaped jar, a modeled owl, and a crudely incised vessel, but there was also a classic Mochica vessel decorated with the characteristic masked warrior figures. Here again we find Mochica associated with different, although contemporaneous, styles.

The chamber of the third grave (M-XII) had been artificially filled with sand. It contained many copper implements, including copper nose plates and face masks of Mochica style and some curious flat clubs unknown elsewhere in Peru. The ceramics here were predominantly of Mochica style, such as a warrior figure with bird mask (Fig. 6), a relief scene of mythological beings, and a spiral motif (Fig. 7). However, one vessel was decorated with a dragonlike animal (Fig. 8), typical of Mochica, but with scrolls on the head like the incised ones on Chavín stone cornices. There was also a grayish-black bottle with relief designs of a divinity with snakes on the head, a snake belt, and animal heads for the feet. This is similar to the vessel from the first grave which was assigned to the coast Chavín style (Fig. 3).

FIG. 5

In résumé, then, all three of these graves belong basically to the Mochica culture. The associated non-Mochica vessels, some of which seem to be a late coast Chavín style, must be contemporaneous. Let us return then to the comparison of this situation with the chronology presented in Viru Valley. There, as mentioned previously, the Chavín and Mochica cultures are said to be separated by several hundred, perhaps a thousand, years. If this is so, the Jequetepeque finds to the north present a difficult problem. One interpretation could be that the coast Chavín style survived for eight or nine centuries in Jequetepeque, although extinguished elsewhere. This is not too convincing. Or, for Jequetepeque, we might move Chavín upward and Mochica downward in time by several centuries each to account for their association in the same graves. Two questions are posed for the Virú chronology. First, has Mochica culture there been given too late a date? Second, is the proposed date for Mochica culture in Virú valid for all manifestations of Mochica? It would seem logical to this writer that Mochica might be considerably earlier in its main center of development in Chicama Valley, particularly if one accepts the principle that the dispersion of a culture begins after it has reached the height of its development at the center.

Fig. 6

Strong bases his classification of epochs, called "Developmental," "Formative," etc., on the excavations in Virú Valley. So long as they are so limited they are acceptable. However, when they are projected to cover all ancient Peruvian cultures, caution must be exercised. The "developmental" aspect of one culture may coincide in time with a similar phenomenon in another culture, but this need not be so. Even admitting that Peru is a close knit unit, an area "co-tradition" in Bennett's terms, the development of culture throughout the whole region need not occur in the same time periods, and field evidence indicates that it doesn't.

In other words, developmental classifications, such as those proposed by Strong and Steward, are not also general chronological ones. My work in Nazca

FIG. 7

FIG. 8

would not suggest a developmental classification similar to the one in Virú, and it would seem inevitable that the situation in the highlands would be chronologically different than on the coast. We generally assume that the originators of Peruvian culture came in from outside the region, presumably from the north, although there is a possibility that they might have come from the south. In any case, the area first settled would have its initial development at an earlier date than the other areas.

This comparison of two North Coast valleys illustrates the difficulties of making sweeping generalizations at the present time. I am still convinced that we should continue to build our chronological classifications on the solid results of field excavations, and leave philosophical speculations for the future.

MAJOR CEREMONIAL AND POPULATION CENTERS
IN NORTHERN PERU[1]

Richard P. Schaedel

The Peruvian North Coast has been reconnoitered but the only published study to date that even attempts to present a synthetic picture of major sites in this zone is Kroeber's (167). The present paper is an attempt to present an over-all picture of the major archeological ruins on the north coast from the valley of Motupe on the North to the valley of Casma on the South. It is based upon a year and a half of intensive reconnaissance conducted by the Instituto de Antropología of the University of Trujillo in collaboration with Dr. Paul Kosok of Long Island University.

For our purposes a preliminary division of major sites was necessary. What we call ceremonial centers are clusters of *huacas* (pyramid-temples) usually with some minor construction in the immediate vicinity which may have served as living quarters for a limited population. Examples are the pyramid clusters of the Huaca del Sol and the Huaca de la Luna in Moche, the Chotuna group in Lambayeque and the Huaca de las dos Cabezas group in Jequetepeque, all described by Kroeber.

Our second major division is the population center, divided into two sub-groupings: the urban elite center and the lay center. The former, by far the most extensive and impressive type of site, is composed of a series of extensive walled compounds and terraced buildings with complicated internal subdivisions, as well as numerous minor structures, cemeteries, etc. Of those already described in the literature, Chan Chan is the most famous. Others are Purgatorio on the Leche river and Pacatnamú on the Jequetepeque river described by Kroeber. The lay centers are characterized by extensive and dense accumulation of house foundations, large refuse deposits, and occasional structures of high grade construction, but generally inferior to the architectural elegance characteristic of the urban elite centers. The majority of the lay centers appear to have served primarily defensive purposes, either as temporary or semi-permanent living quarters for large sectors of the population of a given valley in times of emergency, or as garrison units of a standing army. Almost every North Coast valley shows remains of one or more lay centers at the valley neck in excellent strategic location to protect the intakes of the major irrigation canals and hence control

---

1. Statements in this article are based upon the results of the author's reconnaissance in Peru up to September 1949. Modifications of these statements as a result of subsequent more detailed reconnaissances and excavations of some of the sites mentioned have not been made.

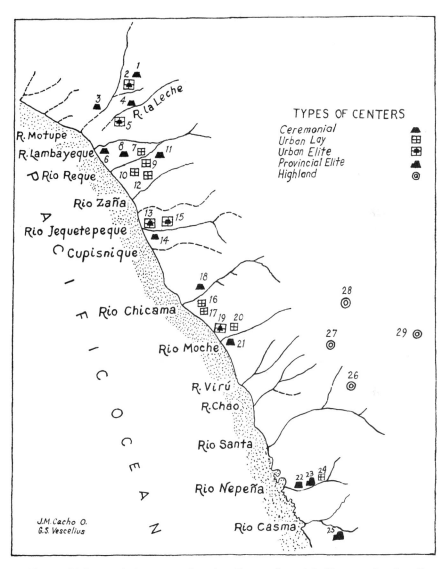

FIG. 1.—Major population centers of northern Peru. *1*, Cerro de la Virgen; *2*, Apurle; *3*, Las Banderas; *4*, Batan Grande; *5*, Purgatorio; *6*, Chotuna; *7*, Pátapo; *8*, Collúz; *9*, Saltur; *10*, Sipán; *11*, Pampa Grande; *12*, Cerro Corbacho; *13*, Pacatnamú; *14*, Huaca de los dos Cabezas; *15*, Farfán; *16*, Chicamita; *17*, Chiquitoy Viejo; *18*, Mocollope; *19*, Chanchan; *20*, Galindo; *21*, Huaca del Sol; *22*, Pañamarca; *23*, Punkuri; *24*, Cerro Pierna' Calzon; *25*, Manchal; *26*, Pashash; *27*, Santiago de Chuco; *28*, Huamachuco; *29*, Chilla.

the water distribution in the valley plain. Unfortunately, none of these lay centers has been described.

From the foregoing classification of major sites the question of chronology has been purposely excluded, since we do not feel that sufficient evidence is at hand from our preliminary survey to assign period occupation to the different types of sites. However, it may be said that the ceremonial centers were built not later than the Early and Middle periods (Florescent and Expansionist). The urban elite centers, or that portion of them which gives them a truly urban, planned form, were erected in the Middle and Late periods (Expansionist and Empire). The majority of the lay centers are the product of the Empire or Late periods, but there are significant exceptions which must be excluded in a brief report.

THE MOCHE AND CHICAMA VALLEYS

The principal ceremonial center for these two valleys was undoubtedly the cluster of ruins known as the Huaca del Sol and the Huaca de la Luna on the south bank of the Moche river. Uhle's excavations and Kroeber's analysis (172) of the collections and architectural details give a sufficiently clear picture of the site; no attempt is made here to elaborate upon it.

In the Chicama, a much larger valley than Moche, there are many more individual pyramid-temples, but with one exception they do not form a cluster. The only ruin which might justifiably be called a ceremonial center was the site of Mocollope, built around a natural hill in the central part of the valley plain. It is composed of a cluster of pyramids, terraced platforms with internal room divisions, and an extensive series of cemeteries. The sherd collection showed an overwhelming percentage of Mochica wares indicating that the site was contemporary with the Huaca del Sol and Huaca de la Luna cluster in the Moche valley.

Chan Chan, which we know from historical sources to have been the capital of the Chimu empire and hence of the entire north coast during several centuries preceding the Inca conquest, is the highest exponent of the elite urban center. It is located on the north bank of the Moche river between the foothills of the Coastal range and the sea. The ruin consists of a "metropolitan area" which, it can be reasonably assumed from the elaborate character of the dwelling units and the richness of the tombs excavated, housed the elite and their retainers. This is the section of the huge walled compounds, each with its palace-like structure decorated with low-relief friezes, plazas, storerooms, and smaller compounds with room divisions which Squier likened to wards of a modern city (319, p. 160). To the north and west of the central area is a vast plain of irrigated land with small walled compounds, interspersed constructions and stone foundations, as well as numerous isolated stone buildings, near irrigation canals and roads, which appear to have been guardhouses.

The intakes for the principal irrigation canals that fed Chan Chan were at the narrowings of the Moche and the Chicama rivers. It is significant that the two largest lay centers for these valleys are directly related to the principal irrigation system for the capital. The large lay center of Galindo is in the Moche valley, occupying the hills and small quebrada openings on the North bank before the valley widens to form the broad plain in which Chan Chan was situated. The site stretches up-valley for eight kilometers. It consists predominantly of numerous stone house foundations, which fill several small quebradas; steep hillsides terraced to provide numerous stone-lined rooms; and several formal compounds, some of stone, some of stone and rubble, and others of adobe. Two of the principal irrigation canals that fed Chan Chan pass through Galindo, and a third has its intake near by. This fact, coupled with a strong percentage of Chimu sherds in our surface collection and one Chan-Chan-like walled compound, is sufficient proof of the contemporaneity of the two sites.

In the Chicama valley, along the course of the large canal that eventually leads to Chan Chan, there is an extensive plain of formerly irrigated land with numerous though dispersed remains of walled compounds and stone buildings. Although in current usage this area is divided into a cluster of ruins called Chicamita, near the present pueblo of Chicama, and Chiquitoy Viejo, near the hacienda Chiquitoy, it probably formed a single interconnected lay center of the Chimu period. Unlike Galindo, its function was not defensive. It represents, probably, a planned agricultural community organized to cultivate a sector of land made usable by large scale irrigation projects.

THE JEQUETEPEQUE VALLEY

Reconnaissance in this large valley was limited to the maritime section and the immediate north and south banks. It seems unlikely, however, from careful review of the aerial photographs that the lower Jequetepeque will provide any ceremonial center other than the Huaca de las Dos Cabezas group sketched by Kroeber. This important cluster at the southern mouth of the Jequetepeque river is similar to ceremonial centers further north, but like many of these it remains undated.

On the opposite bank, situated on a steep cliff overlooking the sea, is the impressive complex of pyramids known as Pacatnamú. As Kroeber observed, the ruin can be divided into a new and an old section. The old section consists of a series of small adobe pyramids, generally oriented in a North-South direction and in a line parallel with the seashore. This section, if proved to be older than the adjoining one, is quite probably a second ceremonial center. The newer section, sketched by Kroeber, has striking architectural similarity to Chan Chan, and could be categorized as urban elite housing. It is hoped that the detailed report by Dr. Heinrich Doering on his excavations in this ruin will establish the relative antiquity of the two sections.

A second elite urban center in the Jequetepeque valley is Farfán, an elongated series of walled compounds with subdivisions that stretches along the Panamerican Highway some few kilometers to the south of Guadelupe. Both from the Chan-Chan-like architecture and the preponderance of Chimu sherds in the surface collection, we are reasonably sure of assigning this center to the Chimu empire.

From a perusal of detailed aerial photographs and information proffered by Dr. Kosok, we were able to locate what appear to be several populous lay centers on the north and south banks of the upper Jequetepeque; our personal reconnaissance did not include these sites.

Similarly in the region of the Rio Seco de San Gregorio to the north of the Jequetepeque, Dr. Kosok located what appears to have been a ceremonial center of the early period, called Moro Viejo; detailed reconnaissance in this area remains to be done.

THE SAÑA VALLEY

Only brief reconnaissance was carried on in this small valley. Evidence from aerial photographs indicates that in the lower Saña there exist one or more ceremonial centers, but they have not been investigated as yet.

There does not appear to be any elite urban center, but the upper and middle Saña contain a number of lay centers. We are able to report on perhaps the largest of these, known as the ruins of Cerro Corbacho, located on the north bank of the river at the narrowing of the valley. This site consists of a dense grouping of terraced platforms on the lower slopes of the hill; stone-walled rectangular compounds suggesting garrison units on the level spurs of the hill somewhat higher up; a series of interconnecting walls joining all parts of this complex of stone structures; and at the base a number of walled adobe compounds, similar in form to those of Chan Chan but with vacuous interiors. Similar in function to Galindo, the ruins of Cerro Corbacho differ in the absence of the stone house foundations and in the presence of the well-constructed stone defensive network on the higher levels.

A detailed study of the architectural elements at this center and in others of a similar type in the Lambayeque valley further north indicates that Cerro Corbacho was occupied successively by the Chimus and the Incas. The walled but empty compounds at the base, both from form and from the sherds in the vicinity, seem to be Chimu garrisons; the stone structures on the upper level appear to be Incaic. In several similar ruins, Chimu sherds were found imbedded in the fill between the stones of the Incaic rectangles. The terraced platforms on the lower slopes possibly will yield evidence of an earlier pre-Chimu occupation, but our surface collections revealed little that was not Chimu or Inca.

THE LAMBAYEQUE VALLEY

By far the largest of the north coast valleys, the Lambayeque contains at least three times as many large sites as any other single valley. Kroeber has sketched the Mocce group, which appears to be a ceremonial center, and the Chotuna group which certainly is. The Chotuna group is quite similar in plan to the ceremonial center of Colluz, also in the Lambayeque valley though some-what further inland. In both centers, the principal structure is a steep-sided pyramid with zig-zag, ascending ramp; there is a secondary structure in the form of a stepped pyramid with central, ascending ramp that cuts the first two terraces; and the pyramids are grouped around an irregular open space or plaza. The Chotuna group is unique in that it contains a pyramid with a courtyard annex (listed on the Kroeber sketch as "sand huaca"), on the interior walls of which are remains of a colored relief frieze. Although there are other somewhat smaller pyramid clusters in the central part of the valley plain, Chotuna and Colluz are the largest. Considerable difficulty arises in assigning period occupa-tion to these sites because of the undefined ingredients of the surface collections. At Colluz, for example, a great number of plain and white-slipped paddle-ware sherds were found with a considerable variety of motives; a representative num-ber of red-on-white-slip pieces, pointing to an undefined style; and a small num-ber of incised and gouge-marked sherds. The small number of Chimu sherds combined with what we considered a regional mixture makes a middle to late occupation most probable. The Chotuna cluster yielded too few sherds for analy-sis. The style of the painted relief frieze, however, on analogy with a similar one in the Huaca "el Dragon" in the Moche valley (296, p. 73), is very similar to the Middle Chimu pressed ware ceramic style, and hence points again to a middle period for the construction of the pyramid.

An up-valley site on the south bank known as Pampa Grande presents what we consider an intrusive ceremonial center in the Lambayeque. The site is com-posed of two adobe pyramids, one of which equals the Huaca del Sol in size. There are in the vicinity remains of adobe wall constructions paralleling the periphery of the major pyramid; most of them can only be distinguished from the air view. At this site Mochica sherds were found both by our expedition and by Dr. Henri Reichlen. Like most ceremonial centers that were in existence some time, at Pampa Grande there is much late period reuse of the area and much of the original adobe structures which are oriented to the large pyramids have been virtually obliterated by what appears to have been Inca reoccupa-tion, the latter consisting of stone walled units.

There is no elite urban center in the Lambayeque valley, but there is a rela-tive abundance of large lay centers. The most important, as in the valleys to the south, are located on the north and south banks at the neck of the valley. The largest, not only in Lambayeque but in the entire north coast, is Patapo, which, as has been frequently observed, is almost surely ancient Cinto. The center of the ruin consists of terraced platforms against a natural hill on some of which small adobe huacas may be discerned. Below these are several Chimu-style com-pounds with few internal subdivisions, probably garrison units. Above these, as at Cerro Corbacho in the Saña valley, is an elaborate chain of stone structures, suggesting lookout stations and garrisons, interconnected by extensive stone walls. The main North-South Inca coastal road passes at the southwest foot of the hill and intersects the ruin at various points. The sherd collection from Patapo supports the architectural analysis. Inca sherds are found in abundance in the upper levels of stone ruins, while Chimu sherds predominate at the base, mixed with local wares.

On the south bank of the Lambayeque at the first narrowing of the valley is the lay center of Saltur. It is generally similar to Cerro Corbacho and Patapo, with the same combination of central terraced platforms, walled compounds of adobe and higher level stone units, all compactly massed on the sides of a large hill. Sherds here were exclusively Chimu and Inca.

Some six kilometers further east of Saltur is a second large lay center, occupying a plain which slopes across from the Lambayeque in a southerly direction to the Saña. The site is known as Sipan or Collique and is connected with Patapo by means of the main North-South Inca highway passing between Saltur and Sipan. The general aspect of the ruins is that of a sprawling agricultural community with small walled compounds at intervals along the irrigation canals. A clustering of unfaced rubble and stone mounds with little evidence of formal terracing is characteristic of the northern sector. One large adobe pyramid and several smaller ones form a small group near these mounds and appear to be an older section, but we were unable to secure any evidence to substantiate this impression. The walled compounds are typically Chimu, and there was no evidence of Incaic structures in the area reconnoitered, although Inca sherds formed a substantial ingredient of the surface collection.

In summary, the ceremonial centers of the Lambayeque, with the exception of the intrusive Pampa Grande site, are located in the central part of the lower valley plain; the large lay centers are situated at the valley neck and along the main North-South line of communication. The latter are predominantly of Chimu and Inca occupation. In fact, Inca influence is stronger in the lay centers of the Lambayeque than in any other north coast valley.

THE LECHE AND MOTUPE VALLEYS

The two rivers form the northern boundary of our reconnaissance, chosen because the density of ruins in this North Coast cultural province terminates with these two valleys.

The principal ceremonial center is a cluster of large adobe pyramids on the mid-Leche river known as Batan Grande. Like the ceremonial centers in the Lambayeque valley, the site of Batan Grande consists in a grouping of pyramids about a roughly defined central area. They have the same steep-sided profiles and the emphasis on the ramp approach as the Lambayeque pyramids. One of the principal pyramids, called the Huaca del Oro, has the remains of a polychrome painted frieze. From the small section which we cleared, it was possible to distinguish what appears to be the figure of an anthropomorphized owl, similar to the frieze of the Huaca Pintada in Tucume (70, p. 585). It is the only painted mural decoration known north of the Chicama valley, just as the

Chotuna reliefs are the only low-relief friezes. By analogy with developments in the Moche valley, it would seem logical to consider a painted frieze antecedent to low relief. Our surface collection from the Batan Grande group contained a considerable proportion of sherds painted red on a cream-slipped base, some incised sherds, and a mixture of Middle and Late Lambayeque forms. In view of the combined evidence—the painted frieze, which in style looks Tiahuanacoid and in technique could be older; the painted ware in the surface collection which points to a Cajamarca-like Early or Middle period style; and the architecture which is local and well developed—we consider the Batan Grande cluster to have been formed in the Middle and possibly Early periods and to have been reoccupied and to some extent rebuilt in Chimu times.

Two smaller pyramid clusters which were reconnoitered are the Las Banderas group on the northwestern extension of the Leche river and the Cerro de la Virgen group near the pueblo of Chochope, further inland than Motupe. In both centers the pyramids were of more modest proportions than the characteristic steep-sided type of the Leche proper and Lambayeque; the forms, although more difficult to ascertain because of the worn condition of the structures, possessed no excessive ramp developments. The surface collections in both sites showed the familiar mixture of elaborate paddle-ware decoration, fine orange-on-white slip wares, and a small proportion of Chimu blackware.

In the center of the Leche valley is the well-known site of El Purgatorio which has all the characteristics of an elite urban center. The ruin consists of numerous pyramids and walled groups, closely massed on three sides of a natural hill, with a large cemetery occupying the remaining space. On the upper slopes and summit of the hill are numerous walls and small platforms and rooms which appear to have been observatories. The excavations of Bennett (34) indicate Chimu occupation of the site which the presence of intrusive-looking walled compounds tends to confirm architecturally. Several stone-faced structures on the summit of the hill are similar to Incaic structures in the lay centers of the Lambayeque and also appear intrusive. The pyramids of the site, however, are typical of those of the Leche river. The approaches are mostly by long platform ramps which project tangent-wise from one of the corners; although some pyramids have the zig-zag approach as in Chotuna and Colluz. Several of the elevated compounds present a new and apparently local urban unit. It shares the principle of numerous room subdivisions with the Chan Chan compound, but in place of the high circumferential wall as the delimiting and defending element, the Purgatorio compound is elevated some fifty feet with a sheer drop to the ground level, and has no exterior wall. As in the Chan Chan compound the entrances are few.

A second urban elite center in this zone of a quite different character from any described so far is Apurle, situated a slight distance from the south bank of the Motupe river. The presence of an urban center the size of Apurle, which is second only to Chan Chan in extent, is somewhat surprising near a river as tiny as the Motupe. Its existence has been satisfactorily explained by Kosok as depending upon the water of the Leche river to the south as well as that of the Motupe. Kosok also holds that Apurle must have existed at a time when water was in turn diverted from the large Lambayeque river to the Leche in order to supplement the water that had been taken northwards for the large settlement of Apurle.

Apurle is a large, spacious urban site centered about a natural hill. The principal structures are clustered at the base; leading out from these are wide avenues and leading in are large irrigation canals. The structural unit here is a rather low pyramidal mound with little to no terracing. The mounds are distributed about a broad area, tending to form clusters generally in a line or at right angles with one another. The sherd collection was very similar to that of the Las Banderas and the Cerro de la Virgen group. Certain large vacuous compounds at the base of the hill probably indicate a certain period of Chimu occupation.

Aerial photographs give abundant evidence of very large settlements in the upper Leche which seem to be lay centers, but our reconnaissance did not include any lay center in this zone.

In comparing the major population centers in the Leche-Motupe valleys with those of Lambayeque, perhaps the most significant fact is the large number of lay centers in Lambayeque and the relative paucity further north. At the same time, the Leche and Motupe valleys boast two elite urban centers, while the Lambayeque has none. Since we are dealing with Middle and Late or Expansionist developments in these sites, it is almost certain that the inter-valley irrigation system had been elaborated by this time and that a similar relation existed between the Leche-Motupe and the Lambayeque valleys as that which existed between the Moche and the Chicama valleys farther south. Thus it is possible that the larger valley (the Chicama and the Lambayeque) was utilized for agricultural exploitation while the nearby smaller valley became the scene for the urban developments of the governing group.

THE SOUTHERN VALLEYS OF THE NORTH COAST

The next two valleys south of the Moche are Viru and Chao which are omitted from this report since Willey has described the settlement patterns in these valleys.[2]

Our reconnaissance of the next valley farther south, the Santa, was confined to the immediate south bank generally and included only a sporadic survey of mid- and up-valley sites, not necessarily the major population centers. For this reason classification of the major centers in this valley is not complete enough to warrant exposition.

Certain observations resulting from our reconnaissance are, however, pertinent. The Santa valley is the northernmost of three successive valleys—the

2. Dr. Gordon Willey's article, "Peruvian Settlement and Socio-economic Patterns," appears in this volume, pp. 195–200.

Santa, Nepeña, and Casma—which reflect strong highland influences in the architecture at unusually low levels. These valleys are dotted with stone "castillos" which in their construction of well-faced cut stone reflect highland and not coastal traditions. These structures give no evidence of having been of Incaic origin; neither do they compare with Chavin or Callejón de Huaylas styles. The sherds found in these sites were not affiliated with any known coast or highland ceramic style. It would seem safest to regard these stone works as the product of a provincial development in the upper parts of the Santa, Nepeña, and Casma rivers.

A second general observation is that beginning with the south bank of the Santa and again including the Nepeña and Casma valleys, in the sites with truly coastal architecture (i.e., excluding the stone works mentioned above) a rather uniform surface collection pertains, at least of utilitarian ware. This ware is usually unslipped, is extravagantly decorated with reed punch marks, gouge marks and incisions; and presents a high proportion of modelled nubbins, as well as vertical and horizontal handles. The ware, for its primitive decoration, suggests a flamboyant development of certain Chavinoid techniques. Perhaps for this reason Kroeber was led to reproduce a few sherds of this type as characteristic of Cerro Sechín (171, Pl. 22). It is, however, a major ingredient of the sherd collections of the coastal sites of these three valleys and appears to be a local ware. It is found in the southern section of the north coast with about the same distribution and density as paddle-ware in the northern section.

In the Nepeña valley, the major ceremonial center is the high-walled site of Pañamarca, in the central valley plain. The design of the principal edifice is not unlike that of the temple of Pachacamac with a series of stepped terraces built against a natural outcrop. It is unlike other north coast centers in form. Remains of painted wall decoration are to be seen in various sections of the high walls, as though murals had existed of some fifty feet in height. The fragments of the paintings do not particularly reflect Mochica influence as has been frequently assumed.

While neither in the Santa or Nepeña valleys is there any true urban elite center, there are in the Nepeña valley and further south relatively small, planned units which demonstrate small-scale urban elegance. Typical of this type of late period site is Punkurí Alto, near the famous Chavinoid temple of Punkurí in the central Nepeña valley. The ruin occupies a natural outcrop and consists of multiple room divisions ingeniously adapted to the natural irregularities of the hill, a series of graded terraces forming the entrance on one side, and on the upper levels two antechambers decorated with niche friezes (in which the design is produced on an adobe wall by removing certain adobes to form the desired figures). Quite similar in size and planning to Punkurí Alto is the site of Manchal on the south bank of the Casma, a ruin bisected by the Panamerican highway. Manchal is built of tapia construction, characteristic of Middle and Late period structures in the central coast, but intrusive in the north. Whatever the function of these small planned units, which we may consider local sub-prefectures, they are consistently found in the smaller valleys of the Central Coast as well as intrusively farther north as in the irrigated area south of Saña.

While personal reconnaissance in the southern section of the north coast brought us to only one lay center, the ruins of Cerro Pierna Calzon on the north bank of the Nepeña river, the aerial photographs indicate several others. The ruins of Cerro Pierna Calzon are similar to the lay centers of Saña and Lambayeque, though on a smaller scale. The site seems to have had a purely defensive function.

Although the southern valleys of the north coast have not been reconnoitered with as much detail as the central and the northern ones, it can be said that they do not contain many true population centers of the size and consequence of those typical of the valleys further north. The role these valleys played in Expansionist and Empire times remains to be established. At the moment the major problem in the study of these valleys is the determination of the significance of the unusually strong highland influence.

NORTH HIGHLAND RECONNAISSANCE

In an effort to establish the boundaries of pre-Incaic cultural provinces in the North Highlands a series of surveys was conducted in the zone of the Tablachaca (Cabana, Huandoval, and Tauca), Santiago de Chuco, and Pataz.

In the reconnaissance of the Tablachaca zone it was possible to establish the site of Pashash as one of the, if not the most important center of the Recuay period. The evidence is based on the abundant ceramic evidence from the surface collection from the site, which is clearly Recuay, and on some thirty odd pieces of stone sculpture taken from the ruin with technically excellent reproductions of Recuay ceramic motives.

The Santiago de Chuco survey was limited to the immediate periphery of the town of that name, and the evidence does not warrant the establishment of a cultural province for this zone, which seems to have been a sub-province of Huamachuco in prehistory.

In the Pataz region limited reconnaissance pointed to Nuñamarka as the probable ceremonial center. The stone sculpture of the site is very similar to that of Pashash and the Callejón de Huaylas in the Recuay period.

SUMMARY

The foregoing presentation has of necessity been brief and general rather than detailed. Even so, certain significant conclusions about north coast prehistory emerge:

1. Major sites on the north coast for the most part pertain to the last one thousand years of Peruvian prehistory, or the Early (Florescent), Middle (Expansionist), and Late (Empire) periods.

2. The pyramid cluster, which we have called the ceremonial center, ante-

dates in all cases the elite urban center, and in most cases antedates the lay urban center.

3. The ceremonial center reflects stylistic architectural differences between individual valleys and between groups of valleys.

4. The population centers reflect the tendency in the Late periods to concentrate large masses of the population, on the one hand in luxurious urban units of the upper class, and on the other in strategically important military and agricultural settlements.

5. Large urban developments are usually related to or dependent upon inter-valley irrigation systems.

6. The population centers are for the most part the product of, and therefore reflect, the economic and political development and expansion of the Chimu state and its subsequent occupation by the Incas.

7. Prior to the formation of the Chimu state, the relative roles played by individual north coast valleys in the struggle for local hegemony fluctuated a good deal and was affected by contemporary developments of alien origin.

The archeological documentation for that phase in the emergence of civilization that Childe calls the urban revolution is perhaps nowhere more complete than on the Peruvian North Coast. If this paper has focused attention of students of civilization on this most important fact, it will have more than served its purpose.

RITUAL RACES AMONG THE EARLY CHIMU

Gerdt Kutscher

Certain motifs which constantly recur among the vase paintings of early Chimu present a unique source for the understanding of this pre-Inca culture of ancient Peru. A frequent theme pictures a line of men moving rapidly forward. T. A. Joyce (152, p. 113) noted that out of a collection of 250 vases which arrived at the British Museum from Valle de Chicama, more than thirty vessels were decorated in this manner. He points out that the frequent occurrence of this kind of representation indicates the exceptional significance with which this scene was endowed in the early Chimu culture (154, p. 180; 152, p. 113).

The old Spanish sources—especially Antonio de la Calancha and Miguel Cabello de Balbao—contain only pitifully sparse information concerning the pre-Inca culture on the Peruvian north coast. It is therefore necessary to infer the significance of these representations iconographically—through a comparative analysis of the works themselves.

Even brief inspection of the vase figures indicates remarkable resemblances in minute, yet certainly not insignificant, detail. It is unlikely that this could be accidental; rather, one may assume that this frequently represented scene must have occurred in definitive, fixed forms which were personally well known to the painters. Furthermore, the ceremonious character of this scene might be inferred from its rigidly determined pattern.

I

The first task is to describe in detail the scene represented on the Chimu vases.

The background is, in all cases, definitely desert-like in character, as is common to the arid regions which separate the river valleys—the seats of culture—along the coast of North Peru. Dunes and chains of low hills are represented by a wave-like ground line as they are in the numerous battle and deer hunts, scenes which are also favored themes for vase painting. Dotting frequently indicates a sandy ground. Sand mounds with wave-like contours sometimes also arise between the various figures, or project from above into the picture. The sparse vegetation is limited to cacti and Tillandsia. Through this sandy desert moves a line of men. Most frequently there are four or five of these figures on the painting, since this number is best suited to the available vase surface.[1] These few

[1]. For illustrations of these details, see the following references: 152, ill. 2; 119, Pl. 94; 175, ill. 39; 240, Pl. 11; 138; 44, No. 14092; 20, Pl. 45/212; 183, Vol. I, Pl. 20, ill. p. 5; 183, II 85, ill. 164, and 176, Pl. 20; 252, ill. 139; 307, ill. 17.

figures, however, represent a much larger column, in the same way as the so frequently repeated pairs of warriors symbolize a multitude of fighters. The line of four or five figures makes a closed circle around the vase circumference, without a leader or starting point being noticeable. In a second kind of painting, however, the column is always ordered in the form of a long drawn-out spiral.

These figures follow, as a rule, in an unbroken line, whether they circle horizontally the body of the vase, or spiral upward so that the end of the spiral approaches the spot where the stirrup-like handle-spout is joined to the body. Both of these forms of composition are only infrequently abandoned for another arrangement such as the one which can be observed on the vase paintings at the Berlin collection (44, No. 13043) in which the figures cover the whole surface with no apparent organization.

The posture of the figures is always the same. Both legs are stretched out in rapid motion so that often only the forward foot is touching the ground. The arms are held at an angle, with closed hands as belt or even chest level. The clothes and jewelry of these figures have a number of peculiarities when compared to the usual kind. The absence of such important pieces of costume as shirt and skirt, which even the simple fishing and seal-hunting people among the Chimu only rarely forego, appears very strange. The upper part of the body is here always uncovered and both nipples are sometimes indicated. With few exceptions (119, Pl. 94; 240, Pl. 11; 142, ill. p. 487), only a dark, simple cloth with a bright, decorated belt covers the loins. The large ear discs, which are otherwise such favorite jewelry pieces, are only rarely observed (119, Pl. 94; 44, No. 14092).

The impression given by the position of the figures is that shirt and skirt have been left off in order to facilitate free and unhampered motion. The head pieces, on the other hand, are usually distinguished by particularly splendid ornaments which are fastened to the front of the head band by a thorn. The richly developed head ornamentation does not occur on other vase paintings, but is reserved for the men who participate in these ceremonies. In any case, the head ornamentation seems to be endowed with great importance since it is sometimes also used as decoration for the handle (307, ill. 17).

Most of the figures hold a very strange emblem in their outstretched hand. The lower half of the object is sometimes disc-like, sometimes drop-like or rod formed. The rest of the object which is not obscured by the fingers consists of two long drawn out pointed ends projecting over the thumb in either a vertical or sickle-shaped curve. The lower half of the object sometimes has two or three horizontally running lines. Some figures in the column have empty hands, and there are some vases on which no figure is provided with this emblem.[2] Only in rare instances do other objects appear in the hands of these figures. For ex-

2. For illustrations of these details see the following references: 183, Vol. I, ill. p. 9, Pl. 23, ill. p. 5; 183, Vol. II, ills. 164, 176; 20, Pl. 45/212; 152, ill. 2; 119, Pl. 94; 240, pl. 11; 175, ill. 38; 245, No. 729; 44, Nos. 62184, 48009; 252, cover.

ample, in the paintings of the Larco Herrera collection, the emblems have a fishbone-like form, while they are reproduced as parallel running lines on the vessels of the Berlin Museum (183, Vol. II, ill. 176; 175, ill. 39).

Besides the white-tailed eagle, we find also humming birds on various pictures accompanying the column and soaring as spirits above the figures. Especially peculiar are the small bean seeds which are strewn in smaller or larger numbers between the figures so that they sometimes fill in the whole space.[3]

Summarizing, the following peculiarities can be established for these representations: the arrangement of the figures moving through desert-like country; the characteristic position of arms and legs which represents rapid motion; the absence of certain pieces of dress; the splendid head ornamentation; the peculiar emblem in the hand of the runners; and, finally, the occurrence of bean seeds as "space fillers."

II

As to the problem of the meaning of this representation, let us first consider Eduard Seler's interpretation (305, p. 295) of the figures as similar to the "Chasquis," the messenger runner of the Inca era. This interpretation, which has also been recently championed by Larco Hoyle (183, II, 90 f.; 180, p. 175), appears at first reasonable. The light dress as well as the characteristic position of the figures is consistent with it. The representation of a long column of runners indicates the participation of numerous messengers in the form of a relay post. According to the chronicler Morua, the "Chasquis" has been introduced only under the government of the Inca Tupac Yupanqui, who conquered the peoples of the north coast. Larco Hoyle (183, II, 122 f.), therefore, assumes this arrangement, originating in the early Chimu period, had been taken over by the Incas from the late Chimu.

A close comparison with the "Chasquis" of the Inca period, who are thoroughly described by various chroniclers, and the figures of runners on these vases shows, however, a number of differences which make Seler's and Larco Hoyle's interpretation questionable. The old reports state very clearly that only *one* messenger was always under way, who then was relieved, after a certain distance, by another runner (83, II, p. 21; *68, p. 169; 226, pp. 33–34). In contrast to this, on the vase paintings there always appear a large number of runners. Larco Hoyle tried to explain this difference by stating that by the presentation of a whole column the continuous, lasting character of the transmission was being expressed, in that the time sequence was visualized by spatial contiguity. This explanation, however, is not convincing because many of the paintings have runners pictured above and beside each other, definitely indicating that *all* runners are *simultaneously* in motion. The Berlin vase paintings also show very clearly that the column of runners is moving ahead, not in a fixed order, but that each participant is striving to be the first to reach the goal.

3. For illustrations of these details see the following references: 175, ill. 38, 39; 44, No. 462193; 240, Pl. 11; 183, Vol. II, Pl. 20, ill. 164, ill. p. 85.

III

A. Baessler offers a more fruitful line of approach. He asserts that we are dealing with "scenes from a festival" in which "men running rapidly" follow each other (20, Pl. 45/212). However, any attempt at a more probable interpretation of these pictures must not permit the characteristic emblem held in the runner's hand to remain unexplained. Baessler interprets the emblem as "an instrument which has not yet been found in the original." Remarkably enough, in the accompanying text to his published relief representations, Baessler has considered a quite different explanation of this emblem (20, Pl. 44/210). Here he speaks of a "purse" which is held in the hand of the runners. Baessler was probably led to this explanation by the semi-spherical shape of the lower part.

Larco Hoyle picks up Baessler's idea and explains the obscure emblem as a purse or small bag (183, II, 90). Larco Hoyle is led to this by a series of excavation findings in the Valle de Santa, among which were some purses of llama leather that were tied together by means of a string. Baessler shows a very similar purse from Chuquitanta (20, Pl. 29/174). The correctness of this explanation is proven by a photograph of Larco Hoyle's in which the discovered leather purse is shown in the hand of one of the finders (183, Vol. II, ill. 87). The result shows surprising similarity to the representations on the vase paintings. The string with which the purse was closed is also clearly recognizable on some vase paintings where it is indicated by a series of horizontal lines (183, Vol. I, ill. p. 144, Vol. II, Pl. 22). The disc-shaped representation in the paintings corresponds to the small semi-sphere in the relief works, on which Baessler based his explanation. The manner in which the purse is represented results in two tips rising up over the hand. We are dealing here with the two corners of the cloth or piece of leather which remain after the two opposite ends have been tied into a knot.

IV

There arises the further question as to the contents of this container. Even if the purse does not directly reveal its content, it is indicated in a different way. The small bean seeds which appear on so many vase paintings between the runners are often in such large numbers that they fill up the whole space. They are not to be viewed simply as "fillers-in," but have a definite meaning. They have the task of explaining the contents of the purse.

There still remains to be explained the above mentioned parallel lines or lines in the form of a fish bone. Comparison indicates that the handle of that familiar vessel of the Baessler collection which presents a deer hunt is decorated with a very similar design (297, ill. p. 189/1). This connection with the representation of a deer hunt indicates that we are dealing with branches of the Algarrobo plant on whose shoots the deer feed. The branches of this tree are represented on the Baessler vases in the same fish-bone-like shape as on the emblem of the runners (419, ill. 20; 150, p. 93; 119, Pl. 96). The runners on the Baessler vases carry twigs in their hands instead of bean-filled purses. In both cases vegetable forms are used as emblems.

But the vessels can also give information about the goal of the column. While most vase paintings limit themselves to the column of runners, the vessels of the Wasserman San Blas collection show the goal of the runners very clearly (407, No. 520). It is a small, temple-like building on the platform of a round step-pyramid. On the narrow ramps, which wind spiral-like around the pyramid, appear two runners who are hurrying up the platform. The emblem which H. Lehmann, compiler of the Wasserman collection, refers to as gift offerings (*ofrendas*) (407, text, ill. 520) are none other than the well known purse with bean seeds. Inside the sanctuary appears a small sitting figure which represents a deity, judging by the characteristic shape of the mouth. A frieze of small plasticly set up snail figures adorns the edge of the ramps. This representation of the Wasserman-San Blas collection finds its counterpart in a vase painting of the Berlin museum. A temple-like structure on the platform of a pyramid is here also the goal of a race (175, ill. 67). The approach to the sanctuary occurs along a sloping ramp similar to the typical imposing "Huacas" of the early Chimu period in Moche, Pacatnamu', etc. (166, p. 62) (109, p. 51). A number of beans associated with the painting of the temple characterize it as a kind of "bean house." Perhaps we should think of it as a mythical home of the bean similar to those which formed the basis of the "Cincalco," the "house of the maize" in Aztec mythology. The small snail figures on the vessels of the Wasserman collection were probably connected with images of moisture and fertility.

The goal of the race is one of the large sanctuaries on the platform of a step pyramid. Through this connection with the sacred temple pyramids of the "Huaca del Sol" of Moche type, these scenes enter into close relation with the religious sphere and gain the character of a sacred action. We are dealing then with "processions" (G. Montell).

V

This interpretation raises the question as to the deeper meaning of these races. For what purpose did this large number of men, with festive head decoration, and bean filled purses or torn off Algarrobo branches, assemble to cross the sandy desert and run rapidly towards a temple pyramid?

It is improbable that these races were only athletic events. Examples from other Indian cultures strengthen the assumption that a sacred act is in process. The ceremonial races which have been passed down by various American peoples served not athletic but magical purposes. The religious background of the races has been worked out especially by K. T. Preuss (270, p. 58), and has also been emphasized by R. Benedict (32, p. 114). In the sacred races of the tribes of northwest Mexico and southwest North America, we are dealing quite obviously with ceremonies which, as Preuss has shown, served the purpose of assuring the fertility of the land. In the rain magic of native populations of Diaguita territory in northwest Argentina, races still play a dominant role (354, p. 79). It appears also from the reports of ancient chronicles that sacred races were known in the Inca period, although in these the relation to the fertility of the land is, as a rule, not easily recognizable. However, the archbishop of Lima, Don Pedro de Villagonez, reports concerning a race which had been arranged by the population of the region of Lima about the time of the Acataymita celebrations (406, p. 173). In the eighteenth paragraph of the forty-sixth chapter of his *Exortaciones*, the Bishop makes the following statements:

Otro abuso más perjudicial que este, es que per el mes de Diciembre que empiezan a madurar las paltas, hacen una fiesta que llaman *Acataymita*, que dura seis días con sus noches, para que madure la fruta. Júntanse Hombres, y mugeres en una placeta entre unas huertas desnudos en cueros, y dende allí corren a un cerro, muy grande trecho, y con la muger que alcanzan en la carrera tienen acceso. Preceden a esta fiesta por vigilia cinco días de ayuno, no comiendo sal, ni agi, llegando a mugeres.

Von Tschudi (383, p. 26), who cites this report, emphasizes that this festival which had been preserved as late as the first third of the seventeenth century, represented no "beastly sexual intermingling" but "hangs together with the Palta fruit and its ripening." That we are dealing here with a ceremony of great importance appears from the elaborate preparations involving feasting and abstinence.

This same idea of the use of sacred races to stimulate fertility of specific plants is also the basis of the scenes which are frequently treated in the vase paintings of early Chimu. It is sufficiently apparent that in almost all cases interest is focused on the bean seed; for in that time the bean provided the population of these densely populated river valleys with the actual basis of existence (175, p. 62).

If these races are interpreted as fertility rites which stood in magical relation to the maturing of the bean seeds, it then becomes obvious why this theme is so frequently depicted on the Chimu vases. The artistic representations of these races occupied the vase painters of that early period because they were dealing with that ceremony which, according to their belief, assured the nourishment of the community. The sacred races of the early Chimu are perhaps the most important religious rites which the culture possessed.

VI

The interpretation of this group of vase paintings is enriched by consideration of another group of paintings in which a curious mixture of animal and human forms appear. Not only the desert-like surroundings, but also clothes, ornament, and emblems of the runners are the same as on the paintings of the first group.

Joyce (154, Text ill. 15; 152, p. 117) saw in these paintings the representation of masked dances and interpreted the figures as masked men in ceremonial habit. These masked dances—which have been brought down in similar form from the Inca period—grew out of the totemistic image world of that era. Baessler (20, Text to Pl. 46/213) had already thought of "men with bird masks" in relation to his published paintings. Larco Hoyle (183, II, 395, Text Pl. 22), on the other hand, sees in these beings idealized messengers whose mixed form was supposed to have expressed symbolically the swiftness, cleverness, etc., of the script scholars.

While Larco Hoyle's interpretation fails because the Chimu—in common with the other Peruvian peoples—possessed no script; Joyce's and Baessler's notions are also unconvincing because we are dealing, as we saw above, not with dancers but with runners. A second difficulty arises when attempting to explain these mixed figures as men wearing masks, for this would lead to the highly improbable conclusion that the ceremony was sometimes conducted with masks and sometimes without masks. Further, if these figures are men wearing masks, then there remain no representations of deities and demons themselves and the manifold god world of the ancient Chimu. We cannot therefore be dealing, here or in the other paintings, with representations of masked dancers but with the demonic beings themselves in whom human and animal features have been combined. These paintings do not present scenes of Chimu life, but rather mythical scenes in which the demons themselves appear.

The goal of these races is sometimes also represented. The goal in some paintings, as in that of the Berlin collection, is a temple pyramid. In other vessels of the same collection it is an enthroned deity accompanied by an owl demon, armed with a whip (175, ill. 50). A four-cornered cloth is spread out in front of the owl demons, on which two bean seeds lie; the cloths that had been knotted together into purses could have been of the same kind. The deity who is expecting the approach of the column may be identified as the moon god Si who, according to reports by Antonio de la Calancha, stood at the head of the Pantheon of the late Chimu. Another vase painting shows two animal demons provided with typical emblems carrying the litter of the moon god (175, ill. 37). Si fits the picture of this deity which Calancha presents. He brings this god into direct connection with the growth of fruit.

In any case, we can conclude from these representations in which the various animal demons appear as runners that according to the belief of the early Chimu not only humans but also gods and demons ran such races. Special significance can be attached to another statement of Calancha's (175, p. 100), that it was the belief of the Chimu that the demons participated in visible form at their dances, drinking bouts, and festivities. Plastic relief representations in the Baessler collection and in the Stuttgart museum point in the same direction. In these a motley crowd of animal demons and men can be seen running along (20, Pl. 44, 211; 336, No. 93345). Representations of this kind permit hardly any other interpretation than that demons themselves participated at the races of men and joined in with the column of runners in order to cross the deserts together on the way to the sanctuary—probably, the temple of the moon deity.

Perhaps still another thought lies at the basis of this curious parallelism between the doings of gods and men. As D. G. Brinton (65, p. 17) once expressed it—the magic actions of men represent nothing but an imitation of godly doings. In the faithful, faultless imitation of the godly model lies also the magic power which exists within the ceremony. Perhaps there was also the notion that in the far distant past these sacred races had been revealed to the gods and demons themselves and that their magic powers originated from this source. Conceptual complexes of the most varied kinds may thus have arisen around these ceremonies whose great importance can be seen in the art of the early Chimu.

THE TECHNICAL DEVELOPMENT OF WHISTLING VASES IN PERU

Adrian Digby

The conception of a whistling vase requires a definite, though probably rudimentary and empirical working hypothesis as to the nature of fluids. That is to say, it must be realized that in whatever form these fluids may be, they occupy a definite amount of space, and if displaced from one place they must go elsewhere. It is unlikely that the ancient Peruvians realized that gases such as air differed from water and other liquids by being capable of compression into a smaller space, and with the weight of fluid involved in everyday use in Peruvian pottery, air would hardly be compressed at all. But even an inaccurate hypothesis, a half-truth which conceived of gases and liquids as having enough body to occupy space, is quite enough to enable them to conceive the idea of a whistling vase, and to understand its mechanism. Without some knowledge of this sort it is difficult to see how the idea of using air to blow a whistle, still less of using the weight of water to force air through a whistle could have occurred. But, given the empirical knowledge the author has postulated, he believes he can show how at least one phase of the development occurred.

In a previous paper (108) it was suggested that the double-spout vases and stirrup-spout vases were made to secure easy pouring through a narrow orifice by providing an alternative means of ingress for the air which was drawn in to replace the outgoing liquid. The simplest form, of course, is the double-spout vase, especially characteristic of Nazca and late Chimu styles. Variants of this include figure-and-spout vases in which a small hole has been pierced in the head of the spout, and some curious vases in which there is a handle and one spout, but with a breathing hole at the end of the handle farthest from the spout. The British Museum has two such vessels, both undocumented. One (British Museum No. 1938.10-17.1) is of Nazcoid appearance with a conventionalized centipede and trophy head ornament. The other (British Museum No. 1933.7-13.61) is of plain white ware, unslipped, which apparently belongs to the Paracas necropolis style. In the former, the breathing hole (if one may use such a term), emerges where the handle bevels over to join the spout; in the latter, it is in the body of the pot just behind the handle.

The stirrup spout is only a modification of the idea of a vase with two openings, in which they are both trunked into one spout. Water flows out through the lower half of the stirrup, and through the spout, and provided the pot is not tilted so steeply that the rush of water chokes the spout, air can get in and flow through the upper part of the stirrup into the pot without interruption. It might be argued that this explanation of the reasons for making the double spout and stirrup is at best hypothetical. But very strong evidence in support of the theory is to be found in an unusual stirrup pot in the British Museum (No. 1947. AM, 10–12) which has a perfectly normal, though small stirrup spout, and a breathing hole perforated through the center of the head. This pot is a little hard to place stylistically, and unfortunately it is, like the two others I described, undocumented. The general appearance suggests the Mochica culture, but it does not seem to fit into the normal Mochica pattern. The flanged lip to the spout, and a certain amount of incised work on the eyebrows and headdress give it some affinities with Cupisnique. The style of the headdress is paralleled by vases from the Salinar culture, illustrated by Larco (181), and by a vase of Paracas Cavernas type from Ocucaje, illustrated by Kroeber (171). The orbits give the impression of formerly carrying an inlay possibly of metal. The pot is of well fired paste, light in weight with a one color slip of cinnamon brown. On the whole, the author is inclined to think that it is an early sub-style of Mochica, or possibly a sort of formative Mochica closely allied with Cupisnique.

For our immediate purpose the most interesting fact is the small breathing-hole in the head, which should be entirely unnecessary for a stirrup-spout vase. A simple experiment showed that if the breathing-hole was stopped up the pot would not pour steadily, but gulped irregularly. If, however, the breathing-hole was opened it poured very well. An X-ray examination showed that there was no defect in the stirrup, but the design was faulty, in that when the pot was tilted for pouring, if the pot was more than half full the water level rose above the level of both ends of the stirrup and prevented air getting in. Therefore it is reasonable to assume that due to this defect, the pot would not pour properly, and to remedy this and give it the good pouring properties expected from a stirrup pot, a breathing-hole was bored in the head of the vase.

These considerations seem to show fairly conclusively that both the stirrup and the double spout with its derivatives had their *raison d'être* in the desire for easy pouring, and that a knowledge of the properties of fluids postulated at the beginning of this paper was understood.

The stirrup spout was in common use on the North Coast of Peru from almost the earliest ceramic times through all periods down to the late Chimu. The double-spout, and head-and-spout types are known in the Salinar, and most North Coast styles, with the notable exception of the Mochica who seem to have specialized like the Cupisnique culture in the stirrup spout. They also occur in the south, in Nazca and Coastal Tiahuanaco styles.

We have, therefore, evidence that the knowledge required for the purely intellectual concept of a whistling vase existed throughout the coastal regions of Peru from very early times, and Larco (182), illustrates a figure-and-spout vase with a whistle from the early Viru culture. The author believes that the whistling vase was first achieved accidentally by a small lip of clay left adhering to the inside of the "breathing-hole" pierced in the bevel of a figure-and-spout vase before firing. This would be sufficient to set up turbulence in the air stream passing through it and cause a whistling noise. The author is strengthened in this belief by an unusual head-and-spout vase of Nazca Y style (British Museum No. 1937-13), which whistles when blown gently, though not when blown hard. X-ray examinations show no sign of any whistle. There is, however, a thickening behind the breathing-hole, caused by restoration at some time before the pot came into the possession of the British Museum. The effect of this is to cause a thickening on one side of the breathing-hole, which is similar in effect to that of a small piece of clay on the inside of the breathing-hole suggested above. This pot is obviously, therefore, an accidental whistler. If an accident can happen once it can happen again, and while this particular example is late, there is no reason why similar accidents may not have occurred in much earlier times, and given rise to the idea of a true whistling vase.

In all Peruvian whistling vases which the author has examined, the whistling mechanism is of one type, consisting of a hollow sphere, from about $\frac{1}{2}$ to 1 inch in diameter, with a small circular orifice, so mounted that a jet from a small circular hole passes obliquely across it. The actual placing of this varies considerably. The earliest method which the author has been able to study in England, where vases from the Viru and Salinar cultures are very scarce, is that used in Mochica pottery, which for the purposes of this paper the author proposes to call mounting A. The whistle-sphere is placed inside the head of a figure, which serves as a resonator. Openings are cut in the eyes and mouth and allow for the escape of sound, and two circular holes, usually in the neck, serve as stops and enable three notes to be produced. This method, characteristic of Mochica vases, is also found in a degenerate form in late Chimu vases, in which the stops are reduced to mere pinholes or eliminated altogether. There is also, in the British Museum, a vase with this type of whistle (No. 1938-20) that appears to be of Nazca Y style.

The general layout of vases with this type of whistle-placing is usually of the two-chamber or double-vessel type, one chamber being in the form of a bird or animal or human figure, the other being globular with a cylindrical spout joined by a bridge handle to the head of the front vessel.

Many Mochica vases, however, are single-chamber vessels with dummy stirrup spouts, one end of which is blocked. The use of a true stirrup spout with a whistling vase is a functional anomaly, for the whistle would provide the necessary secondary air-vent for easy pouring. In fact it is skeuomorphic and functions in the same way as an ordinary straight spout. The impression given by this arrangement is that the Mochica potters, who had a well established tradition, borrowed the whistle from some other culture (probably Salinar or Viru), but endeavored to retain the outward traditional form of their products. These vases sometimes take the form of a sub-spherical body surmounted by a head and stirrup.

Another form of whistling vase is the parrot. One in the British Museum has a bulbous appendix in place of a tail, which might be thought to be a second chamber, but an X-ray photograph shows that this is not so. This type would not therefore be expected to whistle when tilted, but a parrot-form Mochica vase in the Cambridge University Museum has a stirrup of unusually large diameter. The column of air moving up and down this is sufficiently large to blow the whistle when the pot is rocked. Thus, while the Mochica potters made a few double vases, presumably as whistlers, they were also able to achieve the same results without the double vessel and without departing from their traditional shapes.

Turning back to the whistle-mounting, the next type, which we may call B, is found in a number of vases where the whistle is concealed in a thickening of the flat bridge handle where it joins the figure on the front part of figure-and-spout vessels, the air duct passing through the figure. This method is characteristic of vases in the cursive modeled style, the dating of which still seems uncertain, but which the majority of opinion places as contemporary with coast Tiahuanaco. It is also common in a style with thin red bands on white, which is generally similar in form to ordinary black ware of Chimu style, and of course it is very well known in black ware vessels of the later style where a flat bridge handle is used. The two remaining types of whistle-mounting (C and Ci) we have to consider, are those in which the whistle is simply enclosed in any convenient projecting part of the pot, usually the head of a figure. There is a further simplification in which the whistle itself forms part of the external decoration of the vessel, often the head, belly, or posterior of an animal perched on the top of the spout. The former (C), which seems to be earlier in technological sense, is probably the rarer. The earliest example known to the author occurs in a head-and-spout vase which has the appearance of being a hybrid of the Nazca and Tiahuanaco styles. Other examples are not unknown in late Chimu blackware. The latter (Ci) is only found, as far as the author is aware, in late Chimu or Chimu Inca and early post-Conquest ware.

The author has endeavored to show that throughout the coastal area of Peru, the knowledge required for the manufacture of the whistling vases was present from very early times. An example of an accidental whistling vase has been shown which may represent the kind of happy type of accident by which the idea of a whistling vase was conceived. It is clear from the examples cited that the whistling vase is most thickly distributed in the northern coastal area of Peru, but sporadic examples have been found in styles associated with Central or South Coast cultures. In all of the vases examined the actual method of mounting the whistle can be subdivided into four types: (A), (B), (C), and (Ci). According to the author's information, (A) occurred in the Mochica and continued in a degenerate form into late Chimu, but was probably derived from an earlier or contemporary culture, probably Salinar or Viru. (B), which is slightly later, started with Kroeber's cursive modeled style and also continued into late Chimu. (C) and (Ci) are basically late Chimu. The combination of the single type of whistle in all known vessels with the gradual increase in the number of technical methods of mounting it, points to a single point of origin either contemporary with or before Mochica, and somewhere in the northern coastal area. Taken with the general understanding of the nature of fluids there is reason to believe that the whistling vase was invented in Peru, possibly somewhere near the Chicama valley.

Against this must be set the view held by Kidder, Jennings, and Shook that Peruvian whistling vases owe their origin to Meso-American types which appear to be dated about 500 A.D. In the general layout of the whole vessel there is a fairly close resemblance between Figure 77 and Figure 79b in their work on Kaminaljuyu (158, pp. 190–93, Figs. 77–79) which is typical of late Chimu whistling vases. But a closer comparison shows some difference. Compared with a radiograph of a vase with a type A mounting, we see a difference at once. The spherical whistle in the Peruvian type is made separately and mounted on a stem which forms the nozzle from the body of the pot. In that illustrated by Kidder, the whistle-chamber seems to be modeled integrally with the head. The difference, though slight, is material, and before forming any definite conclusions the author wrote to Dr. Kidder, asking him whether the opening in the whistle-chamber was flat or circular. Dr. Kidder very courteously undertook to examine the vessel in question, but was unable to see inside the pot. He was, however, of the opinion that in all probability the opening was elliptical or flattened like that in other Central American whistles. At this point it is of particular interest to compare whistles of the two areas in question.

There is in the British Museum a mold-made whistle figurine (No. 1923.5-10.1) depicting a man with exaggerated canine teeth who is playing panpipes and wearing an owl mask with wings. This specimen is undocumented but is claimed to come from Truxillo. It is interesting in the present connection because the whistle at the back of it is precisely similar to that on Peruvian whistling vases, a small spherical whistle-chamber across which air is blown after entering a conical structure with a single escape hole. This is in striking contrast to a whistle figurine from Lubaantun in which the conical structure itself forms the whistle-chamber, and a flat stream of air is directed against a flat lip.

Although we have the interesting phenomenon of whistle vases and whistle figurines in both areas, the general type of whistle used is so different that it is possible to believe in convergent development rather than diffusion for the whistling vases in two areas. Should the form of whistle prove to be the same in the whistling vases discovered in Middle America as it is in Peru, the coincidence of general layout and whistle type will be so remarkable that it will be very hard to avoid the belief in diffusion of this trait from one area to another. But it has been shown that the whistling vase is of long standing in Peru, and that Peruvian potters had been experimenting for a long time with an empirical form of pneumatics and hydraulics which would present the opportunity for the invention of the whistling vase. It therefore seems likely that the diffusion must have taken place from the Andes to Middle America. Force could be added to this view by the fact that Middle American whistling vases would be shown to be equipped with a type of whistle which is alien to Middle America but common in Peru.[1]

1. Since writing the above, the author has had his attention drawn by Dr. A. V. Kidder to four small whistles of Miraflores horizon, which have been discovered at Kaminaljuyu. These are identical in *construction* to all the Peruvian whistles described in the above paper, and one in particular is similar in *mounting* to type C which occurs only in the Late Chimu and Inca periods. The chronological implications are baffling, since we have a type which occurs at the beginning of the Meso-American sequence and at the end of the Andean sequence, but quite clearly identical in form, and there is no reason to doubt the dating of either group.

COLONIAL PORTRAITS OF INCA NOBLES

John Howland Rowe

In the Archeological Museum at Cuzco there is a series of five full length portraits which, though not artistic masterpieces, are noteworthy cultural documents (Figs. 1–5). Two of them represent women, richly dressed in what is obviously ancient Inca style; the other three represent men, two dressed in a curious mixture of Spanish and Inca styles and the third in pure Spanish costume but with an Inca headdress. I would like to call attention to some of the implications of these pictures for Inca cultural history, especially for the light they throw on the position of the Inca nobility in the Colonial period and its role in the preservation of Inca artistic and cultural traditions.[1]

The first painting (Fig. 1) shows a man of middle age in rich Spanish dress wearing the Inca royal diadem and standing beside the Spanish royal standard. In the upper right is a coat of arms, to be discussed later, and in the lower right hand corner a dwarf attendant supports a white oval containing a lengthy inscription of which all but the two bottom lines are well preserved and perfectly legible. It begins:

Don Marcos Chiguan Thopa, Inca noble, catholic gentleman, by the grace of God *Alférez real* (royal standard bearer) and one of the twenty-four elected deputies of the noble Incas of the eight parishes of this great city of Cuzco. Descendant of royal blood of Capac Lloque Yupangui Inca, who was third king of these realms; graduate of the Royal College of St. Francis of Borja, *Cacique principal* and proprietary governor in two provinces with title from the supreme government.

Following this identification is a long list of Don Marcos' Spanish honors with the names of the five viceroys under whom they were granted. Don Marcos was Cacique of Huayllabamba in the Marquisate of Oropesa and of Colquepata in the province of Paucartambo; he was aide de camp of the Marquis of Oropesa and *Alférez real* in the Marquisate, and in Cuzco in the year 1720. He enjoyed the privileges of bearing arms, maintaining a personal guard of Cañari Indians and lancers, and taking his law suits direct to the Audiencia of Lima.[2]

1. The data on which this study is based were gathered on a research visit to Cuzco in 1946. The trip was financed by a grant from Peabody Museum, Harvard University, and sponsored in the field by the National University of Cuzco. Grateful acknowledgment is due to the Rector of the latter Institution and to the Director of the Archeological Institute of Cuzco for the facilities they so freely placed at my disposal. All photographs, unless otherwise credited, were taken for the author by Martín Chambi.

2. The full Spanish text of this inscription will be found in Appendix A.
The Royal College of St. Francis of Borja was a Jesuit school for the sons of the Inca nobility founded in 1621. It was merged with another school at the time of Independence to form what is now the Colegio Nacional de Ciencias.
It is a surprise to find Cañari Indian guards mentioned in this inscription. The Cañaris were

258

This inscription enables us to date the portrait within very narrow limits. The periods of office of the viceroys named in it cover the years 1707 to 1745, and the date 1739 is mentioned in it. Hence, it was probably painted between 1740 and 1745. The Spanish costume which Don Marcos wears as *Alférez real* fits well with this date and there is no reason to think that the inscription is a later addition.

The next portrait (Fig. 2) shows a somewhat older man wearing an Inca-type tunic, mantle and sandals, with the Inca royal diadem on his head. His feather collar and earplugs are also in the Inca tradition. Spanish influence is evident, however, in his knee breeches and in the gold lion masks which he wears on his shoulders, knees, and sandal tops; also, the gold sundisk he wears around his neck is probably a Hispanicized rendering of an Inca ornament. The subject holds on his left arm the same coat of arms observed in the previous portrait. This picture also had an inscription in an oval in the lower right hand corner but it has been defaced and painted over with black paint.

Enough seemed to be left of the inscription on this portrait to justify an experiment and through the courtesy of the Director of the Museum I was able to have an X-ray photograph made of it at the Cuzco hospital.[3] The first six lines of the inscription could be clearly read on the X-ray plate, identifying the subject as Don Alonso Chiguan Inca, like Don Marcos a descendant of the Inca emperor Lloque Yupanqui. No dates could be read, but it is evident from the style of the painting and of the inscription that it is nearly contemporary with the portrait of Don Marcos.[4]

The third portrait (Fig. 3) shows a younger man in a costume with somewhat fewer Inca elements than that of Don Alonso. His tunic, the Inca royal diadem beside him, and the presence of the same coat of arms which appears in the other two portraits, however, mark him as a member of the same Colonial nobility. The inscription oval in the corner of this picture has been scraped off so that not a letter of the original inscription could be recovered even with the use of X-rays and the subject's name is consequently unknown. The style indicates an early eighteenth century date for this portrait.

The fourth picture (Fig. 4) shows a lady in full Inca court dress, precisely as described by Bernabé Cobo and Felipe Guaman Poma.[5] She carries a spindle in

---

natives of the region around Cuenca (Ecuador) and a contingent of them was brought to Cuzco by Huayna Capac. They joined the Spaniards early in the wars of the conquest and were regularly used as honor guards in the sixteenth and early seventeenth century. As far as I know this is the first reference to them in the eighteenth century.

3. My esteemed colleague, Dr. Sergio A. Quevedo, Professor of Anthropology, made the necessary arrangements with the hospital and assisted the radiologist, Dr. Ignacio Pinto de la Sota, in conducting the experiment. We believe that this is the first time a painting has been subjected to X-ray examination in Peru.

4. The Spanish text of this inscription is reproduced in Appendix B.

5. For Conquest period Inca court costume see Rowe (281, pp. 233–36), Cobo (85, Book 14, chap. ii), Guaman Poma (134, pp. 115, 145, 159, 126, 136, 138).

Fig. 1.—Portrait of Don Marcos Chiguan Thopa, painted about 1740. Museo Arqueológico, Cuzco.

Fig. 2.—Portrait of Don Alonso Chiguan Inca, early eighteenth century. Museo Arqueológico, Cuzco.

Fig. 3.—Portrait of a young Inca nobleman, early eighteenth century. Museo Arqueológico, Cuzco.

Fig. 4.—Portrait of an Inca lady, early eighteenth century. Museo Arqueológico, Cuzco.

one hand and a bunch of red *qantut* flowers in the other. Except for the design on her silver shawl pin, no Spanish influence is apparent in her costume, yet the style of the landscape in the background indicates that this picture also dates from the early eighteenth century. There is a dwarf attendant, also in Inca dress.

The fifth portrait (Fig. 5) is in a somewhat more formal style which perhaps indicates a slightly earlier date, probably late seventeenth century. The lady in this picture also wears full Inca court dress and is attended by a dwarf carrying a feather parasol. The royal diadem lies on the table beside her and in the upper left hand corner of the picture is a coat of arms blazoned differently from that of the three men.

This portrait is the only one of the five of which a photograph has already been published (409, Pl. 83*b*). Two of the portraits were illustrated in lithographs as long ago as 1854, at which time Castelnau (79) published a series of four Inca portraits in Part 3 of the report of his South American expedition. His Plate 59 represents our Figure 1 and his Plate 57 our Figure 2. The other two portraits illustrated by Castelnau represent Inca ladies with Spanish-type lace sleeves added to their native dress; Castelnau's lithographs of these pictures are reproduced in our Figures 6 and 7. While it is difficult to date these two pictures from the lithographs, they are probably of early eighteenth century date also. I have not seen the originals.

Castelnau's Plate 59 is reproduced in our Figure 8 in order to facilitate comparison with its original, our Figure 1. In the lithograph the inscription oval in the lower right hand corner was omitted entirely and the picture is captioned: "Inca Prince in Spanish costume of the time of the Conquest"—a patent anachronism. This peculiar inaccuracy of Castelnau's has been responsible for a remarkable chain of error. Urteaga and Romero reproduced Castelnau's lithograph in their edition of Titu Cusi's relation (377, opposite p. 1) with a caption identifying it as a contemporary portrait of Inca Sayri Topa, the implication being that it was painted in 1558! Cúneo-Vidal copied the picture, identification and all, in his history of the wars of the last Incas (101, pp. 202, 207). Finally, in 1946 the lithograph appears in Imbelloni (143, pp. 219, 238), still identified as Sayri Topa and with the following comment: "The only portrait document with some authenticity in the whole of Inca history(!)" Such is the penalty of uncritical copying.

In considering this group of portraits, one is struck first of all by the very full survival of Inca dress style and even details of pattern as late as the eighteenth century. Such vitality for the Inca style was completely unexpected. Next, perhaps, one is impressed by the sumptuousness of the costumes. The people who sat (or rather stood) for these portraits were evidently persons of considerable wealth who lived luxuriously and in state. This is a completely different class of Indian from the badgered and starving tribute-payer who figures so largely in the documents about social conditions in Peru in the eighteenth century.

It is also very clear from these pictures that this native nobility was very

Fig. 5.—Portrait of an Inca lady, late seventeenth century. Museo Arqueológico, Cuzco.

Fig. 6.—Portrait of an Inca lady, probably early eighteenth century. Cuzco, exact whereabouts unknown. (Lithograph by Champin from Castelnau, 1854, Pl. 58.)

Fig. 7.—Portrait of an Inca lady, probably early eighteenth century. Cuzco, exact whereabouts unknown. (Lithograph by Champin from Castelnau, 1854, Pl. 60.)

Fig. 8.—Portrait of Don Marcos Chiguan Thopa (Fig. 1) as lithographed by Champin (in Castelnau, 1854, Pl. 59). The lithograph bears the legend: "Prince Incas, en costume espagnol du temps de la Conquête, d'après un tableau conservé à Cuzco (Pérou)."

proud of its descent from the Inca kings. This pride is shown clearly in the symbols of Inca royalty with which all the portraits are furnished. The Inca royal diadem, for example, is worn or displayed in all but one of the seven pictures illustrated. It is clearly the royal crown of ancient times and the three traditional elements can all be recognized: the *llawt'u*, a braid wrapped several times around the head; the *suntur pawqar*, a pompom rising from the front of the braid; and the *maska paycha*, a red fringe hanging down from the braid in the middle of the forehead. The fringe was the special symbol of royalty; the other parts of the diadem could be worn with variations by commoners simply as a sign of Inca nationality: thus, in these portraits the attendant dwarfs wear braids and often have some ornament stuck in the front. It is interesting to note, however, that the royal diadem has become more ornate by comparison with the ancient ones illustrated by Guaman Poma (134); jewels have been added to the braid and the pompom has become a miniature castle adorned with banners— the "trophy castle" which appears on Colonial textiles and keros as an Inca symbol.

The coats of arms are Spanish symbols, of course, but they too indicate descent from the Inca royal family in their elements—serpents, red fringes, etc. The most interesting coat of arms is that displayed by Don Marcos, Don Alonso, and the unknown subject of Figure 3. This is the coat of arms granted to the Inca quisling Paullu Topa Inca as a reward for services rendered to the Spanish crown during the conquest. It was granted by a royal *cédula* dated at Valladolid, May 9, 1545, of which a number of copies have been preserved with minor differences in the text. The earliest and best version was published by Ramos Gavilán in his *Historia del célebre santuario de Nuestra Señora de Copacabana* (272), and matches exactly the arms in the portraits.[6] Of course the Chiguan Incas had no right to use this coat of arms, but by the eighteenth century its origin had become somewhat obscure and any noble family that could claim descent from the Inca royal house felt free to adopt it. Several of the families using it, such as the Choquehuancas of Azángaro, the Uchu Incas and the descendants of Luís Guaman Paucar Inga, based their claim to it on copies of the original *cédula* in which the names had been altered. The falsification of genealogies and patents of arms is no North American monopoly.[7]

The lengthy inscription on the portrait of Don Marcos Chiguan Thopa contains a number of references to his offices and honors which suggest another line of investigation. My search for information that would clarify these references led me to the manuscript papers preserved in the office of the Rector of the University of Cuzco, and especially to the twelve volume scrap book of genealogical papers accumulated by Vicente José García about 1770–1790. García was a Spanish officer who married a lady of Cuzco named Doña María Gertrudis de Avendaño y Betancur and he collected these papers to promote his wife's

6. The description of this coat of arms is quoted from the *cédula* in Appendix C.

7. For the falsified *cédulas* see Vargas Ugarte (405, pp. 344, 367); Luna (207, pp. 82–83).

fraudulent claim of being a descendant of the Inca Topa Amaru who was killed in 1572.[8]

Several members of the Betancur family were Inca deputies for the house of Huayna Capac and held the position of *Alférez real* at one time or another so that the García collection contains a considerable amount of information about these offices.

The royal Inca ayllus elected deputies to a council called the Twenty Four (*los veinticuatros*), a custom with obscure Spanish antecedents. I have found references to groups called *veinticuatros* in other parts of America but have not been able to discover how they functioned in Spain. The Inca group met every year in June or July at an assembly presided over by the *Juez de naturales* with the *Protector de naturales* and an interpreter also present. On this occasion they elected one of their number to be *Alférez real de los Incas* for the feast of Santiago (St. James' day, July 25th). After his election the *Alférez* plighted homage and received the royal standard. There were two masses and processions, one at vespers of the 24th and the other on the 25th, and the Inca nobles were supposed to ride in both processions with their *Alférez* at their head. This whole organization was already referred to as an "ancient custom" in 1595. By the late eighteenth century the *veinticuatros* were no longer elected but appointed for life by the *Corregidor de naturales* and confirmed by the Viceroy. The corregidor presided at their meetings. The last election of *Alférez* of which we have specific reference was that of 1781 but the custom probably lasted somewhat later. In addition to the *Alférez real de los Incas* Cuzco had a Spanish *Alférez real* who had bought the honor from the king, and Esquivel y Navía reports squabbles over privileges between the two *Alférez* in 1746 and 1748.

Besides the council of Twenty Four, which apparently was purely honorary and had no political power, there was a parish organization which performed the actual administration of Cuzco's Indian population. Each of the eight parishes of the city had its *Alcalde* and its *Cacique principal* (the former probably elective and the latter probably hereditary). Over the parish *alcaldes* was an *Alcalde mayor* of the city. There was, of course, a parallel but separate administration for the Spanish population. The *Alcalde mayor* and the *Alférez real* had the curious privilege of wearing the Inca royal fringe for the feast of Santiago, thus providing an annual public symbol of the survival of Inca traditions.[9]

8. A summary list of the García papers will be found in the bibliography; the only volume that has been published is listed under its date of publication (125). I am delighted to see that our Peruvian colleague, Daniel Valcárcel, has discovered this collection and is publishing a detailed index of it in the journal *Letras*, of Lima (402, 404). The fraudulent character of Doña María's claim to Inca descent will be apparent to anyone who checks the anachronisms in the published summary of her case (125). The lawsuit in which the claim was aired was directed against the famous Inca rebel José Gabriel Condorcanqui ("Tupac Amaru") and the case is of great historical importance. Condorcanqui wrote a masterly refutation of the Betancur claims which has been published (97). It reveals him as a critical historian of most unusual talent for his time.

9. García MS, Betancur genealogy, Vol. I, fols. 289r–295v, being extracts from the *Libro del Estandarte* (election records of the Inca *Alférez*) for 1595 to 1675 in a copy made for García in 1780 (García, 124, pp. 58–59, 65–66, 75–77; Esquivel y Navía, 118, pp. 130, 394, 431–32).

Additional light on Don Marcos' position in the Marquisate of Oropesa is found in a document in García's collection which names him specifically. It is a commission from Don Pascual Enríquez de Cabrera, Duke of the City of Rioseco, Marquis of Alcañizes and Oropesa, etc., dated at Madrid, March 15th, 1738. The commission is directed to the Rector of the Society of Jesus in Cuzco and empowers him to depose Don Marcos Chiguan Thopa from his position as *Cacique* of Huayllabamba, a town in the valley of Yucay, ". . . forasmuch as I have been informed of the extorsions, violences and tyrannies which Don Marcos Chiguantopa . . . has exercised and is exercising on the Indians of that village, to the point of committing the cruel act of branding them on the buttocks like mules." He goes on to state that Don Marcos, a native of the province of Paucartambo, holds the caciqueship through his wife, and accuses him of appropriating lands belonging to the Marquisate as well as of ill-treating the Indians.[10]

The Marquisate of Oropesa was a feudal holding in the valley of Yucay held by Enríquez de Cabrera by virtue of his descent from Sayri Topa Inca and hence administered somewhat differently from the rest of the country. However, the caciqueships were hereditary offices all over Peru and the caciques were everywhere accused at times of excesses comparable to those with which Don Marcos was charged. They were supposed to be agents of the Spanish administration compelling the Indians under their orders to obey the commands of the corregidores and other Spanish officials without having any power to govern on their own initiative or even to give the Indians a measure of protection against the excessive demands of their superiors. If the corregidores ordered extra tribute collected or forced sales of unwanted goods, the caciques had to execute their orders, and it is evident from repeated complaints that they often did so with great brutality. One of the stock defenses of the Spanish administrators was that it was really the native caciques and not the Spaniards who mistreated the Indians.

These five portraits in Cuzco, then, represent members of the Inca nobility resident in Cuzco at the beginning of the eighteenth century and claiming descent from the Inca royal line. Honored but not trusted by the Spanish government, their positions as hereditary caciques made it possible for them to maintain a very considerable state and to preserve even two hundred years after the conquest the major part of Inca court dress and symbolism. I am certain that more of these portraits can be found with a little search and their study may be very rewarding. After all, this eighteenth century nobility in 1780 formed the heart of the great Inca rebellion of Tupac Amaru which shook the Viceroyalty of Peru to its foundations and it formed also the core of loyalist sentiment by which the rebellion was crushed. We need to know these servant-princes better.

Appendix A.—Text of the inscription on the portrait of Don Marcos Chiguan

10. The text of this commission is reproduced as Appendix D.

Thopa (Fig. 1). The abbreviations have been expanded and the dates of rule of the viceroys named are added in brackets by the author.

Don Marcos Chiguan Thopa
Coronilla Ynga Cauallero Catholico por la
gracia de Dios Alferez Real de su Magestad y vno de los 24
Electos diputados de los Yngas Nobles de las 8 Parroquias desta
    gran Ciudad del
Cuzco Desendiente de Sangre Real de Ccapacc Lloque Yupangui Ynga,
3. Rey que fue de estos Reynos: Colegial del Real Colegio de
San Francisco de Borja Casique Principal Gouernador propietario en
dos Prouincias con titulo del Supremo Gouierno El Exelentisimo
    Señor Marques de
Castel Duos rios [viceroy 1707–1710] le amparo en su noblesa y
    le dio titulo de Ca-
sique Principal y Gouernador de la Villa de Guaillabamba
    Marquesado de Oropesa—Y el
Exelentisimo Ylustrisimo Señor Don Diego Ladron de Gueuara
    [viceroy 1710–1716] le consedio Licensia de Espada y
Daga; asimesmo el Exelentisimo Señor Principe de Santo Buono
    [viceroy 1716–1720] le Onrro con la plasa
de Maestre de Campo de dicho Marques y le consedio Baston de
    dicho Empleo y
Lisencia para traer todas las Armas de Guerra y le amparo
    en su Noble—
sa; y por el año de 1720 El Exelentisimo Ylustrisimo Señor
    Don Diego Mursillo Rubio de
Auñon [viceroy 1720–1724] bino a esta Ciudad fue Enbajador del
    dicho Marquesado de Oropesa y le dio
titulo de Casique Principal y Gouernador del Pueblo de San
    Gerónimo de Colquepata, Prouincia
de Paucartambo—Y siendo Virrey El Exelentisimo Señor Marques
    de Castelfuerte, [viceroy 1724–1736] bajo a la
Audiencia de Lima dos veses a difinir pleitos, le amparo con
    diferentes Prouisiones Reales
sobrecartadas y le hizo merced de Yndios Cañares y lanzas para el Or-
nato y defensa de su persona y por vna Prouision Executoria del
    Real Acu-
erdo de Iusticia Expedio el Rey Nuestro Señor Phelipe 5 que Dios
    guarde el
año de 1739. onrrandole por su limpisima Sangre que ninguna Ius-
    ticia Ordinaria de las Ciudades, Prouincias, Villas y Señorios
    deste Reyno no
conoscan de sus Causas, sus parientes deudos y Familiares
    Yniuiendo su
conosimiento a la Real Audiencia y se le nombró Iues aparte para
    sus causas
y el Exelentisimo Señor Marques de Villa Garcia Virrey Gouernador
    y Capitan General
destos Reinos [viceroy 1736–1745] le boluio nueuamente a ampararle
    en el Casicasco

del Marquesado y por el año de 1720 fue Alferez Real en dicho
Marquesado Y el año de 1720 saco la Real Bandera en esta
[two lines cut off at the bottom; probably «... ciudad del Cuzco ...»].

Appendix B.—Text of the inscription on the portrait of Don Alonso Chiguan
Inca (Fig. 2).

Don Alonso
Chiguan Ynga Visnato de Cca-
pac Lloque Yupangui Ynga tercer
Monarca y Señor Natural que fue destos
Reynos, este fue el primero q' res[ibio el] Agua
del Santo Bautismo siendo Gentil en la Conquista por-
esta f . . . . la San . . . . en la
Ma . . . . S. . . . . hi
so merced . . . . rmas consediendole todas la
Onras . . . . el y sus . . . .
por su limp . . . . Sangre Real
de la Villa . . . .
Se . . . .
D . . . . dor que
q . . . .
. . . .
. . . .
[the dots indicate portions of the inscription too badly
destroyed to be read even in the X-ray].

Appendix C.—Description of the arms granted to Don Cristóbal Paullu Topa
from the royal *cédula* of May 9, 1545 (Valladolid).

... vn escudo fecho dos partes, que en la vna dellas esté vn aguila negra, rauipante
[*sic* for rampante] en campo de oro, y a los lados dos palmas verdes, y en la otra parte
debaxo vn tigre de su color y, ensima del vna borla colorada, que solia tener por corona
Atabalipa vuestro hermano, y a los lados del dicho tigre dos culebras coronadas de oro
en campo azul, y por orla vnas letras que digan AVE MARIA, y entre medio de las dichas
letras, ocho Cruces de oro de Hierusalem en campo colorado, con perfiles de oro, y por
timbre vn hielmo cerrado, y por diuissa vn aguila negra rampante con sus tres colores, y
dependencias a follages de oro y azul.

[from Ramos Gavilán (272, pp. 158–59); for other versions of the same *cédula*
see also Vargas Ugarte (405, p. 368); Cúneo-Vidal (101, pp. 171, 173); Temple
(351, XIII, 66–68, n. 190)].

Appendix D.—Text of the commission to depose Don Marcos Chiguan
Thopa from his post of Cacique of Huayllabamba.

Sello Quarto, 1738
   Don Pasqual Enrriquez de Cabrera Duque de la Ciudad de Rioseco, Conde de
Modica, Melgar, Colle y Ossona, Marques de Alcañizes y Oropesa Vizconde de Cabre-
ra, y Bas, Señor de las Varonias de Alcamo, Cacamo, Calata, Fimy, Villavelli, Belver, y
Cabreros, Hayó Montecodesal y su tierra, y de las Casas de Almanza, y Loiola, y
Adelantado maior de Yucay Etra.
   Por quanto me hallo informado de los extorsiones, violenzias, y tiranias, q. Don
Marcos Chiguantopa Cacique del Pueblo de Guahillabamba ha ejecutado, y ejecuta

con los Yndios de aquel Pueblo asta cometer la crueldad de errarlos como á Mulas en las nalgas, cuio Cacicazgo tiene por su Muger, y de cuios excesos, y graves delitos constan al Sr. Virrey y a los Señores de la Real Audienzia de Lima Y por quanto asimismo me tiene vsurpadas muchas y diversas posessiones y terrazgos del citado mi estado de Oropesa sito en aquel Reyno del Perú, y Provincia del Cuzco; Y que en otros diferentes Pueblos de el asi mismo me estan vsurpadas muchas haciendas y territorios: Por tanto: vsando de mi derecho y regalias, que me competen Y me estan concedidas en los previlegios y Cedulas, con que gozo, y poseo el referido estado, deseando la paz, y tranquilidad de aquellos mis Vasallos, y que en todo se haga justizia, y camino con la equidad, que previene, y la Ley natural enseña, para obiar semejantes excesos, y poner Corrientes todas mis rentas y efectos, doi facultad al Rmo. Padre Rector de la Casa grande de la Compañia de Jesus de la Ciudad del Cuzco que al presente es, Y en adelante fuere, y á quien tengo dado mis poderes amplios y facultativos para la administrazion politica, y economica de aquel mi estado, deponga al referido Don Marcos Chiguan tupa del expressado Cacicazgo, asi por los motivos tan justificados, que quedan expressados, como por no ser natural del Marquessado, sino es de la Provincia de Paucartambo, nombrando al que le parezca Conveniente en su lugar; Y tambien doi facultad al mismo Padre rector que es, ó fuere, ó persona que nombrare para que haga la visita de Yndios, y tierras que me pertenecen, incorporando en aquel mi Patrimonio todas las que sean y esten vsurpadas, cobrando de los que indebidamente las han posehido, las rentas, y vsufructo, que han debido, y deben produzireme, que para todo les subrrogo, y doi todo mi poder y facultad, y el que de derecho me perteneze, y tengo: Y para q. anse ejecute, mandé despachar la presente firmada de mi mano, sellada con el sello de mis armas, y refrendada del infra escripto secretario; de que tomará la razon la contaduria pral. de mi Casa, y estados: De Madrid á quinze de Marzo de mil setezientos y treinta y ocho.

(*signed*) EL MARQUES DE ALCAÑIZES Y OROPESA

Tomó la Razon
(*signed*) JOSEPH DEL PRADO
          GUEMES   Por mandado de S.E.
                                           (*signed*) JOSEPH DEL PRADO GUEMES

V.e. da Comision y facultad al Padre Rector que es, ó fuere de la Compañia de Jesus de la Ciudad del Cuzco, para que deponga del Cacicazgo de Guahillabamba a Don Marcos Chiguantupa, y ponga en su lugar a la persona que le pareciere conveniente, y para que haga la visita de Yndios y tierras de V.S.
[notarization follows]
[from García MS, 126, Vol. I, No. 28, fols. 535r.–536v.].

COMPARATIVE

CULTURAL RESEMBLANCES IN NUCLEAR AMERICA
PARALLELISM OR DIFFUSION?

WILLIAM DUNCAN STRONG

This problem is one of perennial interest and basic importance to Americanists. It has been attacked time and time again from the comparative horticultural, linguistic, ethnographic, archeological, historical, socioceremonial,
mythological, and evolutionary standpoints.[1] Twenty-one years ago, the last
time the International Congress of Americanists met in New York City,
Kroeber summed up certain aspects of this same problem. In 1928, he stated,
"The breadth of the topic is oppressive." The present writer agrees. Kroeber
focused his approach on the then current status of Peruvian archeology and,
on this basis, made such comparisons with Mexico-Guatemala prehistory
as seemed justifiable. He concluded his consideration by pointing out that
at that date, 1928, we still knew nothing of beginnings or early linkages in
either Meso-America or the Andean regions, and that the earliest known cultures in both areas met us full blown. To quote: "Of what lies beyond . . . we
have so far only the most fragmentary glimpses, so fragmentary and limited that
schemes built upon them are of necessity guesses. [However] when we reflect
that but twenty-eight years ago, in 1900, the Mexican Archaic was wholly
unknown; the exacter Mayan chronological correlations in their infancy and the
Old and New Maya epochs not yet formulated; Peruvian history only just carried back to Tiahuanaco, Early and Late Chimu undistinguished, the great arts
of Nazca and Chavin undiscovered—when we reflect on the progress since then,
we should realize how much unsuspected knowledge the next twenty-eight years
are likely to bring to this field."

Today, twenty-one years later, we propose to discuss what certain of these
more recent anthropological discoveries and correlations predicted by Kroeber
have been and what they may mean, not only for Nuclear America, but for the
comparative study of world culture history as well. My own contribution, however, is more limited, being primarily concerned with a very brief cultural and
dynamic comparison between various developmental epochs in the history of
Andean and Meso-American cultures, based, primarily, on the archeology of the
former area with which I am the most familiar.

There seems little need to sum up the general status of Peruvian archeology
prior to 1942 since this has also been done by Kroeber (171) and others (Ben-

---

1. Including: Herzog (139), Seler (304), Joyce (154, 153), Uhle (391, 392), Schuller (302),
Lehman (185), Spinden (315), Rock (279), Rivet (277), Krickeberg (163), Kroeber (168), Jijon
y Caamano (148), Sauer (294), Lothrop (202a), Means (222), Kidder II (159), Strong (331),
Steward (321, 324, 323), among others.

nett, 33; Strong, 332). Summaries of Meso-American archeology, however, are much less adequate despite the greater amount of work and many amazing discoveries which have been made in recent years in all parts of Mexico, in Guatemala, and in Honduras. Spinden's excellent little handbook (315) is now badly out of date, but, as yet, it has no successor as a brief summary report. A bibliography on Meso-American anthropology would be vast and there is a crying need for a Meso-American Handbook similar to the Handbook of South American Indians published by the Smithsonian Institution. Hence, while the following very tentative correlation between Andean and Meso-American culture epochs employs only a few specific sources, it may be checked against much monographic material. In passing, I may state that the regional designation of Nuclear America, as well as the native culture areas which it includes is derived from Kroeber (165).

In the limited space at my disposal I intend to very briefly correlate and compare a series of nine archeological cross sections ranging from southern Peru to central Mexico, attempting to point out certain widespread similarities in pre-Conquest material complexes and patterns which, according to generally accepted estimated dates, seem to be remarkably synchronic. The point of departure in this thumb-nail sketch is the archeological work of the Institute of Andean Research in Peru between 1942 and 1946 (Strong, 331, 333; Bennett, 39). The methodology for comparison of major culture groupings, or epochs, is derived from the very fruitful Chiclin Conference of August 7, 8, 1946 (Willey, 412). This Conference, held at the Museo Rafael Larco Herrera, Hacienda Chiclin, was called together by its Director, and our host, Rafael Larco Hoyle, and the writer, to correlate the current tentative findings of the Viru Valley Project with those of Larco and other Peruvian archeologists. At the Chiclin Conference only two cultural sequence charts were presented, one by Larco and the other by Strong (Willey, 1946). These were quite similar in major cultural epoch designations, but differed in important regards concerning the earlier cultural periods and alignments (compare Larco, 179, and Strong, 333, 332. Larco's culture epoch and sequence chart was based on his earlier stylistic and grave stratigraphic studies (compare Larco, 182; 179), while that of Strong was based primarily on the various refuse heap stratigraphic studies of the Viru Valley Project in 1946 (Strong, 332), as well as the earlier Viru Valley studies of Kroeber, Bennett, and Larco. Particularly important in regard to establishing the evolutionary-cultural epoch sequence for the North Coast of Peru was the objective definition in 1946 of the very early San Pedro-Chicama and Huaca Prieta cultures, as well as the stratigraphic demonstration of the priority of the Gallinazo to the Mochica culture occupations in the Viru Valley (Bird, 60; Strong, 333, 332). While the two culture sequence schemes presented by Larco and Strong at the Chiclin Conference were hotly debated, it was generally agreed that the adoption of some such developmental, functional system for Peruvian prehistory was in order.

Later, at the Viking Fund Conference on "A Reappraisal of Peruvian Archae-ology" in New York, July 17–19, 1947, similar culture epoch systems, with varying terminologies, were advanced, for Peru by Bennett and Willey; for Meso-America by Armillas, and for Nuclear America by Steward (see Bennett, 38). Recently Bennett's version of the Chiclin system has been employed in the "Andean Culture History," Handbook of the American Museum of Natural History by Bennett and Bird (40). It is therefore apparent that the general sys-tem of major epoch terminology proposed by Larco and Strong at the Chiclin Conference has already caught on. Since the functional-developmental method it employs is unique among Peruvian classificatory systems (see Strong, 332), it may well be termed the "Chiclin system," whatever the specific epoch designa-tions which may be employed according to new knowledge, personal predilec-tion, or area of application.[2] The Chiclin system, with modifications where needed, seems quite applicable to Meso-America where a somewhat similar but less extensive functional-historical epoch approach has already come into vogue (Thompson, 374, 373). The Chiclin System is therefore employed here to suggest cultural comparisons between certain Andean and Meso-American cultures on a synchronic (epoch) as well as a diachronic (sequential archeological) basis.

Before considering the chart (Table 1) in horizontal cross section to compare major epoch characteristics in the nine selected regions of Nuclear America, we may first consider the three Peruvian columns vertically. It is interesting to note that in south coastal Peru no new basic cultures have been added to our knowledge in the last twenty-one years (compare Kroeber, 168, pp. 9, 10, with Table 1). However, in central coastal Peru the positions of the Interlocking and White on Red cultures have since then been transposed through stratigraphic excavation, and in north coastal Peru three whole epochs (Formative, Incipient Agriculture, Pre-Agriculture) have been added, including five culture periods (compare Kroeber, 168, p. 11, with Table 1). This marked progress in Peru has been more than paralleled in the Meso-American field. Progress in both Nuclear fields, therefore, obviously confirms Kroeber's optimistic prediction at the last New York meeting of this Congress in 1928.

Turning now to a comparison of the earliest known cultural or human mani-festations in Nuclear America, from the Valley of Mexico to northern Peru, we will consider Table 1—from left to right. The present cultural evidence from this earliest known or Pre-Agricultural epoch is at present very scant. However, it may range in time from 3,000 to perhaps 10,000 years B.C. It includes the Tepex-

2. The Chiclin system, the result of much-needed and progressive co-operation between numerous archeologists (see Margain, 218), is dynamic and subject to indefinite adaptation and refinement as its present variant usage indicates. This is the hallmark of a truly developmental-functional classificatory system. The "Uhle," "Uhle-Kroeber," etc., temporal systems formerly had this quality, but the *temporal*, as a sole criteria for classification, in Peru is now outgrown. It is probably the subjectivity and lack of adaptability of the "Tello system," more than any-thing else, that have limited its general adoption. As knowledge advances, all systems of classi-fication must change.

TABLE 1

Culture Epochs and Periods in Nuclear America (Tentative as of 1949)

NORTH ←   SELECTED REGIONS   → SOUTH

Epochs	Vera Cruz (Tamaulipas)	Valley of Mexico	Oaxaca	Highland Guatemala (Chiapas)	Yucatan	Northwestern Honduras	Peru (North Coast)	Peru (Central Coast)	Peru (South Coast)	Guess Dates
Colonial										
Imperial or militarist	Huasteca 6	Aztec	Monte Alban 5 (Mixtec)	Quiche-Kakchiquel (Maya)	Mexican Absorption (Maya)	Naco (Mexican, etc.)	Inca / Chimu	Inca / Chancay	Inca / Late Ica	1521+
Fusion	Huasteca 5	Chichimec / Toltec	Monte Alban 4 (Zapotec)		Mexican Occupation	Ulua-Yojoa	North Coast Tiahuanaco (and) Lambayeque	Ancon {Late / Middle}	Middle Ica / Pacheco	1000
Florescent	Huasteca 4–3 (Cerro de las Mesas)	Teotihuacan 4, 3, 2	Monte Alban 3	Pamplona-Amatle / Esperanza	Tepeu / Tzakol	Polychrome	Mochica {Late / Early}	Early Lima	Nazca {B / A}	
Formative	Huasteca 2–1 (Early Tres Zapotes)	Teotihuacan 1 / Ticoman Tlatilco-Zacatenco	Monte Alban 2, 1	Miraflores / Las Charcas	Chicanel / Mamom	Playa de los Muertos Yojoa Monoch.	Gallinazo Salinar Cupisnique Guanape	Interlocking White on Red Early Ancon	Necropolis Cavernas	A.D. / B.C.
Incipient agriculture	La Perra Focus			Las Islona de Chantuto ?		Copan pre-ceramic ?	Huaca Prieta	Chilca ?		
Pre-agriculture	Diablo Focus	Chalco (Chupicuaro) / Tepexpan, etc.					San Pedro-Chicama			3000

pan skeleton found near Mexico City (de Terra, Romero, Stewart, 105), various chipped, lithic remains such as those of the Chalco culture from sites adjacent to Tepexpan, the Diablo Focus in Tamaulipas, and others like those from Chupicuaro in Michoacan (information from Muriel Porter) and, in Peru, the well retouched, flaked stone work from the "Quebradas Cupisnique" and "de los Fosiles" (San Pedro Chicama, Table I) (Bird, 60) in north coastal Peru. To these we should add the retouched flint and polished bone work reported from rock shelters near Huancayo (Tschopik, 382) in the central highlands of Peru. As known at present, this early lithic cultural material provides relatively little range for cultural comparison. However, in all the half century or more since Holmes (140, p. 285) described flaked stone implements from near Mitla, until the recent Tepexpan man excitement, very few archeologists seem to have paid attention to such simple stone and bone remains in the Nuclear American region of temples and rich post-ceramic artifacts. In the light of Bird's earlier discoveries (59) of cultural remains on Magellan Strait in Argentina dating back to perhaps 5,000 years, these lithic Mexican and Peruvian links with the northern Paleo-Indian remains are very important. It is easy to predict that, in the not too distant future, this "Pre-Agriculture epoch" (Table 1) will be subdivided, not only into numerous regional and temporal cultures, but also into better defined lithic epochs as well.

The epoch of Incipient Agriculture in New World archeology became a reality in 1946 when Strong and Evans first dug into the pre-ceramic, farming evels at Guañape in northern Peru and Junius Bird combined and greatly enlarged these findings at Huaca Prieta at the mouth of the Chicama Valley not far to the north (Strong, 333, 332; Bird, 60; Bennett and Bird, 40). In Tamaulipas, above the Diablo Focus, MacNeish also reports a pre-ceramic horizon, the La Perra Focus, which has maize and cotton weaving but no ceramics (115, p. 79) and, in Bat Cave in central New Mexico (Mangelsdorf and Smith, 217) just north of the major area under consideration, primitive maize types have been discovered in strata stated to range in time from 2500 B.C. to A.D. 500–1000 (ibid., p. 39). Presumably most of the Bat Cave association is pre-ceramic, but full published data is lacking. An outstanding feature in the Peruvian pre-ceramic is that the Huaca Prieta horizon (Bird, 60, p. 24) lacks maize entirely, but yielded specimens "of cotton, gourds, squash, aji peppers, beans (Canavalia), two varieties of 'fijol de guava' and what may be 'lenteja bocono (Dolichos lablab)' " (ibid.), plus certain definitely wild plants and fruits. The maximum age of the Huaca Prieta horizon is estimated at 3211 B.C. (Bird, 60, p. 28, and Table 1). Considering that Mangelsdorf and Reeves (216) were previously inclined to predicate the original domestication of maize in southeastern South America it is obvious that these recent discoveries, some three thousand miles apart, have enriched, complicated, but not solved the problem of New World horticultural origins. Elsewhere, there is a possibility that Drucker's discovery (112) of a pre-ceramic horizon, underlying ceramic deposits at Las Islas de Chantuto on the coast of

Chiapas, like the pre-ceramic horizon reported by Longyear (197) at Copan, may prove to pertain to the epoch of Incipient Agriculture rather than the epoch of the Pre-Agriculture. However, only pollen or other tests can demonstrate this.

With the Formative epoch we arrive at much richer evidence of cultural similarities in both the extremities and the center of Nuclear America (Table 1). In the "Middle Cultures" of the Valley of Mexico (Vaillant, 395), Huasteca (Ekholm, 114) Monte Alban (Caso, 74), Early Tres Zapotes (Drucker, 110), Las Charcas-Miraflores(?) (Kidder, 157), Mamom (Thompson, 374), Playa de los Muertos-Yojoa Monochrome (Strong, 330), the newly discovered Monagrillo culture on the Parita River in Panama (Stirling, 326a), and the various Chavinoid cultures in Peru (Strong, 331, 332), we have quite early horticultural horizons positively characterized in considerable part by maize horticulture; true weaving; a predominance of plain, incised or rocker-stamped pottery; hand-modeled female figurines; jade work in the north, a little hammered gold in the south; often a feline deity, or half human, half feline effigies (Tlatilco, Tres Zapotes, Cupisnique, see cover Larco, 182, for example). Negative characteristics shared are also important, but cannot be discussed here. From the Valley of Mexico south, these early Formative cultures occur respectively in Vera Cruz, Oaxaca, Chiapas, highland Guatemala, the Peten, northwestern Honduras, Panama and Peru. While simple, the majority of these cultures represent, in varying degrees, fully formed horticultural-ceramic complexes. The most primitive with which I am familiar are the Yojoa Monochrome in Honduras (Strong, 330); the Monagrillo culture in Panama (reported on at this Congress by Willey), and the Early Guañape phase of the Coastal Chavín culture in Peru which seems closely related to the underlying pre-ceramic (but horticultural) Huaca Prieta culture (Strong, 332). Interestingly enough, the great majority of authorities agree in placing these cultures at a time period not long before the birth of Christ. Thus, we now have objective evidence of an early, horticultural Formative epoch, rather similar to that Spinden postulated in the "Archaic" (315), which is either an historically connected and diffused unit in both the north and south of Nuclear America, or else represents a most amazing series of parallel culture growths. Here, for the first time, we come to close grips with the major problem posed in the title of this paper. If these early Formative cultures were known to be continuous between the Valley of Mexico and Peru, there would seem little likelihood of any other interpretation than that of historical unity. However, there still exists a break formed by our stratigraphic ignorance concerning the earlier periods in Colombia and Ecuador. Fortunately, the recent discovery of the Monagrillo culture in Panama suggests that this gap is closing. When it *is* closed, we can, in all probability, answer the problem of cultural unity in the affirmative. However, problems of origin as well as diffusional methods and directions will still remain.

Skipping over the long transitional period of the later Formative epoch cultures, we come to a relatively brief, but brilliant period in the course of the development of the higher cultures of the New World which some call the Classic but which I prefer to call the Florescent epoch (Table 1). In Mexico the great Teotihuacan (II–IV) civilization is perhaps typical. Characterized by huge and elaborate ceremonial structures, complex religious symbolism and ritual, excellent painted ceramic and other arts, wide trade, a priesthood, class structure, and status burial, these northern Florescent cultures apparently relied to a considerable extent on Chinampa farming, terracing and irrigation canals (Armillas, 17, p. 106). Religious symbolism included emblematic monsters including the jaguar, quetzal, humming-bird, owl, and snake. Gods of rain, plant, and water symbolism, and little emphasis on warfare, seem to be characteristic. The great period at Monte Alban (III), Esperanza, and Cerro de las Mesas were similar in many regards, as were the great Maya ceremonial centers of the Initial Series period (Tzakol and Tepeu, Table 1), except that the latter put unusual emphasis on calendric and astronomical activities. In Peru, great Florescent cultures like the Mochica and the little known Nazca shared the majority of these traits, although, judging from the belligerent aspects of Mochica art and the Nazca trophy head cult (Kroeber, 168, p. 10), warfare was more important during the Peruvian Florescent. Irrigation was highly developed in both the Mochica and Nazca cultures. Metal work is quite common in Peru throughout the Later Formative epoch, and gold, copper, and silver were well worked in Mochica times. However, only simple gold work is reported from Nazca graves (Kroeber, 168, p. 10). As to the age and duration of the Florescent in the Mexico-Guatemala region, we can be quite definite. The Maya Florescent or Initial Series era lasted from about A.D. 300 to 900, a period of 600 years, and the other Florescent centers or cultures seem to have had about the same time range (Armillas, 17, Table 6, p. 116). In Peru, however, I believe that the peak of the Mochica and Nazca cultures came somewhat later and that they flourished for a shorter period (see Kuebler, 173), but methods for more than relative dating in Peru are not yet available. In any event, just before the close of the first millennium A.D., the great Florescent centers in both Mexico and Peru were either abandoned, burned, or replaced by other less flamboyant cultures. Perhaps, as Armillas reasons (17, p. 108), population pressure, exorbitant religious demands, and inadequate social and technological equipment brought about these widely separated but more or less simultaneous catastrophes. If so, these also are parallels of no mean order! On the other hand, in both Mexico and Peru, the close of the Florescent epoch precedes, and may even result from, a marked period of folk wandering and militarism. If like conditions can be demonstrated as extending the length and breadth of Nuclear America, the downfall of many of the Florescent centers may be a phenomenon of contact. If, however, their downfall was internal and independent, certain most important, but as yet only vaguely sensed, laws of diachronic culture dynamics would seem to have been involved. The problem is posed—but the final answer awaits the extension of truly creative archeology.

In Meso-America it may be futile to attempt to distinguish between what I have called the epoch of Fusion and the Imperial epoch (Table 1). Armillas (17, p. 108 and Table 6) essayed such a distinction but, at least temporarily, abandoned it. However, in the general region from the Valley of Mexico south to Nicaragua, to judge from linguistic distributions and legendary history, there was a considerable period marked by Chichimec, Toltec, Pipil, Mixtec and many other interminglings, shiftings, and even extensive migrations, militaristic and otherwise. This is the period when metals really became important in Meso-America, plumbate pottery was widely distributed, and fortifications came into vogue (Armillas, 17). Such a period of fusion, or confusion, seems likewise to have occurred at about the same time in Peru-Bolivia (Table 1) with its main marker being the Tiahuanacoid cultures; and, probably, peoples moving to the north, and the black pottery-making, Lambayeque culture-bearers moving to the south (Larco, 179). In both cases, judging from the cultural fragmentation observable in the respective archeological remains, this epoch preceded the period of large empires. This is a confusing epoch in both the north and the south and one that is very poorly known, especially in Peru. However, if the establishment of such an epoch of Fusion in Nuclear America proves to be justified, we are then faced by another aspect of the same basic problem raised in the preceding paragraph and in the title of this paper.

The Imperial epoch in the north and the south of the Nuclear area brings into sharp focus the differences, as well as the underlying similarities, which seem to have developed throughout Mexican and Peruvian pre-history. For Peru, with its great, closely knit Inca empire and its somewhat earlier Chimu and other coastal predecessors, the term Imperial epoch seems very fitting. For Mexico, with the unco-ordinated tribute empires of the Aztec and other Mexican peoples, the term is perhaps not so apt. For this reason I have employed the terms "Imperial or Militarist" for the closing epoch in native Nuclear America (Table 1). It is my own impression that the Aztec empire covered a wider range of space and peoples, with more co-ordinated control than did its predecessors. If so, the northern cultures of Nuclear America were still in step with their southern contemporaries in Peru, despite their looser organization, calendric orientation, emphasis on human sacrifice, etc. This, however, is a matter that may only be decided by experts in Meso-American native history, linguistics, and archeology.

Coming now to our original question, it is my opinion that the marked resemblances in all known stages of the development of culture in the northern and southern portions of Nuclear America are due to original historical unity and later indirect diffusion, rather than to independent, parallel or convergent evolution. That these epochs were remarkably synchronic is now rather strongly indicated by archeological research. The matter of *indirect* contact and diffusion between such extreme points as Peru and Mexico should be stressed; for the reported Peruvian designs and trade objects found in Mexico (Kroeber, 168, p. 15 and Lothrop, 202a) seem rather unconvincing, whereas not even one piece of jade, so highly valued in Mexico-Guatemala, nor any other indubitable Mexican artifact, has been reported from Peru. For these and other reasons the various theories of Maya invasions of South America, and vice versa, seem untenable. It would seem that it was more by culture interpenetrating adjacent culture, peoples in trouble jostling other peoples until the trouble or idea spread, rather than by actual migrations, that the higher cultures of the American continent kept in step. Of this basic unity Kroeber, having criticized certain extreme migration theories, states: "All the foregoing should not be construed as a hesitation to accept the fundamental unity of Mexican and Peruvian civilization, in fact of all the cultures of Middle America in the larger ethnic sense of that term. There is too much in common to believe otherwise: the economic base of life, a whole series of cultivated plants, the textile, ceramic, and metallurgical arts, the type of clothing, architecture, the quality of artistic achievement, the building of states. As against this basic common element, it matters little that Mexico grew cacao and the agave, Peru the potato and the peanut, that Mexico alone developed lime mortar and cement, a day count calendar, writing and paper, Peru, wool spinning and the balance. Many Mexican peoples, the Maya and Tarasca for instance, differ almost as much among themselves" (168, p. 20).

Thus, we come to the same conclusion as did Kroeber twenty-one years ago, but there is one important difference. This is the fact that in the interval archeology, despite the still great geographical and other gaps in the record, can now demonstrate the major steps whereby these great northern and southern empires of the New World arose from a simple Formative culture pattern and developed in apparently synchronous fashion to their final common destiny, That these epochs in the development of New World civilization seem remarkably similar to those which, several millennia earlier,[3] led to the development of Old World civilizations opens important theoretical vistas, but this is another. though connected, problem which cannot be considered here.

3. Compare Childe (81, 82), Graham Clark (84), Curwen (102), and Steward (323).

THE ROLE OF POLITICAL ORGANIZATION IN THE DEVELOPMENT OF MAN, WITH SUGGESTED APPLICATIONS IN THE NEW WORLD

RICHARD THURNWALD

Consideration of the history of Old World cultures has led to the postulation of a general theory of political development. In this paper I will present a rough synthesis of the conclusions reached with some of the evidence as it occurs in the Old World (Part I), and make certain suggestions for the application of these conclusions to interpretation of social and cultural features of the New World (Part II). The underlying assumption involved in applying this theory to the New World is that the *psychic stimulations* and the *social reactions* are undoubtedly of the same kind in the two hemispheres.

I

The evolution of society is due to the *accumulation* of new devices and insights into the nature and processes of life. This progress depends on experiences which are the result of the particular kind of life led by the group. Of central importance in this evolution are the particular patterns developed for the acquisition of food. Various conditions for obtaining subsistence must have led to different devices and specializations of the cultural pattern since each method will require the development of different abilities.

The earliest stages of political organization we may imagine are probably represented in the life of small clusters of people organized into hordes, or, if knitted together more tightly, packs. These groups maintain life in various ways conforming to the nature of the environment; to the kinds of plants to be gathered or animals to be snared. Several factors are decisive: the plants and animals available, the contrivances at the disposition of the horde, or the tendency or capacity of the horde to adapt its institutions to new conditions of life.

A remarkable change in the method of acquiring food occurred in the Old World at the end of the Pleistocene. The receding glaciers which caused inundations and floods probably limited the securing of fruits, roots, and hunting of animals. A new fashion of procuring alimentation obtruded itself on Homo sapiens, namely, not to plunder the natural environment but to *help* it produce more. This change in *psychic attitude* and in the planning of economic activity was one of the decisive steps taken by humanity. Two new directions became possible—the agricultural and the pastoral.

The cultivation of the soil by the digging stick, hoe, and spade made possible a more peaceful, sedentary life, including the building of houses and villages.

However, it was still necessary to search for new land after the original was exhausted, e.g., in the Africa the Bantu Negro gently invaded the southern part of the continent in search of new land.

Quite another way of life and consequent psychic attitude was taken by the herdsman who kept sheep, goats, cattle, or, in more humid areas, pigs. Since herds had to be defended against predatory animals and men, the herdsmen developed skill in the use of weapons. The breeder, who regarded his flock as his property, displayed haughty, fighting attitudes, while the food collectors and agriculturists were able to meet more on an equal footing. However, since the keeper of cattle needed and wanted the products of the agriculturists—their wheat, flour, and handicraft work—barter between herdsmen and producers developed. But in time and due to the military superiority of the herdsmen, the agriculturists became degraded to bondsmen.

This procedure, which I have depicted here in very summary fashion, represents the origin of what is called *stratification*.

Stratifications have occurred also among tribes with different kinds of subsistence economies, i.e., the Polynesians and Micronesians, who as navigators display many similar characteristics to herdsmen. However, before any two groups amalgamate into one stratified society, there must always be a basis of *reciprocal aid*, with the more military of the two groups eventually asserting their power.

Once stratification has occurred, it may either recede or take other courses such as the establishment of an artistocracy. Intermarriage between conqueror and conquered is sometimes an instrument for a type of equalization in which the two strata merge. On the other hand, where the conquerors maintain strict endogamy, aristocracies tend to develop, e.g., Micronesian and Polynesian. The aristocracy in turn may lead to a kingship if one of the dominant families establishes itself as supreme through military conflict, e.g., Rundi in Central Africa.

Before stratification, society is based on the full equality of the individual. This attitude is so deep-rooted that in the first stages of stratification only groups were distinguished, not individuals. As stratification proceeded, a system of grading the individuals within the stratum developed, so that complicated layered-societies resulted. This was evidenced in the germinating of castes, guilds, and corporations, e.g., among the African Hausa.

The growth of stratification in a society is particularly exemplified in the power intrusted to chiefs. It is a long way from the man of authority in a small community who may be asked for special functions to the despot or god-king. In a primitive society, the members of the horde may excel in their personal specialties and be treated as experts accordingly. Stratification, however, engenders a kind of *general* superiority which the dominant families arrogate to themselves and which is given recognition by the whole group. This can be observed in the advent of the mariner-peoples of Polynesian origin among the Papuans. The dominant families impose their interpretations of the emerged stratification on the rest of the group which accepts them in their now changed world. Since nearly all knowledge and intelligence is considered to be the result of superhuman powers, the political and economic organization is closely connected with religion and its cult. Therefore, feasts and ceremonies become the chief's main duties.

II

What do the various stages of stratification and of graded society mean in connection with Americanist studies? Do we encounter similar institutions in ancient America, and how closely do they correspond to certain phases or gaps of the Old World pattern?

It seems that these socio-psychological phases can be used in a way like geological strata, for, on the average, similar situations lead to similar results. Of course I speak of "similar" situations, for absolutely identical situations never recur. When we find stratification in a tribe, we can infer from our theory that two ethnic units have merged in some way; and the layers at first assume certain features which with the lapse of time tend to shift to other configurations and structures. The details of development, the "melody" of events, will never be absolutely identical, but the main features of the series are the same.

The last ten or twenty years of Americanist research have secured an immense mass of new facts about pre-Columbian American civilizations (395, 228, 325). Although the absolute dates are still in dispute, we encounter stratification among the forerunners of the Aztecs and Mayas as well as the early Peruvians. The astounding fact is that in all these societies, stratified communities arise out of a population of food gatherers. All three cases show a certain parallelism in development. In Mexico as well as among the Maya, we find privileged families and a headman. The officials and priests of the clan come from these same privileged families. Aristocratic clans have succeeded in vanquishing other tribes and making them tributary. Some tribes succeed in founding a city-state, much like what happened among the ancient Sumerians of Mesopotamia.

The cult of the gods is politically important. Not only were the images of the gods carried on the back of the headman of the clan, but vanquished tribes also were compelled to accept the cult of the victors—again, just as among the Sumerians and Babylonians. Actually there is somewhat of a merging of the two cults, but it remains under the control of the victors. This kind of development is reminiscent of what we observed in the Old World in the relationship of herdsmen or navigators towards agriculturists.

In Peru the social structure was particularly interesting. From the earliest known times, stratification seems to have prevailed and to have been combined with paternal authority and succession in an extended family, the *ayllu*, that inhabited one house and was endogamous. It indicates a marked isolation which coincides with the characteristic units of "boatloads" in the Malayan area.

The Peruvian ayllus were administered by a chief, the curaca, who possibly held a hereditary position. During Inca time the ayllus were used for purposes of administration, as similarly, the old Slavic derevnia was transmuted by the Czars into the Russian "mir."

A hypothesis may be constructed that the close association within the ayllus resulted from the close connection between boat mates during long passages at sea. These seafarers must have reached the Peruvian coast in early times and started the ayllus, introduced metal-working, pottery, and weaving, as well as the use of the spade-plough handled by men. This spade-plough is the same type as that used in New Zealand by the Maoris. It serves to tear up the ground. The clods are beaten to pieces by women. It is unlikely that this resemblance is coincidental. Most probably this tool once started from India or China and was brought to Indonesia or the Philippine Islands. Some navigators may have taken it to New Zealand, others to the Peruvian coast.

The Peruvians excel in breeding the llama and alpaca, the only quadrupeds domesticated in the Americas. The tribes of the southern regions, however, *hunt* the llama and alpaca, or rather its ancestors, the guanaco and vicuña. The llama does not like the coast and its domestication must have occurred in the mountains of Peru which the newcomers probably had climbed. Mariners may have been particularly inclined for such a task. The domestication had been completed in the earliest known period of the Chavin culture or before.

If one compares the Old World pattern, which I have tried to expound as a kind of model of man's political development, with what I have tried to induce from the events and social configurations in the Americas, one will find a gap between some levels in the American sequence:

1. The first immigrants into America were already at the lower paleolithic stage of culture.

2. The isolation of the scant clusters of immigrants was an impediment to their advancement. During the corresponding period in the Old World, particularly in Western Asia and around the Mediterranean coasts, active contact of various societies engendered much progress.

3. In the New World we do not find groups representing some of the phases of stratification which occurred in the Old World, but rather a contrast between early food collectors who lived similarly to the Onas, Yagans, or California hunting tribes, and the highly stratified, culturally developed groups of the Northwest Coast, Mexico, Guatemala, and Peru, with their arts of spinning and weaving, ceramics, metal work including casting, stone sculpture, complicated time reckoning, picture writing, and so on. It seems impossible that the early tribes who came over the Bering Straits could have achieved such progress in a few centuries without innumerable experiences and diversified learning from contact with many different tribes—contact which did not occur. This gap, then, clearly indicates that the later achievements which show up rather suddenly do not represent a local evolution, but were brought by newcomers from Asia.

4. The stratification initiated by the newcomers from Asia took on, in the course of time, successive forms which I have sketched for the Old World and which can be found represented in various stages among the Maya, the Toltecs, and the Aztecs, and the establishment of a god-kingship among the Incas.

The contribution of Americanist studies to our conception of political organization in the ascent of man lies in its incitement to extended investigation of the social and psychological conditions and circumstances in the lower paleolithic that led to agriculture, to keeping of domesticated animals, and to an ordered family life; that is, to the germs of higher civilization.

My hypotheses may be interpreted as an endeavor to gain heuristic hints for further research.

¿EXISTE ALGUNA RELACIÓN ENTRE "LOS DANZANTES" DE MONTE ALBÁN EN MÉXICO Y LOS MONOLITOS DE CERRO SECHÍN EN EL PERÚ?

Emilia Romero

El principal objeto de este trabajo es señalar objetivamente el parecido—a mi entender notable—que he encontrado entre algunos de los monolitos existentes en Cerro Sechín, cerca de Casma, Perú y los conocidos con el nombre de "Los Danzantes" en Monte Albán, Oaxaca, México.

En 1939 tuve oportunidad de visitar los monolitos de Sechín en compañía del Dr. Julio C. Tello, quien los había descubierto en julio del año de 1937. Grande fué mi sorpresa al visitar Monte Albán en 1947 y ver allí piedras labradas que me recordaron vívidamente las que diez años antes había visto en el Perú.

Los monolitos de Sechín pertenecen, según el Dr. Tello al horizonte inferior de la cultura Chavín (348), una de las más antiguas del Perú, de la que han derivado otras grandes culturas tales como las de Paracas, Muchik, Nazca, Chanka e Inka y tiene una enorme área de propagación. El Dr. Tello señala para esta cultura una antigüedad aproximada de 1000 años antes de Cristo (349, las tables de distribucion de las culturas).

En el XXVII Congreso de Americanistas celebrado en México, el Dr. Tello dió cuenta del descubrimiento de esta cultura Chavín y con este motivo señaló la importancia de los hallazgos realizados por él en Sechín (350). Pero el Dr. Tello no conoció las ruinas de la comarca arqueológica de Oaxaca y nos imaginamos cual habría sido su sorpresa si hubiese podido visitar Monte Albán y contemplar "Los Danzantes."

Cerro Sechín se halla en la costa del Perú a 7 kilómetros al este de Casma. En dicha huaca el Dr. Tello desenterró 96 monolitos, unos altos y alargados que él llama *monolitos mayores* de 1.80 a 4.40 metros de alto y otros pequeños, casi en forma cúbica que él llama *monolitos menores*, de 0.60 a 1.20 metros de alto.

Parte de los monolitos mayores llevan grabada en plano relieve una figura humana y los menores una cabeza humana. Estas figuras de Cerro Sechín si bien están emparentadas con la cultura Chavín tienen rasgos comunes característicos y que difieren en algunos detalles de las representadas en las otras estelas y monolitos de esta cultura. Tienen una sencillez de presentación de que carecen las demás. Los personajes en ellas representadas tienen la nariz chata y ancha; los labios gruesos y abiertos que dejan ver cuatro o cinco dientes; la barba está en el mismo plano que los labios, sin saliente alguna. Las cabezas siempre están de perfil (menos en las representadas en la Fig. 1), aunque en las mayores el cuerpo pueda estar de perfil o de frente. El cuello es en extremo corto, casi inexistente y en las manos y pies los pulgares tienen unas uñas enormes. Las figuras ocupan toda la piedra y parece que ésta hubiese sido cortada antes de que se esculpiera la figura. Algunas llevan adornos de plumas a manera de taparrabo y en las manos una insignia ceremonial. En la cabeza algunas llevan un tocado sencillo (Fig. 2). Otras como la Figura 3 tiene un brazo levantado y tiene tal movilidad que parece que estuviera en actitud de ejecutar una danza.

"Los Danzantes" de Monte Albán (Fig. 4) fueron revelados al mundo por el coronel Guillermo Dupaix en 1806 en viaje hecho a México por orden del Rey de España. Dupaix hizo de ellos esta descripción: "Hay unas losas grandes y cuadrilongas de varios tamaños de piedra berroqueña y por la superficie plana representa gravadas de resalto, unas figuras o personajes con la boca abierta, algo agigantadas, con diversas actitudes y movimientos, sentadas y en pié, todas perfiladas y dirigiendo la vista y cuerpo de Sur a Norte, hacia lo interior de las cinco que se han podido dibujar por tener integridad. ... Lo que me llena de ideas confusas son las actitudes grotescas y la flexibilidad aparente de los miembros varoniles contenidas de relieve en las losas citadas ..." (113, p. 248).

Casi cien años después de que Dupaix describiera los cinco primeros "danzantes" el Dr. Solunguren y el Lic. Belmar descubrieron ocho más; el Dr. Leopoldo Batres encontró nuevas figuras de este tipo en 1902 (25, p. 28) y en las exploraciones que el Instituto de Arqueología e Historia de México lleva a cabo periódicamente en Monte Albán han sido descubiertas las restantes que se conocen y se han hecho estudios sobre ellos (74, 77, 78).

El Dr. Alfonso Caso señala que estas figuras estilo "danzante" pertenecen a la Época I de Monte Albán; es decir, que tienen considerable antigüedad; pero manifiesta que esa cultura I de Monte Albán está ya altamente desarrollada y dice: "está muy lejos de ser 'primitiva,' y como no hemos encontrado vestigios anteriores tenemos que concluir que estos habitantes no desarrollaron esa cultura en Monte Albán y en general en el Valle de Oaxaca, sino que vinieron de algún lugar que por el momento ignoramos." Encuentra luego el Dr. Caso que pueden tener conexiones con la civilización arcaica de México y "con ciertos objetos de barro y de jade llamados 'olmecas' que se encuentran ampliamente distribuídos desde Michoacán hasta Guatemala" (72, pp. 20-21).

En la descripción que de "Los Danzantes" hace el Dr. Caso vemos algunos rasgos que podríamos encontrar en común con las figuras humanas representadas en los monolitos de Cerro Sechín: "La nariz chata y ancha y la boca con labios abultados, mostrando casi siempre dos dientes (en Sechín se muestran cuatro o cinco). ... Las cabezas están siempre de perfil, pero los cuerpos se representan de perfil o de frente. Se ve con claridad que se cortó la piedra, en la que se iba a esculpir la figura y luego se procuró que ésta llenara el mayor espacio posible. ... La boca está siempre abierta. La barbilla a diferencia de las figuras "olmecas" nunca es saliente con relación al plano de los labios. El cuello es tan corto que prácticamente no existe. El cuerpo es robusto, más bien rechoncho. ..."

Luego, refiriéndose a un segundo tipo de danzantes, dice: "Las uñas de los dedos del pulgar de la mano y el pie son enormes" (71, p. 128).

En cuanto a la forma cómo las figuras parecen haber sido grabadas la encontramos muy parecida. El Dr. Tello describe la técnica empleada en Sechín que quizá podría aplicarse a "Los Danzantes": "La técnica empleada en la presentación de las figuras grabadas sobre las piedras es uniforme en todas ellas. No se encuentran diferencias fundamentales. Todas parecen haber sido trabajadas por un mismo artista o por artistas entrenados en las normas tecnológicas de una misma escuela. Los surcos, hendiduras y rebajos no ofrecen huellas de herramientas contundentes. Los surcos son escasos. Las hendiduras anchas han sido producidas por una herramienta que actúa por frotación desgastando la superficie hasta ahondarla; el fondo y los bordes de estas hendiduras revelan el delicado trabajo de frotación por medio de una herramienta que desgasta la piedra suave y lentamente. Es posible que esta labor se haya realizado mediante el auxilio del agua o de alguna otra substancia que cohesione la arenilla desgastante dentro del surco y facilite el manejo de las herramientas. Nada diferente se nota tampoco en los rebajos del fondo de las figuras. La misma herramienta raspa y alisa las aristas de las hendiduras. ... La operación del desgaste lento de la piedra debió estar precedida por el dibujo incindido de la silueta de la figura ..." (350, p. 247).

Hay que recordar que la principal diferencia que hay entre unas y otras figuras incindidas es—naturalmente—la ausencia total de jeroglíficos en los monolitos peruanos.

En vista de las coincidencias que se encuentran entre estas figuras situadas a tan gran distancia unas de otras, me he preguntado muchas veces si no sería conveniente recomendar a los arqueólogos del Perú y México que tuvieran en mente los rasgos comunes a fin de iniciar un estudio comparativo en ambas zonas que podría dar como resultado un mejor conocimiento de ambas antiguas culturas y la posibilidad de hallar alguna relación entre ellas.

El arqueólogo alemán Max Uhle emitió la teoría de que las culturas peruanas eran de origen maya. El Dr. Tello—que siempre impugnó las ideas de Uhle en este punto—refiriéndose a esta teoría dejó escrita esta frase: "La cultura lítica Chavín es la única que tiene un lejano parecido con la centroamericana, pero esto no justifica su filiación genética" (350, p. 95). Ese lejano parecido lo encontramos—tal vez más cercano—con algunos signos y dibujos que aparecen en la zona mexicana de Oaxaca, dentro del horizonte zapoteca y quizás el olmeca.

El parecido que hemos señalado entre los monolitos peruanos y los mexicanos podría tal vez ser originado por el empleo de técnicas semejantes en pueblos de idéntico nivel cultural; pero podría también ser fruto de una invasión cultural realizada en épocas remotas y esto es lo que la arqueología comparada está en la obligación de desentrañar. Hasta el momento no sabemos que personas que tengan profundos conocimientos en la ciencia arqueológica del Perú y de México

FIG. 1

FIG. 3

FIG. 4.—Algunos "Danzantes" de Monte Albán (Oaxaca), México

288

Fig. 2.—Monolitos encontrados por el Dr. Julio C. Tello en Sechín, Perú

hayan realizado trabajos arqueológicos comparativos entre las culturas peruanas y mexicanas. Consideramos, pues, imperiosa, la necesidad de emprender trabajos de arqueología comparada en ambos países, pues sin ellos será imposible realizar una obra completa.

Y esta necesidad urgente de ampliar los horizontes de estudio de los arqueólogos mexicanos y peruanos, abandonando estrechos nacionalismos y cooperando generosamente, es lo que señalo a la atención de los americanistas. En mi opinión existe un parecido entre los monolitos de Cerro Sechín y "Los Danzantes" de Monte Albán, al punto de que creo que de encontrarse alguna vez nexos entre las culturas centro y sudamericanas ha de ser mediante el estudio de las culturas Chavín en el Perú y zapoteca y olmeca en México.

Diez años después de que el Dr. Tello presentase su trabajo básico sobre la cultura Chavín en el Perú, la arqueóloga peruana, Rebeca Carrión Cachot, acaba de publicar su trabajo *La Cultura Chavín*. En estas páginas señala para esta cultura una antigüedad de más de 4500 años (347, p. 78), basándose para ello en el hecho de que diversos cataclismos azotaron el territorio del Perú en tiempos de que la historia no conserva memoria alguna, pero que los estudios geológicos y arqueológicos actuales están poniendo en claro. Estos cataclismos, al parecer, borraron por completo las huellas exteriores de la cultura Chavín que había alcanzado un notable nivel cultural. La destrucción llegó al punto de que los habitantes del Tawantinsuyo habían perdido por completo la memoria de dicha civilización a la llegada de los españoles en el siglo XVI y, por lo tanto, fué ignorada por completo por los cronistas de la Conquista. Esta inteligente interpretación de la señorita Carrión, comprobada científicamente, es sumamente importante en el supuesto de que haya existido una invasión cultural ya fuera de sur a norte (de América del Sur a Mesoamérica) o bien de norte a sur (de Mesoamérica a América del Sur). Y de haber sido de sur a norte podría explicarse por la fuga de los supervivientes de las zonas castigadas por la naturaleza, a través del continente, en busca de un nuevo hogar, llevando en la memoria el recuerdo de sus templos, de sus esculturas, de sus grecas con el signo escalonado y demás signos ornamentales, su culto por el jaguar, etc.

Mientras tanto, queda abierta la fascinante interrogación: ¿Existe realmente alguna relación entre las esculturas de Cerro Sechín en el Perú y "Los Danzantes" de Monte Albán, en Oaxaca, México?

LE PERSONNAGE COUCHÉ SUR LE DOS: SUJET COMMUN DANS L'ARCHÉOLOGIE DU MEXIQUE ET DE L'EQUATEUR

HENRI LEHMANN

Depuis longtemps déjà les archéologues et ethnologues ont remarqué la parenté qui existe entre certains objets de la zone Maya et de l'Amérique Centrale (avant tout Chorotega) d'une part, et ceux des régions côtières de l'Equateur d'autre part. Qu'il suffise de mentionner les très nombreux travaux de Max Uhle (385, 387, 388, 389, 390, 392, 393), les études de Jijón y Caamaño (148, 149) et de Raoul d'Harcourt (106). J'ai trouvé moi-même, au cours d'un séjour sur les côtes du Pacifique (Guerrero et Michoacán) quelques objets qui ont nettement un aspect sudaméricain. J'en ai parlé au dernier Congrès des Américanistes à Paris (184). Il me semblait possible de faire remonter ces relations encore plus vers le Nord, vers Colima et Nayarit.

En étudiant le travail de M. d'Harcourt sur l'archéologie d'Esmeraldas, j'ai été frappé par un certain type de statuettes, représentant toutes un personnage étendu sur le dos et ligoté sur sa couche. Un certain nombre d'objets du même genre ont été trouvés dans une région aussi éloignée de la première que Colima. Bien qu'il y ait entre eux des différences de détail sensibles, ils présentent une analogie qui semble indiquer que des liens existaient entre les deux civilisations qui leur ont donné naissance.

Nous allons décrire ici et tenter d'interpréter quelques statuettes provenant de chacune des deux régions et nous les mettrons en parallèle avec un troisième groupe d'objets analogues de l'époque aztèque. La liste des objets pourra sans doute être élargie, au fur et à mesure qu'on étudiera le matériel existant dans les différents musées.[1]

Les céramiques d'Esmeraldas publiées par Raoul d'Harcourt (106) ont été trouvées à La Tolita, sans doute sur la plage, car leur surface semble rongée par un contact constant avec l'eau. Deux des personnages sont de sexe masculin, le troisième de sexe féminin (Figs. 1 à 3). Aucun des personnages n'est vêtu, le sexe est très visiblement indiqué. Ils portent pourtant tous une coiffure; un des hommes (Fig. 1) porte le bonnet très typique qui épouse la forme de la tête et

---

1. Depuis que cet article a été écrit, nous avons eu l'occasion de visiter l'University Museum de Philadelphie, où nous avons effectivement trouvé une confirmation de notre thèse. Ce musée possède en effet quatre statuettes du même type et provenant des mêmes régions, dont deux d'Esmeraldas, Equateur (29–51–89 et 29–51–111), une de Michoacán (NA 2123) et une de Mexico (11301). Celle de Michoacán correspond stylistiquement aux objets de Colima, celle de Mexico est aztèque.

qui est si fréquent à Esmeraldas. Le même personnage a un collier de perles. Tous les trois ont des boucles d'oreilles.

Les bras sont allongés contre le corps. Il semble que les mains s'accrochent au bout d'un bâton horizontal placé sous les jambes, très apparent dans le cas de la statuette féminine (Fig. 2) et qui provoque une légère flexion des genoux chez les différents personnages. Ce bâton qui fait penser à un billot se trouve légèrement au-dessous des mains dans le personnage (Fig. 3). La tête de la femme repose sans doute sur un appuie-tête, à en juger par les protubérances semicirculaires qui se trouvent symétriquement de chaque côte des joues.[2]

Les trois personnages sont ligotés, à la hauteur de la poitrine, par un bandeau qui emprisonne les bras. Celui du personnage à collier ne fait qu'un seul tour et couvre la poitrine jusqu'au nombril; le collier est placé sur le bandeau. Le bandeau de la femme se trouve à la même hauteur, mais il fait deux tours. Celui du troisième personnage est un peu différent et couvre le corps entier au-dessus du sexe sans toutefois le recouvrir. Il fait quatre tours en tout, le tour inférieur passe sous les bras, sans doute pour libérer les mains.

Une des plaques porte deux trous de suspension: elle était sans doute portée autour du cou ou suspendue.

Quant aux statuettes de Colima, l'une d'elles enregistrée sous le no. 24.13.2022., se trouve dans les collections du Musée de l'Homme (Fig. 4). Un personnage est couché sur un lit à quatre pieds (dont l'un, cassé, manque). Il est immobilisé sur la couche au moyen d'un triple bandeau à hauteur de la poitrine et d'un double bandeau à hauteur des mollets. Les bras emprisonnés dans le bandeau sont collés contre les hanches. Comme le bandeau supérieur comprime la poitrine, le ventre, resté libre, est proéminent. Le sexe est indiqué. La tête repose sur un appuie-tête concave; elle est coiffée d'un bonnet qui en épouse la forme et qui touche le bord semicirculaire du lit.

Une petite statuette de sujet analogue a été trouvée à Las Animas, Colima (Fig. 5). Elle se trouve dans la collection de Diego Rivera à Mexico. Le personnage qui est étendu sur une couche presque plate, y est fixé au moyen d'un double bandeau. Ce bandeau couvre une partie de la poitrine et les bras entre le coude et l'épaule. Les jambes sont écartées pour laisser une place à un petit chien assis, sans doute gardien de sa maîtresse. Au-dessous de la tête se trouve une protubérance qui sert d'appuie-tête.

Un troisième objet du même type et provenant de la même région—Colima ou Nayarit—se trouve dans la collection de M. Ohly à Londres (Fig. 6). Il se distingue des autres par la manière dont le personnage est fixé sur la couche: deux bandeaux disposés en croix qui couvrent la plus grande partie de son corps. Un troisième bandeau, celui-ci du type usuel, retient les jambes. Ajoutons que le personnage porte une *nariguera*, insigne de son rang, et de grandes boucles d'oreille.

Tandis que les statuettes d'Esmeraldas sont réalistes dans le détail—elles suivent en cela le style local—les statuettes de Colima, de type archaïque, sont

2. Un fragment d'objet du même type a été publié par Uhle (387, p. 25 et 56, Lam. 21, 2).

FIG. 1   FIG. 2   FIG. 3

FIG. 4

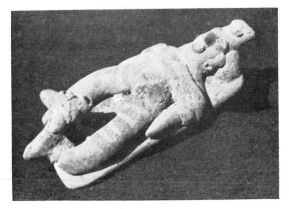

FIG. 5

plus stylisées; des détails comme les doigts ou les pieds sont à peine indiqués. Mais il n'est guère douteux qu'il s'agisse de la même représentation.

Que peut être le sujet représenté? Est-il possible de l'interpréter? Nous avons vu que tous les personnages sont couchés sur le dos, que certains ont la tête placée sur un appuie-tête qui les empêche de bouger et qu'ils sont tous enveloppés dans une étoffe qui emprisonne les bras. Ceci semble indiquer une position forcée.

Cependant il me semble qu'il faut rejeter l'hypothèse suivant laquelle ces personnages représenteraient des prisonniers, sujet assez fréquent dans la céramique du Pérou. La représentation d'une femme et le fait qu'un des personnages porte un collier de perles bien disposé au-dessus du bandeau, ne sont pas

Fig. 6

de nature à soutenir cette hypothèse. Uhle (387) interprète le fragment d'une statuette analogue comme représentant un châtiment ou un sacrifice, tandis que d'Harcourt (106) voit dans les personnages que nous décrivons, des gens qui se soumettent à un rite.

Ne s'agirait-il pas plutôt de représentations de malades? Le fait que les bras sont emprisonnés a nécessairement une signification particulière. Il s'agissait évidemment d'empêcher l'individu de s'en servir. Les bandeaux peuvent être mis en parallèle avec notre camisole de force, à laquelle on a recours dans certains cas de crises de démence. Tandis que la camisole de force rappelle vaguement la forme d'une chemise, le vêtement dont nous nous occupons ici, est une longue bande dans laquelle on enroule le malade. Les mains n'ayant plus aucune possibilité d'action efficace, une fois les bras emprisonnés, elles pouvaient rester libres, comme c'est particulièrement apparent dans la statuette Figure 3.

Outre les bras emprisonnés qui font penser qu'il s'agit de représentations de malades, nous avons observé dans plusieurs de nos statuettes, qu'un billot maintient les genoux en légère flexion. C'est apparemment une coutume qui s'est conservée jusqu'à nos jours: nous mettons un traversin sous les genoux des malades, notamment quand il s'agit de maladies de longue durée pour soulager les articulations. Il ne me semble guère douteux que le billot avait le même but que le traversin actuel.

Si nous admettons que les personnages couchés sur le dos sont des malades, nous pouvons nous expliquer aussi la présence du petit chien dans la statuette de Colima. Il tient compagnie à sa maîtresse immobilisée par la maladie, et en cela il ne se distingue guère des chiens de nos jours. Les artistes de Colima, malgré leur stylisation qui supprime parfois une main et parfois un pied, aiment toutefois des scènes narratives comme celle que nous venons d'évoquer.[3]

FIG. 7

Etudions encore un troisième groupe de statuettes, celles-ci d'origine aztèque et provenant sans exception de la Vallée de Mexico. Toutes les pièces que je donne pour exemples figurent dans les collections du Musée de l'Homme. Les personnages sont représentés ligotés et couchés, à une exception près, dans un lit profond à bords relevés. Il est à remarquer que les pieds reposent généralement sur le bord inférieur du lit. Un seul personnage no. 78.1.789. (Fig. 8) a les pieds à l'intérieur du cadre. Celui-là n'est pas enveloppé dans un bandeau et ses mains reposent sur les cuisses. Il ressemble dans cette position à un défunt.

Tous les autres sont entourés d'un bandeau. Celui du personnage no.

3. Dans le même ordre d'idées je pourrais citer la conception réaliste de nombreuses scènes domestiques ou de danse à plusieurs personnages qui sont très fréquentes dans l'art de Colima. Il existe entre autres un sujet à deux personnages (Fig. 7): une femme couchée dans un lit et une autre femme debout occupée à fixer sur le lit un arceau au-dessus de la tête de la première. Un autre arceau identique est fixé au pied du lit. La poitrine et les bras de la femme couchée sont emprisonnés par deux bandeaux parallèles. La tête repose sur un appuie-tête. Le ventre est proéminent, le sexe à découvert. Ce ventre proéminent fait penser à une femme enceinte; toutefois, il n'est pas impossible qu'il s'agisse simplement d'une femme malade; n'oublions pas que l'homme couché (fig. 4) a lui aussi un ventre proéminent ce qui semble provoqué par les liens qui compriment la poitrine. Si le sujet (Fig. 7) semble différent des autres statuettes, il s'en rapproche tout au moins par la position allongée sur le dos.

78.1.715. (Fig. 9) est particulièrement large et couvre toute la partie supérieure du corps y compris les bras; il laisse à découvert les épaules, les mains et les cuisses. Un arceau va d'un bord à l'autre du cadre à mi-hauteur du corps, arceau apparemment flexible, sous lequel le personnage est coincé, peut-être de force. Les yeux, bien qu'à peine indiqués, semblent trahir une expression de souffrance. La jambe droite est partiellement détériorée; toutefois il ne fait pas de doute qu'elle était identique à la jambe gauche qui ne possède pas de pied. Mais il se peut que la statuette ait été limée à cet endroit.

Le personnage no. 78.1.791. (Fig. 10) ressemble au précédent. Le tronc est également enveloppé dans un bandeau assez large qui laisse libres les épaules, mais il n'y a pas d'arceau supplémentaire. La coiffure consiste en un bonnet, avec deux protubérances sphériques en avant. Cette coiffure se trouve dans un grand nombre de statuettes du même style. Les pieds sont placés sur le bord du cadre; ils ne sont pas coupés comme ceux de la statuette précédente (fig. 9). Remarquons que ces deux dernières statuettes ont chacune deux trous de suspension, l'un au-dessus de la tête, l'autre entre les jambes.

Le personnage no. 87.101.498. (Fig. 11) est d'une taille plus réduite. Il repose sur un lit sans bords relevés. Le bandeau qui entoure le corps est très large. Il passe sous les bras qui sont allongés. Il est à remarquer que les genoux sont pliés et que les jambes pendent. Ceci indique que le personnage repose sur une couche qui s'arrête au-dessous des genoux. La statuette est malheureusement en partie détériorée. La coiffure a des protubérances sphériques comme tant d'autres.

Le sexe n'est indiqué sur aucun des personnages de style aztèque que nous venons d'analyser.

Malgré les différences stylistiques entre ces dernières statuettes et celles de Colima et d'Esmeraldas, il me semble certain que le sujet est le même. Quelques détails comme les bras emprisonnés, les jambes qui pendent, semblent souligner le bien fondé de notre supposition, suivant laquelle il s'agit, dans les statuettes de personnages couchés sur le dos, de représentations de malades. L'imagination des artistes a pu se trouver particulièrement frappée par ce sujet.

A titre comparatif, nous voudrions mentionner ici deux groupes de statuettes, aztèques elles aussi, qui pourraient facilement induire en erreur et qui n'ont aucun rapport avec le sujet que nous venons de traiter.

Le premier groupe est représenté par les deux statuettes nos. 78.1.795. et 925 (Fig. 12). Elles sont creuses et légèrement bombées à l'envers et ont dû être utilisées comme hochets (l'une d'elles est partiellement détruite). Elles représentent chacune un personnage de sexe féminin, assis à l'intérieur d'un siège à baldaquin. Le vêtement consiste en un ou plusieurs bandeaux qui font quelques tours autour du corps en l'enveloppant au-dessous des seins, y compris une partie des cuisses. Il semble même que les personnages soient attachés à l'aide de ces bandeaux au fond de leur siège. Les avant-bras sont pliés vers le haut, les mains sont ouvertes, les paumes en avant. Chaque main a quatre doigts. La bouche du 78.1.795. est largement ouverte; elle fait entrevoir une deuxième bouche comme celle qu'on connaît dans des représentations de Xipe Totec, bien

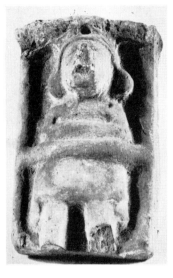

FIG. 8

FIG. 9

FIG. 10

FIG. 11

FIG. 12

FIG. 13

que cette dernière divinité soit toujours de sexe masculin. Les yeux sont hori-
zontalement incisés en rectangle. La coiffure est semblable à celle des autres
statuettes aztèques, avec deux protubérances sphériques sur les côtés. Un autre
motif sphérique, semblable à celui du bonnet, apparaît sur chacune des épaules
des deux personnages. Les boucles d'oreilles sont discoïdes.

Le deuxième groupe comprend douze statuettes, dont deux fragments (Fig.
13). Elles représentent des personnages masculins et féminins, bien que le sexe ne
soit indiqué clairement qu'une seule fois (No. 78.1.1638). Ces personnages sont
adossés à des couches ou sièges inclinés. Ils ont une tablette ou une barre hori-
zontale devant eux à hauteur du ventre. Il semble qu'il s'agisse là d'une position
de contrainte qui pourrait se comparer à la statuette no. 78.1.715. (Fig. 9) qui
est fixée au cadre par un arceau horizontal. Toutefois aucun de ces personnages
n'est ligoté, les bras, libres, reposent sur la barre.

Ainsi qu'on le voit, il s'agit ici exclusivement de personnages assis qui ne
doivent par conséquent pas être confondus avec les personnages allongés des
trois séries précédentes.

En résumé, nous trouvons le même sujet traité dans la céramique de trois
régions différentes. Seuls les objets de la troisième peuvent être datés avec
certitude: ils sont tous aztèques, de la dernière période, du XVème siècle, et sans
aucun doute beaucoup plus récents que ceux de Colima et Nayarit. Faute de
fouilles méthodiques, il n'est pas encore possible de dater la céramique figurative
de ces deux régions de l'Occident mexicain, pas plus d'ailleurs que celle de la
région d'Esmeraldas.

Toutefois, on peut admettre que Nayarit et Colima ont influencé Esmeraldas.
En effet, on sait que le Mexique est, par excellence, le pays des petites têtes en
céramique qu'on y trouve depuis les époques archaïques. Le nombre de ces
petites têtes s'amenuise au fur et à mesure qu'on se dirige vers le Sud. Plutôt
rares en Colombie, elles disparaissent presque complètement au Pérou. La région
de l'Equateur peut être considérée dans ce sens comme un îlot en Amérique du
Sud, et, avant tout, la région côtière.

On peut admettre que la représentation du personnage couché sur le dos
a suivi le même chemin que les petites têtes, de la côte du Pacifique (Colima-
Nayarit) à Esmeraldas, par la côte, à une époque antérieure aux Aztèques. Plus
tard, à l'époque aztèque, un deuxième mouvement aurait amené cette représentation de la côte du Pacifique (Colima-Nayarit) à la vallée de Mexico.

Comme par ailleurs le courant d'influence Nord-Sud semble avoir eu une
contre partie dans un mouvement Sud-Nord, ainsi que nous avons déjà essayé
de le démontrer (184), on peut en conclure qu'il existait un mouvement
d'échanges commerciaux continus entre les deux continents. Toutefois les documents type sud-américain sont encore plus rares au Mexique que ceux du type
mexicain à Esmeraldas.

Quoi qu'il en soit il me semble que l'apport Colima-Nayarit est au moins
aussi important pour la céramique de l'Equateur que celui des Maya et Chorotega établi par Uhle.

SIGNIFICANT PARALLELS IN THE SYMBOLIC ARTS OF SOUTHERN ASIA AND MIDDLE AMERICA

Robert Heine-Geldern and Gordon F. Ekholm

Seventy years ago Edward Tylor (384, pp. 116–31) pointed out that the ancient Mexican game of patolli was similar in its details to the game of pachisi, played in India and in the whole region of southern Asia from Syria to the Philippines. "It seems clear," he wrote, "that the Mexican game must have come from Asia." Subsequently, Stewart Culin (100, pp. 854–55) showed that even the cosmic meaning of the patolli game, its relation to the four quarters of the world and to the colors ascribed to them, was essentially the same as in pachisi, particularly in that form in which the latter is played in Burma.

In the latest edition of his *Anthropology* Dr. Kroeber (165, pp. 550–51) in discussing the two games, observes that "the mathematical probability of two games invented separately agreeing by chance in so many quite specific features is very low" and that "long odds could be laid against so complex a coincidence." The close correspondences between the rules of the two games would rather indicate a real connection. However, Dr. Kroeber felt troubled by the supposed absence of other traces of Indian influence in Mexico. He thought it unlikely that the people who brought the game would have brought just that and nothing else. Therefore he decided that we must for the present leave the problem unsolved. He expressed the hope that "fuller and more accurate knowledge may some day resolve the dilemma."

It is precisely some additional facts that we wish to submit for consideration in solution of this problem.

One of the most frequent motifs of early Indian art is the lotus plant. As applied on architraves and in border designs it shows not only the flowers and leaves, but the whole plant, including the rhizome, a kind of root-like stalk which grows horizontally under water and from which the stalks, bearing each a single flower or leaf, rise above the surface. While the flowers and leaves are often represented in a strikingly naturalistic manner, the rhizome is transformed into a purely decorative undulating creeper (Fig. 1, *B*). The same kind of lotus motif occurs in America at Chichen Itzá—as a border in the reliefs of the lower room of the Temple of the Tigers (Fig. 1, *A*). It is certainly remarkable that in India, as well as in Middle America, the rhizome, a part of the plant not normally visible because it is submerged and deeply buried in mud, should have been made the basic element of a whole motif and, moreover, be stylized in the same unrealistic manner as an undulating creeper.

There are still other correspondences, however. In the early art of India the

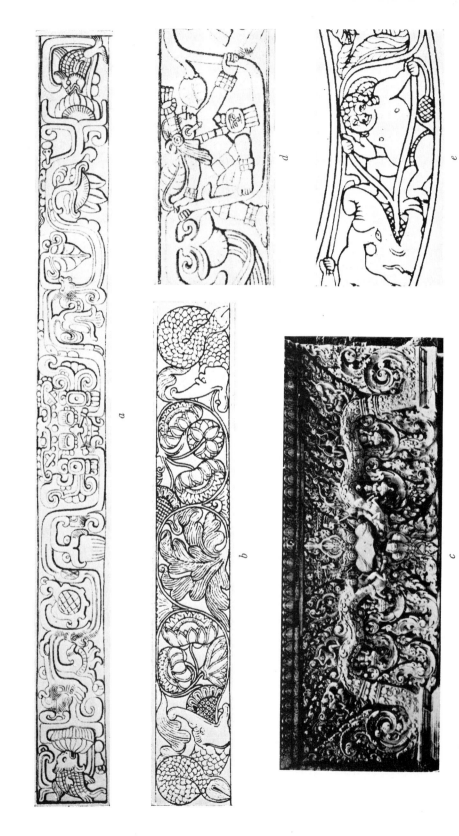

Fig. 1.—The lotus motif in Asia and America. *a, d,* Chichen Itza, Mexico, after Maudslay; *b, e,* Amarāvatī, southern India, after Coomaraswamy; *c,* Angkor, Cambodia, after Stern.

lotus plant is often used as a kind of imaginary landscape animated by human figures. The same is true in America at Chichen Itzá. As is to be expected, the figures differ in racial type and in costume, but the motif is essentially the same. The similarity is particularly striking in the case of figures shown in a reclining position, holding on to the rhizome of the lotus, such as occur at Amarāvatī, on the east coast of southern India in the second century A.D., and in America at Chichen Itzá (Fig. 1, E, D).

In India the lotus rhizome frequently surges from the mouths of makaras, sea monsters with fish-like bodies and elephant-like trunks. At Chichen Itzá we see stylized figures of fish at both ends of the lotus plant, in the same position as the makaras in India (Fig. 1, A, B). Such a combination of highly specific details cannot be accidental. It suggests the existence of some kind of relationship between Maya art and, not only Buddhist art in general, but the school of Amarāvatī of the second century A.D. in particular. This raises important problems of chronology. In order to clarify this point it is necessary to say a few words about the role which the style of Amarāvatī probably played in the early Hindu-Buddhist art of Southeast Asia.

The earliest Hindu-Buddhist kingdoms of the Malay Peninsula, Indo-China, and Indonesia were founded in the first and second centuries A.D. We know from inscriptions and Chinese reports that some of them soon expanded into powerful empires, that their kings had sumptuous palaces, that Brahman and Buddhist sanctuaries existed, and that they were centers of Buddhist learning. Yet, out of more than half a millennium of vigorous political and cultural activity not a single locally produced work of art seems to have survived. The reason for this would appear to be that the temples, palaces, monasteries, and sculptures of that period were all built or wrought of wood, as is still largely the case in Burma, Laos, and Bali.

We know, however, that close links existed between the early Hindu-Buddhist colonies in Southeast Asia and the centers, such as Amarāvatī, in the eastern coastal regions of southern India. It is from a script used in that area that the earliest script of Southeast Asia was derived. The dynastic legends of the early kings of Southeast Asia, particularly those of Funan, are related to those of the Pallava kings of southern India. Even more significant, about a half dozen Buddha statues of the Amarāvatī school, ancient imports from southern India, have been found in Annam, Siam, Sumatra, Java, and Celebes. We have, therefore, every reason to assume that the style of Amarāvatī may have exercised a powerful influence on the lost art of the first half millennium of Hindu-Buddhist culture in Southeast Asia.

Naturally, local developments must have taken place in the course of those centuries. Moreover, Southeast Asia was in constant touch with India, and stylistic changes in the art of the mother country were, to a certain extent, reflected in that of the colonies. As a result, when at last the architects and sculptors of Southeast Asia began to use stone, in Cambodia in the seventh, and in Java in the eighth century A.D., the characteristic elements of the Amarāvatī style, which once must have existed there, had either completely disappeared or had been deeply transformed. This would indicate then that if the lotus motif in its particular Amarāvatī aspect was transmitted to Middle America via Southeast Asia, as seems most likely, this transmission probably took place between approximately A.D. 100 and 600, in the period of most vigorous Indian colonial expansion. This would agree very well with the archeological situation in Southeast Asia, since some of the earliest traces of Hindu-Buddhist culture have been discovered, not in the regions nearest to India, where we might expect them, but further east, in Annam, East Borneo, and Celebes.

The lotus motif survived both in India and Southeast Asia into later periods, but it was gradually transformed into either totally unrealistic, purely decorative designs of foliage-like scrolls, or into a kind of garland. Moreover, it was eventually combined with another motif, a demonic lion face, which appears in Indian art in the Gupta period. This combination seems to be found for the first time in the Pallava art of the seventh century A.D. It became a favorite in the art of Southeast Asia, particularly in that of Cambodia and Champa. On Cambodian door lintels of the ninth to eleventh centuries the creepers with ornamental foliage which had replaced the lotus are frequently shown as surging from both sides of the mouth of a demonic face without lower jaw (Fig. 1, C). In Bali, the motif survived until recent times. Lotus rhizomes emanating from both sides of the mouth of a demonic face without lower jaw occur also at Chichen Itzá (Fig. 1, A). This indicates that contacts between Southeast Asia and America were not confined to the period prior to A.D. 600, but may have continued until some later date.

The so-called fire serpent of Aztec art and its counterpart in that of the Maya differ from the numerous more realistic representations of serpents of the same areas by their trunk-like upper jaws. They correspond in so many details (fish-like bodies, elephant-like trunks, forms of the teeth, etc.) to the makara, the mythical sea monster of Hindu-Buddhist art, that the assumption of relationship to the latter seems practically unavoidable. Both in Hindu-Buddhist art and in that of the Maya, variants with paws occur, which resemble a crocodile rather than a fish, and in both regions a human figure often emerges from the mouth of the monster (Fig. 2, A, B).

Atlantean figures appear in India in the second century B.C. They played an important role in Indian art and are found even on very recent Siamese Temples. In America, they can be seen at Tula in Central Mexico and at Chichen Itzá.

Gods or ceremonial figures standing on crouched human figures are found in India from the second century B.C. onward. In Middle America they occur in many Maya sculptures, notably at Palenque. Also the so-called "diving god" of Mexico has his close counterpart in Southeast Asia.

Equally striking is the similarity between the so-called "cross" of Palenque, a stylized tree with a demonic face in its branches, and the representation, in shadow play figures from Java, of the celestial tree on the top of Mount Meru, the cosmic mountain, again with a demonic face in its branches (Fig. 2, *D, C*). These Javanese specimens are, of course, recent, but the fact that the motif appears in an already highly conventionalized form among the reliefs of Angkor Vat in Cambodia, at about the middle of the twelfth century, indicates that it must be of considerable antiquity.

We may also compare the stairways flanked by serpent balustrades in Southeast Asia and Middle America. If we include the stairways flanked by serpent-like makaras, the trait can be traced back in Southeast Asia as far as the eighth century A.D.

The use of half columns flanking the doors and of groups of small columns set in panels is characteristic of Cambodian architecture. These features are particularly conspicuous in the tenth century, although certainly of somewhat earlier origin. Highly similar combinations appear in certain Maya buildings of Puuc style (Fig. 2, *E, F*).

We believe that the correspondences shown so far can be fitted into the chronological framework of both Asiatic and American archeology without particular difficulty. The case is somewhat different, however, with regard to the temple pyramids of the Cambodian and Mexican-Mayan areas and the use of the corbelled arch in both regions. As far as our present knowledge of the archeology of Cambodia goes—and the country has been fairly well explored—temple pyramids do not antedate the eighth century and became important only in the ninth and tenth centuries. Thus, they are later than many of the similar American monuments. Although fully aware of this difficulty, we nevertheless think that the similarities are so striking that they warrant at least a tentative comparison.

Chronological discrepancies do not exist, however, in the case of the Asiatic similarities to the building known as the Mercado at Chichen Itzá. As a vaulted gallery, closed by a wall on one side and with pillars along the other, it cannot fail to remind anyone familiar with the archeology of Cambodia of the galleries which are so conspicuous in the architecture of that country and eventually culminate in the galleries of Angkor Vat, dated to about the middle of the twelfth century. It is precisely in the twelfth century that the Mercado and similar buildings at Chichen Itzá have been dated. We may add that the gradual development of these galleries follows very much the same pattern in both Cambodia and in the architecture of the northern Maya area.

The comparisons we have made do not by any means exhaust the correspondences between Hindu-Buddhist and Mayan-Mexican art. Moreover, these correspondences are matched by those in other fields, only a few of which will be pointed out here.

The close relationship between the patolli game of Mexico and the pachisi game of India has already been mentioned. William MacLeod (209, pp. 551–61) has called attention to the similarity between the Mexican volador ritual and the Indian rite of hook-swinging. In the volador the performers usually, al-

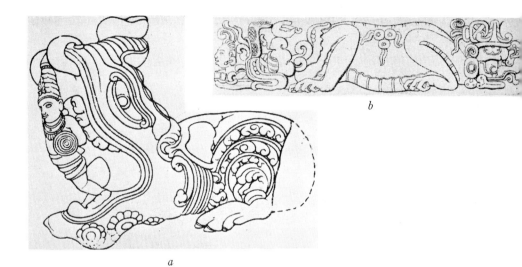

FIG. 2.—Some Asiatic-American resemblances. *a*, Mysore, India, medieval period, after Coomaraswamy; *b*, Copán, Honduras; *c*, Javanese shadow play figure; *d*, Palenque, Mexico; *e*, Cambodia; *f*, Labna, Mexico (*b* and *f* after Maudslay.

f

e

Fig. 2—*Continued*

though not invariably, hang by their feet, and in India by their shoulders. We have found, however, an old description and illustration of hook-swinging in India in which the voluntary victims are attached by their feet as in the volador (68, p. 405). Even more important, a relief of the Bayon, the central temple of Angkor Thom in Cambodia, appears to represent a rite similar to the Mexican volador (178).

No less striking is the use of the parasol as a sign of royalty and rank among the Maya. In Asia, it has been used as such ever since the third millennium B.C. and is still so used in India and Southeast Asia. The frescoes of Chacmultun, in Yucatan, show two types of parasols, both of which correspond to two types still in use in Southeast Asia. To this may be added the use of the throne, of the litter, and of fans mounted standard-like on long poles as insignia of rank and royalty, all of them closely resembling similar paraphernalia of rank and royalty in southern and eastern Asia. Certain aspects of this complex are also shown in the frescoes of Bonampak and on the Maya painted pottery.

In reading descriptions of the palace and court of the Aztec Emperor, anyone familiar with Southeast Asia cannot fail to be reminded of the courts of Burma, Siam, and Cambodia, not only in a general way, but even in minor details. The same applies to the form of government. Thus, the institution of four chief officials in Mexico corresponds to the four ministers of state and governors of the four quarters of the kingdom in the Hindu-Buddhist empires of Southeast Asia. In both cases this institution is based on cosmological principles. In general, the great stress laid on the four quarters of the world and on the colors attributed to them in both Southeast Asia and Mexico seems particularly significant since it indicates a similar conception of the world.

The large number of highly specific correspondences in so many fields precludes any possibility of mere accidental coincidence. Nor would it help us to take refuge in any kind of explanation based on some alleged psychological laws. There is no psychological law which could have caused the peoples on both sides of the Pacific to stylize the lotus plant in the same manner and to make it surge from the mouth of a jawless demon's head, to invent the parasol and use it as a sign of rank, and to invent the same complicated game. There is no explanation other than the assumption of cultural relationship. We must bow to the evidence of facts, even though this may mean a completely new start in our appraisal of the origin and development of the American Indian higher civilizations.

It is significant that while in Mexico and among the Mayas, traits of apparently Hindu-Buddhist origin abound in the fields of art, religious architecture, government, kingship, cosmology, mythology, and iconography, there seems to be little evidence of Indian influence in material culture and technical fields, in so far as these do not touch upon art and architecture. This is a phenomenon which, to a somewhat lesser extent, can be observed also in the various branches of Indian colonial cultures in Asia, notably in Tibet and Southeast Asia. It allows speculation concerning the classes of people who, apart from merchants, primarily participated in colonial movements emanating from India and from the Indianized countries of Asia. What is even more important from our point of view, it also allows tentative conclusions concerning the nature of those relations which we assume to have existed between Southeast Asia and America.

The character of the correspondences which we have indicated precludes the possibility of attributing Hindu-Buddhist influence in Mexico and among the Maya to mere accidental contacts, such as might have resulted from ships driven to the coast of America by storms and ocean currents. Such ships would have carried sailors and merchants, neither of whom we could expect to have been accomplished architects and sculptors or experts in cosmological lore and similar fields. Artists and astrologers do not usually sail into the blue. They would embark for an ocean voyage only if they knew where they were going and if they had reason to expect that their services would be appreciated. This indicates the existence of some kind of two-way traffic between Southeast Asia and America in ancient times.

On the basis of what we know about the history and practices of religion in India and Southeast Asia, we may take it for granted that Buddhist and Brahman missionaries would not have missed the opportunities offered by such contacts in order to spread their respective religions. The traces of Hindu-Buddhist influence in Mexico and among the Maya correspond in kind precisely to those cultural elements which in Southeast Asia were introduced by Buddhist monks and by Brahmans. The fact that at the time of the Spanish Conquest neither Buddhism nor Hinduism existed in Middle America does not by any means preclude the possibility that both religions may have played a certain role at an earlier date. We know from the history of Southeast Asia how easily they may disappear or be submerged in local paganism. Among the Cham of Annam, Hinduism and Buddhism had been firmly established from the second to the fifteenth century, thus through almost a millennium and a half. Yet, Buddhism disappeared completely after the fall of the Cham kingdom in A.D. 1471, and Hinduism degenerated so rapidly that its remnants are at present hardly recognizable. Among the non-Mohammedan Badui and Tenggerese of Java traces of Hinduism and Buddhism are exceedingly slight, although these must have been the predominant religions as late as the sixteenth century. The Batak of Sumatra were subjected to Buddhist and Hindu influences from probably the third to the fourteenth century, but in the nineteenth century they were pagans and some of their tribes were even cannibals. We have little doubt that a sober but unbiased comparative analysis of the Mexican and Mayan religions will reveal many traces of the former influences of either Hinduism or Buddhism or of both. To mention but one instance, the conceptions of hell and of the punishments inflicted there resemble those of Buddhist and Hindu belief to such an extent, both in a general way and in specific details, that the assumption of historic relationship is almost inevitable.

There appears to be little doubt but that ship-building and navigation were sufficiently advanced in southern and eastern Asia at the period in question to have made trans-Pacific voyages possible. As early as the time of Ptolemy, in the second century A.D., Indian ships sailed to the Malay Peninsula and Indonesia, not coastwise, but across the Bay of Bengal. In the third century, horses were exported from India to the Malay Peninsula and Indo-China, an indication that there must have been ships of considerable size. The recent discovery of a large metropolis in Cochinchina yielding Roman objects of the second century A.D. testifies to the intensity of sea traffic. When the Chinese Buddhist scholar Fa-hien returned from India around A.D. 400 he embarked on a ship which carried more than two hundred sailors and merchants and which therefore must have been larger than the ships of Columbus and other early Spanish explorers. This ship sailed directly across the ocean from Ceylon to Java. From Java, Fa-hien traveled in another merchant vessel which again carried more than two hundred persons. This ship too sailed not along the coasts, but right across the China Sea to northern China. Ships of that size able to cross the Indian Ocean and the China Sea with their dangerous cyclones could certainly cross the Pacific as well.

Although it would be too much to expect any definite analysis of the chronological problem at this early stage of the investigation, we wish to offer a few tentative suggestions in this respect. As already mentioned, there are indications that the contacts in question may have begun between A.D. 100 and 600. As seen from Asia, the third to fifth centuries would seem most likely. On the basis of the American evidence, the establishment of contacts must have taken place not later than the middle of the Classic period of Middle America since some traits of Hindu-Buddhist affinity appear in the Maya area at that time. This does not, however, preclude an earlier date. Contacts with Southeast Asia seem to have been either intensified or renewed around the end of the Classic period and the beginning of the Mexican or so-called New Empire period. This indicates that they may have continued through many centuries.

The great chronological gap between the lotus designs of Chichen Itzá and those of Amarāvatī—approximately one millennium—need not unduly trouble us. Instances of the persistence of decorative or symbolic motifs through far longer periods abound. Connecting links must, of course, have existed. Actually the lotus occurs in Maya art as early as the middle of the Classic period, several hundred years earlier than the date of the Chichen Itzá reliefs. We can properly assume, moreover, that wooden sculptures and buildings may have existed in Middle America and have carried on the tradition; much as was probably the case during the first half millennium of Hindu-Buddhist art in Southeast Asia. Saville has shown how important wood carving was among the Aztec and there is no reason to believe that it was not equally as important in earlier times.

The fact that in Asia the correspondences with Mayan-Mexican art are spread over approximately one millennium is important from more than one point of view. As already mentioned, the lotus designs of Chichen Itzá with interspersed human figures and with fishes on both ends point to the first half of the first millennium A.D., when elements of the Amarāvatī school of South India must have been strongly represented in Southeast Asia. Atlantean figures and the motif of gods standing on crouching human figures may have come about the same time.

The makara may very well have been introduced several times over a prolonged period. A more detailed comparison of the various forms in which it appears in Asia, as well as in America, some day may yield valuable chronological clues.

The combination of the jawless demon mask with the lotus motif would seem to indicate contacts in the period from the ninth to the twelfth century.

The so-called diving god and the celestial tree, as represented in the "cross of Palenque," probably also belong to a relatively late period in the history of Southeast Asiatic and Middle American relations.

The similarities between the buildings of the Puuc style and Cambodian temples, particularly those of Iśvarapura, indicate connections around the tenth century A.D.

Finally, the Mercado at Chichen Itzá can be linked to Cambodian galleries of the eleventh and twelfth centuries.

Vague as these hints still are, they seem to suggest that contacts between Southeast Asia and Middle America either persisted from the first centuries to the twelfth century A.D. or, if temporarily interrupted, were frequently renewed.

There are indications that Java and possibly Sumatra may have participated in trans-Pacific contacts with America. Certain similarities in sculpture, not mentioned in this paper, also would point to Champa, the easternmost of the ancient kingdoms of Indo-China, in what is now Annam. The close correspondences with Cambodia suggest, however, that in the period from the ninth or tenth to the twelfth century trans-Pacific traffic originated mainly in that country. The harbors from which that traffic was carried on must have been located on the coast of what now is Cochinchina, a region Cambodia lost to the Annamites in the eighteenth century.

After a period of unprecedented political power and cultural achievements around A.D. 1200, the Cambodian empire suddenly collapsed in the thirteenth century, mainly as a result of the revolt of the Thai and their subsequent attacks upon the core of the kingdom. This political collapse may very well have been the cause for the cessation of trans-Pacific voyages.

We hope that we have succeeded in contributing to some extent toward the solution of the problem that Dr. Kroeber indicated. As seen in its wider cultural context, the patolli game and its puzzling similarity to the pachisi game of India will, perhaps, no longer appear as a kind of ethnological freak, but as just *one* item among a number of cultural elements which in ancient times found their way to America from across the Pacific.

BIBLIOGRAPHY

1. Acosta, Jorge R. "Exploraciones en Tula, Hidalgo," *Revista mexicana de estudios antropológicos* (Mexico City), IV (1940), 172–94.
2. ———. "Los últimos descubrimientos arqueológicos en Tula, Hidalgo," *ibid.*, V (1941), 239–48.
3. *Album de colecciones arqueológicas.* Seleccionadas y arregladas por Franz Boas, ilustraciones por Adolfo Best, texto por Manuel Gamio. ("Publicaciones de la Escuela Nacional de Arqueología y Etnología Americanas.") Mexico City, 1921.
4. Almaráz, Ramón. "Apuntes sobre la Pirámide del Sol en Teotihuacán," *Comisión Científica de Pachuca* (Mexico City), 1865, pp. 349–58.
5. Andrews, E. Wyllys. *The Archaeology of Southwestern Campeche.* ("Carnegie Institution of Washington Publications," No. 456; Contr. No. 40.) Washington, D.C., 1943.
6. ———. "Chronology and Astronomy in the Maya Area." In *The Maya and Their Neighbors*, pp. 150–61. New York: Appleton-Century Co., 1940.
7. ———. "Glyph X of the Supplementary Series of the Maya Inscriptions," *American Anthropologist*, XXXVI (1934), 345–54.
8. ———. "Glyphs Z and Y of the Maya Supplementary Series," *American Antiquity*, IV (1938), 30–35.
9. ———. "Notes on Glyph G of the Maya Inscriptions," *Maya Research* (New Orleans), III (1936), 306–8.
10. ———. "The Phonetic Value of Glyph C of the Maya Supplementary Series," *American Anthropologist*, XL (1938), 755–58.
11. ———. "Some New Material from Cobá, Quintana Roo, México," *Ethnos* (Stockholm), III (1938), 33–46.
12. Antze, Gustav. "Metallarbeiten aus dem nördlichen Peru," *Mitteilungen aus dem Museum für Völkerkunde im Hamburg* (Hamburg), Vol. XV (1930).
13. Apenes, O. "The 'Tlateles' of Lake Texcoco," *American Antiquity*, IX (1943), 29–32.
14. Armillas, Pedro. "Fortalezas mexicanas," *Cuadernos americanos* (Mexico City), V (1948), 143–63.
14a. ———. "La Serpiente emplumada, Quetzalcoatl y Tlaloc," *ibid.*, XXI, Part I (1947), 161–79.
15. ———. "Los Dioses de Teotihuacán," *Anales del Instituto de Etnología Americana* (Mendoza), VI (1945), 35–61.
16. ———. "Notas sobre sistemas de cultivo en Mesoamérica: Cultivos de riego y humedad en la cuenca del Río de las Balsas," *Anales del Instituto Nacional de Antropología e Historia* (Mexico City), III (1949), 85–113.
17. ———. "A Sequence of Cultural Development in Mesoamerica." In Bennett, Wendell C. (ed.), *A Reappraisal of Peruvian Archaeology*, pp. 105–11. ("Memoirs of the Society for American Archaeology," Vol. IV.) Menasha, Wis., 1948.
18. Arnold, J. R., and Libby, W. F. *Radiocarbon Dates.* Chicago: University of Chicago, Institute for Nuclear Studies, 1950.
19. *Atlas arqueológico de la República mexicana.* ("Publications of the Instituto Panamericano de Geografía e Historia," No. 41.) Mexico City, 1939.

20. BAESSLER, ARTHUR. *Altperuanische Kunst: Beiträge zur Archeologie des Inca-Reiches*, Vols. I-IV. Berlin: A. Asher & Co., 1902–3.

21. BANCROFT, HUBERT H. *The Native Races of the Pacific States*, Vol. IV. San Francisco: A. L. Bancroft & Co., 1883.

22. BARRERA VÁSQUEZ, A., and RENDÓN, SILVIA. *El Libro de los libros de Chilam Balam*. Mexico City and Buenos Aires: Fondo de Cultura Económica, 1948.

22a. BARRERA VÁSQUEZ, A., and MORLEY, S. G. *The Maya Chronicles*. ("Carnegie Institution of Washington Publications," No. 585; Contr. No. 48.) Washington, D.C., 1947.

23. BASTIEN, RÉMY. "La Pirámide del Sol en Teotihuacán." Unpublished Master's thesis, Escuela Nacional de Antropología e Historia (Mexico City), 1947. Pp. 74.

24. BATRES, LEOPOLDO. *Exploraciones en Huexotla, Texcoco y el Gavilán*. Mexico City: Guerrero & Co., 1904.

25. ————. *Explorations of Mount Alban, Oaxaca, Mexico*. Mexico City: Gante St. Press, 1902.

26. ————. "Memoria en extracto de las exploraciones llevadas a cabo por mandato oficial en las ruinas de Teotihuacán durante los años de 1905 a 1911," *Boletín de la Sociedad de Geografía y Estadística* (Mexico City), Quinta época, IX (1919), 253–61.

27. ————. *Teotihuacán: Memoria que presenta Leopoldo Batres*. Mexico City: Imprenta de F. S. Soria, 1906.

28. BEALS, RALPH. "Review of Kaj Birket-Smith's *The Origin of Maize Cultivation*," *American Anthropologist*, XLIX (1947), 289–90.

30. BECERRA, MARCOS E. *El antiguo calendario chiapaneco*. Mexico City: Imprenta Mundial, 1933.

31. BELMONT, G. E. "The Secondary Series as a Lunar Eclipse Count," *Maya Research* (New Orleans), II (1935), 144–54.

32. BENEDICT, RUTH. *Patterns of Culture*. New York: Penguin Books, Inc., 1946.

33. BENNETT, WENDELL C. "The Archeology of the Central Andes." In STEWARD, JULIAN H. (ed.), *Handbook of South American Indians*, II, 61–147. (Bureau of American Ethnology Bull. 143.) Washington, D.C., 1946.

34. ————. *The Archaeology of the North Coast of Peru*, pp. 1–153. ("American Museum of Natural History Anthropological Papers," Vol. XXXVII.) New York, 1939.

35. ————. *Excavations at Tiahuanaco*, pp. 359–494. ("American Museum of Natural History Anthropological Papers," Vol. XXXIV.) New York, 1934.

36. ————. *Excavations in Bolivia*, pp. 329–507. ("American Museum of Natural History Anthropological Papers," Vol. XXXV.) New York, 1936.

37. ————. *The North Highlands of Peru*, pp. 1–114. ("American Museum of Natural History Anthropological Papers," Vol. XXXIX.) New York, 1944.

38. ————. "The Peruvian Co-tradition." In his *A Reappraisal of Peruvian Archaeology*, pp. 1–7. ("Memoirs of the Society for American Archaeology," Vol. IV.) Menasha, Wis., 1948.

39. ———— (ed.). *A Reappraisal of Peruvian Archaeology*. ("Memoirs of the Society for American Archaeology," Vol. IV.) Menasha, Wis., 1948.

40. BENNETT, WENDELL C., and BIRD, JUNIUS. *Andean Culture History*. ("American Museum of Natural History Handbook Series," No. 15.) New York, 1949.

41. BERLIN, HEINRICH. "A Critique of Dates at Palenque," *American Antiquity*, X (1945), 340–47.

42. ————. "Notes on Glyph C of the Lunar Series at Palenque," *Carnegie Institution of Washington, Notes on Middle American Archaeology and Ethnology* (Cambridge), I (1943), 156–59.

43. BERLIN, HEINRICH. "Un Templo olvidado en Palenque," *Revista mexicana de estudios antropológicos* (Mexico City), VI (1942), 62–90.

44. BERLIN MUSEUM. Catalogue numbers in American Ethnology Section: 14092, 13043, 48009, 62193.

45. BEYER, HERMANN. "Another Mayan Hieroglyph for 'Day,' " *American Antiquity*, II (1936), 13–14.

46. ———. "Das Zeichen für Zwanzig in den Maya-Inschriften," *El México antiguo* (Mexico City), IV (1938), 155–61.

47. ———. "The Date on the Cornice of House C of the Palace at Palenque," *ibid.*, III (1935), 53–55.

48. ———. "Decipherment of a Greatly-damaged Inscription at Palenque," *ibid.*, IV (1936), 1–6.

49. ———. "Las dos estelas mayas de Tila, Chis.," *ibid.*, II (1926), 235–50.

50. ———. "Lunar Glyphs of the Supplementary Series at Piedras Negras," *ibid.*, IV (1937), 75–82.

51. ———. "The Lunar Glyphs of the Supplementary Series at Quirigua," *ibid.*, III (1936), 1–11.

52. ———. "Mayan Hieroglyphs: Glyph G8 of the Supplementary Series," *American Anthropologist*, XXXVIII (1936), 247–49.

53. ———. "Mayan Hieroglyphs: The Variable Element of Introducing Glyphs as Month Indicator," *Anthropos* (Vienna), XXVI (1931), 99–108.

54. ———. "Note concerning the Moon-Count at Palenque and Tila," *Maya Research* (New Orleans), III (1936), 110–11.

55. ———. "The Relation of the Synodical Month and Eclipses to the Maya Correlation Problem," *Studies in Middle America*, pp. 301–19. ("Middle American Research Institute Publications," No. 5.) New Orleans, 1933.

56. ———. "The Variants of Glyph D of the Supplementary Series." In *Los Mayas antiguos*, pp. 62–71. Mexico City: Colegio de México, 1941.

57. ———. "Zur Konkordanzfrage der Mayadaten mit denen der Christlichen Zeitrechnung," *Zeitschrift für Ethnologie* (Berlin), LXV (1933), 75–80.

58. ———. "Zur Konkordanzfrage der Mayadaten mit denen der Christlichen Zeitrechnung," *ibid.*, LXVII (1935), 43–49.

59. BIRD, JUNIUS. "Antiquity and Migrations of the Early Inhabitants of Patagonia," *Geographical Review* (New York), XXVIII (1938), 250–75.

60. ———. "Preceramic Cultures in Chicama and Viru." In BENNETT, WENDELL C. (ed.), *A Reappraisal of Peruvian Archaeology*, pp. 105–11. ("Memoirs of the Society for American Archaeology," Vol. IV.) Menasha, Wis., 1948.

61. BLOM, FRANS, and LA FARGE, OLIVER. *Tribes and Temples.* ("Tulane University Middle American Research Series," No. 1.) New Orleans, 1926–27.

62. BOGGS, STANLEY H. "Informe sobre la tercera temporada de exploraciones en las ruinas de Tazumal," *Tzunpame* (San Salvador), V (1945), 33–45.

63. BOWDITCH, CHARLES P. *Notes on the Report of Teobert Maler.* ("Memoirs of the Peabody Museum," Vol. II, No. 1.) Cambridge, 1903.

64. ———. *The Numeration, Calendar Systems, and Astronomical Knowledge of the Mayas.* Cambridge: At the University Press, 1910.

65. BRINTON, DANIEL G. *The Myths of the New World.* 3d ed. Philadelphia: D. McKay, 1896.

66. BULTER, M. "A Pottery Sequence from the Alta Verapaz, Guatemala." In *The Maya and Their Neighbors*, pp. 250–67. New York: Appleton-Century Co., 1940.

67. BURLAND, C. A. "A 360-Day Count in a Mexican Codex," *Man*, XLVII (1947), 106–8.

68. CAMPBELL, WILLIAM. *British India in Its Relation to the Decline of Hindooism and the Progress of Christianity.* London: J. Snow, 1839.

69. CANBY, JOEL S. "Excavations at Yarumela, Spanish Honduras." Ph.D. thesis, Harvard University, Cambridge, 1949.

70. CARRION CACHOT, REBECCA. "La Luna y su personificación ornitomorfa en el arte Chimú," *Proceedings of the XXVIIth International Congress of Americanists,* pp. 571–87. Lima, Peru, 1939.

71. CASO, A. "Calendario y escritura de las antiguas culturas de Monte Albán." In OTHÓN DE MENDIZÁBAL, MIGUEL, *Obras completas,* I, 113–43. Mexico City, 1947.

72. ———. *Culturas mixtecas y zapotecas.* Mexico City: Ediciones encuadernables el nacional, 1942.

73. ———. "El Mapa de Teozacoalco," *Cuadernos americanos* (Mexico City), Año VIII, XLVII (1949), 145–81.

74. ———. *Exploraciones en Oaxaca, quinta y sexta temporadas 1936–1937.* ("Publications of the Instituto Panamericano de Geografía e Historia," No. 34.) Tacubaya, 1938.

75. ———. "La Correlación de los años azteca y cristiana," *Revista mexicana de estudios antropológicos* (Mexico City, III (1939), 11–45.

76. ———. *Las Estelas zapotecas.* Mexico City: Secretaría de Educación Pública, 1928.

77. ———. *Las Exploraciones en Monte Albán, temporada 1931–32.* ("Publications of the Instituto Panamericano de Geografía e Historia," No. 7.) Tacubaya, 1932.

78. ———. *Las Exploraciones en Monte Albán, temporada 1934–35.* ("Publications of the Instituto Panamericano de Geografía e Historia," No. 18.) Mexico City, 1935.

79. CASTELNAU, FRANCIS COMTE DE. *Antiquités des Incas et autres peuples anciens, recueillies pendant l'expédition dans les parties centrales de l'Amérique de Sud ... pendant les années 1843 à 1847.* (Part III of the whole report.) Paris: P. Bertrand, 1854.

80. CHARENCEY, L. F. H. G. DE. "Recherches sur le calendrier zotzil," *Revue d'ethnographie* (Paris), III (1885), 398–401.

81. CHILDE, V. GORDON. *Man Makes Himself.* London: C. A. Watts & Co., Ltd., 1948.

82. ———. *What Happened in History.* New York: Penguin Books, Inc., 1946.

83. CIEZA DE LEÓN, PADRE. *The Second Part of the Chronicle of Peru.* Edited by SIR C. R. MARKHAM. ("Hakluyt Series," Vol. LXVIII.) London, 1883.

84. CLARK, GRAHAME. *From Savagery to Civilization.* London: Cobbett Press, 1946.

85. COBO, BERNABÉ. *Historia del Nuevo Mundo.* Edited by MARCOS JIMÉNEZ DE LA ESPADA. 4 vols. Seville: Sociedad de Bibliófilos Andaluces, 1890–93.

86. *Codex Becker I.* Museum für Völkerkunde, Neue Hofburg, Vienna I.

87. *Codex Bodley.* Bodleian Library, Department of Western Manuscripts, Oxford.

88. *Codex Borgia: Eine altmexikanische Bilderschrift der Bibliotek der Congregatio de propaganda fide.* 3 vols. Berlin, 1904–9.

89. *Codex Dresden: Die Maya-Handschrift der Königlichen Bibliothek zu Dresden.* Dresden, 1892.

90. *Codex Fejervary-Mayer.* Free Public Libraries, Carnatic Hall, Liverpool.

91. *Codex Laud.* Bodleian Library, Department of Western Manuscripts, Oxford.

92. *Codex Selden.* Bodleian Library, Department of Western Manuscripts, Oxford.

93. *Codex Vindobonensis.* Museum für Völkerkunde, Neue Hofburg, Vienna I.

94. *Codex Waecker-Götter.* Department of Manuscripts, British Museum, London.

95. *Codex Zouche-Nuttall*. Department of Ethnography, British Museum, London. Also "Publications of the Peabody Museum," Vol. I, No. 4. Cambridge, Mass., 1902.

96. COLLIER, DONALD, and MURRA, JOHN V. *Survey and Excavations in Southern Ecuador*. ("Anthropological Series of the Field Museum of Natural History," Vol. XXXV.) Chicago, 1943.

97. CONDORCANQUI, JOSÉ GABRIEL. "Genealogía de Túpac Amaru." In LOAYZA, FRANCISCO A. (ed.), *Los pequeños grandes libros de historia americana*, Ser. 1, X, 5–59. Lima, 1946.

98. COOK, SHERBURNE F., and SIMPSON, LESLEY B. *The Population of Central Mexico in the Sixteenth Century*. Berkeley: University of California Press, 1948.

99. COOPER, JOHN M. "Areal and Temporal Aspects of Aboriginal South American Cultures," *Primitive Man* (Washington), XV (1942), 1–38.

100. CULIN, STEWART. "Chess and Playing-Cards," *Report of the U.S. National Museum for 1896*, pp. 854–55.

101. CÚNEO-VIDAL, RÓMULO. *Historia de las guerras de los últimos Incas peruanos contra el poder español (1535–1572)*. Barcelona: Casa Editorial Maucci, 1925.

102. CURWEN, E. CECIL. *Plough and Pasture*. London: Cobbett Press, 1946.

103. DEEVEY, E. S. "Pollen Analysis and Mexican Archaeology: An Attempt To Apply the Method," *American Antiquity*, X (1944), 135–49.

104. DE LANDA, DIEGO. *Relación de las cosas de Yucatán*. Merida: E. G. Triay e hijos, 1938.

105. DE TERRA, HELMUT; ROMERO, JAVIER; and STEWARD, T. D. *Tepexpan Man*. ("Viking Fund Publications in Anthropology," No. 11.) New York, 1949.

106. D'HARCOURT, RAOUL. "Archéologie de la province d'Esmeraldas (Equateur)," *Journal de la Société des Américanistes de Paris* (Paris), XXXIV (new ser.; 1942), 61–200.

107. DIBBLE, C. A. "El antiguo sistema de escritura en México," *Revista mexicana de estudios antropológicos* (Mexico City), IV (1940), 105–28.

108. DIGBY, A. "Radiographic Examination of Peruvian Pottery Techniques," *Actes du XXVIIIe Congrès international des Américanistes*, pp. 608–9. Paris, 1948.

109. DOERING, HEINRICH. *Auf den Koenigstrassen der Inka*. Berlin: E. Wasmuth, 1941.

110. DRUCKER, PHILIP. *Ceramic Sequences at Tres Zapotes, Veracruz, Mexico*. (Bureau of American Ethnology Bull. 140.) Washington, 1943.

111. ———. *Some Implications of the Ceramic Complex of La Venta*. ("Smithsonian Miscellaneous Collection," Vol. CVII, No. 8.) Washington, D.C., 1947.

112. ———. "Preliminary Notes on an Archaeological Survey of the Chiapas Coast," *Middle American Research Records* (New Orleans), I, No. 2 (1948), 151–69.

113. DUPAIX, GUILLERMO. "Monuments of New Spain." In KINGSBOROUGH, E. K. (ed.), *Antiquities of Mexico*, V, 248. London, 1830–48.

114. EKHOLM, GORDON F. *Excavations at Tampico and Panuco in the Huasteca, Mexico*. ("American Museum of Natural History Anthropological Papers," Vol. XXXVIII, Part V.) New York, 1944.

115. ———. "Middle America—Notes and News," *American Antiquity*, XV (1949), 77–79.

116. EMERSON, R. A. "A Preliminary Survey of the Milpa System of Maize Culture as Practiced by the Maya Indians of the Northern Part of the Yucatan Peninsula." Ithaca, N.Y.: Cornell University(?), n.d. Mimeographed.

117. ESCALONA RAMOS, ALBERTO. "Cronología y astronomía maya méxica: Un nuevo

sistema de correlación calendarica," *Proceedings of the XXVIIth International Congress of Americanists*, pp. 623–30. Mexico City, 1939.

118. ESQUIVEL Y NAVÍA, DIEGO. *Anales del Cuzco, 1600 á 1750.* Edited by RICARDO PALMA. Lima: Biblioteca Nacional del Peru, 1901.

118a. FORD, J. A., and WILLEY, G. R. *Surface Survey of the Viru Valley, Peru.* ("American Museum of Natural History Anthropological Papers," Vol. XLIII, Part I.) New York, 1949.

119. FUHRMAN, ERNST. *Peru II.* Hagen, i.W., and Darmstadt: Volkwangverlag, 1922.

120. GAMIO, MANUEL (ed.). *La Población del Valle de Teotihuacán.* 3 vols. Mexico City: Secretaría de Educación Pública, 1922.

121. GANN, THOMAS. *Ancient Cities and Modern Tribes.* New York: Charles Scribner's Sons, 1926.

122. ———. *In an Unknown Land.* London: Duckworth & Co., 1924.

123. GARCÍA PAYÓN, JOSÉ. "La Cerámica del Valle de Toluca," *Revista mexicana de estudios antropológicos* (Mexico City), V (1941), 209–38.

124. GARCÍA RODRIGUEZ, VICENTE JOSÉ. "Arbol genealógico que principia por el decimosegundo emperador Huayna-Capac Inga del Perú," *Revista universitaria* (Cuzco), 2a. época, Año XXII, No. 65 (1933), pp. 31–102.

125. ———. MS, Documents relating to the Betancur case in the lawsuit over descent from Topa Amaru. 4 vols. of MSS in the Rectorado of the University of Cuzco.

126. ———. MS: "Genealogía de la casa y descendencia de don Diego Sairitupac. ..." 4 vols. Rectorado of the University of Cuzco. 1790.

127. ———. MS: "Genealogía de la casa, y familia de Dn. Diego Felipe de Betancur, y Tupac Amaro, Hurtado de Arbieto. ..." 2 vols. Rectorado of the University of Cuzco. 1790.

128. ———. MS: "Genealogy of the Garcia Family." 1 vol. Rectorado of the University of Cuzco.

129. GOODMAN, J. T. "The Archaic Maya Inscriptions." Appendix to MAUDSLAY, ALFRED P. *Archaeology.* London: R. H. Porter & Dulau, 1899–1902.

130. ———. "Maya Dates," *American Anthropologist*, VII (1905), 642–47.

131. GORDON, GEORGE B. "The Hieroglyphic Stairway, Ruins of Copan," *Peabody Museum Memoirs* (Cambridge), I (1902), 149–86.

132. ———. "Prehistoric Ruins of Copan," *ibid.*, pp. 1–48.

133. ———. "Researches in the Uloa Valley, Honduras," *ibid.*, Vol. I (1902).

134. GUAMAN POMA DE AYALA, FELIPE. *Nueva corónica y buen gobierno (codex péruvien illustré).* Edited by PAUL RIVET. ("Travaux et mémoires de l'Institut d'ethnologie," Vol. XXIII.) Paris, 1936.

135. GUTHE, CARL E. "The Maya Lunar Count," *Science* (Lancaster), LXXV (1932), 271–77.

136. ———. "Notes on the Eclipse Table in the Dresden Codex," *ibid.*, LXXVI (1932), 572.

137. ———. "A Possible Solution to the Number Series on Pages 51 to 58 of the Dresden Codex," *Peabody Museum Papers* (Cambridge), Vol. VI, No. 2 (1921).

138. HAMBURG MUSEUM. Catalogue numbers in the American Ethnology Section: 22, 28, 292.

139. HERZOG, WILHELM. "Über die Verwandtschaftsbeziehungen der Costaricensische Indianersprachen mit denen von Central- und Sud-Amerika," *Archiv für Anthropologie*, XVI (1884), 623–27.

140. HOLMES, W. H. *Archaeological Studies among the Ancient Cities of Mexico.* ("Field Columbian Museum Anthropological Series," Vol. I, No. 1.) Chicago, 1895).

316 THE CIVILIZATIONS OF ANCIENT AMERICA

141. HUMBOLDT, ALEXANDER VON. *Sites des Cordillères et monuments des peuples indigènes de l'Amérique*. Paris: Guérin & Cie., 1869.
142. IMBELLONI, JOSÉ. "L'antico Peru." In BIASUTTI, RENATO (ed.), *Le Razze et i popoli della terra*, Vol. III: *Oceania-America*. Turin, 1941.
143. ———. *Pachacuti, IX (El incario crítico)*. Buenos Aires: Humanior, Biblioteca del Americanista Moderno, D-2, 1946.
144. JIJON Y CAAMAÑO, J. *Contribución al conocimiento de los aborígenes de la provincia de Imbabura*. Madrid, 1914.
145. ———. *El Ecuador interandino y occidental antes de la conquista castellana*. 4 vols. Quito: Editorial Ecuatoriana, 1940–47.
146. ———. "Nueva contribución al conocimiento de los aborígenes de la provincia de Imbabura," *Boletín de la Sociedad de Estudios Históricos* (Quito), IV (1920), 1–120 and 183–245.
147. ———. *Puruhá: Contribución al conocimiento de los aborígenes de la provincia del Chimborazo*. 2 vols. Quito, 1927.
148. ———. "Una gran marea cultural en el Noroeste de Sud-America," *Journal de la Société des Américanistes de Paris* (Paris), XXII (1930), 107–97.
149. ———. "Un Vaso 'Thin Orange' del país Caranquí, Ecuador," *American Antiquity*, XIV (1949), 226–28.
150. JIMENEZ, BORJA ARTURO. *Moche*. Lima: Lib. Studium, 1938.
151. JIMENEZ DE ARBALAEZ, EDITH. "Cultura del bajo Magdalena," *Boletín del Museo Arqueológico de Colombia* (Bogotá), Año II (1944), pp. 3–18.
152. JOYCE, THOMAS A. "The Clan Ancestor in Animal Form as Depicted on Ancient Pottery of the Peruvian Coast," *Man* (London), XIII (1913), 113–17.
153. ———. *Mexican Archaeology*. London: P. L. Warner, 1914.
154. ———. *South American Archaeology*. London: Macmillan & Co., Ltd., 1912.
155. JOYCE, THOMAS A.; GANN, T.; GRUNING, E. L.; and LONG, R. C. E. "Report on the British Museum Expedition to British Honduras, 1928," *Journal of the Royal Anthropological Institute* (London), LVIII (1928), 323–50.
156. KEMPTON, J. H. "Preliminary Report of the Agricultural Survey of Yucatan of 1935." Washington, D.C.: Carnegie Institution of Washington(?), n.d. Mimeographed.
157. KIDDER, ALFRED V. "Kaminaljuyu, Guatemala: Addenda and Corrigenda," *Carnegie Institution of Washington, Notes on Middle American Archaeology and Ethnology* (Cambridge), III (1948), 224–32.
157a. ———. "Archaeological Problems of the Highland Maya." In *The Maya and Their Neighbors*, pp. 117–25. New York: Appleton-Century Co., 1940.
157b. ———. *The Artifacts of Uaxactun, Guatemala*. ("Carnegie Institution of Washington Publications," No. 576.) Washington, D.C., 1947.
157c. KIDDER, ALFRED V., and THOMPSON, J. E. "The Correlation of Maya and Christian Chronologies." In *Cooperation in Research*, pp. 493–510. Washington, D.C.: Carnegie Institution of Washington, 1938.
158. KIDDER, ALFRED V.; JENNINGS, J. D.; and SHOOK, E. M. *Excavations at Kaminaljuyu, Guatemala*. ("Carnegie Institution of Washington Publications," No. 561.) Washington, D.C., 1946.
159. KIDDER, ALFRED II. "South American Penetrations in Middle America." In *The Maya and Their Neighbors*, pp. 441–59. New York: Appleton-Century Co., 1940.
160. KIRCHHOFF, PAUL. "Mesoamérica: sus limites geográficos, composición etnica y caracteres culturales," *Acta Americana* (Mexico), I (1943), 92–107.
161. KREICHGAUER, DAMIAN. "Anschluss der Maya-Chronologie an die Julianische," *Anthropos* (Vienna), XXII (1927), 1–15.
162. ———. "Neue Beziehungen zwischen Amerika und der Alten Welt." In

Festschrift: Publication d'hommage offerte au P. W. Schmidt, pp. 366–78. Vienna: Mechitharisten-Congregations-Buchdruckerei, 1928.

163. KRICKEBERG, W. "Mexikanische-peruanische Parallelen." In *Festschrift: Publication d'hommage offerte au P. W. Schmidt*, pp. 379–93. Vienna, 1928.

164. KROEBER, ALFRED L. *Anthropology.* New York: Harcourt, Brace & Co., 1923.

165. ————. *Anthropology.* New rev. ed. New York: Harcourt, Brace & Co., 1948.

166. ————. *Archaeological Explorations in Peru*, Part I: *Ancient Pottery from Truxillo.* ("Field Museum of Natural History Anthropology Memoirs," Vol. II, No. 1.) Chicago, 1926.

167. ————. *Archaeological Explorations in Peru*, Part II: *The Northern Coast.* ("Field Museum of Natural History Anthropology Memoirs," Vol. II, No. 4.) Chicago, 1930.

168. ————. *Cultural and Natural Areas of Native North America.* ("University of California Publications in American Archaeology and Ethnology," Vol. XXXVIII.) Berkeley, 1939.

169. ————. "Cultural Relations between North and South America," *Proceedings of the XXIIIrd International Congress of Americanists*, pp. 5–22. New York, 1928.

170. ————. "Los Métodos de la arqueología peruana," *Letras* (Lima), No. 22 (2° cuatrimestre) (1942).

171. ————. *Peruvian Archaeology in 1942.* ("Viking Fund Publications in Anthropology," No. 4.) New York, 1944.

172. ————. "The Uhle Pottery Collections from Moche," *University of California Publications in American Archaeology and Ethnology* (Berkeley), XXI (1925), 191–234.

172a. KROEBER, ALFRED L., and STRONG, W. D. "The Uhle Pottery Collections from Ica," *University of California Publications in American Archaeology and Ethnology* (Berkeley), XXI (1924), 95–133.

173. KUBLER, GEORGE. "Towards Absolute Time: Guano Archaeology." In BARRETT, WENDELL C. (ed.), *A Reappraisal of Peruvian Archaeology*, pp. 29–50. ("Memoirs of the Society for American Archaeology," Vol. IV.) Menasha, Wis., 1948.

174. KUNIKE, HUGO. *Haguar und Mond in der Mythologie des andinen Hochlandes.* Leipzig, 1915.

175. KUTSCHER, GERDT. *Chimu: Eine altindianische Hochkultur.* Berlin: Gebr. Mann, 1950.

176. ————. "Religion und Mythologie der frühen Chimu (Nord Peru)," *Actes du XXVIIIᵉ Congrès international des Américanistes*, pp. 621–31. Paris, 1947.

177. LA FARGE, O., and BYERS, D. S. *The Year Bearer's People.* ("Tulane University Middle American Research Series," No. 3.) New Orleans, 1931.

178. "L'Amérique précolombienne et l'Asie méridionale," *Bulletin de la Société des études indo-chinoises de Saïgon* (Paris), Vol. XVIII, Nos. 1 and 2 (1943).

179. LARCO HOYLE, RAFAEL. *Cronológia arqueológica del norte del Perú.* Buenos Aires: Sociedad Geográfica Americana, 1948.

180. ————. "A Culture Sequence for the North Coast of Peru." In STEWARD, JULIAN H. (ed.), *Handbook of South American Indians*, II, 149–75. (Bureau of American Ethnology Bull. 143.) Washington, D.C., 1946.

181. ————. "La Cultura salinar," *Revisto geográfico americano* (Buenos Aires), XXIII (1945), 327–36.

182. ————. *Los Cupisniques.* Lima: Casa ed. "La Crónica" y "Variedades," 1941.

183. ————. *Los Mochicas*, Vols. I and II. Lima: Emp. ed. "Rimac," 1938–39.

184. LEHMANN, HENRI. "Résultat d'un voyage de prospection archéologique sur les

côtes du Pacifique ... ," *Actes du XXVIIIe Congrès international des Américanistes*, pp. 423–39. Paris, 1948.

185. LEHMANN, WALTER. *Zentral-Amerika.* 2 vols. Berlin: D. Reimer, 1920.

186. LEHMANN, WALTER, and DOERING, HEINRICH U. *Kunstgeschichte des alten Peru, erläutert durch ausgewählte Werke aus Ton und Stein, Gewebe und Kleinode.* Berlin: Wasmuth, A.G., 1924.

187. LINCOLN, J. STEWARD. *The Maya Calendar of the Ixil of Guatemala.* ("Carnegie Institution of Washington Publications," No. 528; Contr. No. 38.) Washington, D.C., 1942.

188. LINDER, L. L. *Peruvian Pits.* Copenhagen, 1882.

189. LINNÉ, SIGVALD. *Archaeological Researches at Teotihuacan, Mexico.* ("Publications of the Ethnological Museum of Sweden," new series, No. 1.) Stockholm, 1934.

190. ———. *Darien in the Past: The Archaeology of Eastern Panama and Northwestern Colombia.* Göteborg: A. Elanders Boktryckeri Aktiebolag, 1929.

191. ———. *Mexican Highland Cultures.* Stockholm: Håkan Ohlssons Boktryckeri, 1942.

192. LIZARDI RAMOS, CÉSAR. "El Glifo B y la sincronología Maya-Cristiana." In *Los Mayas antiguos*, pp. 245–59. Mexico City: Colegio de México, 1941.

193. LONGYEAR, JOHN M. III. "Copan Ceramics: Their Chronological and Historical Significance." Ph.D. dissertation, Harvard University, Cambridge, 1940.

194. ———. *Cultures and Peoples of the Southeastern Maya Frontier.* ("Carnegie Institution of Washington, Theoretical Approaches to Problems," No. 3.) Washington, D.C., 1947.

195. ———. Revised edition of his thesis (1940), being prepared for publication.

196. ———. "A Southern Maya-Peten Pottery Correlation," *American Antiquity*, VII (1942), 396–98.

197. ———. "A Sub-pottery Deposit at Copan, Honduras," *ibid.*, XIII (1948), 248–49.

198. LOTHROP, SAMUEL K. *Atitlan: An Archaeological Study of Ancient Remains on the Borders of Lake Atitlan, Guatemala.* ("Carnegie Institution of Washington Publications," No. 444.) Washington, D.C., 1933.

199. ———. "Gold and Silver from Southern Peru and Bolivia," *Journal of the Royal Anthropological Institute* (London), LXVII (1937), 305–25.

200. ———. "Gold Artifact of Chavín Style." Unpublished MS.

201. ———. "Gold Ornaments of Chavín Style from Chongoyape, Peru," *American Antiquity*, VI (1941), 250–62.

202. ———. *Pottery Types and Their Sequence in El Salvador.* ("Indian Notes and Monographs," Vol. I, No. 4.) New York: Heye Foundation, 1927.

202a. ———. "South America as Seen from Middle America." In *The Maya and Their Neighbors*, pp. 417–29. New York: Appleton-Century Co., 1940.

203. ———. "The Southeastern Frontier of the Maya," *American Anthropologist*, XLI (1939), 42–54.

204. LUDENDORFF, HANS. *Das Mondalter in den Inschriften der Maya.* ("Untersuchungen zur Astronomie der Maya," No. 4.) Berlin, 1931. Reprinted from *Sitzungsberichten der Preussischen Akademie der Wissenschaften.*

205. ———. *Über die Reduktion der Maya-Datierungen auf unsere Zeitrechnung.* ("Untersuchungen zur Astronomie der Maya," No. 2.) Berlin, 1930. Reprinted from *Sitzungsberichten der Preussischen Akademie der Wissenschaften.*

206. ———. *Zur astronomischen Deutung der Maya-Inschriften.* ("Untersuchungen zur Astronomie der Maya," No. 10.) Berlin, 1936. Reprinted from *Sitzungsberichten der Preussischen Akademie der Wissenschaften.*

207. LUNA, LIZANDRO. *Choquehuanca, el amauta.* Lima: Imprenta Gráfica Stylo, 1946.

208. LUNDELL, CYRUS LONGWORTH. *Ruins of Polol and Other Archaeological Discoveries in the Department of Peten, Guatemala.* ("Carnegie Institution of Washington Publications," No. 436; Contr. No. 8.) Washington, D.C., 1934.

209. MacLEOD, WILLIAM C. "Hook-swinging in the Old World and in America: A Problem in Cultural Integration and Disintegration," *Anthropos* (Vienna), XXVI (1931), 551-61.

210. MAKEMSON, MAUDE W. *The Astronomical Tables of the Maya.* ("Carnegie Institution of Washington Publications," No. 546; Contr. No. 42.) Washington, D.C., 1943.

211. ———. *The Maya Correlation Problem.* ("Vassar College Observatory Publications," No. 5.) Poughkeepsie, N.Y., 1946.

212. MALER, TEOBERT. "Explorations in the Department of Peten, Guatemala: Tikal," *Peabody Museum Memoirs* (Cambridge), V (1911), 3-135.

213. ———. "Explorations in the Upper Usumatsintla and Adjacent Region: Altar de Sacrificios; Seibal; Itsimte-Sacluk; Cankuen," *ibid.*, IV (1908), 1-49.

214. ———. "Researches in the Central Portion of the Usumatsintla Valley," *ibid.*, II (1901), 1-75.

215. ———. "Researches in the Central Portion of the Usumatsintla Valley," Part II, *ibid.*, II (1903), 77-216.

216. MANGELSDORF, PAUL C., and REEVES, R. G. *The Origin of Indian Corn and Its Relatives.* (Texas Agricultural Experiment Station Bull. 574.) Texas, 1939.

217. MANGELSDORF, PAUL C., and SMITH, EARLE C., JR. "A Discovery of Remains of Primitive Maize in New Mexico," *Journal of Heredity*, XL (1949), 39-43.

218. MARGAIN, CARLOS R. "Review of Rafael Larco Hoyle's *Cronología arqueológica del norte del Perú,*" *Boletín bibliográfico de antropología americana* (Mexico City), XI (1949), 203-8.

219. MARQUINA, IGNACIO. *Estudio arquitectónico comparativo de los monumentos arqueológicos de México.* Mexico City: Secretaria de Educación Pública, 1928.

220. MARTÍNEZ HERNANDEZ, JUAN. *Significación cronológica de los ciclos mayas.* Mérida, Yucatán, 1928.

221. MAUDSLAY, ALFRED P. *Archaeology.* London: R. H. Porter & Dulau & Co., 1899-1902.

222. MEANS, PHILIP A. "The Philosophic Interrelationship between Middle American and Andean Religions." In *The Maya and Their Neighbors*, pp. 430-40. New York: Appleton-Century Co., 1940.

223. MENA, RAMÓN. *Notas acerca de Xochicalco.* Mexico City: Imprenta del Gobierno Federal, 1910.

224. MERRILL, ROBERT H. "A Graphical Approach to Some Problems in Maya Astronomy," *American Antiquity*, XII (1946), 35-46.

225. MERWIN, R. E., and VAILLANT, G. C. "The Ruins of Holmul," *Peabody Museum Memoirs* (Cambridge), Vol. III (1932).

226. MONTESINOS, FERNANDO. *Memorias antiguas historiales del Peru.* Edited by P. A. MEANS. ("Hakluyt Series," Vol. XLVIII, 2d ser.) London, 1920.

227. MORLEY, FRANCES R., and MORLEY, SYLVANUS G. *The Age and Provenance of the Leyden Plate.* ("Carnegie Institution of Washington Publications," No. 509; Contr. No. 24.) Washington, D.C., 1939.

228. MORLEY, SYLVANUS G. *The Ancient Maya.* Stanford, Calif.: Stanford University Press, 1946. Spanish ed., 1947.

229. ———. "Archaeological Investigations of the Carnegie Institution of Washington in the Maya Area of Middle America, during the Past Twenty-eight Years,"

Proceedings of the American Philosophical Society (Philadelphia), LXXXVI (1943), 205–19.

230. ———. *Check List of the Corpus Inscriptionum Mayarum and Check List of All Known Initial and Supplementary Series.* ("Carnegie Institution of Washington, Division of Historical Research.") Cambridge, 1948.

231. ———. "Combinations of Glyphs G and F in the Supplementary Series," *Carnegie Institution of Washington, Notes on Middle American Archaeology and Ethnology* (Cambridge), II (1945), 153–58.

232. ———. "The Initial and Supplementary Series of Stela 5 at Altar de Sacrificios, Guatemala," *ibid.*, pp. 222–28.

233. ———. *The Inscriptions at Copan.* ("Carnegie Institution of Washington Publications," No. 219.) Washington, D.C., 1920.

234. ———. *The Inscriptions at Peten.* 5 vols. ("Carnegie Institution of Washington Publications," No. 437.) Washington, D.C., 1938.

235. ———. *An Introduction to the Study of the Maya Hieroglyphs.* (Bureau of American Ethnology Bull. 57.) Washington, D.C., 1915.

236. ———. "The Maya New Empire." In *Cooperation in Research*, pp. 533–65. Washington, D.C., Carnegie Institution of Washington, 1938.

237. ———. "The Supplementary Series in the Maya Inscription." In *Holmes Anniversary Volume*, pp. 366–96. Washington, D.C.: Privately printed, 1916.

238. MOTOLINIA, T. *Historia de los indios de la Nueva España.* Barcelona: Herederos de J. Gili, 1914.

239. MUELLE, JORGE. "Filogenia de la estela Raymondi," *Revisto del Museo Nacional* (Lima), VI (1937), 135–50.

240. MUELLE, JORGE, and BLAS, CAMILLO. *Muestrario de arte peruano precolombino.* Vol. I: *Cerámica.* ("Publications of the Instituto de Arte Peruano," No. 1.) Lima, 1938.

241. MULLER, FLORENCIA. *Cerámica de la cuenca del Río Lerma: El Occidente de México.* Mexico City: Soc. Mexicana de Antropología, 1948.

242. ———. *Chimalacatlán.* ("Acta antropológica," Vol. III, No. 1.) Mexico City, 1948.

243. ———. "Exploración preliminar de la zona arqueológica de Chalco-Xico." MS. 1943.

244. ———. "Tepoztlán." MS. 1947.

245. MUNICH MUSEUM. Catalogue number in American Ethnology Section: 729.

246. NOGUERA, EDUARDO. "Cerámica de Xochicalco," *El México antiguo* (Mexico City), VI (1947), 273–98.

247. ———. "Excavaciones en El Tepalcate, Chimalhuacan, México," *American Antiquity*, IX (1943), 33–43.

248. ———. "Exploraciones en Xochicalco," *Cuadernos americanos* (Mexico City), XIX (1945), 119–57.

248a. ———. *Guia para visitar las principales ruinas arqueológicas del estado de Morelos: Xochicalco.* ("Publicaciones de la Secretaría de Educación Pública," Vol. XXI, No. 3.) Mexico City, 1929.

249. ———. "La Cerámica de Tenayuca y las excavaciones estratigráficas." In *Tenayuca*, pp. 141–201. Mexico City: Departamento de Monumentos de la Secretaría de Educación Pública, 1935.

250. NOLL-HUSUM, H. "Grundlegendes zur Zeitbestimmung der Maya," *Zeitschrift für Ethnologie* (Berlin), LXIX (1937), 54–63.

251. NORDENSKIÖLD, ERLAND. *The Copper and Bronze Ages in South America.* ("Comparative Ethnographical Studies," Vol. IV.) Göteborg, 1921.

252. ————. *De sydamerikanska indianernas kulturhistoria.* Stockholm: A. Bonnier, 1912.

253. ————. *Origin of the Indian Civilization in South America.* ("Comparative Ethnological Studies," Vol. IX.) Goteborg, 1931.

254. NOTTEBOHN, KARL-HEINZ. "A Possible Lunar Series on the Leyden Plate," *Carnegie Institution of Washington, Notes on Middle American Archaeology and Ethnology* (Cambridge), II (1944), 21–22.

255. NÚÑEZ DE LA VEGA, FRANCISCO. *Constituciones diocesanas del obispado de Chiappa.* Rome, 1702.

256. OSGOOD, C., and HOWARD, G. D. *An Archaeological Survey of Venezuela.* ("Yale University Publications in Anthropology," No. 27.) New Haven, 1943.

257. PALACIOS, ENRIQUE JUAN. *El Calendario y los jeroglíficos cronográficos mayas.* Mexico City: Editorial Cvltvra, 1933.

258. ————. *En los confines de la selva Lacandóna: Exploraciones en el estado de Chiapas, Mayo-Agosto, 1926.* Mexico City: Secretaría de Educación Pública, 1928.

259. ————. "A Maya-Christian Synchronology of Calendrical Correlation." In *Middle American Papers,* pp. 147–80. ("Middle American Research Institute Publications," No. 4.) New Orleans, 1932.

260. ————. "What the Hieroglyphics of the Great Monument of Xochicalco Say," *Thirty-second Annual Archaeological Report: Appendix to the Report of the Minister of Education, Ontario.* Toronto, 1920.

261. PAVÓN ABREU, RAUL. "Morales, una importante ciudad arqueológica en Tabasco," *Campechano* (Campeche), Año II, III (1945), 166–38.

262. ————. *Nuevas fechas mayas.* Mexico City, n.d.

263. PEÑAFIEL, ANTONIO. *Monumentos del arte mexicano antiguo.* Berlin: A. Asher & Co., 1890.

264. PÉREZ DE BARRADAS, JOSÉ. *Arqueología agustiniana.* Bogotá: Imprenta Nacional, 1943.

265. ————. *Arqueología y antropología de Tierra Adentro.* Bogotá: Imprenta Nacional, 1937.

266. PIÑEDA, EMETERIO. *Descripción geográfica del departamento de Chiapas y Soconusco.* Mexico City, 1845.

267. PIÑEDA, VICENTE. *Historia de las sublevaciones indígenas habidas en el estado de Chiapas: Gramática de la lengua Tzel-tal y diccionario de la misma.* San Cristóbal las Casas, Chiapas: Tipografía del Gobierno, 1888.

268. POLO DE ONDEGARDO, JUAN. "Report by the Licentiate Polo de Ondegardo." In MARKHAM, C. R. (ed.), *Narratives of the Rites and Laws of the Incas.* ("Hakluyt Series," Vol. XLVIII.) London, 1873.

269. POPENOE, DOROTHY H. "Some Excavations at Playa de los Muertos, Ulua River, Honduras," *Maya Research* (New Orleans), I (1934), 61–85.

270. PREUSS, KONRAD T. "'Sport' unter den eingeborenen Amerikas." In MALLWITZ, A., and MINDT, E. (eds.), *Das Museum für Leibensübungen,* pp. 55–59. Berlin, 1930.

271. PROSKOURIAKOFF, TATIANA, and THOMPSON, J. ERIC. "Maya Calendar Round Dates such as 9 Anau 17 Mol," *Carnegie Institution of Washington, Notes on Middle American Archaeology and-Ethnology* (Cambridge), III (1947), 143–50.

272. RAMOS GAVILÁN, ALONSO. *Historia del celebre santvario de Nvestra Señora de Copacabana, y sus milagros, e inuención de la cruz de Carabuco.* Lima: Geronymo de Contreras, 1621.

273. REICHARD, GLADYS A. "Form and Interpretation in American Art," *Proceedings*

of the XXIIIrd International Congress of Americanists, pp. 459–62. New York, 1930.

274. *Relaciones de Yucatán*. Vol. I. ("Colección de documentos inéditos relativos al descubrimiento, conquista y organisación de las antiguas posesiones españoles de ultramar," Vols. XI and XIII.) Madrid, 1898–1900.

275. *Revista del Museo Nacional*. ("Nota bibliográfica," Vol. XI, No. 2.) Lima, 1942.

276. RICKETSON, O. B., and RICKETSON, E. B. *Uaxactun Guatemala, Group E, 1926-1931*. ("Carnegie Institution of Washington Publications," No. 477.) Washington, D.C., 1937.

277. RIVET, PAUL. "Les Éléments constitutifs des civilisations du nord-ouest et de l'ouest Sub-Américain," *Proceedings of the XXIst International Congress of Americanists*, Part II, pp. 1–20. Göteborg, 1925.

278. ———. "Prehistorie de la Columbia," *Journal de la Société des Américanistes de Paris* (Paris), XXVI (1932), 210–11.

279. ROCK, FRITZ. "Altamerikanische Kulturbeziehungen zwischen Nord-, Mittel-, und Sud-Amerika," *Proceedings of the XXIst International Congress of Americanists*, Part I, pp. 200–211. The Hague, 1924.·

280. ROOT, W. C. "The Metallurgy of the Southern Coast of Peru," *American Antiquity*, XV (1949), 10–37.

281. ROWE, JOHN HOWLAND. "Inca Culture at the Time of the Spanish Conquest." In STEWARD, JULIAN H. (ed.), *Handbook of South American Indians*, II, 183–330. (Bureau of American Ethnology Bull. 143.) Washington, D.C.: Smithsonian Institution, 1946.

282. ROYS, R. L. "The Maya Correlation Problem Today," *American Anthropologist*, XXXV (1933), 403–17.

283. ———. "Moon Age Tables," *Carnegie Institution of Washington, Notes on Middle American Archaeology and Ethnology* (Cambridge), II (1945), 159–69.

284. RUBIN DE LA BORBOLLA, DANIEL F. "Orfebrería Tarasca," *Cuadernos americanos* (Mexico City), Año III, XV (1944), 127–38.

285. RUPPERT, KARL, and DENISON, JOHN H., JR. *Archaeological Reconnaissance in Campeche, Quintana Roo, and Petén*. ("Carnegie Institution of Washington Publications," No. 543.) Washington, D.C., 1943.

286. RUZ LHUILLIER, ALBERTO. "Arqueología Maya: trayectoria y meta," *Cuadernos americanos* (Mexico City), Año IV, XXII (1945), 139–55.

287. ———. "Report on First Season's Excavations at Palenque, with Discussion of Inscriptions of J. E. S. Thompson." In press.

288. SAHAGUN, BERNADINO DE. *Historia general de las cosas de Nueva España*. 5 vols. Mexico: Pedro Robredo, 1938.

289. SATTERTHWAITE, LINTON, JR. *Concepts and Structures of Maya Calendrical Arithmetic*. ("Joint Publications of the Museum of the University of Pennsylvania and the Philadelphia Anthropological Society," No. 3.) Philadelphia, 1947.

290. ———. "Further Implications of Thompson's Readings of Maya Inscriptions at Copan," *Proceedings of the XXVIIIth International Congress of Americanists*, pp. 467–93. Paris, 1948.

291. ———. "Moon Ages of the Maya Inscriptions: The Problem of Their Seven-Day Range of Deviation from Calculated Mean Ages," *Proceedings of the XXIXth International Congress of Americanists*. New York, 1949.

292. ———. "New Photographs and the Date of Stela 14, Piedras Negras," *Carnegie Institution of Washington, Notes on Middle American Archaeology and Ethnology* (Cambridge), I (1943), 182–88.

293. ———. *Piedras Negras Archaeology: Architecture*, Part IV: *Ball Courts*. Philadelphia: University of Pennsylvania, University Museum, 1941.

294. SAUER, CARL O. "American Agricultural Origins: A Consideration of Nature and Culture." In *Essays in Anthropology in Honor of A. L. Kroeber*, pp. 279–97. Berkeley: University of California Press, 1936.

295. ———. *Colima of New Spain in the Sixteenth Century*. ("Ibero-Americana," Vol. XXIX.) Berkeley: University of California Press, 1948.

296. SCHAEDEL, RICHARD P. "Uncovering a Frieze on the Peruvian Coast," *Archaeology* (Cambridge), II (1949), 73–75.

297. SCHMIDT, MAX. *Kunst und Kultur von Peru*. Berlin: Propylaenverlag, 1929.

298. SCHULZ, R. P. C. "Apuntes sobre cálculos relativos al calendario de los indígenas de Chiapas," *El México antiguo* (Mexico City), VI (1942), 6–14.

299. ———. "Beiträge zur Chronologie und Astronomie des alten Zentralamerika," *Anthropos* (Vienna), XXXI (1936), 258–88.

300. ———. "Zur Chronologie der Maya," *Zeitschrift für Ethnologie* (Berlin), LXVII (1935), 49–68.

301. ———. "Zur Chronologie der Maya. II," *ibid.*, pp. 321–31.

302. ———. "Zur Korrelation des Mayakalendars mit der europäischen Zeitrechnung," *ibid.*, LXV (1933), 396–99.

303. SCHULLER, RUDOLF. "Zur sprachlichen Verwandschaft der Maya-Qu'itse mit den Carib-Aruac," *Anthropos* (Vienna), XIV–XV (1919–20), 465–91.

304. SELER, EDUARD. "Alterthümer aus der Alta Vera Paz." In *Gesammelte Abhandlungen zur amerikanischen Sprach und Altertumskunde*, III, 670–87. Berlin, 1908.

305. ———. "Die buntbemalten Gefässe von Nasca im südlichen Peru und die Hauptelemente ihrer Verzierung." *Ibid.*, Vol. IV. Berlin, 1923.

306. ———. "Die Ruinen von Xochicalco." *Ibid.*, Vol. III. Berlin, 1908.

307. ———. "Ein altperuanisches besticktes Gewebe," *Jahrbuch der königlich Preussischen Kunstsammlungen* (Berlin), XXXVII (1916), 181–201.

308. ———. *Gesammelte Abhandlungen zur amerikanischen Sprach und Altertumskunde*. Berlin, 1902–23.

309. SHOOK, EDWIN M. "Archaeological Discovery at Finca Arizona, Guatemala," *Carnegie Institution of Washington, Notes on Middle American Archaeology and Ethnology* (Cambridge), II (1945), 200–221.

310. ———. "Guatemala Highlands," *Carnegie Institution of Washington Yearbook*, No. 47, pp. 214–18. Washington, D.C., 1948.

311. SMITH, R. E. "Ceramics of Uaxactún: A Preliminary Analysis of Decorative Technics and Design." ("Carnegie Institution of Washington, Division of Historical Research.") Guatemala, 1936. Mimeographed.

312. ———. "Preliminary Shape Analysis of the Uaxactún Pottery." ("Carnegie Institution of Washington, Division of Historical Research.") Guatemala, 1936. Mimeographed.

313. SMITH, A. L., and KIDDER, A. V. *Explorations in the Motagua Valley, Guatemala*. ("Carnegie Institution of Washington Contributions to American Anthropology and History," No. 546.) Washington, D.C., 1943.

314. SOCIEDAD DE ARTE MODERNO. *Mascaras mexicanas*. Mexico City, 1945.

315. SPINDEN, HERBERT J. *Ancient Civilizations of Mexico and Central America* ("American Museum of Natural History Handbook Series," No. 3.) 3d ed. New York, 1928.

316. ———. *Maya Dates and What They Reveal*. ("Brooklyn Institute of Arts and Sciences Bull.," Vol. IV, No. 1.) Brooklyn, 1930.

317. SPINDEN, HERBERT J. *Maya Inscriptions Dealing with Venus and the Moon.* ("Buffalo Society of Natural Science Bull.," Vol. XIV, No. 1.) Buffalo, 1928.

318. ———. *The Reduction of Maya Dates.* ("Papers of the Peabody Museum of American Archaeology and Ethnology," Vol. VI, No. 4.) Cambridge, 1924.

319. SQUIER, EPHRAIM G. *Peru: Incidents of Travel and Exploration in the Land of the Incas.* New York: Harper & Bros., 1877.

320. STEGGERDA, MORRIS. *The Maya Indians of Yucatan.* ("Carnegie Institution of Washington Publications," No. 531.) Washington, D.C., 1931.

321. STEWARD, JULIAN H. "American Culture History in the Light of South America," *Southwestern Journal of Anthropology* (Albuquerque), III (1947), 85–107.

322. ———. "The Circum-Caribbean Tribes." In STEWARD, JULIAN H. (ed.), *Handbook of South American Indians,* IV, 1–41. (Bureau of American Ethnology Bull. 143.) Washington, D.C., 1948.

323. ———. "Cultural Causality and Law: A Trial Formulation of the Development of Early Civilizations," *American Anthropologist,* L (1949), 1–27.

324. ———. "A Functional Developmental Classification of American High Cultures." In BENNETT, WENDELL C. (ed.), *A Reappraisal of Peruvian Archaeology,* pp. 103–4. ("Memoirs of the Society for American Archaeology," Vol. IV.) Menasha, Wis., 1948.

325. ———. (ed.). *Handbook of South American Indians.* (Bureau of American Ethnology Bull. 143.) 6 vols. Washington, D.C.: Smithsonian Institution, 1945–50.

326. ———. Preface, *ibid.,* IV (1948), xv–xvi.

326a. STIRLING, MATTHEW W. "Exploring the Past in Panama," *National Geographic* (Washington), XCV (1949), 373–99.

327. ———. "Great Stone Faces of the Mexican Jungle," *ibid.,* LXXVIII (1940), 309–34.

328. STONE, DORIS Z. *Archaeology of the North Coast of Honduras.* ("Memoirs of the Peabody Museum of Archaeology and Ethnology," Vol. IX, No. 1.) Cambridge: Harvard University, 1941.

329. ———. "A Delimitation of the Area and Some of the Archaeology of the Sula Jicaque Indians of Honduras," *American Antiquity,* VII (1942), 376–87.

330. STRONG, W. DUNCAN. "The Archaeology of Honduras." In STEWARD, JULIAN H. (ed.), *Handbook of South American Indians,* IV, 71–120. (Bureau of American Ethnology Bull. 143.) Washington, D.C., 1948.

331. ———. *Cross-sections of New World Prehistory.* ("Smithsonian Miscellaneous Collection," Vol. CIV, No. 2.) Washington, D.C., 1943.

332. ———. "Cultural Epochs and Refuse Stratigraphy." In BENNETT, WENDELL C. (ed.), *A Reappraisal of Peruvian Archaeology,* pp. 93–102. ("Memoirs of the Society for American Archaeology," Vol. IV.) Menasha, Wis., 1948.

333. ———. "Finding the Tomb of a Warrior-God," *National Geographic* (Washington), XCI (1947), 453–82.

334. ———. "The Uhle Pottery Collections from Ancon," *University of California Publications in American Archaeology and Ethnology* (Berkeley), XVI (1925), 135–90.

335. STRONG, W. D.; KIDDER, A. V. II; PAUL, A. J. D. *Preliminary Report on the Smithsonian Institution–Harvard University Archaeological Expedition to Northwestern Honduras, 1936.* ("Smithsonian Miscellaneous Collection," Vol. XCVII, No. 1.) Washington, D.C., 1938.

336. STUTTGART MUSEUM. Catalogue number in American Ethnology Section: 93345.

337. TAYLOR, WALTER W. *A Study of Archaeology.* ("Memoirs of the American Anthropological Association," No. 69.) Menasha, Wis., 1948.

338. TEEPLE, JOHN E. "Astronomía maya," *Anales del Museo Nactional de México* (Mexico City), Época V (1937), pp. 479–581.

339. ———. "Factors Which May Lead to a Correlation of Maya and Christian Dates," *Proceedings of the XXIIIrd International Congress of Americanists*, pp. 136–39. New York, 1930.

340. ———. *Maya Astronomy*, pp. 29–115. ("Carnegie Institution of Washington Publications," No. 403.) Washington, D.C., 1931.

341. ———. "Maya Inscriptions: Further Notes on the Supplementary Series," *American Anthropologist*, XXVII (1925), 544–49.

342. ———. "Maya Inscriptions. IV," *ibid.*, XXIX (1927), 283–91.

343. ———. "Maya Inscriptions. VI," *ibid.*, XXX (1928), 391–407.

344. ———. "Maya Inscriptions: Glyphs C, D, and E of the Supplementary Series," *ibid.*, XXVII (1925), 108–15.

345. ———. "Maya Inscriptions: Stela C at Copan," *ibid.*, XXIX (1927), 287–82.

346. TELLO, JULIO C. "The Discovery of the Chavín Culture in Peru," *American Antiquity*, IX (1943), 135–60.

347. ———. *"La Cultura Chavín.* Lima, 1948.

348. ———. "Los Resultados de la expedición arqueológica al Marañon de 1937," *El Comercio* (Lima), January 9, 1938.

349. ———. "Origen y desarrollo de las civilizaciones prehistóricas Andinas," *Actas del XXVII° Congreso Internacional de Americanistas*, pp. 589-723. Lima, 1942-43.

350. ———. "Sobre el descubrimiento de la cultura Chavín del Peru," *ibid.*, pp. 231–52. Mexico, 1942.

351. TEMPLE, ELLA DUNBAR. "La Descendencia de Huayna Capac," *Revista histórica* (Lima), XI, Nos. 1–2, 93–165; No. 3, 284-323; XII, 204–45; XIII, 31–77 (1937–40).

352. THOMPSON, EDWARD H. "The Home of a Forgotten Race," *National Geographic* (Washington), XXV (1914), 585–608.

353. THOMPSON, J. ERIC. "Apuntes sobre la estela num. 5 de Balakbal, Quintana Roo," *Revista mexicana de estudios antropológicos* (Mexico City), IV (1940), 5–9.

354. ———. *Archaeology of South America.* ("Chicago Museum of Natural History, Department of Anthropology Leaflets," No. 33.) Chicago, 1936.

355. ———. *Archaeological Investigations in the Southern Cayo District, British Honduras.* ("Field Museum of Natural History Anthropology Series," Vol. XVII, No. 3.) Chicago, 1931.

356. ———. "A Coordination of the History of Chichen Itza with Ceramic Sequences in Central Mexico," *Revista mexicana de estudios antropológicos* (Mexico City), V (1941), 97–111.

357. ———. *A Correlation of Mayan and European Calendars.* ("Field Museum of Natural History Anthropology Series," Vol. XVII, No. 1.) Chicago, 1927.

358. ———. "The Dating of Seven Monuments at Piedras Negras," *Carnegie Institution of Washington, Notes on Middle American Archaeology and Ethnology* (Cambridge), II (1944), 65–82.

359. ———. "The Dating of Structure 44, Yaxchilan . . . ," *ibid.*, III (1946), 62–74.

360. ———. *Excavations at San Jose, British Honduras.* ("Carnegie Institution of Washington Publications," No. 506.) Washington, D.C., 1939.

361. ———. "Hieroglyphic Research," *Carnegie Institution of Washington Yearbook*, No. 43, pp. 172–73. Washington, D.C., 1944.

362. ———. "The Initial Series of Stela 14, Piedras Negras, Guatemala, and a Date on Stela 19, Naranjo, Guatemala," *Carnegie Institution of Washington, Notes on Middle American Archaeology and Ethnology* (Cambridge), I (1943), 113-16.

363. THOMPSON, J. ERIC. "The Inscription on the Altar of Zoomorph O, Quirigua," *ibid.*, II (1945), 189–99.

364. ———. "Jottings on Inscriptions at Copan," *ibid.*, II (1944), 48–64.

365. ———. "Lunar Inscriptions in the Usumacintla Valley," *El México antiguo* (Mexico City), IV (1937), 69–73.

366. ———. *Maya Chronology: The Correlation Question.* ("Carnegie Institution of Washington Publications," No. 456; Contr. No. 14.) Washington, D.C., 1935.

367. ———. *Maya Chronology: The Fifteen Tun Glyph.* ("Carnegie Institution of Washington Publications," No. 436; Contr. No. 11.) Washington, D.C., 1934.

368. ———. "Maya Epigraphy: A Cycle of 819 Days," *Carnegie Institution of Washington, Notes on Middle American Archaeology and Ethnology* (Cambridge), I (1943), 137–51.

369. ———. "Observations on Glyph G of the Lunar Series," *ibid.*, I (1942), 27–29.

370. ———. "Variant Methods of Date Recording in the Jatate Drainage, Chiapas," *ibid.*, II (1944), 133–38.

371. ———. "Maya Chronology: Glyph G of the Lunar Series," *American Anthropologist*, XXXI (1929), 223–31.

372. ———. *Maya Hieroglyphic Writing: Introduction.* ("Carnegie Institution of Washington Publications," No. 589.) Washington, D.C., 1950.

373. ———. "A Survey of the Northern Maya Area," *American Antiquity*, XI (1945), 2–24.

374. ———. "A Trial Survey of the Southern Maya Area," *ibid.*, IX (1943), 106–34.

375. ———. "Un Vistazo a las 'ciudades' mayas: su aspecto y función," *Cuadernos americanos* (Mexico City), XX (1945), 135–49.

376. THOMPSON, J. ERIC; POLLOCK, H. E. D.; and CHARLOT, JEAN. *A Preliminary Study of the Ruins of Coba, Quintana Roo, Mexico.* ("Carnegie Institution of Washington Publications," No. 424.) Washington, D.C., 1932.

377. TITU CUSI YUPANQUI INCA, DIEGO DE CASTRO. *Relación de la conquista del Peru y hechos del Inca Mango II.* Edited by URTEAGA and ROMERO. ("Colección de libros y documentos referentes a la historia del Perú," Ser. 1, Vol. II.) Lima, 1916.

378. TOZZER, ALFRED M. *Excavation of a Site at Santiago Ahuitzotla.* (Bureau of American Ethnology Bull. 74.) Washington, D.C.: Smithsonian Institution, 1921.

379. ———. *Landa's Relaciones de las cosas de Yucatan.* ("Peabody Museum Papers," Vol. XVIII.) Cambridge, 1941.

380. ———. "Maya and Toltec Figures at Chichen Itza," *Proceedings of the XXIIIrd International Congress of Americanists*, pp. 155–64. New York, 1930.

381. ———. "A Preliminary Study of the Ruins of Tikal, Guatemala," *Peabody Museum Memoirs* (Cambridge), V, No. 2 (1911), 93–115.

382. TSCHOPIK, HARRY, JR. "Some Notes on Rock Shelter Sites near Huancayo, Peru," *American Antiquity*, XII (1946), 73–80.

383. TSCHUDI, J. J. VON. "Culturhistorische und sprachliche Beiträge zur Kenntnis des alten Peru," *Denkschriften der Kaiserlichen Akademie der Wissenschaften*, Vol. XXXIX, No. 1. Vienna: Philos.-histor. Klasse, 1891.

384. TYLOR, E. B. "On the Game of Patolli in Ancient Mexico, and Its Probable Asiatic Origin," *Journal of the Anthropological Institute of Great Britain and Ireland* (London), VIII (1879), 116–31.

385. UHLE, MAX. "Civilizaciones mayóides de la costa pacífica de Sudamérica," *Boletín de la Academia Nacional de Historia* (Quito), VI (1923), 87–92.

386. ———. *Die alten Kulturen Perus im Hinblick auf die Archäologie und Geschichte des americanischen Kontinents.* Berlin: Wilhelm Süserott Verlag, 1935.

387. ———. "Estudios esmeraldeños," *Anales de la Universidad Central de Ecuador* (Quito), XXXIX (1927), 107–36.

388. ———. "Influencias Mayas en el alto Ecuador," *Boletín de la Academia Nacional de Historia* (Quito), IV (1922), 205–40.

389. ———. "Las antiguas civilizaciones de Manta," *ibid.*, XII (1931), 5–72.

390. ———. "Las antiguas civilizaciones esmeraldeñas," *Anales de la Universidad Central de Ecuador* (Quito), XXXVIII (1927), 107–36.

391. ———. "Los Principios de la civilización en la sierra peruana," *Boletín de la Academia Nacional de Historia* (Quito), I (1920), 44–56.

392. ———. "Orígenes centroamericanos," *ibid.*, IV (1922), 1–6.

393. ———. "Toltecas, Mayas y civilizaciones sudamericanas," *ibid.*, VII (1923), 1–33.

394. VAILLANT, GEORGE C. "The Anthropological Setting of the Playa de los Muertos Culture," *Maya Research* (New Orleans), I (1934), 87–100.

395. ———. *Aztecs of Mexico.* Garden City, N.Y.: Doubleday, Doran & Co., 1941.

396. ———. "Chronology and Stratigraphy in the Maya Area," *Maya Research* (New Orleans), II (1935), 119–43.

397. ———. "A Correlation of Archaeological and Historical Sequences in the Valley of Mexico," *American Anthropologist*, XL (1938), 535–73.

398. ———. *Excavations at El Arbolillo.* ("American Museum of Natural History Anthropological Papers," Vol. XXXV, Part II.) New York, 1935.

399. ———. *Excavations at Ticomán.* ("American Museum of Natural History Anthropological Papers," Vol. XXXII, Part II.) New York, 1931.

400. ———. *Excavations at Zacatenco.* ("American Museum of Natural History Anthropological Papers," Vol. XXXII, Part I.) New York, 1930.

401. VAILLANT, GEORGE C., and VAILLANT, SUZANNAH B. *Excavations at Gualupita.* ("American Museum of Natural History Anthropological Papers," Vol. XXXV, No. 1.) New York, 1934.

402. VALCÁRCEL, DANIEL. "Documentos sobre gestiones del cacique Túpac Amaru ante la Audiencia de Lima," *Letras* (Lima), XXXV, No. 3 (1946), 452–66.

403. ———. "El Personaje mítico de Pubara," *Revisto del Museo Nacional* (Lima), Vol. II (1932).

404. ———. "Indice de documentos referentes al juicio sobre legítima descendencia del último Inca Túpac Amaru," *Letras* (Lima), Vol. XXXIX, No. 1 (1948); Vols. XL–XLI, Nos. 2–3 (1948); more to be published.

405. VARGAS UGARTE, RUBÉN. *Manuscritos peruanos del Archivo de Indias*, Vol. II. Lima: Biblioteca Peruana, 1938.

406. VILLAGOMEZ, PEDRO DE. *Exortaciones e instrucción acerca de las idolatrías de los Indios del Arzobispado de Lima.* Edited by HORACIO H. URTEAGA. ("Colección de libros y documentos referentes a la historia del Peru," Vol. XII.) Lima, 1919.

407. WASSERMANN–SAN BLAS, B. J. *Cerámicas del antiguo Peru de la colección Wassermann–San Blas.* Buenos Aires, 1938.

408. WAUCHOPE, ROBERT. *Excavations at Zacualpa, Guatemala.* ("Middle American Research Institute Publications," No. 14.) New Orleans: Tulane University, 1948.

409. WEGNER, RICHARD N. *Indianer-Rassen und vergangene Kulturen.* Stuttgart: Ferdinand Enke Verlag, 1934.

410. WEITZEL, R. B. "Maya Moon Glyphs and New Moons," *Maya Research* (New Orleans), II (1935), 14–23.

411. WHORF, BENJAMIN LEE. *The Phonetic Value of Certain Characters in Maya Writing.* ("Peabody Museum Papers," Vol. XIII, No. 2.) Cambridge, 1933.

412. WILLEY, GORDON R. "The Chiclin Conference for Peruvian Archaeology," *American Antiquity*, XIII (1946), 132–34.

413. ———. "Functional Analysis of 'Horizon Styles' in Peruvian Archaeology." In BENNETT, WENDELL C. (ed.), *A Reappraisal of Peruvian Archaeology*, pp. 8–15. ("Memoirs of the Society for American Archaeology," Vol. IV.) Menasha, Wis., 1948.

414. ———. "The Viru Valley Program in Northern Peru," *Acta Americana* (Mexico), IV, No. 4 (1946), 224–38.

415. WILLSON, ROBERT W. *Astronomical Notes on the Maya Codices*. ("Peabody Museum Papers," Vol. VI, No. 3.) Cambridge, 1924.

416. WINNING, H. VON. "The Teotihuacan Owl-and-Weapon Symbol and Its Association with 'Serpent-Head X' at Kaminaljuyu," *American Antiquity*, XIV (1948), 129–32.

417. WISSLER, CLARK. *The American Indian.* 3d ed. New York: Oxford University Press, 1938.

418. WITTFOGEL, KARL A. "Die Theorie der orientalischen Gesellschaft," *Zeitschrift für Sozialforschung* (Paris), VII (1938), 90–122.

419. YÁCOWLEFF, EUGENIO. "La Deidad primitiva de los nasca," *ibid.*, Vol. 2 (1932).

420. YÁCOWLEFF, EUGENIO, and HERRERA, FORTUNATO L. "El Mundo vegetal de los antiguos peruanos," *Revista del Museo Nacional* (Lima), III, 241–322, and IV, 29–102 (1934–35).

421. YDE, J. *An Archaeological Reconnaissance of Northwestern Honduras*. Copenhagen: Levin & Munksgaard, 1938.